Visions of Mughal India • The Collection of Howard Hodgkin

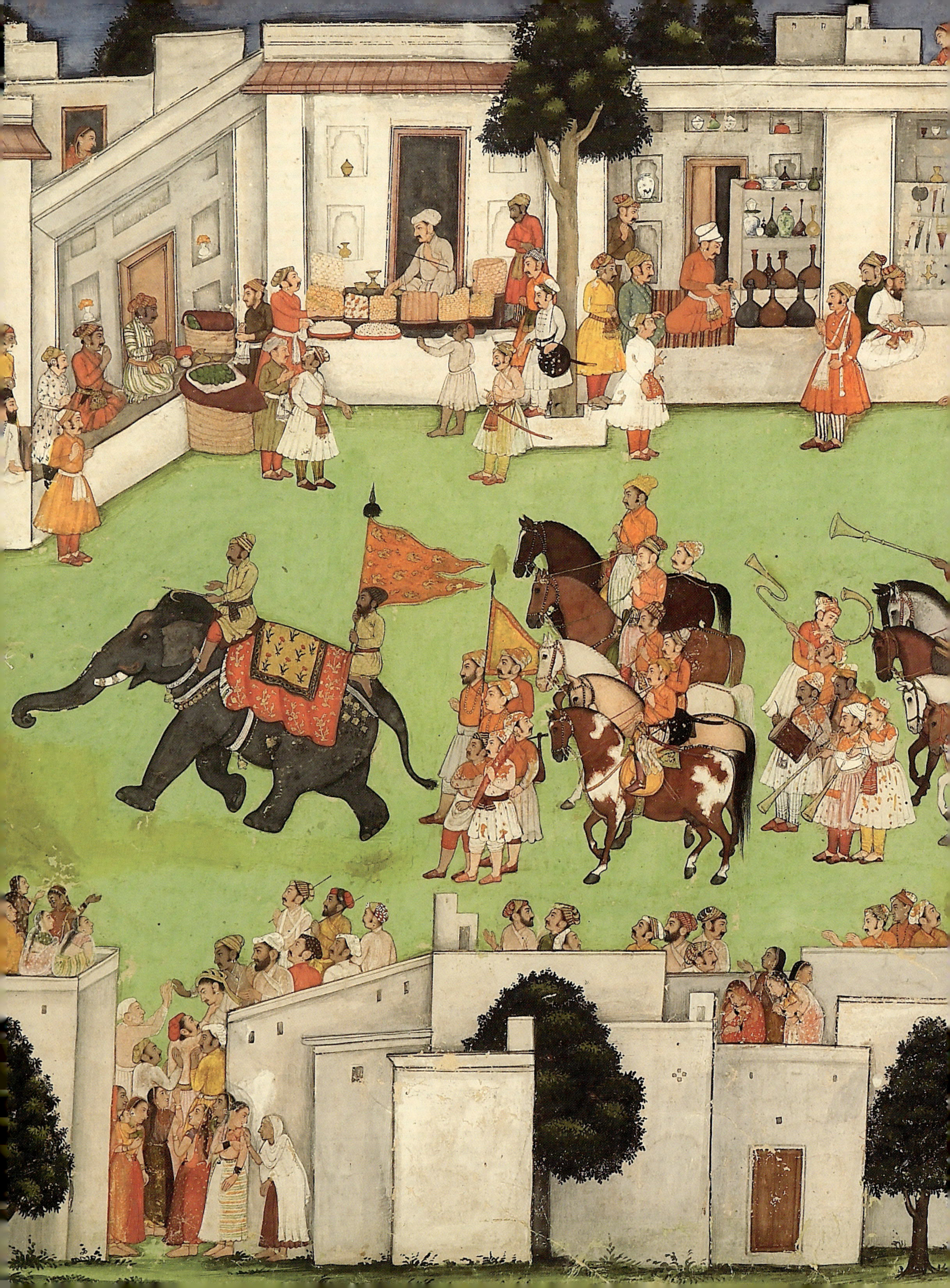

Andrew Topsfield

VISIONS OF MUGHAL INDIA

The Collection of Howard Hodgkin

ASHMOLEAN MUSEUM • OXFORD

Visions of Mughal India: The Collection of Howard Hodgkin

The Ashmolean Museum, Oxford
2 February to 22 April 2012

British Library Cataloguing in Publications Data

A catalogue record for this book is available from the British Library

EAN 13: 978 1 85444 263 5

Catalogue designed by Peter B. Willberg

Printed and bound in Singapore by Craft Print International Ltd

Front cover illustration:
Sultan Ali Adil Shah shooting an arrow at a tiger,
Bijapur, Deccan, *c.* 1660 (cat. no. 37)

For further details of Ashmolean titles please visit:
www.ashmolean.org/shop

The Ashmolean Museum gratefully
acknowledges the support of:
Howard Hodgkin
CHK Charities Ltd

The loans have been made possible by the provision of insurance through the Government Indemnity Scheme. The Ashmolean Museum would like to thank HM Government for providing Government Indemnity and the Department for Culture, Media and Sport and Arts Council England for arranging the indemnity.

ASHMOLEAN

Contents

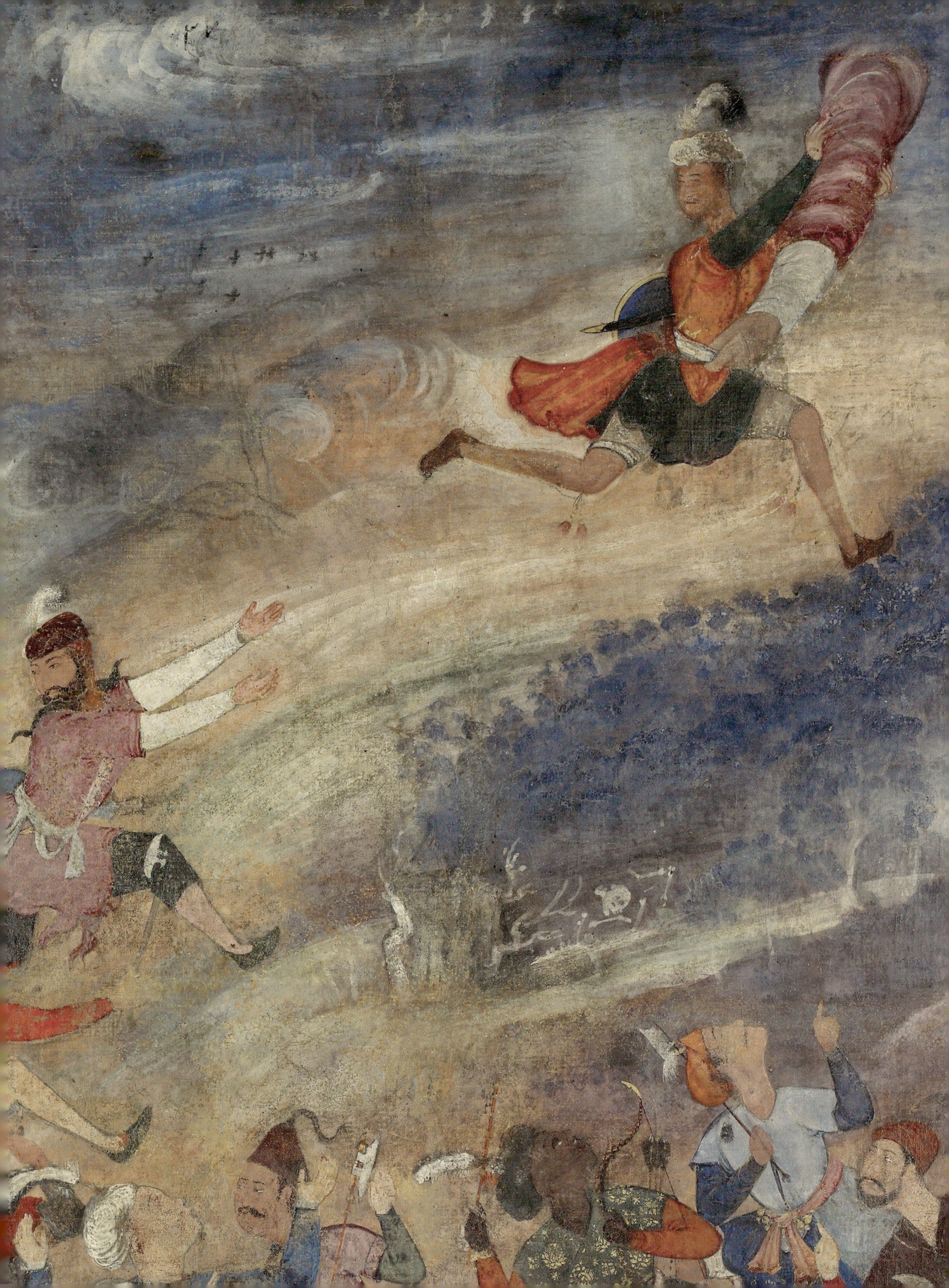

Foreword

Howard Hodgkin is one of the greatest, if not the greatest, contemporary British artist. His work is characterised by a bold and original sense of colour which is clearly related to his long engagement with Indian painting and with India itself. Howard has been collecting Indian pictures since his schooldays and he has travelled regularly to India for much of his adult life. He has gone there above all to observe and experience, forming intense impressions which later found their way into his work. He has seldom painted there, though one of his most important works is the large decorative mural on the facade of the British Council in New Delhi.

At the same time he has constantly added to and refined his collection of Indian paintings and drawings, which has developed within the last forty years into one of the finest and most exciting of its kind in private hands. It is above all a personal collection, formed by the artist's eye. Artistic quality and emotional feeling have always mattered more to Howard than a picture's narrative or historical aspects.

Twenty years ago the Ashmolean Museum was able to exhibit a selection of 42 paintings from the Hodgkin collection, following earlier showings at the Arthur M. Sackler Gallery, Washington, D.C., and the Museum Rietberg, Zurich. That selection was later exhibited, with additions, at the Sainsbury Centre, University of East Anglia, and the British Museum. A further enlarged showing of the collection was held in 1997 at the Museo di Castelvecchio, Verona. This last exhibition, held to mark the 50th anniversary of India's Independence, was staged under the patronage of the President of the Indian Republic.

Howard has long been a friend and great supporter of the Ashmolean and for the last decade a large part of the Hodgkin collection has been on long-term loan to the Museum. Selected pictures have been displayed in our Indian galleries during that time. Howard meanwhile has continued to collect, despite occasional resolutions to the contrary. We therefore thought it time for a fresh and comprehensive viewing of the collection, including many important works which have not previously been shown. This exhibition presents a valuable opportunity both to reassess and to delight in Howard Hodgkin's remarkable achievement as a life-long collector of Indian paintings. We thank him most warmly for his generous assistance in making it possible. On a more personal note, Andrew Topsfield, our specialist in Indian art, and I would like to thank him for his friendship, support and wise advice over many years.

Dr Christopher Brown
Director, Ashmolean Museum, University of Oxford

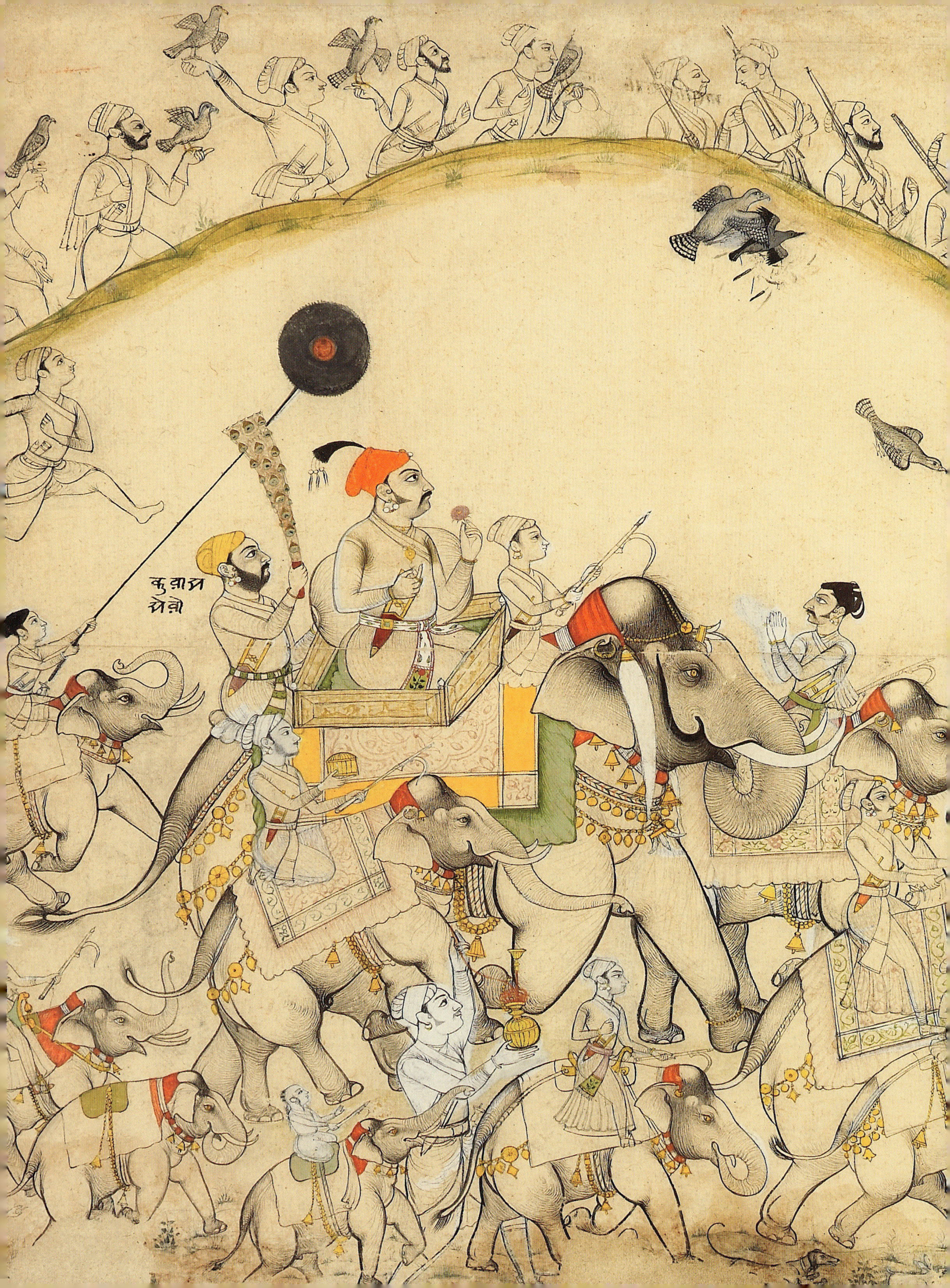

Notes on the Collection (1991)[1]

Howard Hodgkin

I decided to collect Indian paintings a long time ago. I started buying them because I thought they were beautiful. Most definitions of collecting come down to one word – greed. But once the wanting stage has passed, usually when large amounts of money are to be spent on serious acquisitions, and the need for them distorts your life, then you make a horrible discovery that a collection has a life of its own: it makes its own demands. Once its design begins to form in your mind, things have to be acquired out of necessity, as well as passion. And that perhaps is the most dangerous and yet the most creative part of making a collection, because it's no longer obeying the dictates of the heart, or lower organs: the head intervenes as well. You can argue yourself into almost anything, when it's a question of buying another beautiful object.

Collecting Indian paintings may be particularly difficult, partly because it looks so easy: there are many Indian paintings in the world. Most of them of relatively poor quality, but some with the kind of historic, romantic or exotic connotations which make inferior paintings seem desirable. The great old collections were usually made as a result of circumstance, rather than choice. They are accumulations. Until the second half of this century there has been no von Bode of Indian painting. There have been no active, proselytising connoisseurs, apart from Coomaraswamy and in our own day the great Cary Welch.

I particularly like big pictures and don't mind if they are damaged, provided that the original character of the painting survives. The pictures are chosen according to my idea of aesthetic quality, rather than any other criteria. My collection has nothing to do with art history, it is entirely to do with the arbitrary inclinations of one person.

As a European, affected by European art and the history of European painting, I look at Indian pictures in that light. I like large paintings; I prefer broad, architectural compositions rather than small, finicky ones and I only enjoy illustration in the sense that it applies to Giotto – rather than to Arthur Rackham. The trouble with a lot of Indian painting, in so far as one can generalise, is that it is very small in scale – it even thinks small. There is a good reason for this: most Indian paintings were made as glorified manuscript illustrations or, later, as detached, book-scale pictures. They were kept in bundles and opened up and passed around while people were sitting about. They were meant to be held in the hand – often at a voluptuous moment, which is why there are a number of (almost universally poor) erotic Indian pictures. Perhaps they were poor because they had no need to be more than diagrammatic, when your partner was sitting next to you.

One of the great temptations for a European looking at another country's art – you can see it among collectors of African artefacts for example – is to equate the artists you admire so much in

1 This essay first appeared in the 1991 exhibition catalogue *Indian paintings and drawings from the collection of Howard Hodgkin* (by A. Topsfield and M.C. Beach; reprinted 1992, 1994). It appeared again in the 1997 Verona exhibition catalogue, *Indian miniatures and paintings from the 16th to the 19th century: The collection of Howard Hodgkin*, with a brief postscript. It reappears here with minor textual revisions and a new postscript by Howard Hodgkin.

your own culture with the works in another. I could look through my Indian collection and say, there is my Ingres, there is my Poussin, this is like Seurat, this reminds me slightly of a landscape by Claude, this is my Uccello and so on. But that is obviously misleading. It's easy to make mistakes buying pictures on that basis, but very tempting.

I have collected a lot of portraits of men and of elephants. You don't find pictures of women that are actually portraits at all – there is one large picture of a girl singing (cat. no. 97), but that is idealised in that "pin-up" style which one finds across the board in Indian depictions of women. But my pictures of men and of elephants are almost entirely portraits of individuals, or variations on the idea of a portrait – a subject I find fascinating. You rarely find work that, in a European sense, has been done 'directly from life' – possibly the large Mughal profile of *Iltifat Khan* (no. 16) was done from life, possibly not, but you find endless variations on conventions, on the accepted notion of a head of a ruler, for example, the accepted version of what he looked like. The ruler in one case appears as a god from the Hindu Pantheon, as in the great Mandi drawing (no. 51). The same goes for the portraits of elephants – they range from the naturalistic to the virtually iconic or symbolic.

I am, inescapably, a European person looking at Indian painting, but that doesn't mean that I particularly enjoy the kind of Indian painting that apes Western painting. I don't like Company painting.

It's fairly easy to distinguish fine quality calligraphy even when you can't read it. Similarly, I have deliberately not learned about Indian iconography and have in my collection only a few pictures which are of religious subjects. When at last I see them together, I am surprised that my Indian pictures do have something in common: to some extent they do portray life as lived in India between 1570 and the mid-nineteenth century.

I deliberately haven't collected scenes from everyday life; such scenes do not appeal to me when I look at Western painting. One of my best pictures, the large painting of the lake and its palace by Bakhta (no. 110) includes an extraordinary collection of genre scenes. When I found it I felt I was buying a piece of India – it was like hanging a fragment of the sub-continent on my wall. I have never seen most of the activities depicted there – people in full court dress shooting waterfowl outside their palace and so on. But it is a picture of amazing actuality: people who have never been to India experience the same emotion about it that I do. This sense of nearness, of nakedness, of tangible reality, within an art form which is, on the whole, third, fourth and fifth hand is rare. On looking into the bottomless pit of Indian painting, when browsing through a pile of pictures in a large sale, you inevitably find copies of copies of copies. Real pictures, made by individual artists, are elusive. That picture of a lake palace is by the hand of the original artist. It's not a copy from his atelier, not a simplified version. It's moving to come across such authenticity, in the midst of arid acres of stylization and stereotype.

Once you've had that experience, once you've found a picture like that, then you feel differently about looking through daunting piles of pictures or auction catalogues, knowing that where one Indian picture has been reproduced there is probably another just like it somewhere else. A sense of déjà vu makes you despair, yet you continue to turn the pages because every now and then you receive an authentic shot to the heart. Then you are off again and you buy another picture. I have decided that these little shots to the heart must cease. That won't be difficult because I admire and love the pictures in my collection. Many of them were a great struggle to buy, both emotionally and financially;

there aren't many great Indian pictures around. The ones that are available are getting fewer. So the decision has been taken out of my hands: now is the time to stop.

I put the paintings in frames and hang them on the wall so that they become pictures in the Western sense. This is a distortion of the way they would have been looked at originally.

Putting Indian paintings into broad wooden frames makes them part of my life. It means they can be hung on the wall, they can be moved and handled with ease and they retain their physical safety and identity. I don't like putting pictures in mounts of cream coloured board, with a thin little linear frame round the edge, as museums tend to do. I think that distorts them all the more. They don't look like pictures to me, they look like specimens. I have experimented over the years with many different ways of framing. I like the one I use now; though I don't always get the proportions quite right.

I have been very lucky to find a picture framer, who is himself an artist, to make these frames for me. I think it's very important that paintings which people love and admire and want to have, can become part of their lives – rather than remain as objects in a museum. Many of the greatest Indian pictures *are* in museums – thank God for that, since it means I can go and see them, but I believe in private collections and I believe that pictures should have a life outside museums as well. I don't live surrounded by pictures – they are too demanding – but I like to be able to hang them up when I want to look at them.

I use strong colours in my own paintings, so people often imagine that Indian painting has had a great influence on my work. There are one or two pictures in my collection which have very strong colour which could remotely relate to my own work; but I dislike this comparison because it is made so glibly. Indian paintings are small and painted with gouache or opaque watercolour on paper. My pictures are painted with thick oil paint on wood in bright colours. Many of the Indian pictures in my collection are not in fact very coloured. Their predominant shade is one of those beautiful beige colours, the tinted cream of Indian hand-made paper.

Anyway, my own pictures are totally different in subject matter – even when they are portraits. If there *has* been any influence it would be more subtle and oblique and more to do with India itself, as evoked in Indian paintings.

Painting in a studio alone is naturally a lonely occupation. Collecting, on the other hand, brings with it an almost automatic series of international social contacts, with dealers, scholars and occasionally with fellow collectors. The conversations that ensue (particularly with other collectors) can be illuminating, inspiring and sometimes quite extraordinarily childish – even descending to the level of "My picture is bigger and better than your picture...".

Among many friends who have kept me company while this collection was being formed, three names at least should be mentioned here. Robert Skelton, former Keeper of the Victoria and Albert Museum's Indian Section, with whom I first visited India; Stuart Cary Welch [1928–2008], former Curator of Islamic and Later Indian Art at the Harvard Art Museums; and the New York based scholar and dealer Terence McInerney have in their different ways, inspired, argued and helped. I have written more about them in the Fall 1991 issue of the magazine *Asian Art*.[2]

When I started collecting it may have seemed a suitable 'something else to do', apart from painting. But this has not been the case and the passions and pressures of being a collector must stop.

2 Reprinted as Appendix 1 in this book.

Notes on the collection: Postscript (2011)

Collecting is, ultimately, shopping. It's circumscribed only by your budget and by how selective your eye is. Putting a collection on show in a public space forces one to be objective. My collection has been seen before in an incomplete form but it's since grown considerably. Now I'm struck all over again by its quality. I was never interested in covering all or even some of the bases. I never bought paintings or drawings on the tempting but distracting basis of their topography, their school of art, their theme, period or style. I just wanted great art. How amazing that I was able to buy so much.

Quite apart from money, collecting takes an inordinate amount of time and energy. As I have aged I've naturally stopped collecting. Several times. Only to discover, once I'd publicly renounced the habit, that I came across even more wonderful works. This past year Cary Welch's collection came up for sale after his death. He was a very different collector, a rich scholar / pirate / curator. But he had an eye for outstanding quality. There was no sentiment involved in trying to acquire something from his collection. I loved Cary, but I had no illusions about his ruthless pursuit of his own interests. He went to inordinate lengths to stop me buying things he wanted, which he could afford much more easily than I could. He once sat next to me at a Sotheby's sale and held my hand down, to stop me bidding against him. I was so shocked I didn't use my other hand.

I had once set my heart on a work from the collection of Sir Elijah Impey, an eighteenth century Mughal portrait from a shop called Luzac in Great Russell Street. It looked very pretty. I didn't have enough money but I reckoned I would have, if I won a bet at a point to point race. I put my entire term's pocket money on a horse I liked the look of. And lost it all. Somehow that only whetted my appetite. I persuaded my family to give me birthday and Christmas presents in cash and I bought the portrait. That was a valuable experience. Once I owned it I could see that it was an academic, anaemic, dull portrait of a dull ruler. You can learn from your mistakes, as long as they prove expensive. I sold or swapped the portrait eventually, happily. It probably contributed towards the foot of an elephant.

Inevitably I went on making bad purchases. I once bought a piece of Minai pottery from a shop in Oxford's High Street. I spent all the money I had on the bowl. That was my habit then. It's one I've gone back to. Later I realised it was mean and nasty and got rid of it. I've kept nothing back from my early purchases. Nothing survived the weeding out process. But it was probably necessary: owning teaches you to discriminate. By spending far more money than I ever thought possible I have at last, probably, reached the end.

Artists have always collected art. Perhaps because it's something from elsewhere. A professional artist sells what he makes. Buying art fills the void that comes as each work leaves the studio.

Howard Hodgkin

6 October 2011

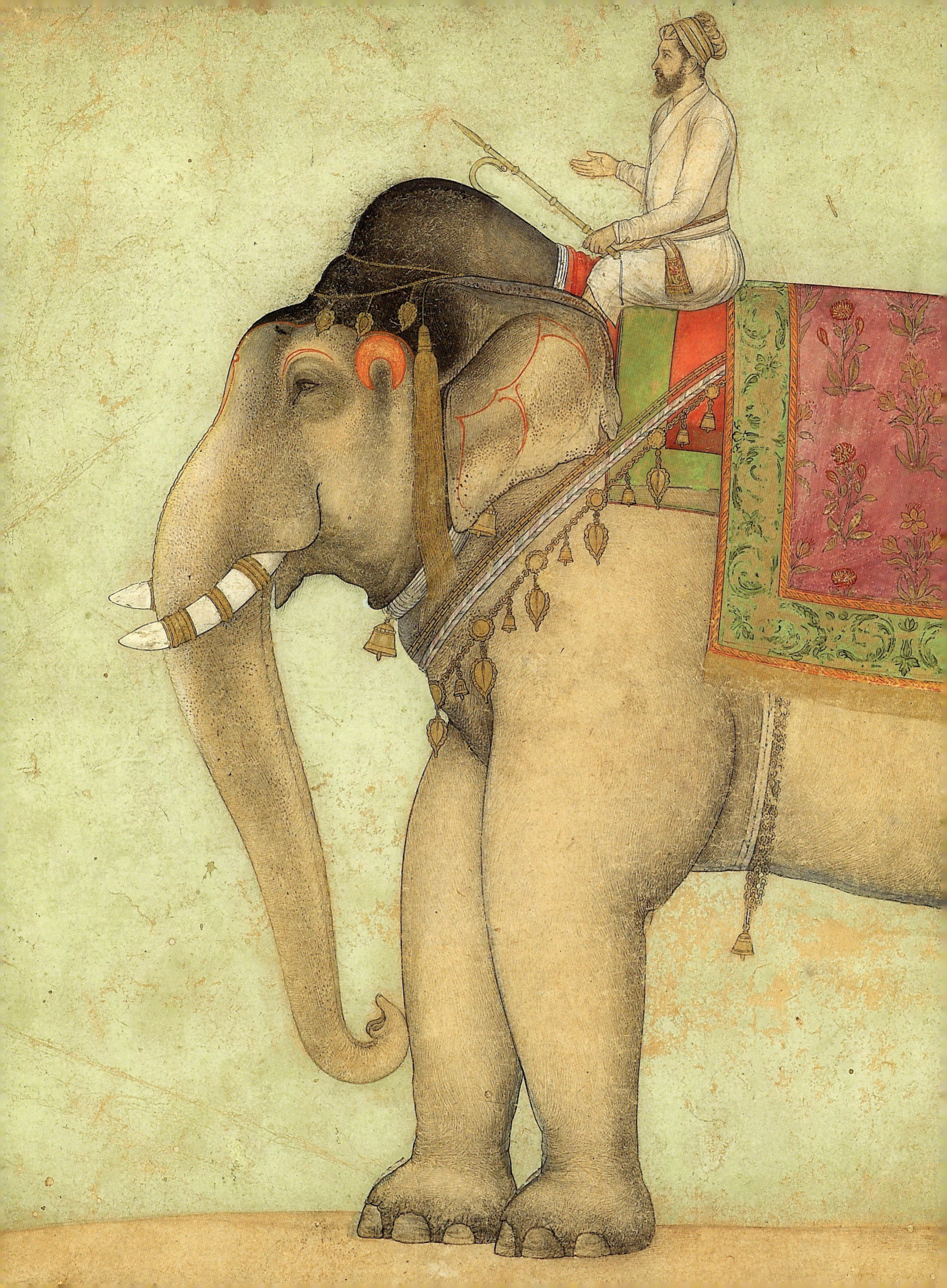

Visions of Mughal India: The Hodgkin Collection

Andrew Topsfield

Howard Hodgkin is one of the foremost artists of our time, one of the distinguished few who continue to extend and enrich the Western tradition of painting. As his introduction and essays in this volume demonstrate, he can also be on occasion a compelling writer and speaker – succinct, illuminating, candid, often unexpected. He has told the story of his early passion for Indian pictures: of how his art master at Eton (before he ran away from that school) showed him pictures from his collection, of his own first purchases at the age of thirteen, followed by a growing sense of their mediocrity, and his steady learning from that experience.

From the very beginning, however, Hodgkin found in Indian painting a pictorial language, a vision of the world, at once intriguing and profoundly congenial. It was for him

> the most extraordinary phenomenon, because it was a system of representation, a microcosmic world, which was completely different, yet not completely different from our own.[1]

As he later told the critic David Sylvester, in a filmed interview in 1981:[2]

> The first Indian paintings I saw astounded me because they depicted a whole world in a way which was completely convincing but totally separate from the tradition of Western art which I was used to. At least it seemed so at the time. I've realised long since that it wasn't nearly as separate as I first thought, but as it was a whole world in which everything was very precise and visible and yet somewhere else, I was very excited by this.

He was impressed particularly by the Indian artists' unselfconscious eclecticism and their great freedom, within certain formal conventions, to improvise:

> ... they seem to have an answer for everything. As a child I looked and I thought, how do you paint a tree? Well, they show you numerous ways of painting a tree, perhaps in the same picture.[3]

Hodgkin's turning-point as a collector came in early 1958, over lunch at the Daquise restaurant in South Kensington.[4] There Robert Skelton, the rising authority on Indian painting at the Victoria and Albert Museum, introduced him to the American scholar-collector Stuart Cary Welch (1928–2008), then in London on one of his regular study and buying trips. Later a curator at Harvard Art Museums, Welch was an inspired collector, writer, teacher and populariser, who did more than anyone over the next half century to inform taste and to open eyes to those exceptional Indian paintings whose quality sets them above the common run. Hodgkin immediately came under the spell of Welch's generous enthusiasms and his example as a collector. They would remain close friends and uneasy rivals for fifty years.[5]

As Bruce Chatwin remarks, the immediate upshot of their meeting was that

> Howard's hunting instincts were thoroughly aroused. He bought, sold and traded; he perfected the tactics of the bazaar; and for over ten years he channelled about half his creative energies into his collection.[6]

Among his earlier finds was the superb Deccani portrait of *Muhammad Adil Shah and Ikhlas Khan riding an elephant* (no. 36), which had appeared at auction in 1961. Another milestone was his acquisition, through Chatwin's mediation, of the early Mughal masterpiece, *Mihrdukht aims her arrow at the ring* (no. 1), which belonged to the widow of an Islamic scholar in Switzerland. It was followed by the great Kota drawing, *Elephants fighting* (no. 80), which Hodgkin had traced to its owner, K. de B. Codrington, the brilliant and by then increasingly eccentric Professor of Indian Archaeology at London, through an illustration in a geographical magazine shown him by an aunt. A persistent elephant theme was already developing in his collecting.

In 1964 Hodgkin visited India for the first time. This was another revelation, and he would return there almost every year. Like Indian painting, the subcontinent was a different world, "somewhere else".[7] Travelling there might involve trials or discomforts, but it also offered sudden epiphanies, what he has called "passionate moments":[8]

> I've never forgotten the first time I went to India and saw a pool surrounded by lilies, in a very unimportant, junky little yard somewhere; it wasn't the yard of a palace or anything. There were birds flying about and there were very bright green trees. They were absolutely similar to the kind of pool, lilies and birds and trees that you would see in an eighteenth century Deccani painting. It was a sort of one-for-one representation.[9]

A twentieth century Indian courtyard was part of the same world – was the same world – as the formally ordered visions of Mughal India he had seen in the paintings.

Hodgkin was also moved by a quality of openness in the daily life of India, the different way (for an Englishman) in which people there seemed to live and interact:

> It's the sort of nakedness of their usually very inhibited emotions. I mean, everything is very visible, somehow, there. Life isn't covered up with masses of objects, masses of possessions, so that the difference being indoors or out of doors and all the sort of functions of life are much more visible, straightforward, than they are here.[10]

On this first trip he travelled in the company of Robert Skelton, whose own first Indian visit had been made two years earlier.[11] They spent time in and around Delhi and Bombay and they toured Rajasthan

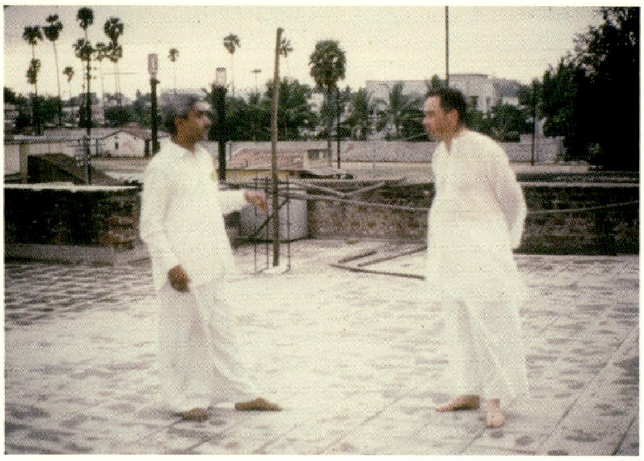

Howard Hodgkin with Jagdish Mittal, Hyderabad, 1964. (Photo: Robert Skelton)

and the Deccan. They saw monuments, museums, palaces and temples. But in the cities Hodgkin was also able to meet and befriend a select band of Indian connoisseurs, who shared his enthusiasm for Indian painting and also possessed a rare eye for quality. They included collectors, dealers and museum curators, who sometimes combined more than one of these roles. Among their number were such knowledgeable and perceptive figures as Jagdish Mittal in Hyderabad, or Kumar Sangram Singh of Nawalgarh in Jaipur. Such encounters gave a further strong impulse and direction to Hodgkin's collecting, which at that period centred mainly on Rajasthani pictures, then abundantly available following the dispersal of many former princely collections in the 1950s and 60s.

But collecting is a passion fraught with anxiety. For Hodgkin it was never a simple process of accumulation, with occasional thinnings out. It was rather a continuous and often painful critical review of every picture he owned. In earlier days, whenever a new masterpiece declaring itself to be indispensable came into view, many other less brilliant pictures had to be traded off to obtain it. After a while this all became too demanding and distracting. He started making resolutions to give up collecting. Around 1979, he removed his Indian pictures from immediate sight by lending them to the V&A. (I was working there at the time, and we were glad to have them for display). But this strategy was only partly successful, as Hodgkin soon became aware. Speaking again to Sylvester in 1981:[12]

> Next year I'll be fifty, and I think I can probably buy the two pictures which will complete my collection, and then I shall just stop, because I think it's something I can't continue dealing with... It's another emotional strain I think I'm too old to contend with... Nearly all my collection is at the V&A. I think that's the first step in stopping collecting. I lent them three years ago, and a great friend of mine said: as soon as you empty your shelves you'll fill them again. And it's quite true. I've made another collection since I lent those.

And so – fortunately for us – it has gone on.

The Hodgkin collection in its present form is several times larger than it was thirty years ago, and twice as large as twenty years ago. It then comprised about sixty pictures, two-thirds of which were included in the 1991–92 touring exhibition shown in Washington, Zurich and Oxford. In the last two decades many more important acquisitions have been made, including in recent years two previously unknown paintings of Raja Balwant Singh by his great artist Nainsukh (nos. 71–72) and the outstanding Bijapur portrait (no. 37) which appears on the cover of this book. Fifteen years ago, 87 of Hodgkin's Indian paintings and drawings were successfully exhibited at the Museo di Castelvecchio, Verona.[13] The present Ashmolean showing of 115 works, held in Hodgkin's 80th year, represents his collection at a still later stage of its evolution and virtually in its entirety. This review of a lifetime's collecting is a valuable opportunity for us – and for the collector himself – to reappraise and take stock, to discern themes and patterns.

Hodgkin is an avowedly unacademic collector. He has always simply sought those works, of whatever school or region, that deliver an authentic "shock to the heart". Even so, in his intuitive way, Hodgkin has shown a great breadth of taste as a collector, embracing much of the full range of Mughal period painting in India. At the present state of play, Mughal paintings – for imperial or sub-imperial patrons – account for almost a third of the collection. Paintings from the Rajput courts of Rajasthan are as ever slightly more numerous. Pahari pictures, from the Rajput courts of the Punjab Hills, comprise about a quarter, and the always rarer works from the Sultanates of the Deccan, less than a tenth. They are catalogued here broadly within these four main regional or stylistic groups, though such divisions are somewhat arbitrary. Many further thematic or stylistic connections can be seen between the works in Hodgkin's collection, running between or throughout these groupings.

The Mughal empire in India was established in 1526 by the Central Asian prince and vivid diarist Babur (r.1526–30). It was consolidated from the 1560s by his dynamic grandson Akbar (r.1556–1605). Under Akbar's keen eye, the Mughal style of painting was also formed at this time, from an inspired synthesis of Persian miniature technique with vigorous local Indian styles and a growing element of European naturalistic influence. Many of Hodgkin's Mughal pictures belong to the Akbar period, before the energetic qualities brought by his enlisted Indian artists were gradually refined out of the imperial style. These works include his three *Hamzanama* pages (nos. 1–3), of which the hitherto unexhibited *Khwaja Umar saved from pursuers* (no. 2) is especially full of movement and drama; the rare elephant procession fragment (no. 4); and a spirited *Harivamsha* page depicting Krishna's defeat of the giant water-snake Kaliya (no. 6).

There are paintings too in the hybrid sub-imperial style, by Mughal-trained artists of lesser rank for noble patrons, some of them Hindu Rajput princes, serving at the Mughal court around 1600 and after. With its assertive geometry, unrestrained pattern-making and heightened emotional sensitivity, *Rama's forest dwelling in Panchavati* (no. 8) was probably made for a Raput patron from Datia in Central India. As Andrew Graham-Dixon has noted, its particular aesthetic accords in some ways with Hodgkin's own vision as an artist:

> To see the two lovers who gaze so intensely at each other, rapt in a field of high artifice, ... is perhaps to sense the deeper, unpredictable affinity between the art of the collector and the art he collects. When Hodgkin succeeds, in his own painting, he engineers a tension between the conventions of pictorial form and the pressures of lived, felt reality which is precisely analogous to the effect of this sixteenth-century picture.[14]

Hodgkin came to post-Akbari Mughal painting, with its more highly refined naturalism, a little later in his collecting career, though he had already acquired the remarkable 1701 drawing *Azam Shah enters Ahmedabad* (no. 31) in the 1960s. His Mughal works of the Jahangir (1605–27) and Shah Jahan (1627–58) periods include a *Padshahnama* durbar scene of attendant figures with elephants and horses (no. 15), two fine – and contrasting – bust portraits of Iltifat Khan and Aurangzeb (nos. 16–17), and superb groups of imperial elephant portraits (nos. 20–25) and bird studies (nos. 12–14). Some of the later works, such as two evocative scenes of noblemen at leisure on terraces (nos. 18–19), or the majestic portrait of the elephant Ganesh Gaj (no. 25), were probably executed away from the imperial centre of Delhi and Agra, and far south in the permanent Mughal military settlements in the Deccan.

In the Deccani Sultanates of Bijapur and Golconda, which would remain independent until 1686–87, the new Mughal conventions of royal portraiture had already been assimilated and transformed by local court artists. Outstanding Bijapur works in Hodgkin's collection include *Muhammad Adil Shah and Ikhlas Khan riding an elephant* and *Ali Adil Shah shooting a tiger* (nos. 36–37). The former composition derives closely from a Mughal model, yet the treatment is wholly Deccani in its subtle richness of colour and the restricted modelling of the darkly massive forms of the royal elephant. In both pictures, painted about fifteen years apart, the Sultan wears an opulent, glowing gold robe. Gold too, in varying shades, permeates the extravagant flowering vase design (no. 43), a superb flight of Deccani decorative fantasy. Yet in contrast, a natural history illustration of bamboo plants (no. 35), an earlier and less typical work from Bijapur which Hodgkin acquired in the 1960s and prizes highly, is stark in its conceptual simplicity and boldly energetic brushwork.

Mughal art was still more influential at the semi-independent Rajput courts in the Punjab Hills, Rajasthan and Central India, many of whose princes were required to attend the imperial court and to serve in its armies. The interaction of Mughal pictorial conventions with indigenous painting styles led to the formation of numerous, distinctive local Rajput schools in the seventeenth and eighteenth centuries. Each was also subject to wide variations of style at different periods.

Among the earliest paintings attributable to a Pahari (Hill) school is the superb Mandi scene of a wedding procession passing though a bazaar (no. 49). This rare and exceptionally detailed view of mid-seventeenth century street life is executed with all the technical facility of Mughal art. (Compare also Hodgkin's later slices of Indian urban life, in the processions of Azam Shah and Ranjit Singh, nos. 31, 77). Yet two generations later at Mandi, a robust indigenous idiom had reasserted itself, as seen in the powerful stippled image of the eight-armed deity Harihara Sadashiva (no. 51). Other Pahari works of the late seventeenth century fall between these stylistic extremes. A pair of vibrantly coloured portraits of Basohli rulers (nos. 61–62) adapt the Mughal portrait convention of a ruler smoking a hookah and make of it something altogether different. In each, the dominant figure of the Raja becomes twice the size of the humbly kneeling hookah-wallah holding the coal-tongs. The red borders and other strong primary and secondary colours, together with boldly assertive carpet and textile patterns, create an atmosphere more intense than serene. Some viewers have again found resonances of feeling here with Hodgkin's own works.

Hodgkin has collected a few paintings of Hindu gods and mythological themes, such as Brahma (no. 52) or the Tantric goddess Bhadrakali (no. 50), but their iconography or symbolic meaning have not interested him much, only their effect as works of art. A quasi-mythological genre that has attracted him particularly, at least in its early Pahari forms at Basohli and other courts (nos. 53–60), is that of *Ragamala* ('Garland of Ragas'). These series of illustrations depicting the ragas, the musical modes of North India, and their *ragini* 'wives' were conceived as representing the essential spirit or ethos of each mode, as originally expounded in musicological texts. In the Hill schools, *Ragamala* images tend to be small, squarish and compactly composed, with strong red borders and yellow or other coloured grounds. Their textually prescribed dramatis personae are usually two or more figures of men, women, animals, snakes, gods or yogis, engaged in a wide diversity of decorous but emotionally charged psychological or physical encounters. Sometimes these tautly conceived engagements of figures are devotional or heroic in feeling (nos. 53 and 59; no. 56), more often they tend to the erotic (nos. 54–55, 57–58, 60).

The resurgence of imperial painting under Muhammad Shah (r.1719–48) brought a further wave of refining Mughal influences to the Hills in the second quarter of the eighteenth century, disseminated especially by wandering painters of the Guler school. The unfinished yet dramatic painting of the monkey Angada's leap to Ravana's golden fortress (no. 67), from the Siege of Lanka series of *c.*1725, reveals Hodgkin's interest in uncompleted works for their disclosure of the artist's first ideas and workings. It is also – like so many of his Indian pictures – a work of unusually large size. Of large scale also are three intriguing works of the 1740s, an unidentified scene of family scandal in an urban setting (no. 70), and two strongly drawn Chamba subjects, an imposing shrine scene and the satirical *Fly-infested feast* (nos. 68–69), both of which experiment with partly coloured drawing styles on a plain ground.

The most gifted Pahari artist of the mid-eighteenth century was Nainsukh of Guler. For much of his career he worked for the minor nobleman Balwant Singh of Jasrota, and the unusually close understanding that he developed with his patron is evident in his many intimate and psychologically revealing studies of the Raja's daily life. Two works certainly attributable to Nainsukh are the elongated hunting scene, in which Balwant Singh and other nobles on horseback surround a huge and defiant tiger (no. 71), and the mysterious, beautifully understated drawing of the Raja's courtyard encounter with a goose (no. 72). Other slightly later works, either by Nainsukh or his close followers, are the *Disrobing of Draupadi*, a restrained and elegant rendering of a famous scene of thwarted sexual humiliation from the *Mahabharata*, set against a boldly striped durree (no. 73), and the sensitive fragmentary study of some Pahari travellers singing by the wayside (no. 74).

Further creative reinterpretations of Mughal models are found among the Rajasthani works which comprise more than a third of the Hodgkin collection. Among the many local court styles of Rajasthan, Hodgkin has valued above all the animated elephant drawings and paintings from Kota (nos. 80–85). From the mid-seventeenth century onward, Kota elephant and hunting pictures were unrivalled in their energy of line and sense of mass in motion, as seen in the tumultuous collision of *Fighting elephants* (no. 80). Nearly a century later, the Kota artists' jungle landscapes, turbulent lakes and swaying bamboo clumps still seethe with life, as in *Madho Singh hunting boar* and the *Elephant hunt* (nos. 105–6). Such compositions derive in part from distant Mughal models, and were also reworked repeatedly in large-scale palace mural compositions by artists at the neighbouring courts of Bundi and Kota. Yet in the hands of a master painter they could still be recreated afresh. This ever renewed creative impulse appears finally at Kota in the mid-nineteenth century under Ram Singh II, as in the exuberant scene of his wedding at Udaipur in 1851 (no. 115).

Elsewhere in Rajasthan, Hodgkin has favoured works from a select group of major and minor courts. There are strong court and hunting scenes from Udaipur, capital of the ancient dynasty of

Mewar (nos. 98–102). Dating from *c.*1700–50, they were painted for the innovative patron Amar Singh II and his grandson Jagat Singh II. With its happily improvised perspective and rectilinear plan view, *Jagat Singh in a lake palace garden* (no. 101) evokes the pleasant hours spent by that hedonistic ruler in admiring his gardens and fountains, while listening to his female musicians. Comparable strong architectural symmetries appear in a slightly later Jodhpur painting, of Maharaja Vijai Singh's water sports with his ladies in his palace at Nagaur (no. 104). An earlier important work from the same region is the resplendent bust portrait of the latter ruler's father Bakhat Singh at a palace *jharoka* window, with his noble profile and tall Rathor turban and the richly varied textile patterns (no. 88).

At the minor courts – lesser kingdoms in the Rajput hierarchy, or else small baronial estates (*thikanas*) – the weight of dynastic history and court protocol was less oppressive, and painters working there could improvise or experiment more freely. At Kishangarh, the prevalent poetic cult of Krishna and his consort Radha led to expressive stylisations of figures and faces with a characteristic elongated eye, as in the magnificent early *picchavai* panel depicting four *gopis* or milkmaids, and the fine study of a singing-girl with a green *tanpura* (nos. 96–97). From the small court of Sawar, also in central Rajasthan, come several freely improvisational works, including a *jharoka*-type portrait of Maharaja Raj Singh in a garden (no. 89), and large scale, partly coloured drawings of his court life (nos. 90–91). *Raj Singh and his elephants* (no. 91) is notable for its accomplished, rhythmical drawing, bold compositional design and shifts of scale in the figure drawing. From Raghugarh, on the fringes of Madhya Pradesh, come a large, refined and strangely minimalist equestrian portrait of the redoubtable Dhiraj Singh (no. 94) and a warmly toned chamber scene of the same Raja watching a dancer (no. 95).

Rawat Gokul Das at the Singh Sagar (no. 110) is a late masterpiece by the master Bakhta, who trained at the major court of Udaipur, but found artistic liberation after moving to work for the Rawats of the Deogarh *thikana* in the late 1760s. This is a large format work but painted mainly on a miniaturist scale. Close viewing reveals abundant, brilliantly observed passages of human and animal life around the Deogarh lake, with its small pleasure pavilion on an island. Less inhibited still than Bakhta was his son Chokha, an ebullient and eclectic artist who worked both at Udaipur and Deogarh in the first quarter of the nineteenth century. Chokha's large scale *Court beauty* (no. 112), painted for Bhim Singh of Mewar, transforms a standard languorous heroine figure, typically found in palace mural paintings, into a supercharged, nubile bombshell with a soulful Kishangarh eye.

While the Hodgkin collection is larger and more diverse than ever, it continues to reveal a coherent vision, rooted in his sensibility as an artist, in his long engagement with the country of India, and in particular themes or technical concerns that have intrigued or resonated with him. It is worth mentioning again at least three leading features of the collection, already alluded to: the matter of size, the interest in drawings and the prevalence of elephants.

Hodgkin has often acquired unusually big pictures. Most Indian paintings on paper were made as manuscript illustrations, or else to be held in the hand and passed round in intimate, appreciative gatherings of nobles or ladies. There are of course many works of those kinds in the collection. But many others are of greater than usual size, some even on the scale of palace wall-paintings, and their expansiveness undoubtedly lends much to their effect. Largest and most imposing of all are the two giant Kota drawings of elephants pushing cannons drawn by bullocks (nos. 108–9), both of them powerful, repetitive compositions. (How often, incidentally, Hodgkin's favoured themes seem to come represented in pairs, or trios, of pictures).

Hodgkin has also collected drawings as keenly as finished paintings, and often also partly coloured works on a plain paper ground – like *Raj Singh receives a yogi* (no. 90) – which occupy an intriguing border area between the two. His interest in drawings is not surprising, since draughtsmanship – the mastery of outline and contour above all – is an essential test of quality in an Indian picture. Indian artists seldom lacked a sure sense of colour, yet only a few at any period could draw at a level above the conventional, or take a received pictorial idea and revivify it as the Kota masters did. Elephant studies, Hodgkin's great predilection, in fact reveal this aptitude most clearly. Even when a painter's human figures remain stiffly conventional – as they often do – it was unheard of for him (or her: no. 11) to produce a lifeless or listless elephant. From earliest times, Indian painters and sculptors have known how to convey a warmly sympathetic sense of this royal animal's massive volumes, its grace in motion, its noble intelligence and playful charm.

Collecting Indian paintings has been almost as deep a passion in Hodgkin's life as painting, and this exhibition is in a sense a summation of his collecting. We hope it will inspire, inform and delight. It is appropriate to leave Howard Hodgkin the last word:

> These pictures have been chosen because I thought they were beautiful, because they touched my emotions, and not for any scholarly purposes. It is a collection made by an artist. I hope you enjoy looking at it.[15]

1 From Hodgkin's talk 'On collecting Indian paintings', reprinted here as Appendix 2: see p. 280.

2 David Sylvester, *London Recordings*, London, 2005, p. 107; recorded for an Arts Council film, the interview was first printed in the catalogue *Howard Hodgkin: Forty paintings 1973–84*, London: Whitechapel Gallery, 1984.

3 Sylvester, *London Recordings*, p. 108.

4 This and some other passages below appeared in a different form in my essay 'Rajput and Mughal paintings in the Hodgkin Collection', in A. Topsfield and M.C. Beach, *Indian paintings and drawings from the collection of Howard Hodgkin*, New York, 1991.

5 See Howard Hodgkin's short memoir, 'Stuart Cary Welch', *Artibus Asiae*, LXVIII, 1, 2008, p. 159.

6 Bruce Chatwin, 'A portrait of the artist', in *Howard Hodgkin's Indian Leaves*, London, 1982, pp. 5–17; reprinted as 'Howard Hodgkin', in Chatwin's *What am I doing here*, London, 1990, pp.70–78; and in E. Juncosa ed., *Writers on Howard Hodgkin*, Dublin and London, 2006, pp. 57–67.

7 Sylvester, *London Recordings*, p. 108.

8 Ibid., p. 110.

9 Hodgkin, 'On collecting Indian paintings', Appendix 2, p. 280

10 Sylvester, *London Recordings*, p. 109.

11 Simon Digby, 'Travels with Robert', in R. Crill, S. Stronge and A. Topsfield eds., *The arts of Mughal India: Studies in honour of Robert Skelton*, London, 2004, pp. 14–19. I am grateful to Robert Skelton for providing his recollections of the 1964 tour with Howard Hodgkin.

12 Sylvester, *London Recordings*, p. 111.

13 G.G. Filippi, *Indian miniatures and paintings from the 16th to the 19th century*, Milan, 1997.

14 Andrew Graham-Dixon, *Howard Hodgkin*, London, rev. ed. 2001, p. 118.

15 From a note Hodgkin added to the 1997 Verona exhibition catalogue: Filippi, *Indian miniatures and paintings from the 16th to the 19th century*, p. 16.

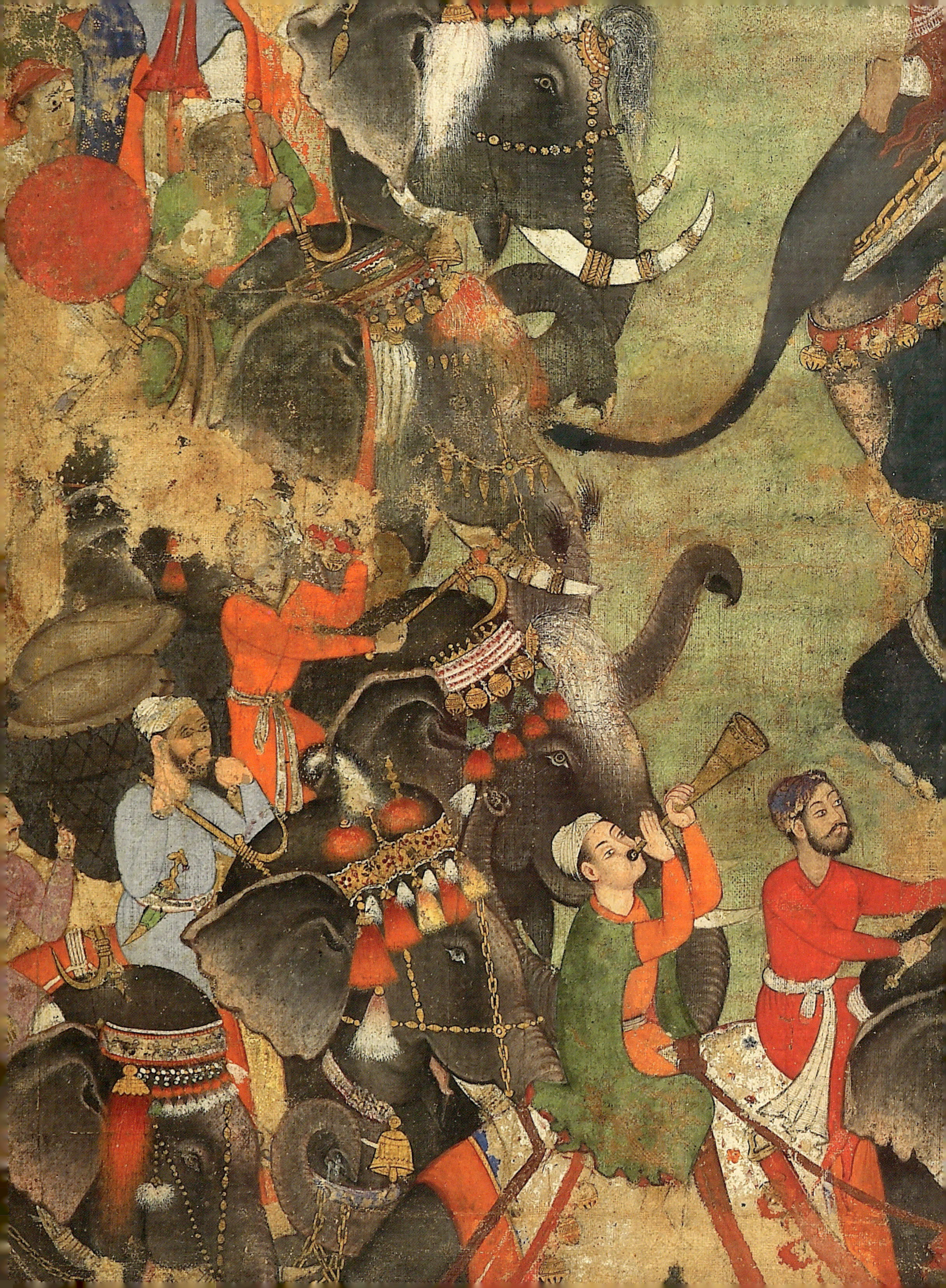

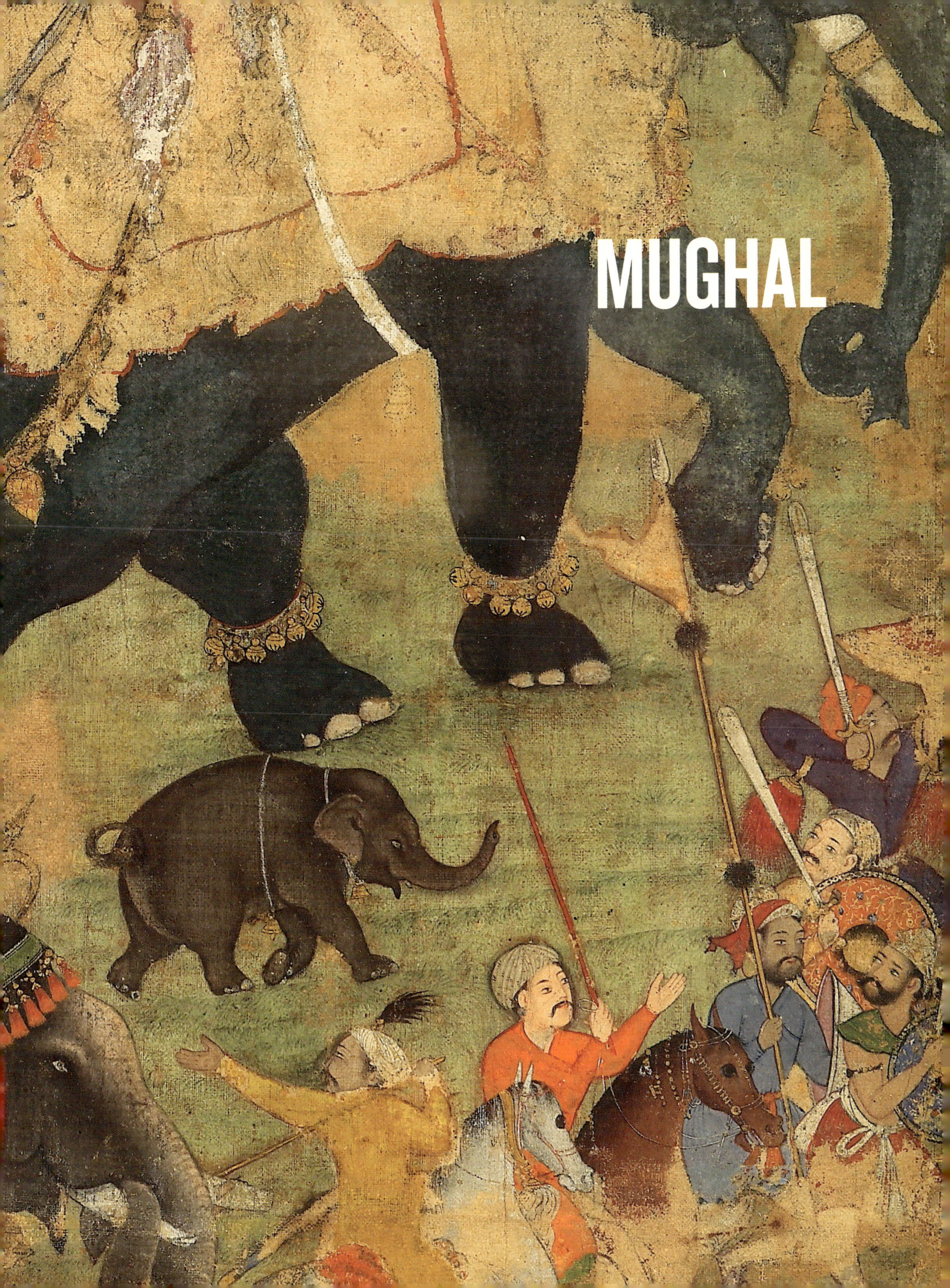
MUGHAL

1 Mihrdukht aims her arrow at the ring

Illustration to the *Hamzanama*
Mughal, *c.* 1570
Gouache and gold on cotton cloth, 67.8 × 52 cm
Hodgkin Loan 1
Published: Glück 1925, Abb. 37; Barrett and Gray 1963, illus. p. 76; Beach and Topsfield 1991, no. 1; Filippi 1997, no. 1; Seyller 2002, no. 76[1]

In his youth the emperor Akbar was enthralled by the action-packed tales of traditional story-tellers (*dastan-gu*) from Persia or Central Asia who visited the Mughal court. A particular favourite was the story cycle centred on the youthful Amir Hamza, a scourge of infidels, demons and dragons. This rambling epic was often recited at court, and in the privacy of his harem Akbar himself would take the role of story-teller and narrate these heroic episodes of love, war and trickery. Early in his reign he set the newly recruited imperial studio to compile an extraordinarily ambitious series of large scale illustrations, as an aid to narration. Painted on cloth with texts on paper on the reverse, the twelve-volume series comprised fourteen hundred paintings in all. Around 180 pages now survive, mostly in Vienna or London. Three are in the Hodgkin collection (nos. 1–3). Unique in its ambition and freedom of expression, the *Hamzanama* series took fifteen years to complete and served as a training-ground for the early Mughal school.

This episode belongs to the tale of Mihrdukht, a beautiful and resourceful young woman and a phenomenal archer, who undergoes various tribulations while in search of her husband Hamid. Here, not for the first time, various suitors are vying for her favours. To see off the unwanted admirers, Mihrdukht declares that she will choose whichever of them can shoot an arrow through a small ring suspended from the mouth of a golden bird at the top of an immensely tall tower. Here she herself calmly performs this feat. Her female attendants watch in amazement, a despairing suitor steals away grey-faced in the foreground, and a watchman leaning on his staff looks on philosophically. Soon after this, a suitor does succeed in shooting through the ring. Fortunately he turns out to be the lost husband Hamid.[2]

This painting has been trimmed slightly at the edges and is now missing its text. Its setting is a luxuriant palace garden whose sandstone architecture recalls Akbar's new capital of Fatehpur Sikri, still under construction at this time. The walls and pavilion in which Mihrdukht aims her arrow at the bird on the minaret-like tower is enriched with arabesque and geometric designs in the Persian manner, while the luxuriant garden with its vigorously painted trees and flowering shrubs is more typically Indian in feeling.

1 Seyller attributes this painting to the artists Jagan and Basawan.
2 Glück 1925, col. pl. 45, with a similar composition to the present painting; also Seyller 2002, fig. 111.

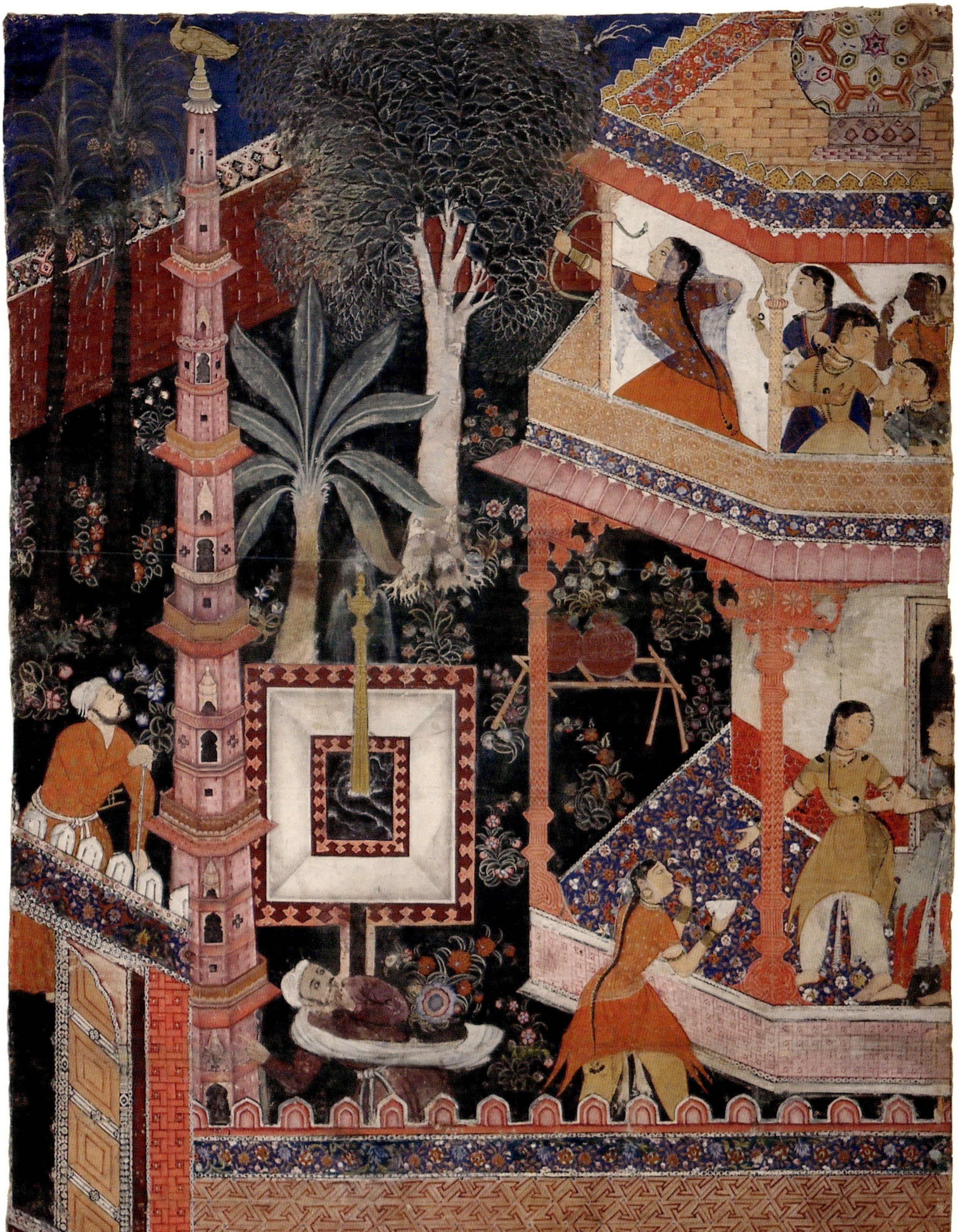

2 Khwaja Umar saved from pursuers

Illustration to the *Hamzanama*
Mughal, *c.*1565–70, attributed in part to Kesu Das
Gouache and gold on cotton cloth, 65.5 × 49.8 cm
Hodgkin Loan 100
Unpublished[1]

See also detail, p. 6

This vigorous page from Akbar's *Hamzanama* series (no. 1) illustrates an unidentified episode,[2] in which the lanky figure of Umar, arch-trickster, master spy and one of Amir Hamza's loyal helpers, is saved from pursuers by a heavenly hand which reaches down to lift him skyward.[3] Hard on his heels are a band of armed warriors who round a sharp bend in a dynamic curve. Several look upward, gesticulating helplessly as Umar rises out of their reach, against dramatic billowing cloud effects in blue, white, tawny gold and cream tones, with a small flight of birds and vivid blue hills and woods below. Like the 'Hand of God' in its modelled crimson sleeve which acts here as a *deus ex machina*, these motifs and painterly effects are adapted from European Baroque sources.

In the foreground three more warriors sprawl helplessly on the ground following Umar's passing. Around them, in the lower corners, are scattered human skeletons and a horse's skull, suggesting that this desolate waste was once a battleground. More bones appear just below the Europeanised, blue-toned forest beneath Umar's flying feet. Such bones and skulls are a new motif in Indian painting, again probably borrowed from European art. The dark Abyssinian (*habshi*) lying on his back at lower left has a shield with unusual devices including a sun and moon.

The freely painted cloudy billows and vivid landscape effects which enhance the drama of Umar's escape in the upper half of the painting, as well other passages, are painted with great verve and licence. Together with the dynamic, swirling composition, they suggest the work of a younger artist experimenting with the novel techniques found in European prints and paintings that were reaching the Mughal court by this time. This was probably Kesu Das, an artist well-known in his later career for his skilful reworking of European subjects and techniques and for similar streaked blue and white skies.[4] Kesu seems to have been the leader of the two hands who worked on the painting and was probably responsible for its overall design.

1 Sotheby's cat., 30 April 2003, lot 23.
2 The painting is numbered 37 at the top of the painting above the group of flying birds.
3 The heavenly hand motif recurs in Book 11 of the series: Seyller 2002, no. 69.
4 I am grateful to John Seyller for first suggesting this attribution. For Kesu Das's career, see e.g. Beach 1976–77; Okada 2011.

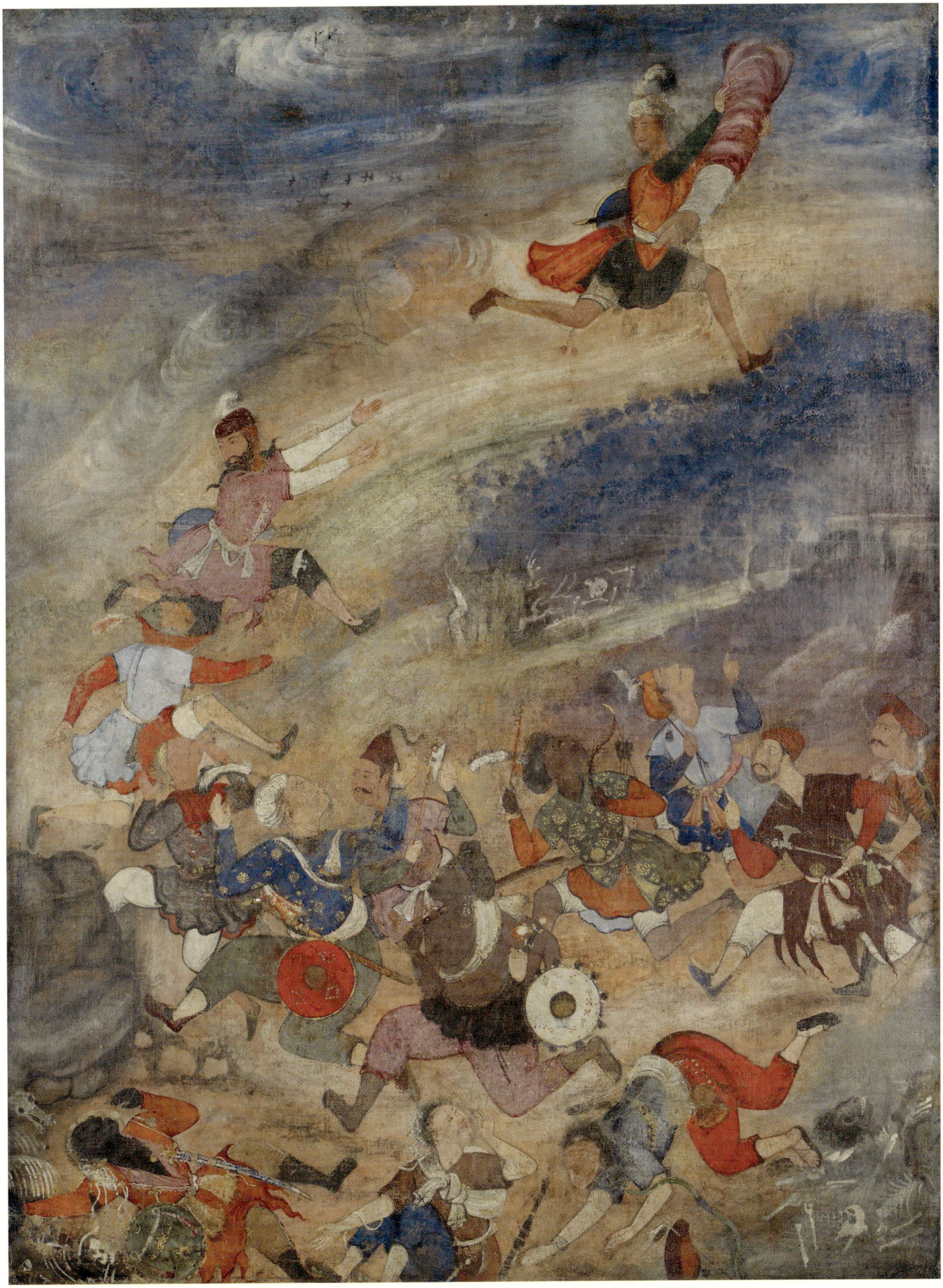

3 A supplicant at a Hindu temple

Illustration to the *Hamzanama*
Mughal, *c.*1570
Gouache and gold on cotton cloth, 70.2 × 53.3 cm
Hodgkin Loan 2
Published: Chandra and Ehnbom 1976, no.24; McInerney 1982, no.1; Filippi 1997, no.2; Seyller 2002, p.271, fig.123

In another unidentified scene from Akbar's *Hamzanama* series (nos.1–2), a worshipper makes a respectful gesture of salutation in the courtyard of a temple, where the priest receives him at the doorway to the shrine. As is proper, the humble supplicant wears no upper garment, but he may be a prince or nobleman as an attendant follows him at the temple gate carrying a bowl of fruit as an offering gift. This scene is watched with gestures of interest or wonder by various yogis and religious mendicants gathered around the courtyard. In the rocky landscape beyond, two woodcutters are seen on their way home, and in the distance a palace complex with a tall minaret.

The architecture of this Hindu temple is largely imaginary, with its flag-bedecked finials, Persian arabesque decoration and geometric tilework. Several sandstone sculptures of Indian deities are however shown, including a seated image with attendant figures on either side at the base of the temple tower, with a *makara* (aquatic monster) panel to the left. In the left niche beside the temple door is a seated goddess, and in the right niche a better preserved, buxom goddess dancing to the music of her flute, which recalls the earlier eastern Indian style of painting.[1] Like many of the surviving pages, this painting is now much rubbed and damaged. But this typical *Hamza* scene still retains much of its expressive power, with its fanciful, colourful buildings and energetic rocks and trees. As sometimes occurred, a later, pious Muslim hand has deliberately smudged the faces of the human and sculpted figures, and in some cases these have been crudely repainted. One wonders if similar iconoclasm may also have followed next in this *Hamza* episode, since idolatry was equally deplored by Amir Hamza and his companions, as doughty champions of Islam[2] – though not of course by the emperor Akbar or his painters, many of whom were Hindus themselves.

1 As remarked by Chandra and Ehnbom, no.24.
2 E.g. Seyller 2002, no.22, for a scene of destruction of similar Hindu idols.

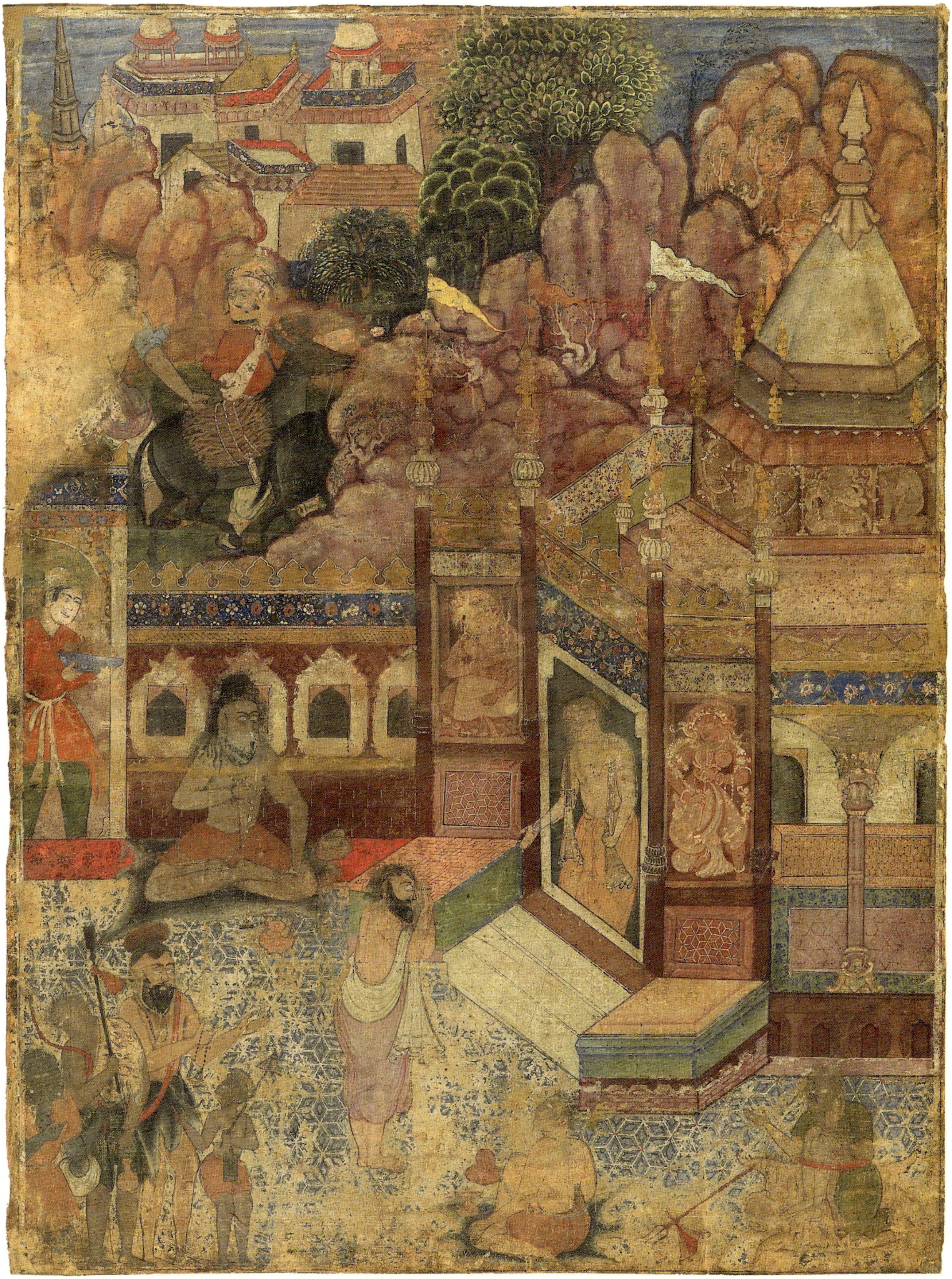

4 A prince riding an elephant in procession

Mughal, *c.*1570

Gouache with gold on cotton cloth, 34 × 39.8 cm

Hodgkin Loan 26

Published: Gray 1937, figs.1–2; McInerney 1982, no.2; Brand and Lowry 1985, no.24; Topsfield and Beach 1991, no.2; Filippi 1997, no.26

See also detail, pp.22–23

The large cloth-painting of which this is a fragment was evidently made for Akbar around the time he moved his court to the new city of Fatehpur Sikri near Agra. It is contemporary with the great *Hamzanama* series, also painted on cloth (nos.1–3), and it shares the same dramatic sense of movement and vigorous drawing and composition.[1] The subject is a procession setting out an expedition from the gate of a large palace: the latter building, crowded with human figures, appears in the surviving upper section of the painting, still in India.[2]

In this lower fragment, a prince rides a large elephant at the head of the procession. Several superbly painted elephants carrying musicians and other attendants follow behind, as well as a small elephant calf. Because of paint loss, the prince's figure is now only faintly discernible in its original under-drawing (more remains of the attendant who clings on behind him). His posture however was evidently animated and commanding, and it is possible that Akbar himself is represented.[3] He was well-known as an expert elephant driver, who

> mounts on every kind of elephant, from the first to the last class, making them, notwithstanding their almost supernatural strength, obedient to his command. His Majesty will put his foot on the tusks, and mount them, even when they are in the rutting season, and astonishes experienced people.[4]

The escorting figures are also depicted with lively gestures, varied expressions and an often vivid palette typical of early Mughal painting.

Like their Mongol ancestors, the emperors spent much of their time living in camp while touring, hunting or campaigning within their domains. Cloth-paintings such as this, of which very few examples survive, were probably displayed in their private tent quarters, in place of the mural paintings that covered their palace walls.

1 E.g. Beach 1987, p.76, figs.55–57, for discussion.

2 Indian Museum, Calcutta: see McInerney 1982 for discussion; also Ray 1975, pl.I, pp.136–39; Beach and Topsfield 1991, p.22, fig.1. The present painting was acquired by Lady Herringham in 1929 and was later owned by Bedford College, London.

3 Basil Gray in Ashton ed.1950, no.644, and Ray 1975 suggest less plausibly that an equestrian figure in yellow exiting the gateway in the Calcutta fragment could be Akbar.

4 Abu'l Fazl, *Ain-i Akbari*, I, p.138.

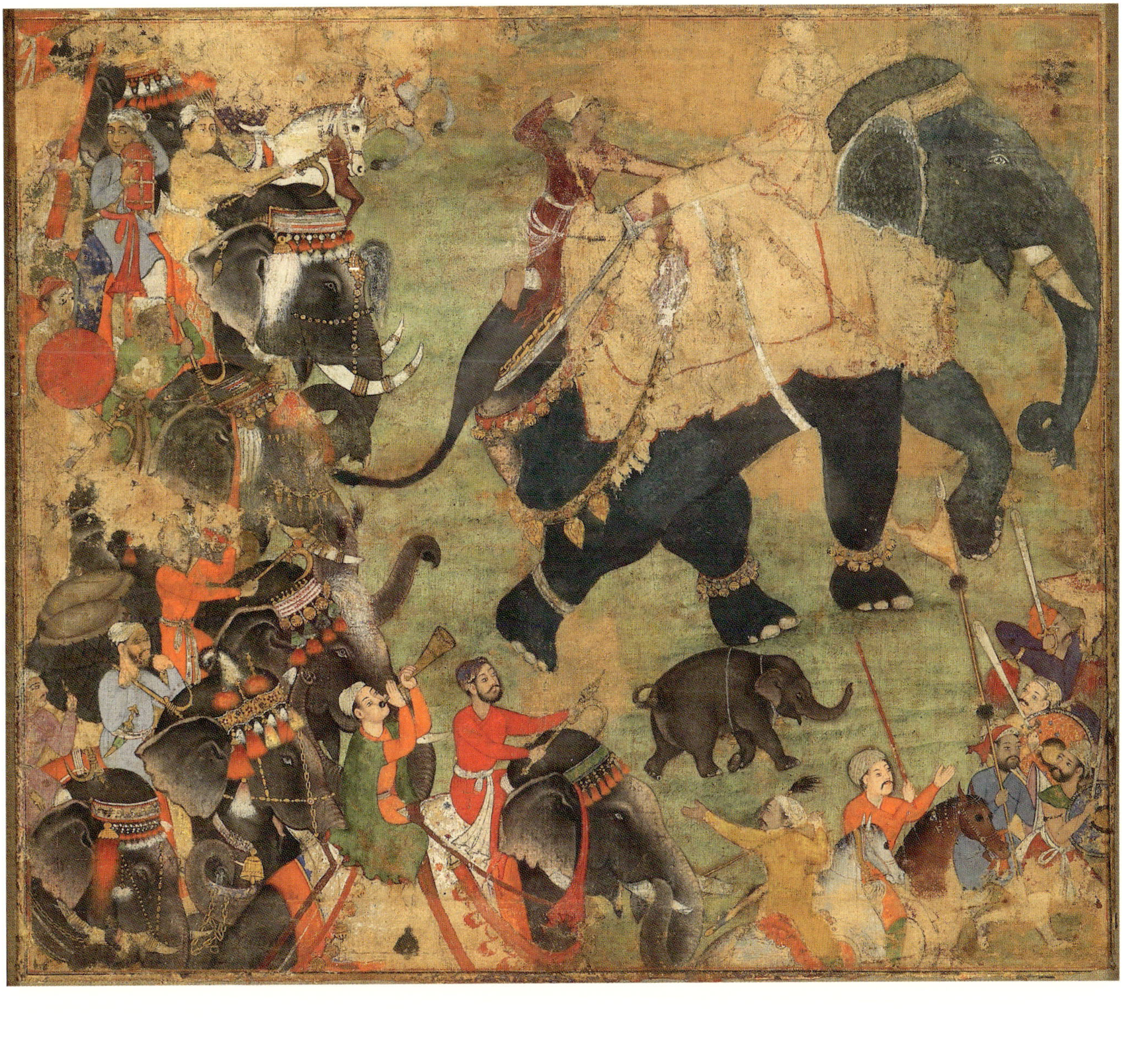

5 A hunter shoots a leopard

Illustration to the *Anwar-i Suhaili*
Mughal, *c.* 1570–75
Gouache with gold on paper, 13.3 × 17.8 cm
Hodgkin Loan 81
Published: Topsfield and Beach 1991, no. 3; Filippi 1997, no. 81

In this tale from a Persian version of the Sanskrit *Panchatantra*, an ancient collection of didactic animal fables, a hunter with a blue bow has shot a bounding leopard which is arrested in mid-stride. A dead dog and fox already lie bleeding on the ground. This spectacle is observed by a lynx in the right corner behind the pink rocks.

In the story, the lynx serves as the attendant of a lion but, distressed by his master's bloodthirsty ways, he decides to leave him. Shortly after, however, he chances upon a mouse which is tormenting a tree by gnawing its root; then a snake which swallows the mouse; a hedgehog which eats the snake; a fox which devours the hedgehog; and then a dog which savages the fox to death:

> The lynx was observing these marvels, each of which was a clear proof of the certainty of retribution, and was in expectancy as to what was next to come from the secret chamber of fate into the expanse of the plain of destiny, when suddenly it beheld a leopard, which rushed out from the corner of the desert, and before the dog was aware, tore its heart from its breast with his life-lacerating teeth. It happened that the leopard had sprung out without observing the ambush of a hunter, who was sitting close by with an arrow fitted to his bow. When he saw the leopard busy with the dog he discharged a heart-piercing shaft at it, which entered its right side and came out at the left.[1]

Subsequently the hunter skins the leopard. Then a horseman arrives on the scene and kills the hunter for the precious skin. As the horseman rides off, his horse stumbles and he too is finally thrown and killed. "Thus the actions of each, since they were based on injury to others, proved, by way of retaliation, injurious to himself." The moral is do no evil to others, or 'As thou judgest, so thou shalt be judged.'

This tightly composed fragment is charred at the edges, as in other surviving pages from this manuscript. The fire damage occurred in 1816 when the house of the Hon. Mountstuart Elphinstone, British Resident at Poona, to whom the manuscript belonged, was attacked and burned by the Marathas.[2]

1 Eastwick tr. 1854, pp. 516–22.

2 See e.g. Leach 1998, no. 3; Fondation Custodia 1986, pp. 5–6. Most of the pages from the Elphinstone manuscript were acquired in the 1930s by the Prince of Wales Museum (now Chhatrapati Shivaji Maharaj Vastu Sangrahalaya), Bombay.

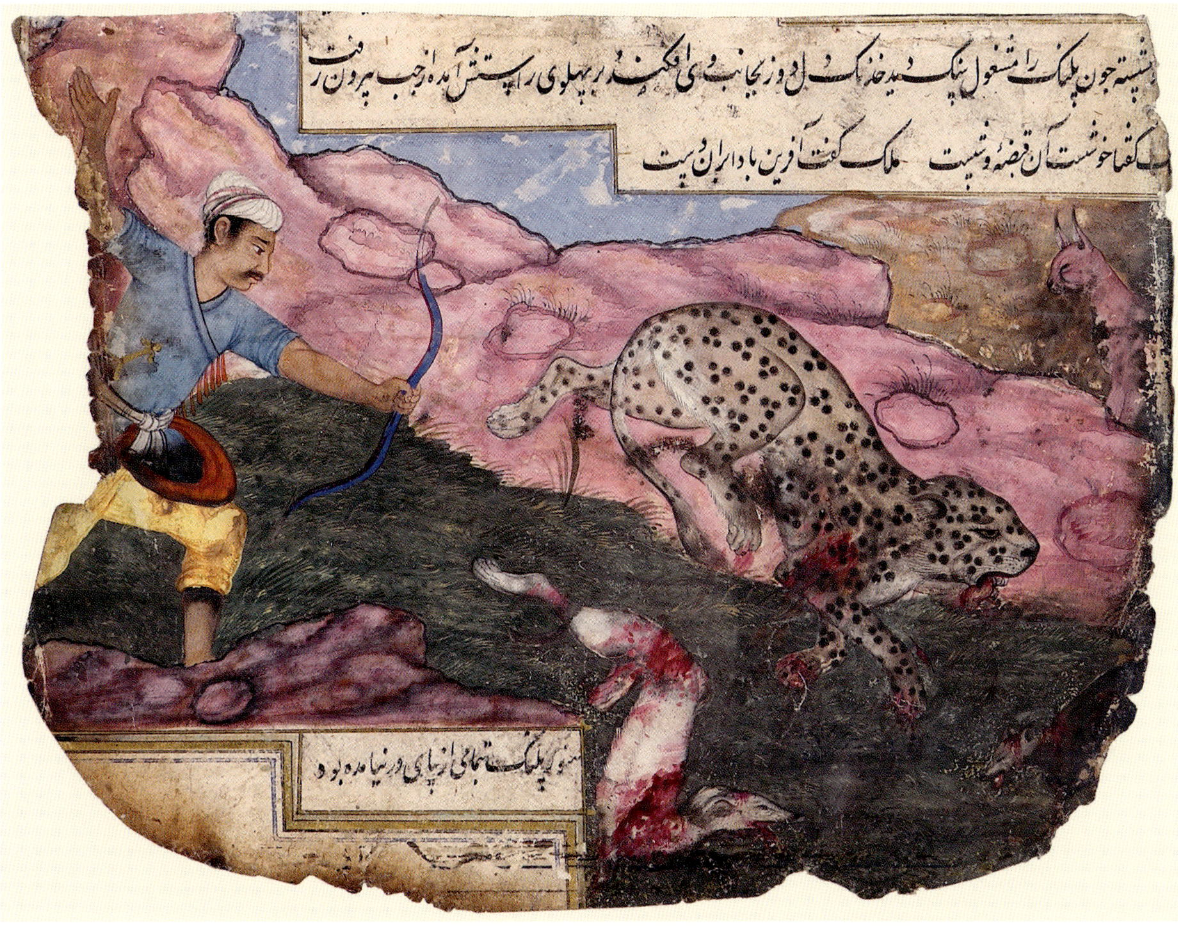

6 Krishna dances on the head of Kaliya

Illustration to the *Harivamsha*
Mughal, *c.*1590–95
Gouache with gold on paper, 29 × 32.2 cm
Hodgkin Loan 101
Unpublished

The god Krishna spent his early youth among the cow-herding villagers of the Braj country near Mathura. Even as an infant he had begun to reveal his divine nature by prodigious feats of strength and the slaying of demons. In this episode the young Krishna vanquishes the many-headed serpent king Kaliya, banishing him from the Jumna river where his presence had threatened the villagers and their cows.

Launching himself from a kadamba tree, Krishna tussled in the water with the mighty serpent. For a while it seemed to the fearful onlookers that the fight was going against him. But then, urged on by his brother Balarama,

> Krishna calmly spread apart his arms and snapped the serpent's stranglehold. Then he planted his foot on the slippery coils and, grabbing hold of the snake's central head, he bent it down and leapt onto the top of his wide-spreading hood. Perched there on the monster's head, Krishna began to dance about, his arm-bands glinting as he moved.[1]

Krishna, in gold crown and yellow dhoti and scarf, is here shown playing his flute in triumph as he pummels Kaliya into submission with his dancing feet. The pale-skinned Balarama meanwhile turns to Krishna's astonished foster-parents Nanda and Yashoda to indicate his victory.

This version of the story comes from the *Harivamsha*, one of several Hindu epics and mythological texts that were translated from Sanskrit into Persian for the free-thinking emperor Akbar. Although painted in the later years of his reign, almost a generation after the *Hamzanama* (nos.1–3), this composition still shows much of the same vigour and narrative drama. Its upper part is dominated by the kadamba tree growing from the rhythmically indented riverbank, its lower part by the monstrous heads and writhing coils of the great snake, amid crisply billowing wavelets with inquisitive fish and slender-snouted gharials.

1 Hutchins 1980, p.48.

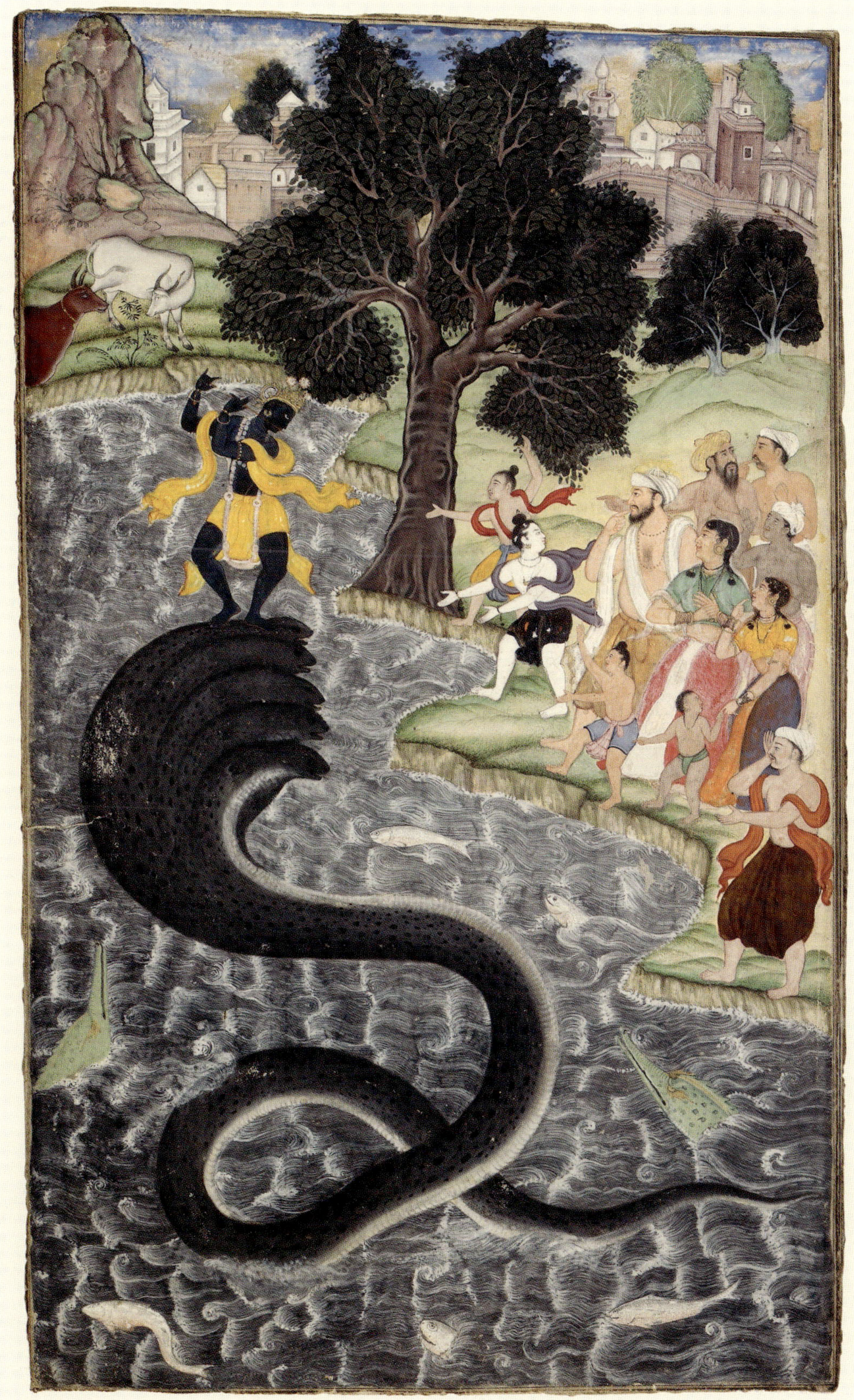

7 Bad news at court

Fragmentary illustration to the *Tarikh-i Alfi*
Mughal, *c.*1592–94
Gouache with gold on paper, 12.5 × 21.6 cm
Hodgkin Loan 94
Unpublished

Something momentous, probably a military defeat, has been announced at court. In this fragmentary lower section of a manuscript page, attendants and courtiers assembled at the foot of a throne area (above) make eloquent gestures of surprise and concern. Several are open-mouthed or cry out with amazement, including the huntsman with his hawk and the groom with a horse in the lower corners.

Despite the Mughal architectural setting, the scene is Arabia in the early days of Islam. This fragmentary folio belonged to a great illustrated history, the *Tarikh-i Alfi* or 'History of a Thousand Years', commissioned by the emperor Akbar in 1581–82, in anticipation of the Islamic millennium ten years later. This "history of all the kings of Islam" was to chronicle the thousand years since the time of the Prophet and "to mention therein the events of whole world."[1] Work on the project became protracted, and the illustrated imperial copy of the text is thought to have been executed finally in 1592–94. It had around three hundred illustrations, of which only a tenth now survive. Its tall pages are often dominated by their text panels, with the illustrations grouped around these in the interstices and borders.

The accompanying text on the present folio fragment is missing, but on its other side (below) the six lines of text appear to relate to the conflicts among he clans of the Quraish tribe in the early seventh century AD.[2] The passage tells of Abu Harb killing a hostile soldier from the army of a certain Mutasem, then departing disguised in a *burqa*. This exciting tale is not depicted in the adjacent illustration, which may show warriors defeated in battle by Mutasem who anxiously await a further attack. Several are gathering rocks and logs by a river. It seems likely also that the scene of the courtiers' consternation (above) may show the announcement of the same defeat to the clan leader and his entourage.

1 See Beach 1981, pp. 91–99; also Brand and Lowry 1986, pp. 70–71.

2 I am grateful to Dr John Gurney for his helpful advice on this passage and for providing an English literal version: "They said that he left and the reason for his departure was that early a soldier from Mu'tasem's army came to his house, dismounted and [but] Harb's wife had obstructed him. The soldier became angry, struck the woman's hand with a stick, and the mark remained until Abu Harb arrived. When Abu Harb saw her state, he immediately laid in wait for the soldier and killed him. And afterwards he covered his own face with a burqa' and took refuge in the mountains of Syria and exhorted the people to 'enjoin the good and forbid the evil' and he related to them the disgraceful deeds of Mu'tasem, and he claimed that he was of the Sufyani. It was said that after a while, when the Sufyani [Sufayaneh] rule will have collapsed, someone from amongst them would be found who will become the ruler of Syria. He said (and the people understood its meaning to be...)".

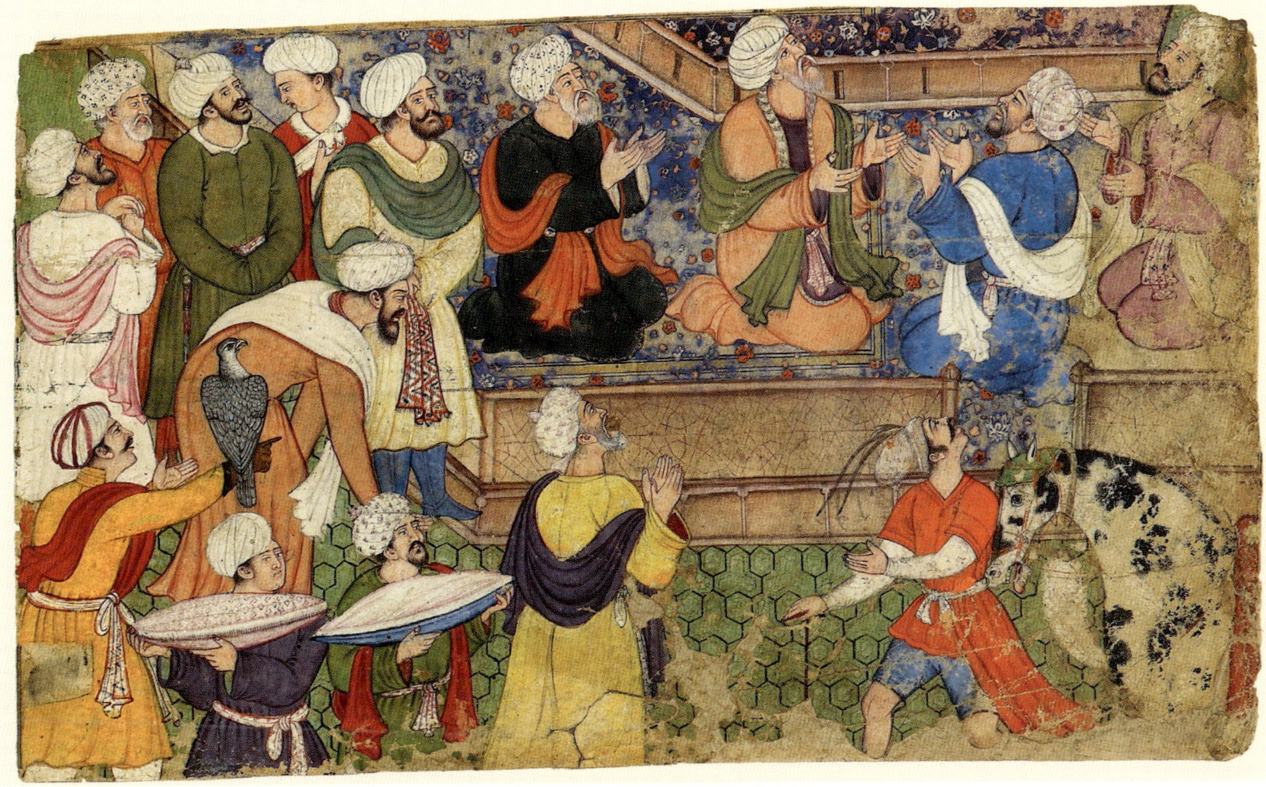

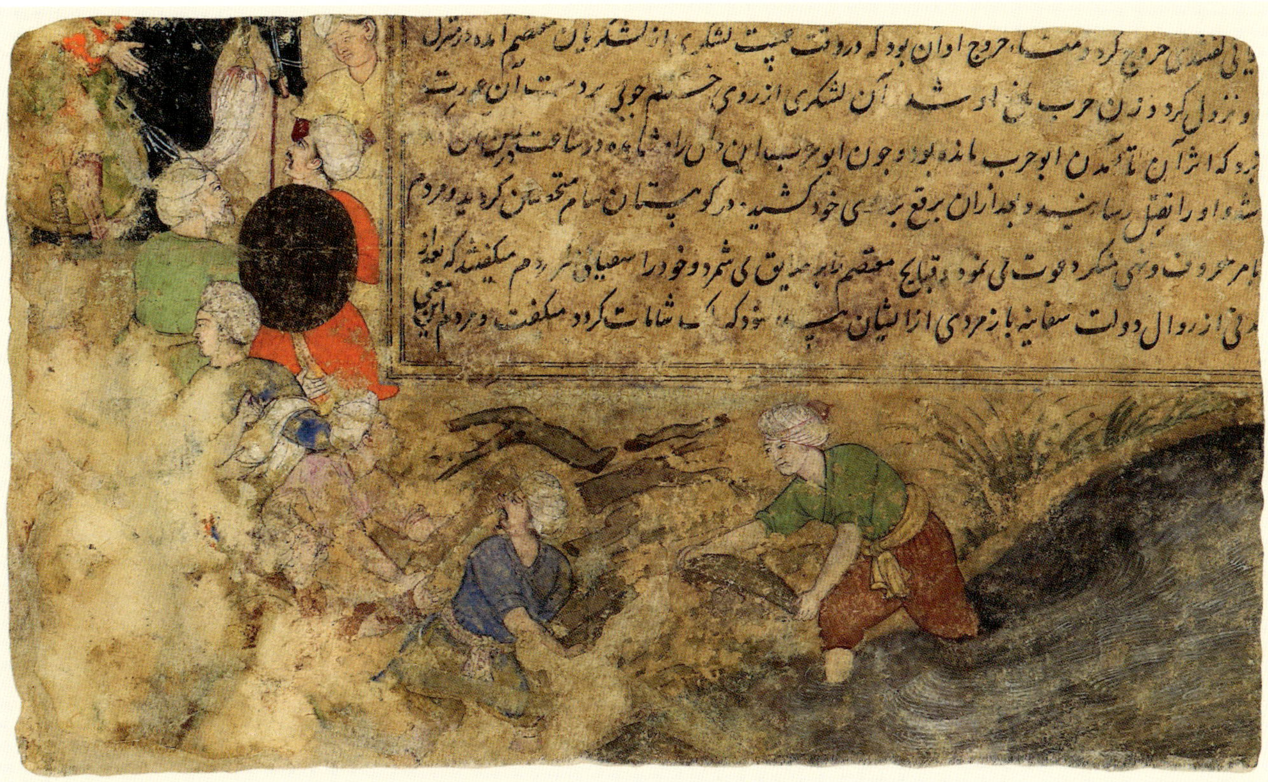

8 Rama's forest dwelling in Panchavati

Illustration to the *Ramayana*
Sub-imperial Mughal, *c.*1605
Gouache with gold on paper, 28.8 × 19.1 cm
Hodgkin Loan 12
Published: McInerney 1982, no.7;
Topsfield and Beach 1991, no.4; Filippi 1997, no.12

In the *Aranyakanda* (Book of the Forest), the third book of the *Ramayana* epic, the divine prince Rama is exiled from his homeland of Ayodhya as the result of a family intrigue against him. Together with his loyal wife Sita and half-brother Lakshmana, he leaves the court to wander in distant forests. There they encounter the sage Agastya, who directs them to build a home in the delightful forest region of Panchavati. Lakshmana constructs for them "a spacious hut with walls of mud, supported by strong stakes made of long graceful bamboos, thatched with boughs of the Shami tree."[1] He uses grasses and creepers to strengthen it, reeds and leaves for its roof.

No such humble materials are seen in this artist's vision of Rama's forest abode. It is an ornate, fantastical Mughal pavilion more befitting a prince or a god, richly coloured and abounding in lively floral arabesques and the rhythmical blue and white patterned floor-spread and chequered tiles.[2] While the figure types and freely painted landscape details are in a sub-imperial Mughal style, the treatment of architecture recalls an older Rajput tradition of flat planes of vibrant colour or pattern. There is great sensitivity and feeling in the way Rama, seated beneath an arching tree with feathery leaves, gazes with direct intensity into the eyes of Sita. Lakshmana meanwhile looks decorously away, keeping watch for game with his bow and arrow in hand.

The patron of this *Ramayana* series[3] was most likely a Rajput noble, as the text passage on the reverse is in the original Sanskrit, not the Persian translation commissioned by Akbar in 1584 as part of his programme to make the Mughal nobility more conversant with Hindu culture. It is thought that this patron was probably Bir Singh Deo Bandila of Datia,[4] a prominent nobleman of Bundelkhand in Central India.

1 Shastri tr. 1957, vol.II, p.35.
2 See Seyller in Mason ed.2001, no.16, and no.6, with attributions of several further pages to the present artist.
3 Chandra 1957–59; see also e.g. Seyller 1999, pp.33–34, figs.12–13; Topsfield ed.2004, no.157, for a similar powerful use (or even surfeit) of contrasting geometric and arabesque architectural patterns.
4 The series was formerly in the Datia Palace collection. Its pages were at some time damaged by fire at the edges in varying degrees.

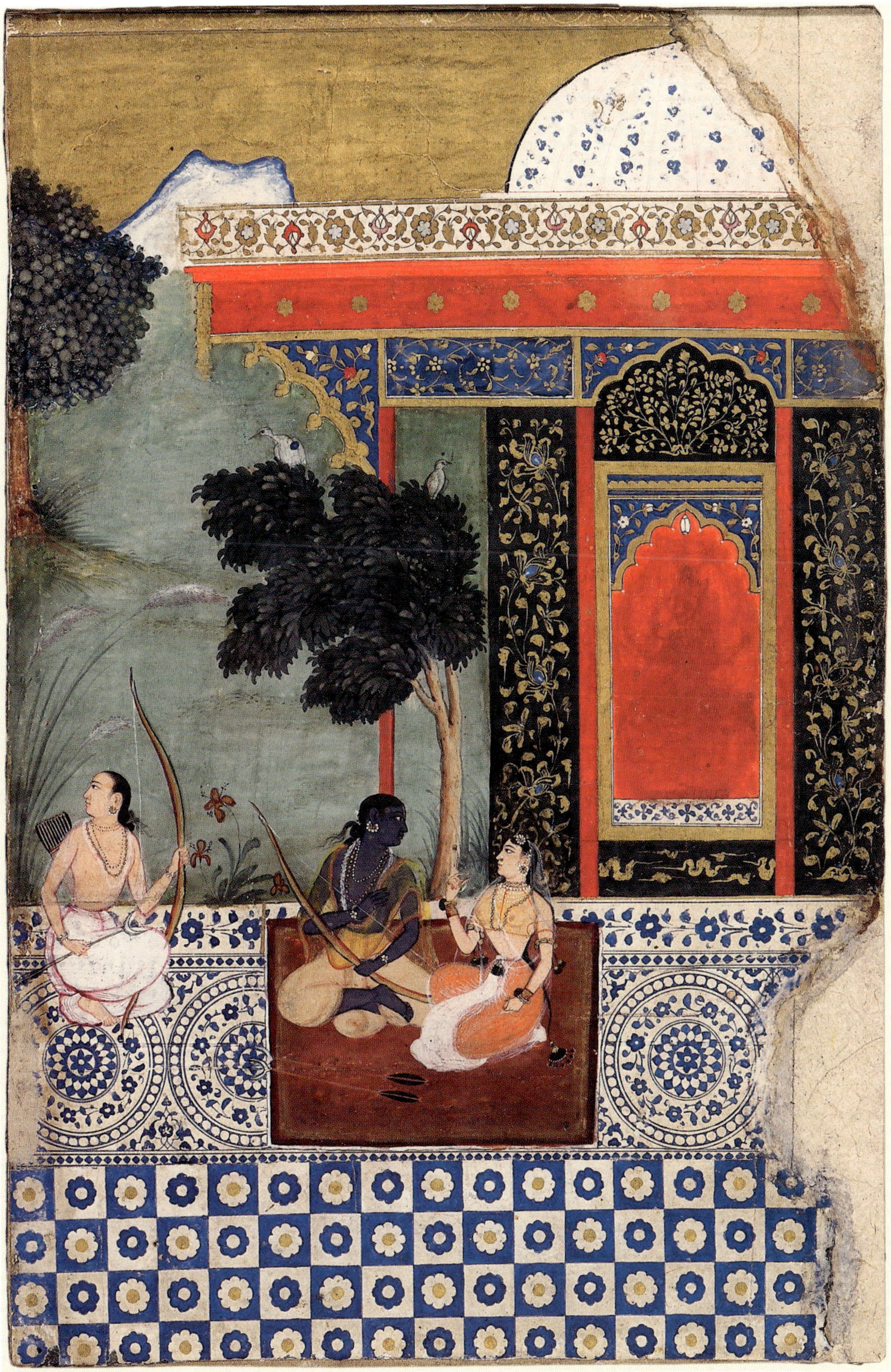

9 Dhritarashtra attacks the statue of Bhima

Illustration to the *Razmnama*
By Qasim. Sub-imperial Mughal, *c.* 1616–17[1]
Gouache with gold on paper, 38.8 × 24 cm
Hodgkin Loan 10
Published: Grube n.d., no. 245;
Topsfield and Beach 1991, no. 5; Filippi 1997, no. 10.

Commissioned by the emperor Akbar in 1582, the *Razmnama* is a Persian translation of the *Mahabharata*, the Indian epic whose central narrative relates the rivalry and war between the Pandava family and their Kaurava cousins. Towards the end, the blind Kaurava king Dhritarashtra meets the victorious Pandava princes again. Overcome by grief for his slain sons, he angrily sets upon the mighty warrior prince Bhima. But the god Krishna, ally of the Pandava brothers, divines his murderous intention. Pulling Bhima aside, he miraculously substitutes an iron statue in his image. The old blind king crushes the iron Bhima with his bare hands before his anger finally passes.

In the painter Qasim's version, Dhritarashtra wrestles with the metal image which also seems to grasp him round the body. The real Bhima stands beside Krishna, gazing in wonder like the other Pandavas and courtiers. The setting is the courtyard of a Mughal pavilion with four doors and slender columns supporting gold leonine capitals, and a roof terrace above with distant trees and pairs of birds. Qasim was an artist employed by Abd ur-Rahim Khankhanan (1556–1626), a leading Mughal courtier and Commander-in-chief of the armies, who was also a poet, scholar and patron of art and literature. This page comes from an incomplete and widely dispersed *Razmnama* manuscript which was prepared around 1616–17 by artists working for the Khankhanan.[2]

1 Inscribed below: *'amal-i qasim*
2 Seyller 1985, Appendix B, lists 68 pages from the present series, this one being no. 19; Seyller 1999, pp. 252–57.

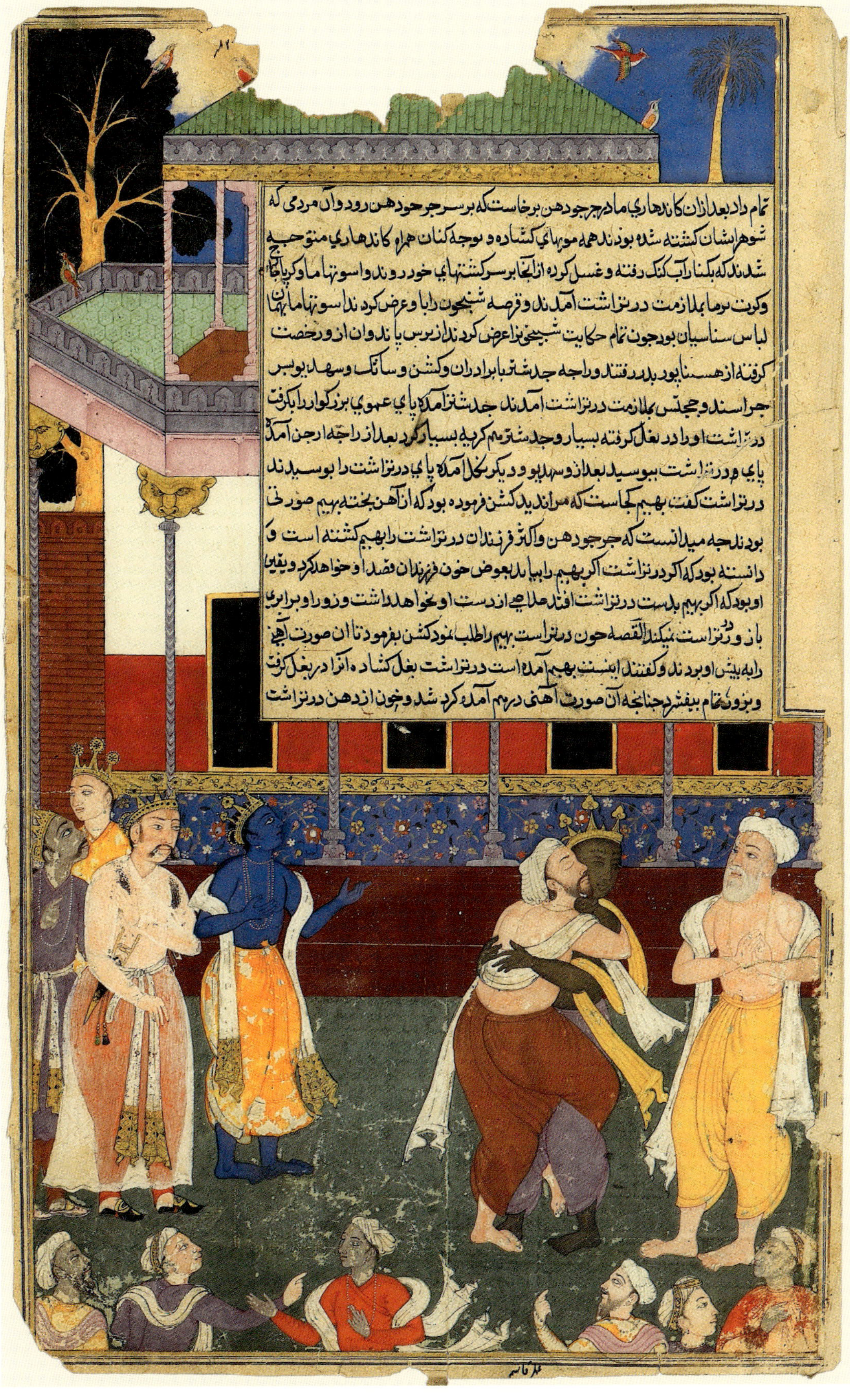
تمام داد بعد از آن کاندهاری مادر جرجودهن برخاست که بر سر جرجودهن رود و آن مردمی که
شوهر ایشان کشته شده بودند همه موهای گشاده و نوحه کنان همراه کاندهاری متوجه
شدند که بکنار آب کنگ رفته و غسل کرده از آنجا بر سر کشتهای خود روند و اسوتهاما و کرپاچارج
و کرت بوما بملازمت درتراشت آمدند و قصه شنیجون را با و عرض کردند اسوتهاما بهمان
لباس سناسیان بود چون تمام حکایت شنیجی را عرض کردند از پس پاندوان از و رخصت
گرفته از هستنا پور بدر رفتند و راجه جدشتر با برادران و کشن و سانک و سهدیو بسر
جراسند و جچلس بملازمت درتراشت آمدند جدشتر آمده پای عموی بزرگوار را بگرفت
درتراشت او را در بغل گرفته بسیار و جدشتر هم گریه بسیار کرد بعد از راجه ارجن آمده
پای درتراشت ببوسید بعد از و سهدیو و دیگر نکل آمده پای درتراشت را بوسیدند
درتراشت گفت بهیم کجاست که مرا ندید کشن فرموده بود که از آهن بجثه بهیم صورتی
بودند چه میدانست که جرجودهن و اکثر فرزندان درتراشت را بهیم کشته است و
دانسته بود که اگر درتراشت اگر بهیم را بیابد بعوض خون فرزندان قصد او خواهد کرد و یقین
او بود که اگر بهیم بدست درتراشت افتد علاج از دست او نخواهد داشت و زور او برابری
باز و درتراست نمیکند القصه چون درتراست بهیم را طلب نمود کشن بفرمود تا آن صورت آهنی
را به پیش او بردند و گفتند اینست بهیم آمده است درتراشت بغل گشاده آنرا در بغل گرفت
و بزور تمام بیفشرد چنانچه آن صورت آهنی درهم آمده گرد شد و خون از دهن درتراشت
عمل قاسم

10 A gathering of dervishes

Mughal, *c.* 1605–10
Gouache with gold on paper, 27.8 × 21.2 cm
Hodgkin Loan 102
Published: Habighorst et al. 2007, fig. 69

Assemblies of dervishes or Sufi mystics became a popular genre subject in seventeenth century Mughal painting, as did the more dissolute gatherings of common drug addicts. In some cases these genres might overlap with satirical intent. The setting of this refined yet subversive picture is a verdant, Persianate hillside with a central chenar tree (Oriental plane), flowering plants and minutely painted, preternaturally glittering gold herbage. At the foot of the chenar a garden water-course has been laid out, and a loose circle of over twenty dervishes has gathered around its central tank. Many if not all are under the influence of *bhang*, a strong decoction of marijuana which is being sieved and prepared by the men seated in the right foreground. Other dervishes meanwhile converse among themselves, pass the *bhang* cup around, or sit slumped in intoxicated languor. One man sprawls against the chenar, while others in the left foreground perhaps admire the beauty of a blue and white vase filled with flowers.

Such scenes of the worldly or otherworldly drunkenness of Muslim and Hindu ascetics generally tend to caricature the participants to humorous effect. As the setting of the present painting suggests, the genre had Safavid Persian antecedents, but it became greatly elaborated by Mughal and other Indian painters from this period onwards.

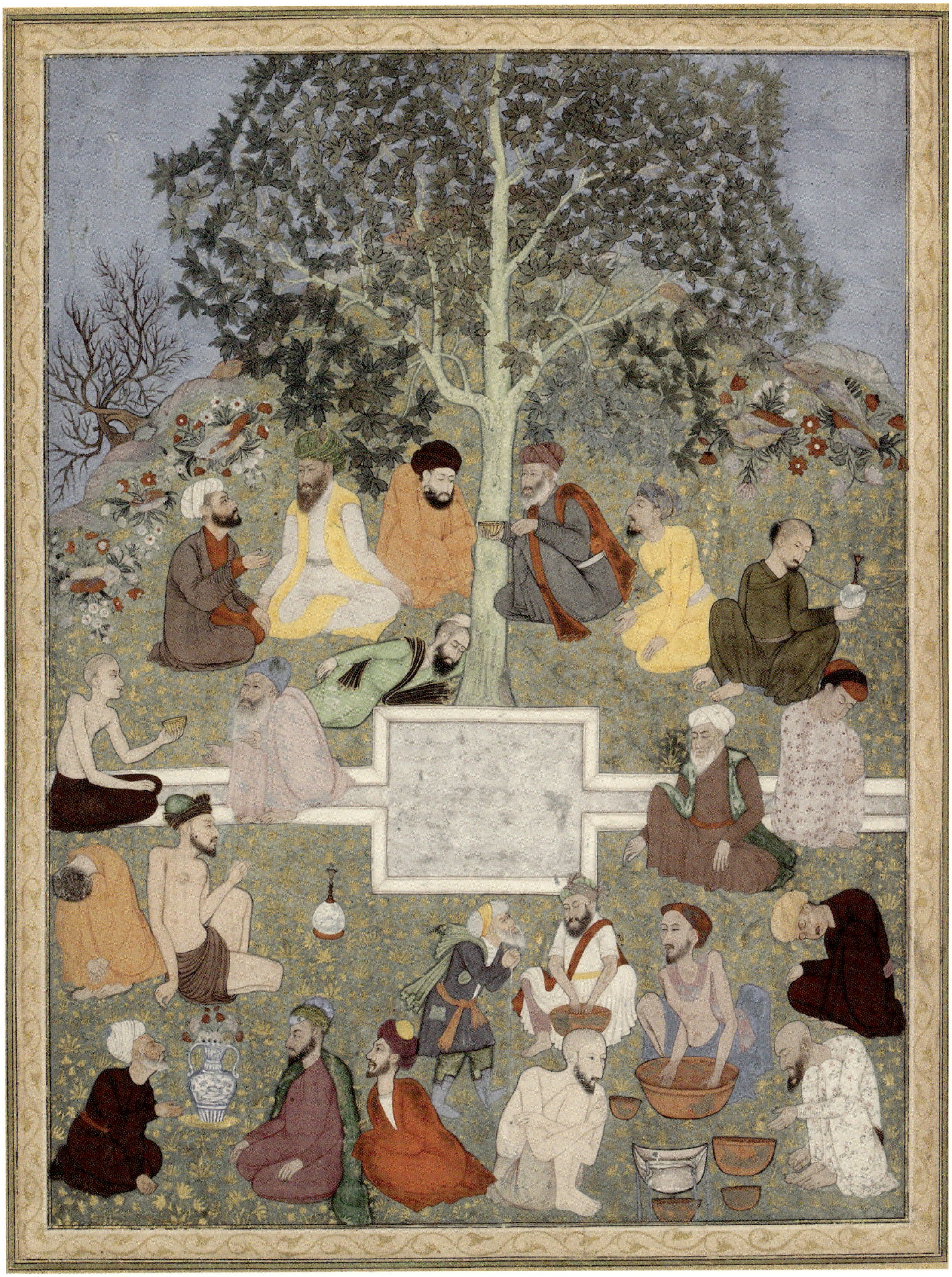

11 Elephants fighting

Mughal, *c.* 1600. By Khurshid Banu
Gouache with gold on paper, 22.5 × 27.7 cm[1]
Hodgkin Loan 97
Unpublished

Elephant fights were among the most popular royal entertainments in Mughal times. One such combat is described by the French traveller Bernier in the mid-seventeenth century:

> "...The two ponderous beasts meet one another face to face, each having a couple of riders, that the place of the man who sits on the shoulders, for the purpose of guiding the elephant with a large iron hook, may immediately be supplied if he should be thrown down. The riders animate the elephants either by soothing words, or by chiding them as cowards, and urge them on with their heels... The stronger or more courageous elephant passes on and attacks his opponent and, putting him to flight, pursues and fastens on him with such obstinacy that the animals can be separated only by means of *cherkys*, or fireworks, which are made to explode between them."[2]

The present fight has become quite spirited as the elephants tussle trunk to trunk. The mahout on the rearing animal on the right drops his ankus and hangs on grimly to the harness ropes, as does his assistant (or *bhoi*) seated behind. The mahout on the left gesticulates with raised arms as he urges his beast to greater deeds.

By the early seventeenth century paintings of such combats were a common Mughal genre. This example, evidently following an earlier model, is unusual for its ascription to a female artist, Khurshid Banu. She is one of several noble ladies of the imperial Mughal household who are known to have received instruction in painting,[3] and this is her only known work.

1 Inscribed below in Persian: *'amal-i khurshid banu*. On the back are three Mughal seals of the 1650s, with the names Itimad Khan and Inayat Khan, courtiers of Shah Jahan, and a librarian of Aurangzeb / Alamgir; also three inscriptions in Persian or devanagari, one of the latter a formulaic inscription dated A.H. 1111 (1699–1700) added at Amber, found on a number of paintings from that royal collection which later passed into the possession of the Maharanas of Mewar. A late 19th century Mewar inventory number (25/232) also appears.

2 Bernier 1916, pp. 267–77. The *charkhi* (or wheel) was a type of Catherine Wheel mounted on a long pole.

3 A tentative identification of Khurshid Banu with a lady of the emperor Humayun's household named Khurshid Kukah (mentioned in Gulbadan's *Humayun-nama*, tr. Beveridge, p. 121) has been suggested by Robert Skelton, though that lady would have been at least 70 by the time this picture was made.

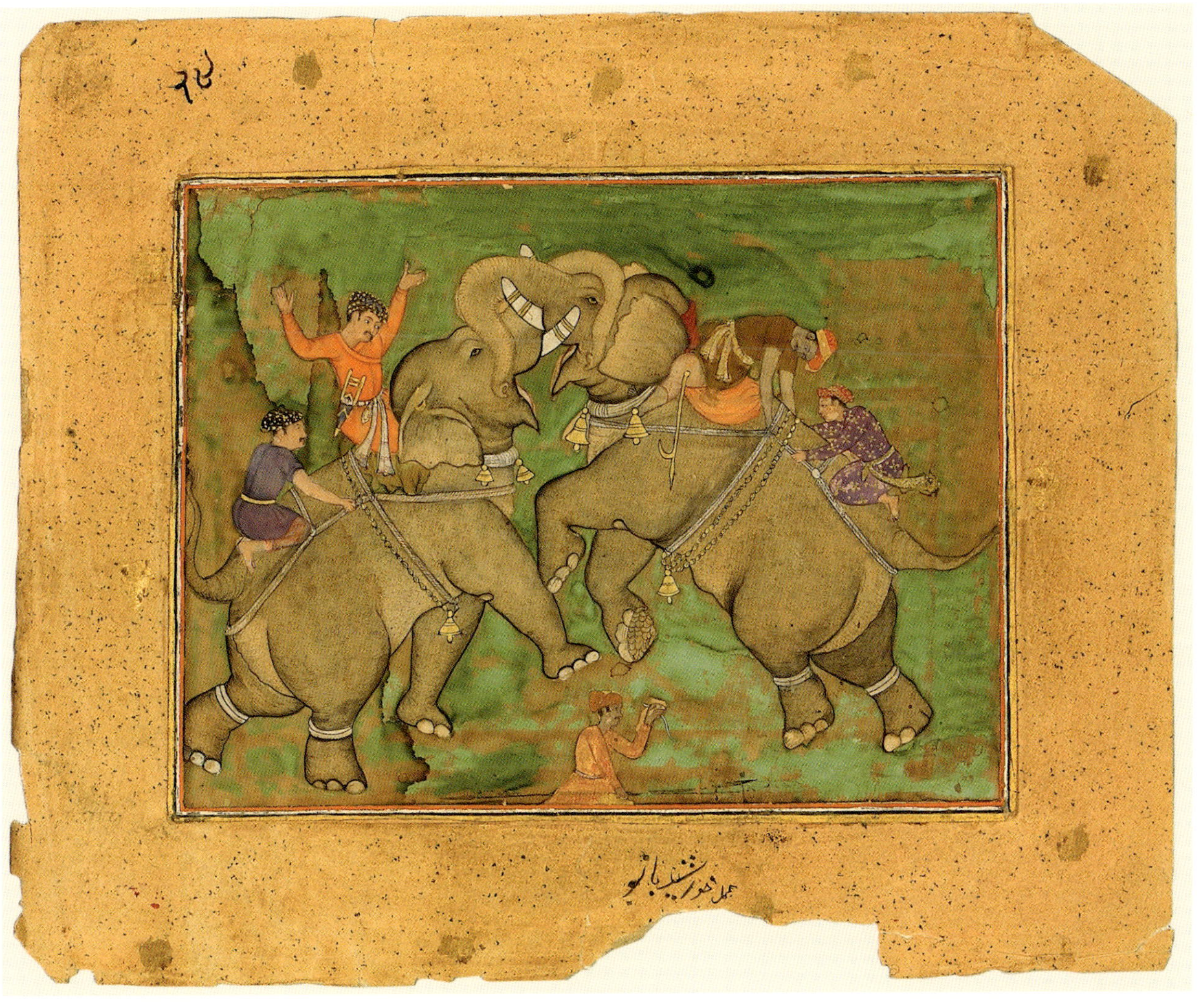

12 Two orioles

Mughal, *c.*1610

Gouache on paper, 15.1 × 8.6 cm[1]

Hodgkin Loan 65

Published: Spink and Son 1987, no.2; Topsfield and Beach 1991, no.6; Filippi 1997, no.65

The upper bird in this artfully composed natural history study is a male Indian Golden Oriole (*Oriolus kundoo*), a species found in southern and central Asia. The lower bird is a male Black-hooded Oriole (*Oriolus xanthornus*), a resident of tropical southern Asia from India to Indonesia. Both are commonly seen birds in India. With their vivid, mainly yellow plumage they complement each other well in this near-symmetrical grouping, as they eye a flying insect.

The early Mughal emperors took a keen interest in the flora and fauna of their new Indian empire. The memoirs of Babur and Jahangir both include firsthand descriptions of birds and plants which had caught their interest, and illustrated copies of those texts include some well-observed depictions of the species that they mention. The arrival of European botanical and natural history prints, brought to the Mughal court by visiting merchants and missionaries, increasingly influenced the ways in which Indian artists composed their studies of plants, birds and animals. This composition of orioles among flowering plants, with one bird about to seize the intervening insect, belongs to a group of works closely related to European natural history studies of the late sixteenth to early seventeenth centuries.[2] Like their Western models, these accomplished Mughal studies tend to isolate their subjects against a plain paper ground, with incidental floral or landscape elements.

1 Mughal seals and devanagari inscriptions on the reverse of the picture indicate that it had several seventeenth century owners before entering the royal collection of the Maharanas of Mewar.

2 For comparable works in the Musée Guimet, Paris, see Bibliothèque Nationale 1986, nos.117–18.

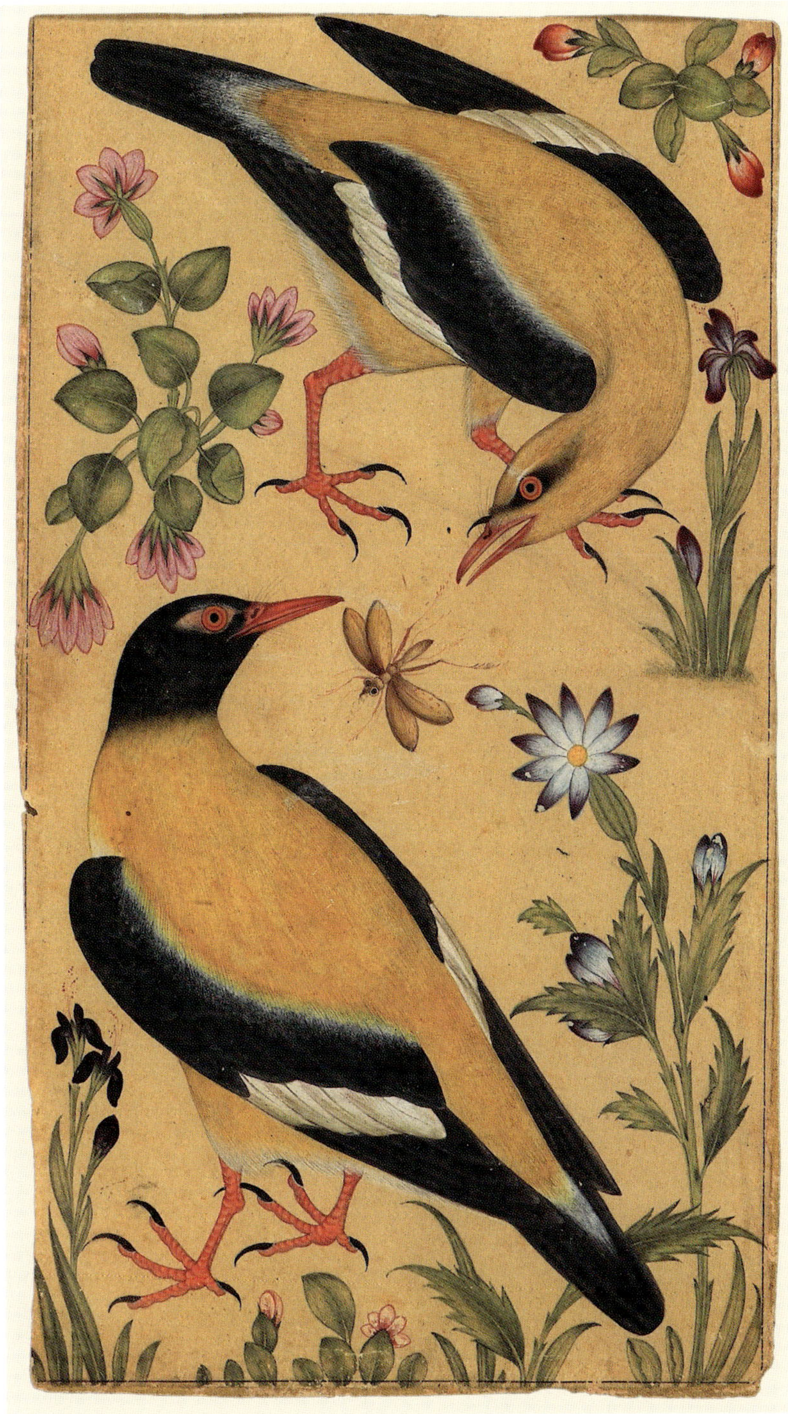

13 A pair of mynas

Mughal, *c.*1620

Gouache on paper, 14.6 × 9.5 cm

Hodgkin Loan 68

Published: Welch 1963b, fig. 20; Filippi 1997, no. 68

In this impressive Mughal bird study, two mynas (the Common or Indian Myna, *Acridotheres tristis*) stand vividly silhouetted against a strong red ground. The painter captures well the mannerisms and natural inquisitive-ness of the species. Standing close together, both birds stare attentively in the same direction, the female turning her head and raising a bunched claw as though poised for motion. The slightly larger male myna opens his beak as though making a warning call to his mate; or he could perhaps even be talking. Often kept as

cage birds, mynas were prized in India as elsewhere for their uncanny mimicry of the human voice and other sounds. Members of the starling family, they frequently colonise man-made structures such as temples and mosques, where it is said they have been known to learn and repeat the daily prayers of the faithful.

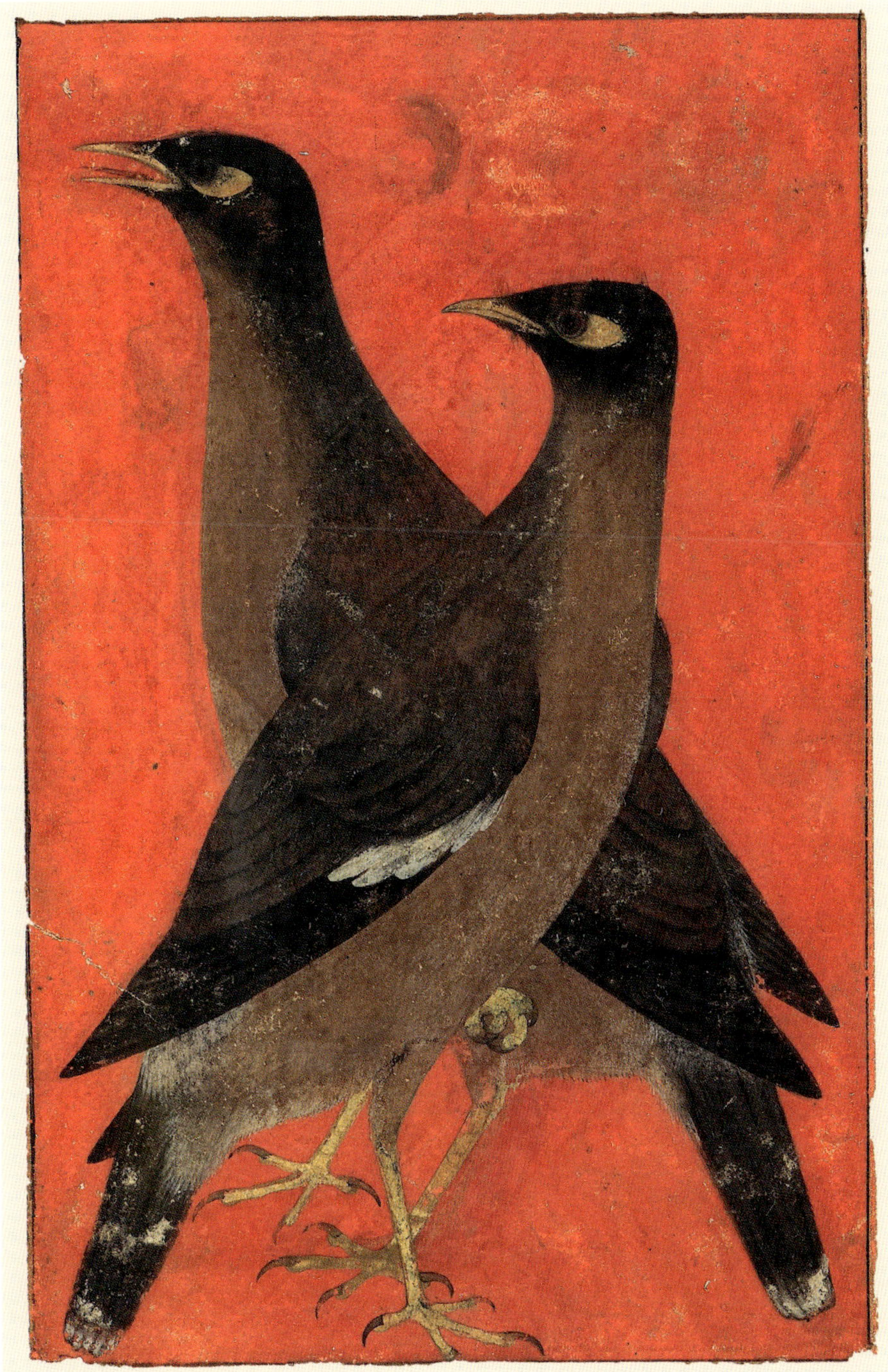

14 Two pigeons

Mughal, *c.*1650
Gouache on paper, 22 × 12.5 cm
Hodgkin Loan 92
Unpublished

In this fine study a pair of Imperial Pigeons stand together, isolated against the plain paper ground, the smaller female bird inclining her head at a slightly different angle to her mate. Their heads and breasts are white, while the wing and tail feathers, carefully delineated in wave-like patterns, are painted in rich blue and grey-blue tones. The legs of the nearer, male pigeon are visible and bear gold rings, suggesting that these are prized birds in imperial possession. The composition follows, in reverse, an earlier painting of pigeons (browner in colouration) in the Bibliothèque Nationale, Paris.[1] It may have been based on a tracing or pounce from that or a similar work.

Pigeon-flying, known as *ishq-bazi* or 'love play', was a favourite pastime of the nobility during the Mughal period. The emperor Akbar was particularly devoted to the sport. According to Abu'l Fazl, "the amusement which His Majesty derives from the tumbling and flying of the pigeons reminds one of the ecstasy and transport of enthusiastic dervishes; he praises God for the wonders of creation."[2] More than twenty thousand pigeons were kept at Akbar's court, of which five hundred were classified as *khasa* or choice imperial birds. Chief among these was "a well-trained pigeon of bluish colour" known as Mohana, on which Akbar lavished special care and which in turn became the progenitor of many more champion birds.

1 Bibliothèque Nationale 1986, no.119; Hurel 2010, no.29.
2 Abu'l Fazl, *Ain-i Akbari*, I, pp.310–14, with a detailed account of pigeon types and behaviour.

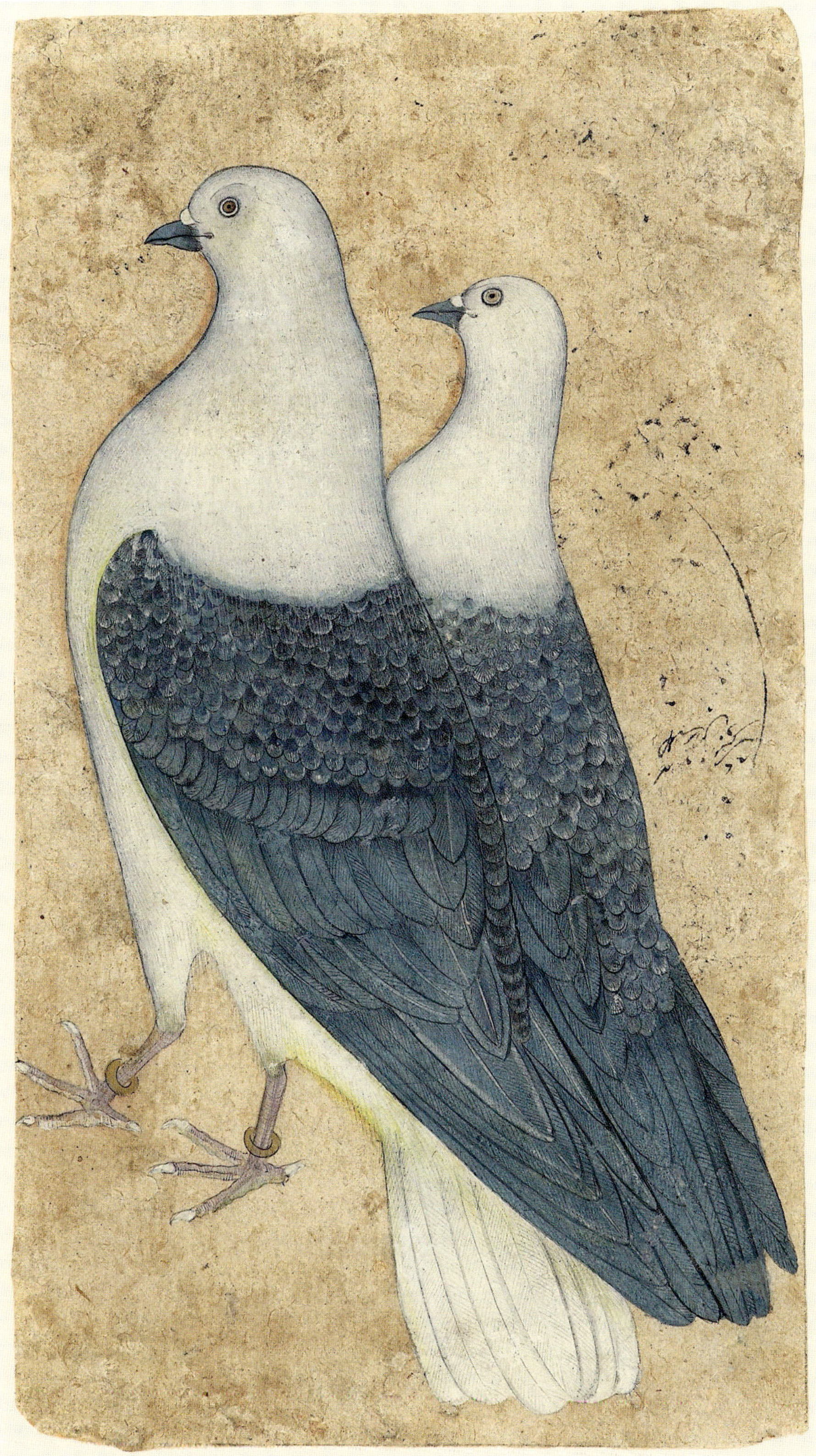

15 Attendants at an imperial durbar

Mughal, *c.*1645. Ascribed to Hunhar[1]

Gouache with gold on paper, 36.8 × 26.9 cm

Hodgkin Loan 14

Published: Beach and Koch 1997, fig.162, p.225, App. U; Filippi 1997, no.14

This right hand page from a double-page composition was probably intended for a manuscript of the *Padshahnama*, the official history of Shah Jahan's reign. In the left hand page, the emperor would be receiving the Persian ambassador in full durbar assembly. Here the lesser grandees and court attendants are assembled. They include several of the ambassador's retinue, standing formally in a row to the left in their Safavid style turbans. In front of them grooms hold two horses. To the right stand a larger and a smaller imperial elephant, magnificently portrayed with their youthful riders. An attendant standing in front of them waves a fragrant censer. Further behind stand three more ranks of minor nobles and courtiers, one of whom smiles directly at the viewer.

Crowning the composition, the musicians of the *naqqarakhana* ('drum house') above the ceremonial gate beat their thunderous kettle-drums with animation, accompanied by the long, sonorous horns and reedy, wailing *shehnais*. The guardians of the gateway stand below exchanging pleasantries. This vignette of imperial ceremonial life is notable not least for the fine portraiture of the two elephants. The painting is ascribed below to the painter Hunhar and is possibly by him.

1 Inscribed below: *kar-i hunhar*.

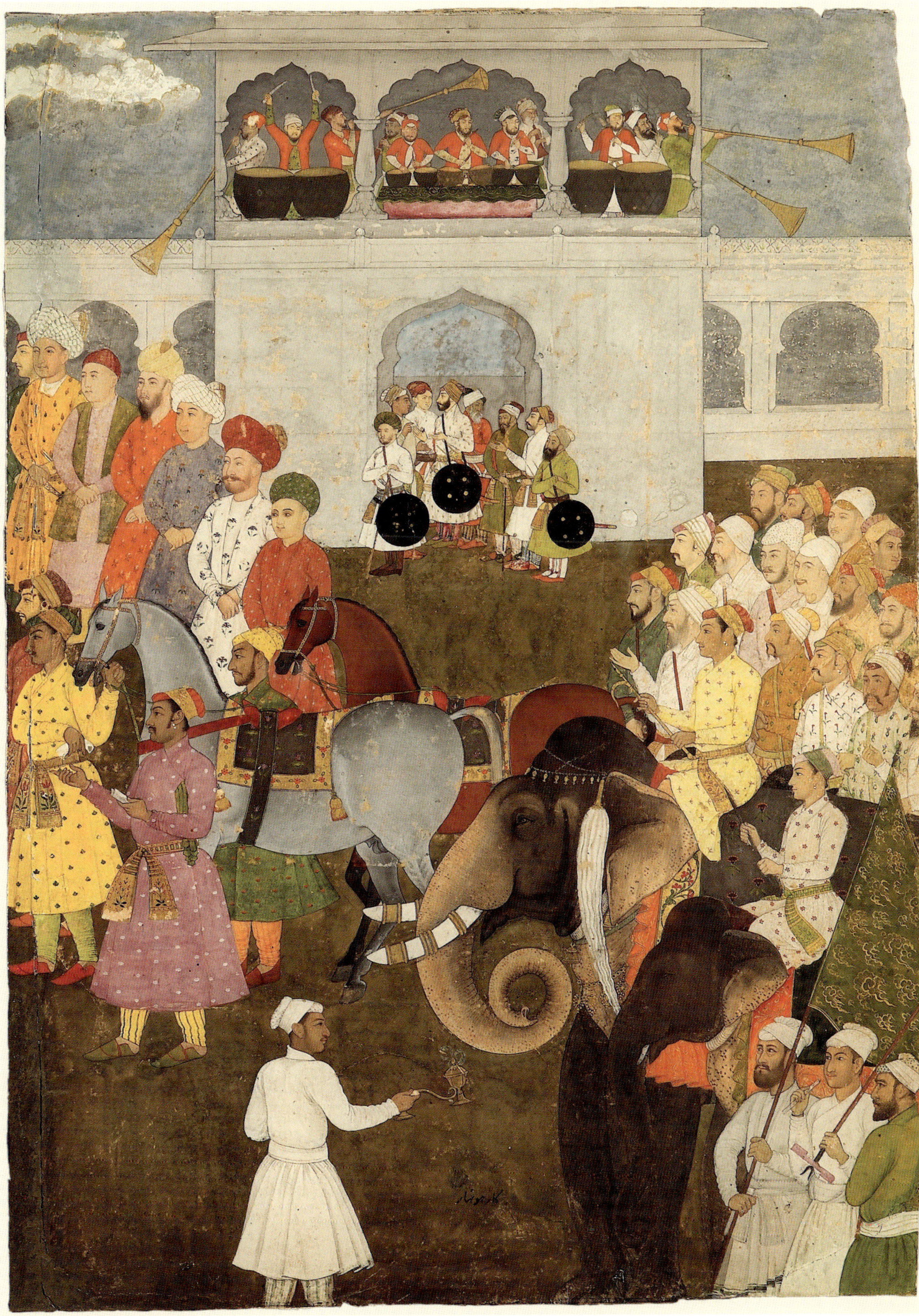

16 Iltifat Khan

Mughal, *c.*1640
Brush drawing with pigment on paper, 43 × 31.6 cm[1]
Hodgkin Loan 35
Published: McInerney 1982, no.14; Hodgkin and McInerney 1983, no.7; Topsfield and Beach, no.12; Brand 1995, no.99; Filippi 1997, no.35

This life-size head of an officer of Shah Jahan's court is a portrait of unusual immediacy. The artist's first outlines and later corrections are clearly visible in his reworking of areas such as the turban and ear. Not intended as a finished work, this vivid drawing from life is a rare surviving study of the kind that Mughal painters might have referred to when called upon to depict a particular courtier in one of the grand imperial durbar scenes of the period. Iltifat Khan appropriately appears in profile, as if standing at attention and looking up at the enthroned emperor. He emanates the sober poise of the seasoned courtier, yet his more personal qualities – an evident intelligence, a fastidious set of the lips – also show through.

This is in fact Iltifat Khan's only known portrait. He seems never to have been depicted in more finished works, either individually or as an attendant figure at a durbar, unlike his father and his son[2] after him. He remained in obscurity largely through an innate lack of ambition or drive. A descendant of the Safavid Persian royal dynasty, he is briefly mentioned by Jahangir in his journals for 1615 as having been "honoured with the title Iltifat Khan."[3] His father Mirza Rustam of Qandahar had taken service under Akbar and became a leading Mughal grandee, marrying his daughters to Parviz, a son of Jahangir, and Shah Shuja', a son of Shah Jahan. Iltifat Khan was also well connected, having married the daughter of Abd ur-Rahim Khankhanan, commander-in-chief and a great patron of the arts (no.9). But after his father's death in 1642, this well-born Mughal under-achiever chose the quiet life. Retiring early from the imperial service, he passed his remaining years 'in ease and freedom from care' at Patna[4] and died there in 1657.

1 Inscribed: *iltaphat khan amir syahjihani*: as the devanagari inscription indicates, this drawing was formerly preserved in a Rajasthani royal collection.
2 E.g. Beach and Koch 1997, pp.161, 165, 172, 201, for durbar depictions of Mirza Rustam Safavi; and Gahlin 1991, no.31, and Crill and Jariwala 2010, no.26, for a portrait of Iltifat Khan's only son Mirza Murad Kam, who later received the title Mukarram Khan from Shah Jahan in 1655.
3 Jahangir, *Tuzuk*, I, p.298.
4 Shah Nawaz Khan, *Maathir ul-Umara*, II, p.247.

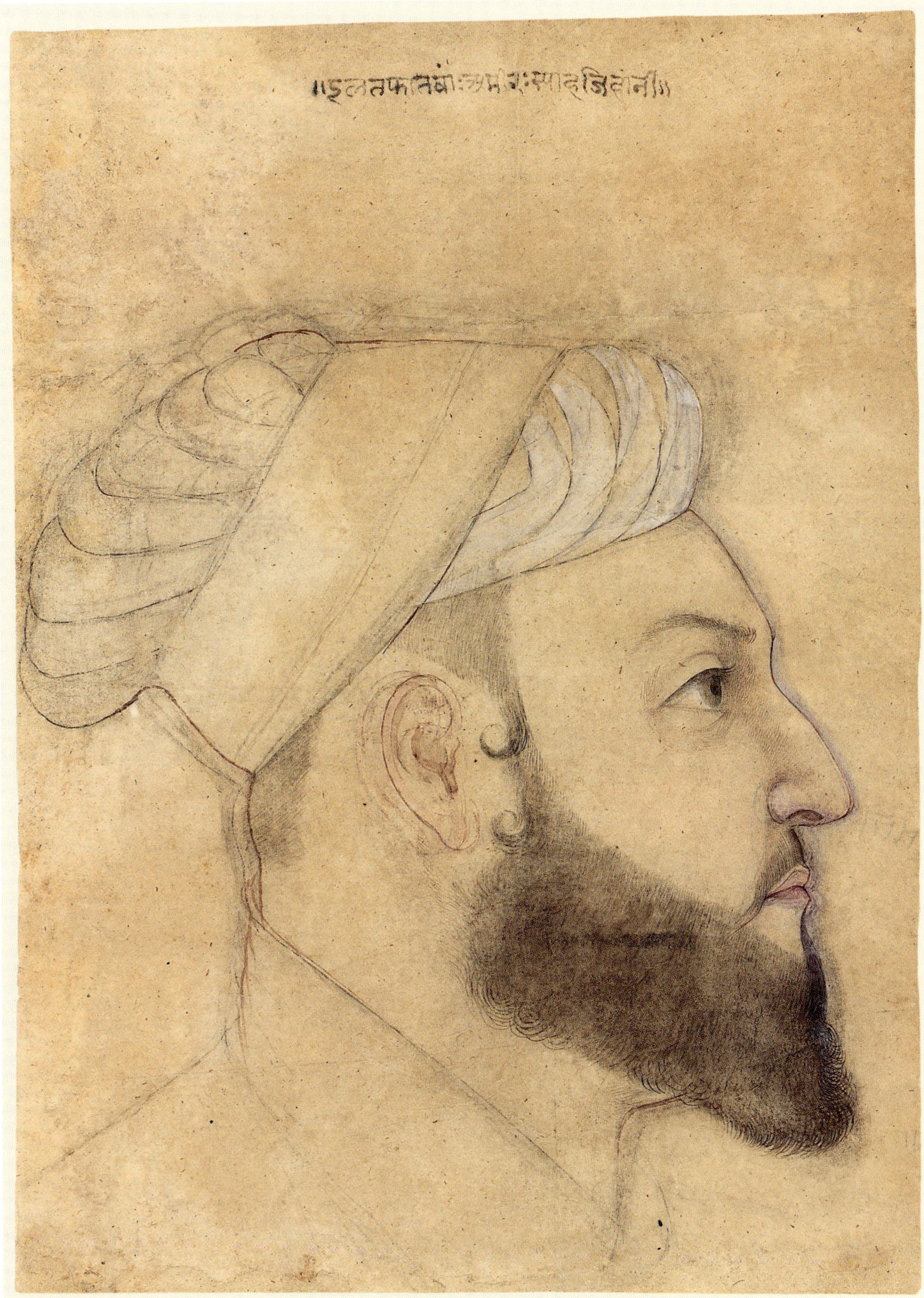

17 Prince Aurangzeb

Mughal style in the Deccan, *c.*1653–55
Gouache with gold on paper, 37.2 × 27.3 cm
Hodgkin Loan 88
Unpublished

The third son of the emperor Shah Jahan, Aurangzeb would eventually depose his father in 1658, succeeding him after a fratricidal war as the emperor Alamgir ('Seizer of the World'). He appears here, in a common Mughal convention, wearing full court dress against a plain green ground, with a draped balcony before him, as though he were appearing ceremonially at a palace *jharoka* window. This fine portrait was most likely painted by a Mughal-trained artist working in the Deccan, possibly at Aurangabad, the Mughal military headquarters in the region. It could date from near the end of Aurangzeb's first term as viceroy of the Deccan (1636–44), or perhaps more likely from early in his subsequent term as governor (1653–57). When he returned to the Deccan in 1653 he was thirty-five. His appearance here may be compared with his portrait as a younger man by Lalchand, dating from the early 1640s.[1]

The artist has strongly delineated the features of the pious warrior prince, accentuating the outlines of the profile, eye and mouth. The formal sobriety of the *jharoka*-type portrait is offset by the rich floral, arabesque and other textile patterns of the turban and robe, throne cushion and balcony cover, and the lavish jewellery, from the pearls and swallowtail pendants suspended from the prince's aigrette to his heavy jewelled necklace and pendant.

1 Chester Beatty Library, Dublin: Leach 1995, I, pp.470–71, no.3.80; Wright 2008, no.86.

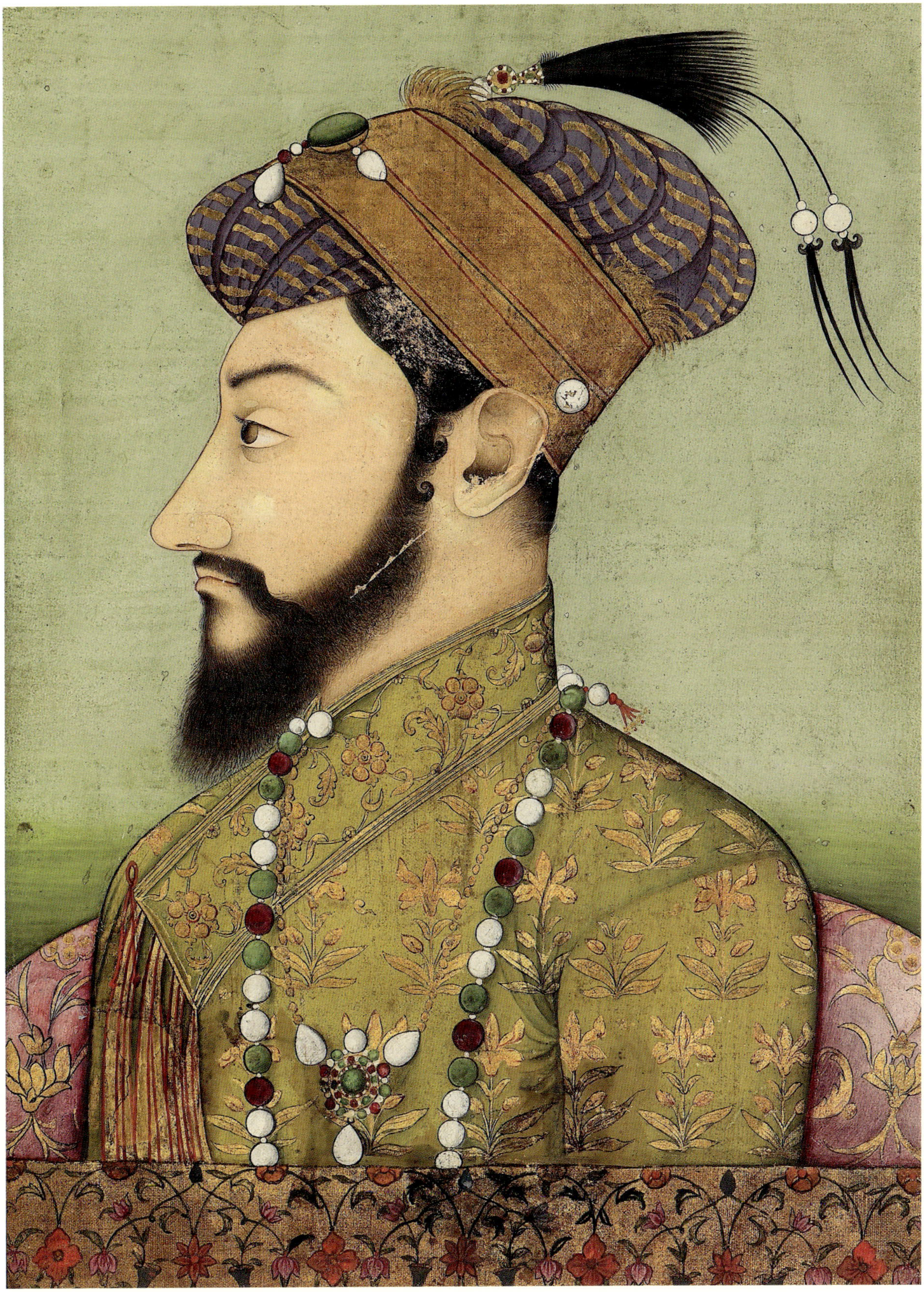

18 Nobleman smoking on a terrace

Mughal or Deccan, *c.*1670. Ascribed to Ali Reza
Gouache with gold on paper, 22 × 18.3 cm[1]
Hodgkin Loan 112
Published: Zebrowski 1983, fig.190; Overton 2011, fig.14, pp.376, 386–89

A Mughal nobleman, probably an officer serving with Aurangzeb's armies in the Deccan, takes his ease on a palace terrace. Wearing a pink floral robe, he rests comfortably against well-filled cushions, his unbuckled dagger beside him. He holds a porcelain wine-cup and the long stem of his Persian hookah, which is held steady by a youth in a flowered gold robe whom he regards with a steady gaze. Two darker-skinned, youthful attendants stand at either side, one making a gesture of greeting. Beyond the Mughal columns, cusped arches and furled brocade screens, a fountain plays in a wide pool. In the distance is a walled garden with symmetrically planted trees.

With its subtly heightened palette and its ambience of dignified, sensuous ease, this painting reveals the interaction between the realism of Mughal portrait conventions and the more imaginative Deccani sensibility that was taking place at Mughal centres in the Deccan such as Aurangabad. It is sometimes debatable whether a Mughal artist is adapting to the Deccan, or a Deccani artist modifying his style for Mughal patrons. From the refined naturalism of his style the artist Ali Reza seems to have been among those Mughal-trained painters who sought employment in the Deccan during the final decades of the seventeenth century.[2] The painting is mounted in a seventeenth century Mughal album page with floral borders, with a specimen of Persian calligraphy on the reverse by the celebrated Muhammad Husain Kashmiri.

1 Inscribed in Persian in lower right corner: *'amal-i 'ali reza*. Among the flaked white paint traces in the shallow bowl in the foreground are black marks which may have belonged to another inscription.

2 Overton 2011 tentatively and not altogether persuasively identifies him with the great Bijapur master whom Zebrowski 1983 calls the Bodleian Painter.

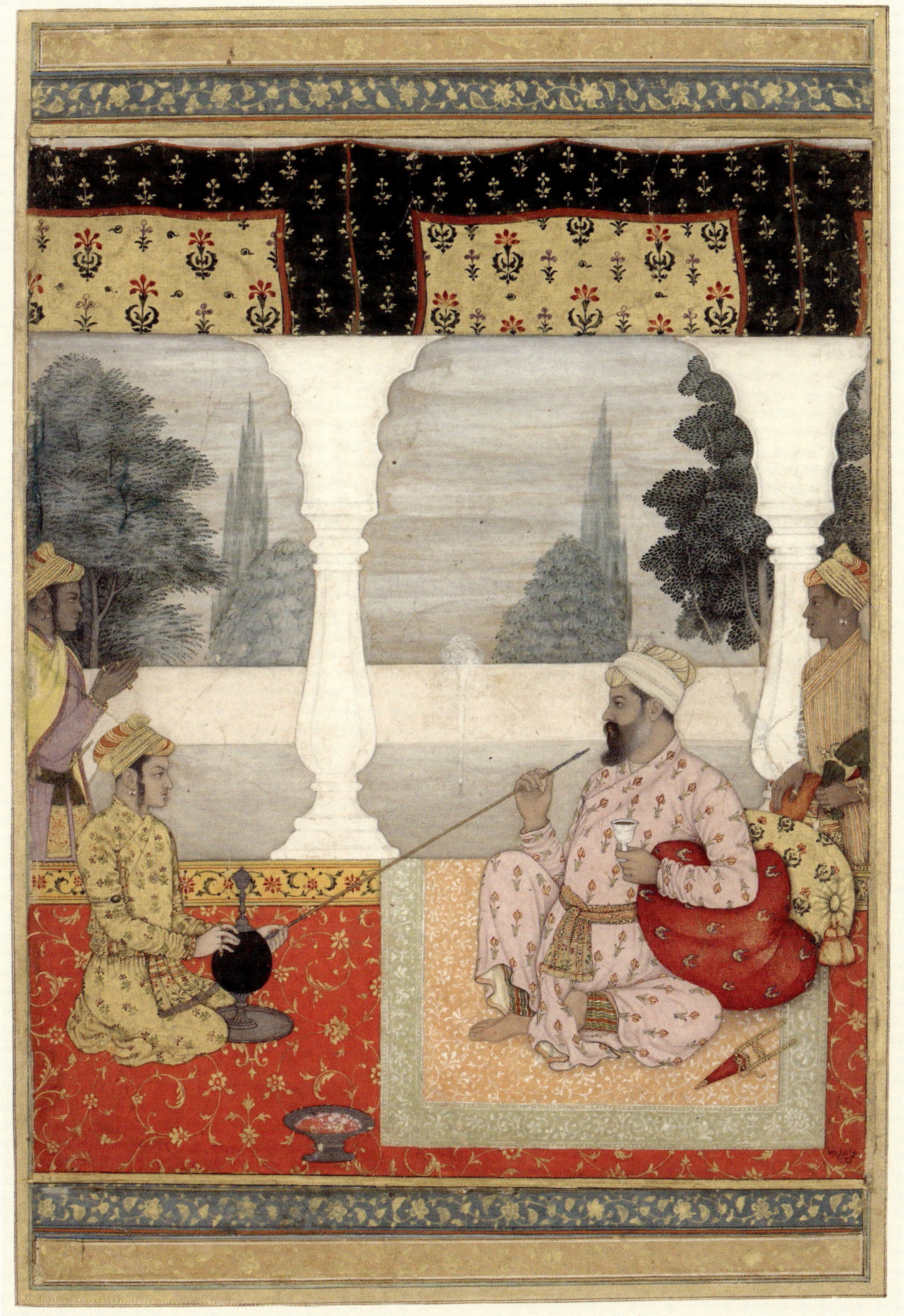

19 Music party on a riverside terrace

Mughal, *c.*1670

Gouache with gold on paper, 36.2 × 26.7 cm

Hodgkin Loan 21

Published: Topsfield and Beach 1991, no.16; Filippi 1997, no.21; Koch 2006, fig.25, p.29

A music party is being held on the terrace of one of the noblemen's *havelis* or garden mansions that lined the riverfronts at Agra, upstream from the Taj Mahal.[1] The frontage of several of these pleasant residences can be seen in the distance across the Jumna river, on which a nobleman's barge and two other craft are plying and a cargo barge is towed by men on the shore.

The Muslim noble who hosts the soirée presides against a flowered gold cushion, an attendant with a peacock feather fan behind him. Holding a rose, he gazes with grave courtesy at his chief guest who shares the same floor-spread. Other nobles, both Muslim and Hindu from the style of their robes,[2] sit to the left, some clasping their shields. While a formal decorum prevails, this is also a scene of relaxed enjoyment as the invited assembly listen with absorption to the musicians performing on the right. The lead singer in pink parts his lips in song, while he and his companion softly clap the *tala* (rhythmic cycle) with their hands. Three instrumentalists playing vina, tanpura and pakhavaj drum accompany them with calm concentration. The underlying animation of the occasion is conveyed more by the rhythmical red railings and the boldly coloured flowers, fronds and tendrils in the carpet, which seem to coil or expand in sympathy with the music.

1 Koch 2006, Ch.1.

2 From Akbar's time it became customary for Muslim nobles to wear the *jama* (court robe) tied on the right side, and Hindu nobles on the left.

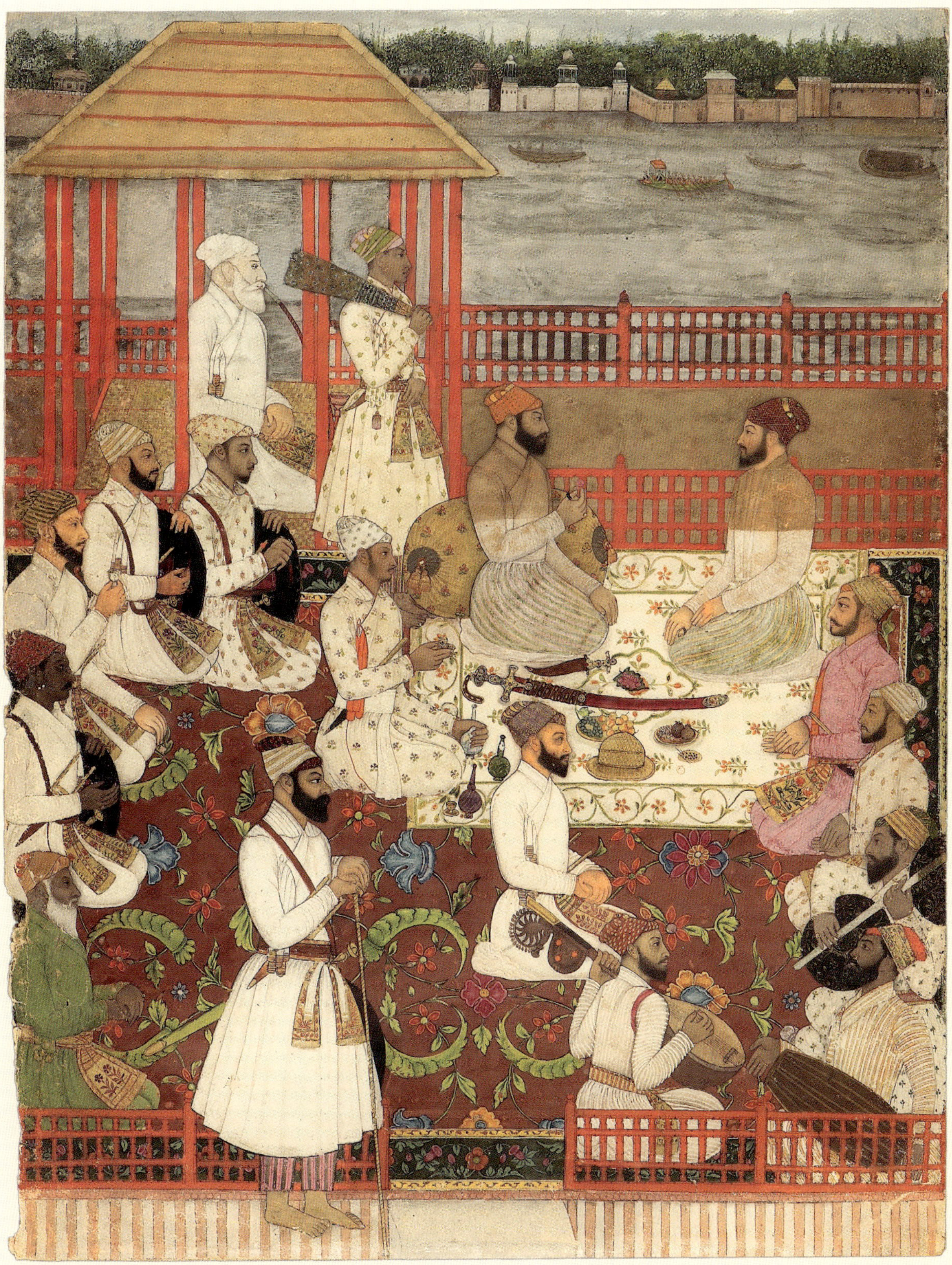

20 Elephant and rider

Mughal, *c.*1640
Gouache with gold on paper, 32 × 40.5 cm
Hodgkin Loan 56
Published: Pal et al. 1989, fig.189; Topsfield and Beach 1991, no.9; Filippi 1997, no.56

Elephants were highly prized by the Mughal emperors, as by other Indian rulers, for their formidable power in battle. As Abu'l Fazl relates,

> This wonderful animal is in bulk and strength like a mountain; and in courage and ferocity like a lion. It adds materially to the pomp of a king and to the success of a conqueror; and is of the greatest value for the army. Experienced men of Hindustan put the value of a good elephant equal to five hundred horses.[1]

Their other main function was as ceremonial mounts ridden on state occasions, where their imposing stature and calm dignity would enhance the ruler's majestic presence. Outstanding elephants were among the most prestigious and valuable gifts that one ruler could bestow on another, and from the early seventeenth century portraits of the finest animals in the imperial stables were increasingly produced by Mughal artists. Often these were annotated, either by scribes or their imperial owners, with the elephant's name and other information.

In this superb example of the Shah Jahan period, an imperial elephant stands patiently in profile for his portrait. His rider, wearing a fine transparent muslin robe, sits with his ankus held ready. The artist renders the animal's benign and intelligent gaze with particular sympathy, meticulously observing the slight fraying of the ear, the wrinkled folds of the trunk and the gentle spiral of its tip. His shaded modelling of the body brings out its massive rounded volumes, in contrast to the arresting flat pattern of the brocade saddle-cloth, decorated with the rows of lilies, tulips and other flowers which had become universal Mughal decorative motifs. The setting, as so often, is minimally suggested, with matching flowering shrubs at each corner and a rich pale yellow ground suggesting the light of gathering evening.

1 Abu'l Fazl, *Ain-i Akbari*, I, pp.123–24.

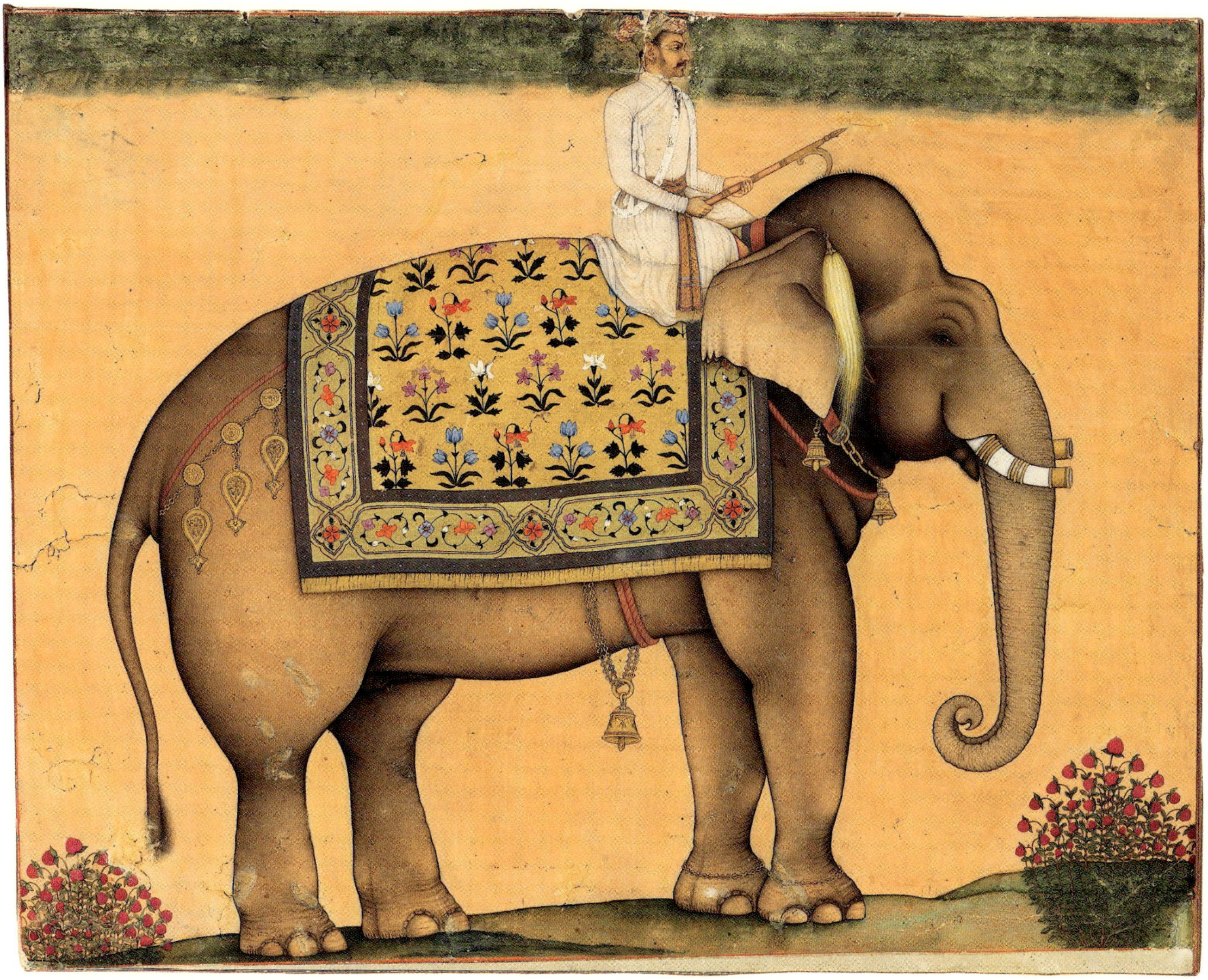

21 The elephant Khushi Khan

Mughal, *c.*1650

Gouache with gold on paper, 26.2 × 35.3 cm[1]

Hodgkin Loan 58

Published: Filippi 1997, no.58

The elephant Khushi Khan ('Lord of Happiness') stands caparisoned with ornamental trappings and bells and a gold-embroidered red and blue saddle-cloth that awaits a royal rider. He is outlined against a plain ground of the pale verdigris colour often used in Mughal portraiture. In a convention of the Shah Jahan period, his name is recorded between his fore and hind-legs, here written in red within a gold cartouche next to the elephant's hanging bell. Such bells were more than decorative, being necessary in any crowded place "to warn the passers-by and give them time to get out of the way; for when an elephant runs, or merely walks, he does not stop like a horse would."[2]

Khushi Khan's skin colour is a rich dark grey, relieved by the mottled pale pink skin of trunk, neck and ear tips. Both the dark colour and the rosy mottling were traditionally considered to be among the many marks of beauty and distinction in elephants.[3] He stands docilely for his portrait, with no mahout to control him. A seasoned campaigner, he evidently had a happy and equable temperament to match his name.

1 Inscribed: *shabih-i fil khushi khan.*
2 Manucci 1907–09, II, p.364.
3 Edgerton 1931, pp.10–11, 54–55.

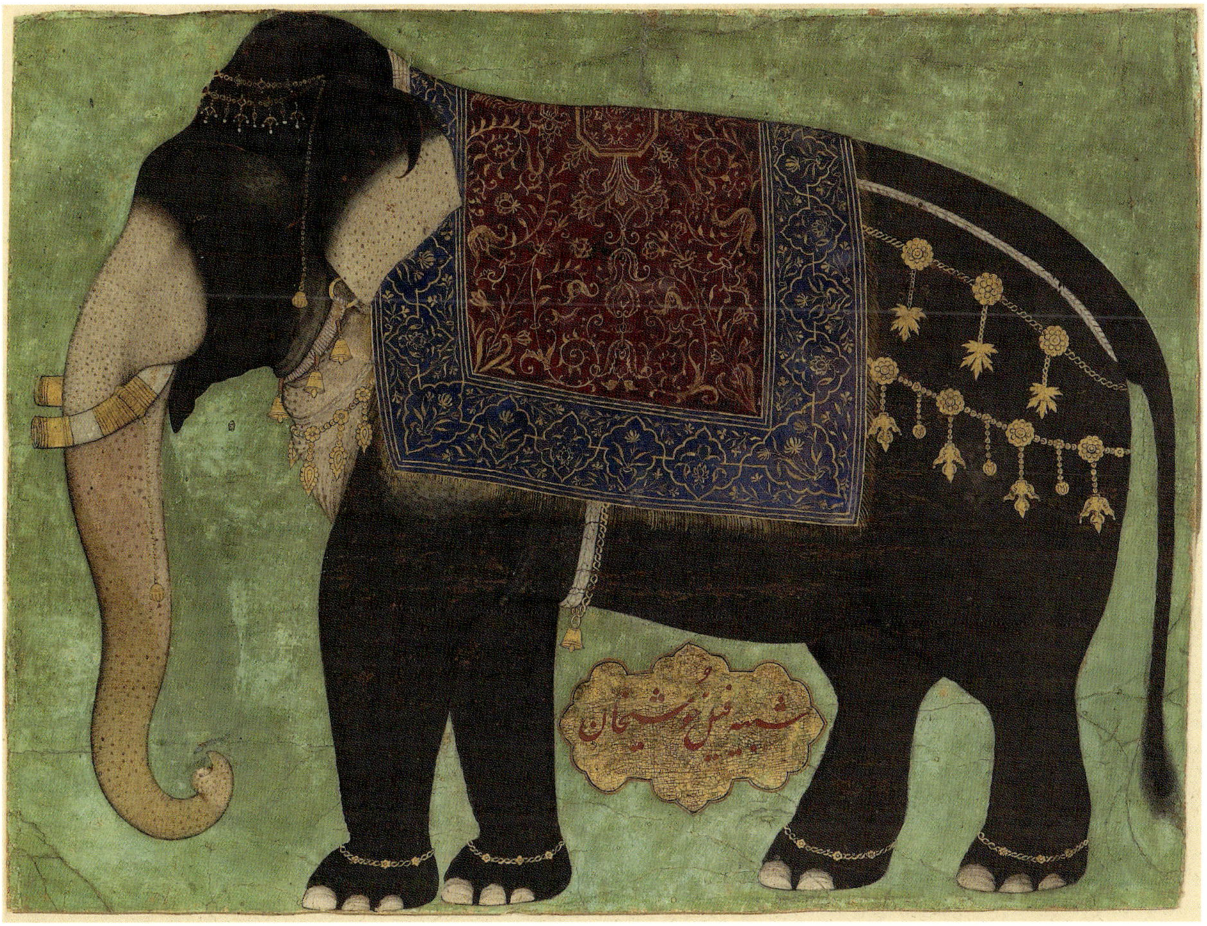

22 Young elephant eating

Mughal, *c.*1650
Gouache on paper, 24 × 27 cm
Hodgkin Loan 48
Published: Filippi 1997, no.48

Set against a plain yellow ground, this young male elephant is of a very dark grey colour, with auspicious mottled pink patches on his trunk and ears. His dark skin may suggest that he is of the type called Mand, which according to Abu'l Fazl is "black, has yellow eyes, a uniformly sized belly, a long penis, and is wild and ungovernable."[1] His forefeet are linked by a chain, presumably in case of unruly behaviour, yet this young bull looks calm and happy with life. He has recently deposited three neat balls of dung. Tethered by his rope, he addresses himself with pleasure to the plantain and banyan leaves and sugar cane left for him by his (unseen) keeper or *meth*. Being off duty, he wears only a junior-size saddle-cloth and small bells on his neck rope and girth chain.

The setting may be an imperial encampment in open country, where his keeper could easily forage for fresh vegetation for him. Under Akbar, the daily feeding of the imperial elephants had been carefully regulated. The basic staple was a nutritious mush, but for the 101 *khasa* or élite elephants, reserved for the emperor's sole use, generous dietary supplements were provided, including sugar, ghee, spiced rice, milk and sugar cane.

This painting was formerly mounted back to back with another portrait of an elephant feeding (no.23), in a Mughal album page formerly in a nineteenth century French collection.[2]

1 Abu'l Fazl, *Ain-i Akbari*, I, p.125 et seq.
2 Sotheby's cat., 27 April 1995, lot 119, pp.111–13.

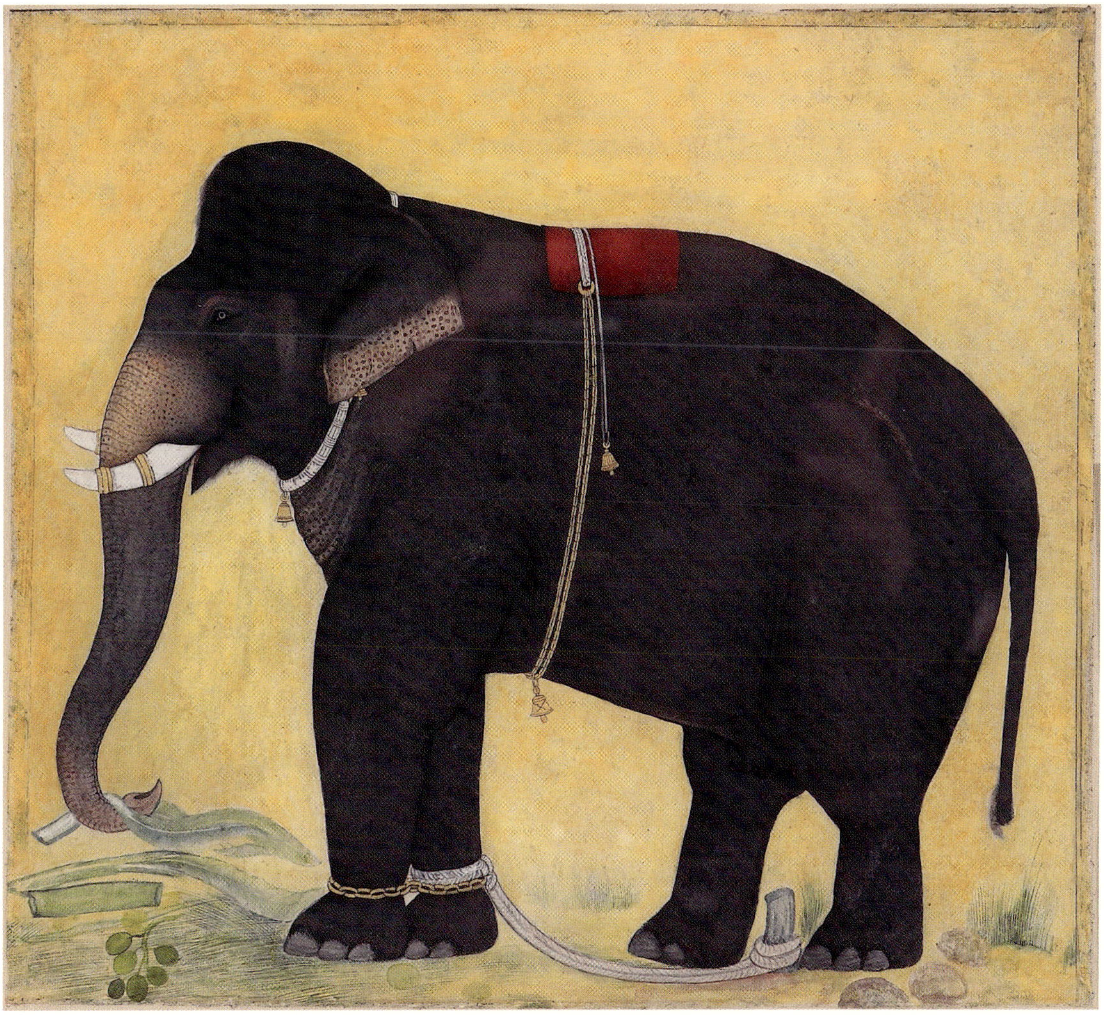

23 An elephant and keeper

Mughal, *c.*1650–60
Gouache with gold on paper, 18 × 22 cm
Hodgkin Loan 46
Published: Filippi 1997, no.46

An imperial elephant stands tethered in open grassland, close to a Mughal army encampment. Tiny groups of foot-soldiers and cavalry are seen drilling or exercising in the distance, as well as elephants, camels and a noblewoman's purdah carriage drawn by bullocks. Further off is a hill-line with trees painted in blue receding tones. It is the elephant's feeding time and he waits expectantly as his keeper strips and prepares sugar cane or other greens for his meal. There is a close intimacy between the two figures.

The names of both the elephant and the artist were given in a damaged inscription below, written in a bold hand resembling that of Shah Jahan. Unfortunately neither name can now be clearly read, though the elephant has been identified previously as Firuz Jang ('Victorious in War'). His body is finely modelled with graduated grey tones, hatching and cross-hatching, speckled mottling of the face and ears and a confident delineation of the folds and wrinkles of his skin. The rich red saddlecloth with gold arabesques is also naturalistically modelled with folds and turned ends, not merely depicted as a flat textile surface pattern. The atmospheric treatment of the camp scene and the informally squatting keeper seen from the rear suggest that the artist had come under the influence of the great Mughal master Govardhan. This feeding scene was later paired with another (no.22), with which it was backed in a single album page, probably in the eighteenth century.

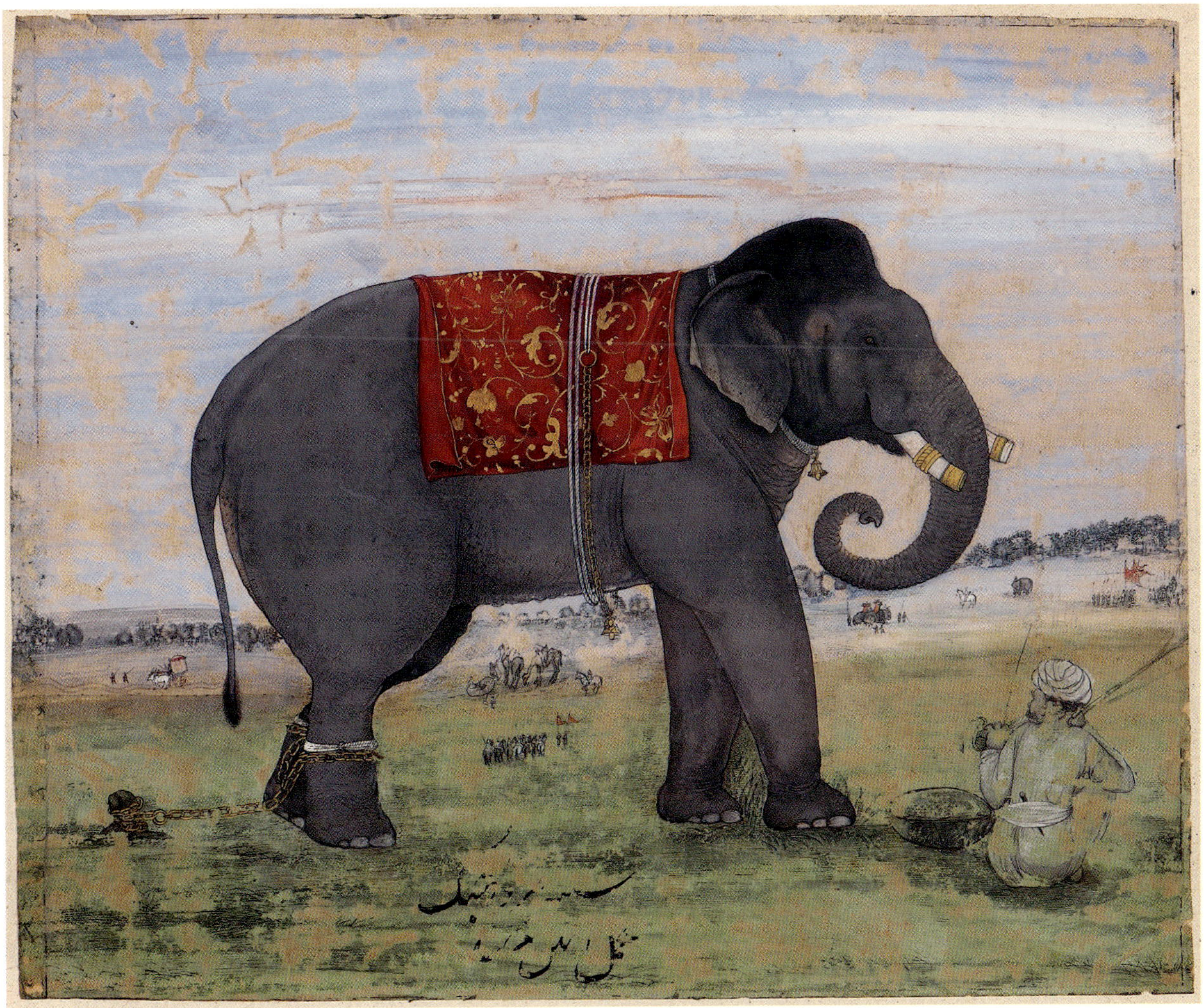

24 Elephant with mahout

Mughal, *c.* 1660
Gouache on paper, 24 × 28.5 cm
Hodgkin Loan 47
Published: Filippi 1997, no. 47

See also detail, p. 13

Set against a conventional pale green ground, this imposing imperial elephant stands quietly obedient to the commands of his mahout. Resting the ankus lightly on the elephant's head, the mahout is depicted in a smaller scale, emphasising the grandeur of the majestic animal. He gestures with his right hand, as though coaxing his mount to stay still.

The elephant is evidently a mature and trusted animal, as he stands untethered and without restraining chains on his legs. Caparisoned with the usual trappings and bells, he also has decorative orange markings painted on his forehead, temple and ear, as though for a festive occasion. An inverted orange crescent is painted around the temporal gland, which becomes inflamed when the elephant is rutting, or in *mast* (no. 81). His everyday red and green saddle-blanket has been overlaid with a finer, gold-embroidered and flower-patterned textile, on which a rider of noble rank may presently sit. As so often in elephant portraits of this kind, the saddle-cloths form the strongest colour accents within the painting.

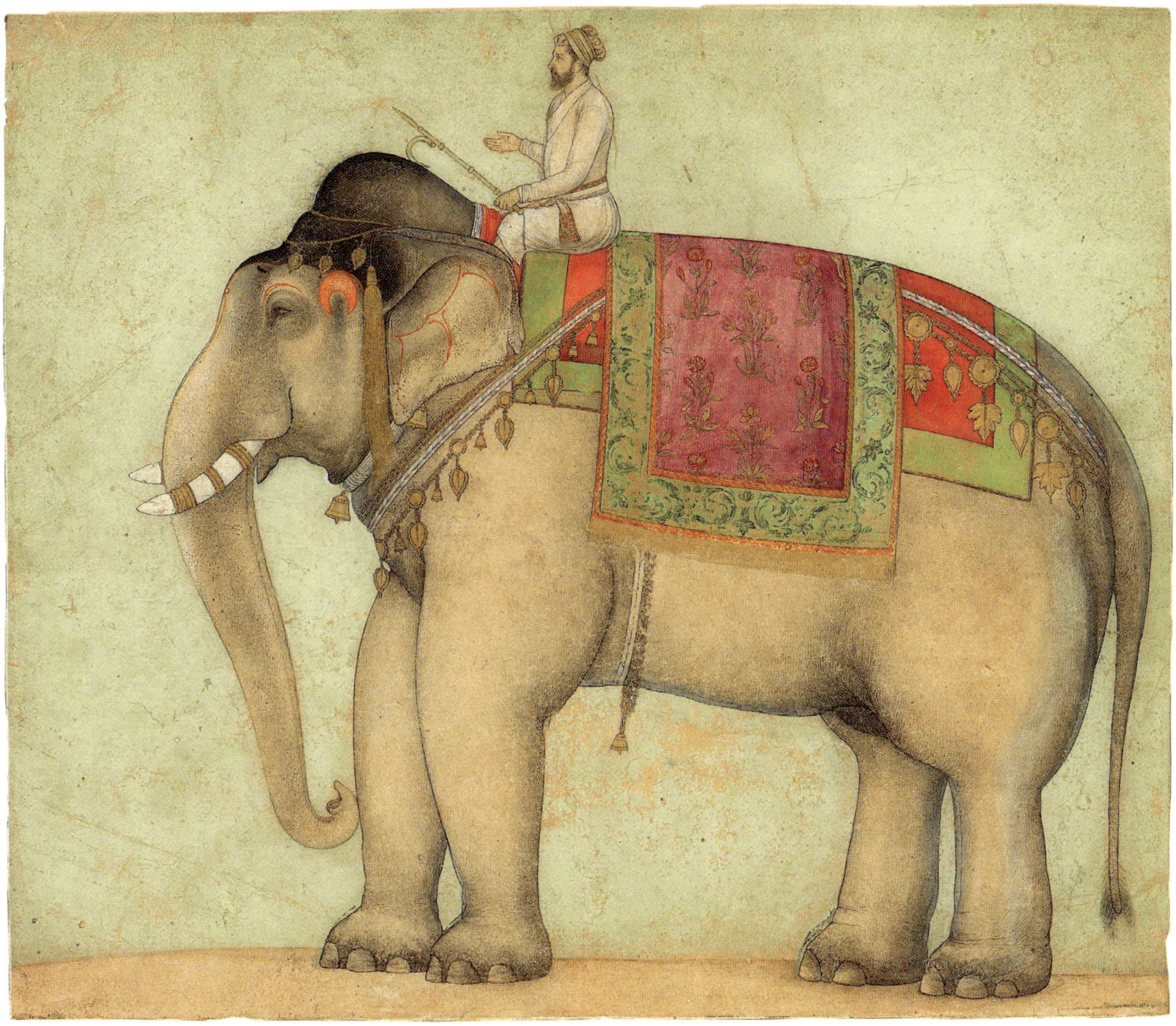

25 The elephant Ganesh Gaj

Mughal, *c.*1660–70
Gouache with ink and gold on paper, 32 × 48.8 cm[1]
Hodgkin Loan 55
Published: Topsfield and Beach 1991, no.11;
Filippi 1997, no.55

See also detail, p.287

Named after the popular Hindu elephant-headed deity, the elephant Ganesh Gaj is an animal of massive size in relation to his princely rider. The low viewpoint and horizon line also help to emphasise his stature. The head and speckled trunk of the noble animal are very finely drawn and modelled. His expression as he gazes down at his keepers conveys a grave dignity and calm. He has markings on his trunk, face and ear, and is missing a tusk. He stands untethered in open country, probably at one of the Mughal camps in the Deccan during Aurangzeb's interminable campaigns there. In the background is a jagged line of hills painted in grey wash tones, in front of which a camel train is passing.

The beardless prince in a flowered gold robe with fur collar who holds the ankus may be intended for one of the sons of Aurangzeb. His figure is highlighted by the white pigment applied around it, as is the contour of the elephant's head and trunk. A conventional band of blue sky and cloud formations appears above. The two keepers, also drawn in a hard-edged way, stand by with their *charkhis*, poles with firework attachments for restraining elephants. The decorative borders with a floral meander pattern at either side suggest this page belonged to a painting album assembled in the period of Aurangzeb, from which (as the inscriptions indicate) it was later removed, before entering a Rajasthani royal collection.

1 Inscribed in Persian: *tasvir-i fil* ('Picture of elephant'); in devanagari and Persian scripts: *pirag das* (perhaps a Hindu valuation clerk or other official) and *qimat 30* ('value 30 [rupees]'); also, in the lower left corner: *patasyah hathi ganesa gaj* ('The emperor's elephant Ganesh Gaj').

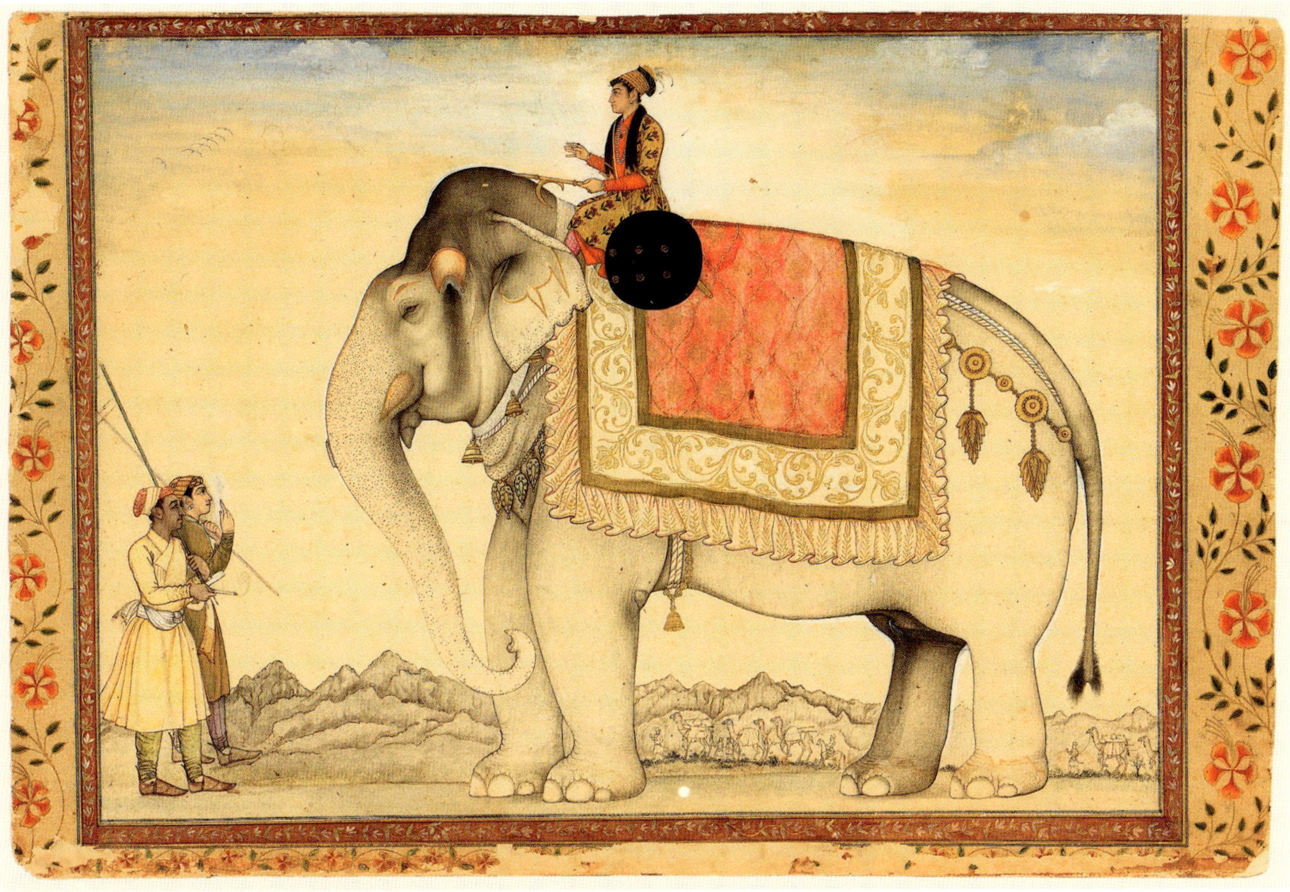

26–28 Three botanical paintings: Geranium, dianthus and composite flower

Mughal, *c.*1630

Gouache on paper, each 17 × 10 cm

Hodgkin Loans 70–72

Published: Filippi 1997, nos. 70–72

Following the emperor Jahangir's rapturous encounter with the spring-time flora of Kashmir, flower painting became a significant genre of Mughal painting during the seventeenth century. While European plant studies provided general pictorial models for these works, Indian artists were given to elaboration or even fantastical exoticisation of their floral subjects, as seen in some of the flower studies in Prince Dara Shikoh's album of the mid-1630s.[1]

Painted around 1630, these three studies from a now dispersed album reveal the sensitivity and growing artfulness that Mughal botanical painters brought to their subjects. The studies of a geranium (26) and a dianthus or carnation (27) are well observed, with near-symmetrical arrangements of the flower-heads or buds and the slightly curling, sinuous leaves against the plain paper ground. Perhaps the most elegantly composed of the three, no. 28 is also the most imaginary, as it depicts a composite plant with flowers and leaves that do not match.[2] In its contrivance it is already on the road to metamorphosis into a Mughal decorative motif of some kind (no. 29). Yet it is again both sensitively painted and carefully observed in the way its four flowers are shown respectively emerging from bud, in different stages of opening, and in full bloom.

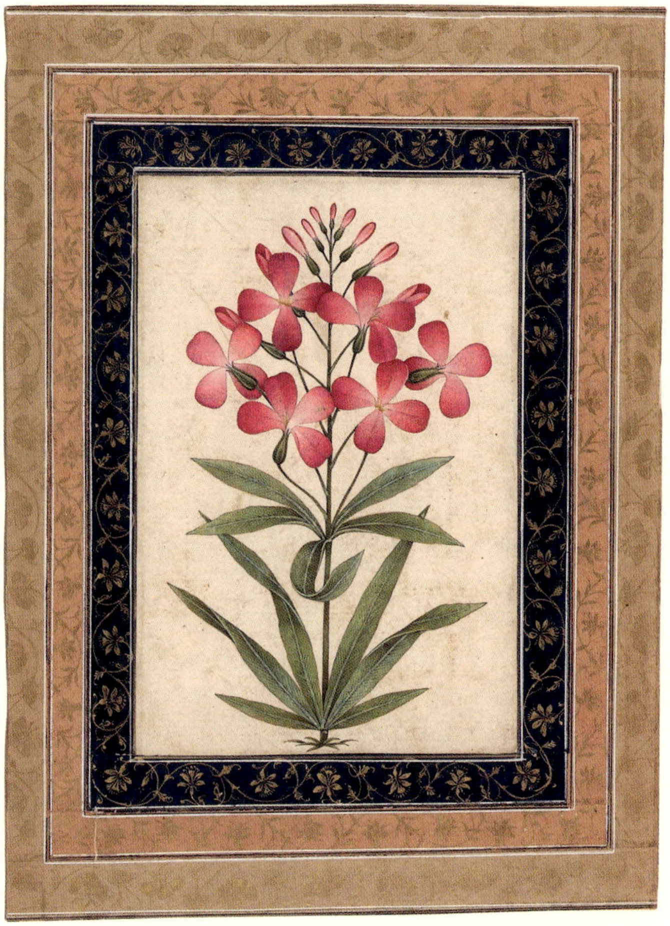

1 British Library, India Office Collections: Falk and Archer 1981, no. 68; for further flower paintings of the Shah Jahan period, see Hurel 2010, nos. 44 (1–26).

2 Dr Stephen Harris comments, 'This image appears to be a mixture of different taxa. The artist has gone to some effort to show the relationship of the four free sepals to the four free petals by moving the petals into unnatural positions. The petals are clearly opposite the sepals, which eliminates all of the likely plant families. The whorled leaves, with the distinctive veination, give the impression of a member of the family Apocynaceae but the floral characteristics are wrong.'

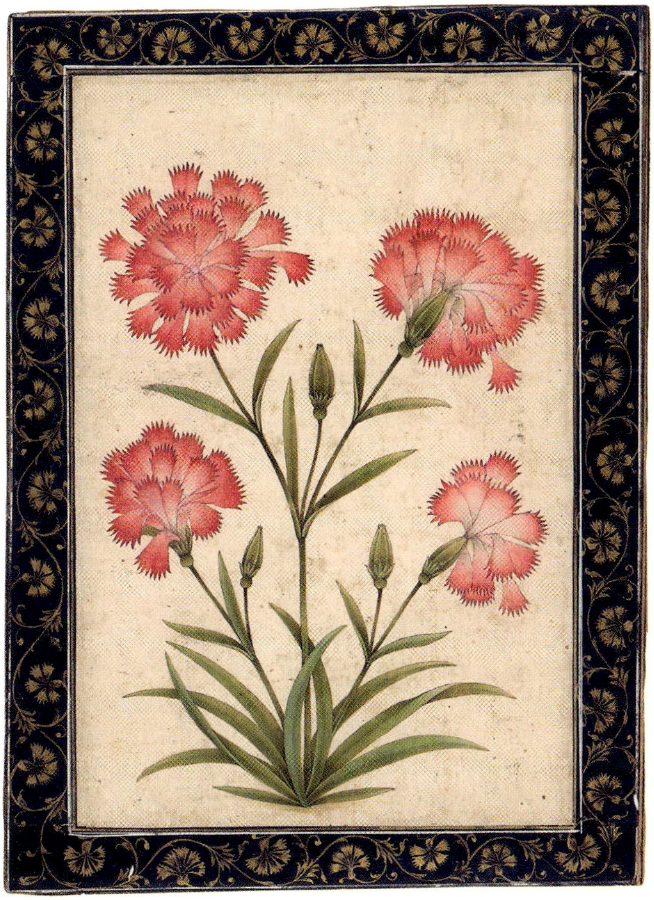

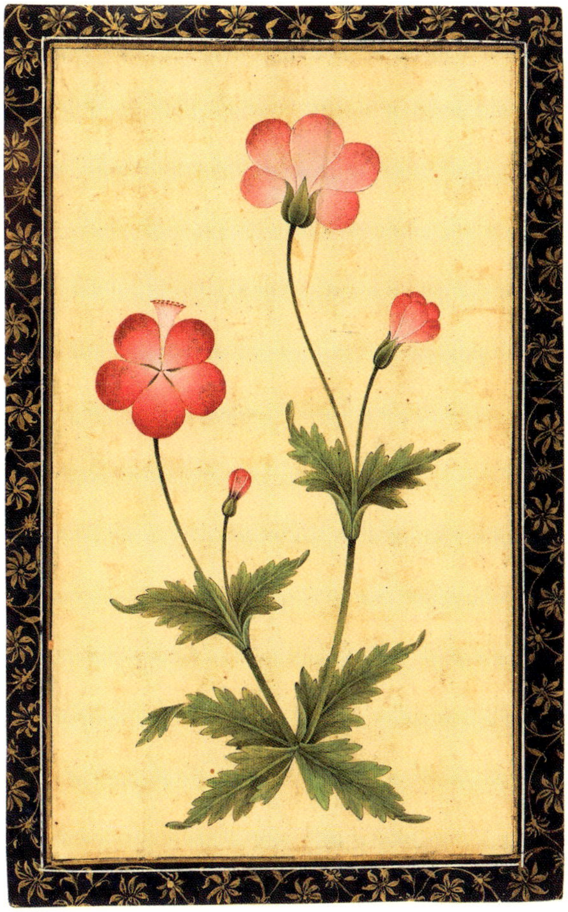

29 A sheet of flower studies

Mughal, *c.*1650

Brush drawing on paper, 20.8 × 26.8 cm

Hodgkin Loan 69

Published: Pal ed.1989, fig.100; Filippi 1997, no.69

This rare surviving sheet of flower studies by a Mughal artist of the Shah Jahan period comprises nineteen flowers or details, loosely arranged in four overlapping rows. Many of the plant stems are diagonally cut at the base, as though they have recently been gathered for drawing. They are carefully modelled with linear veining or shading and occasional traces of pale grey wash, although as so often they show varying degrees of naturalism. Some are meticulously observed, others show more artifice. Such imaginative flights or simplifications were often steps in the development of the classic floral decorative motifs that had become universal in the borders and bindings of Mughal painting albums, in architectural ornament, textiles, metalwork and many other arts.

Most of the present specimens are classic flowers in the Mughal taste.[1] In the top row (from the left), the first and second flower are a lily and narcissus; the third is less identifiable; the rest are an iris, a tulip and what may be a Persian Violet. In the second row are a fritillary, a carnation, two forms of lily and a type of poppy. The third row comprises an anemone; a Trillium or Paris (Melianthaceae); a probable *Silene* or campion; and an unidentified flower. In the bottom row are two unidentifiable plants with stylised leaves and stems, both curling in on themselves as though aspiring to become decorative designs; and finally another *Silene* and an anemone.

1 I am again grateful to Dr Stephen Harris for advice on identifications.

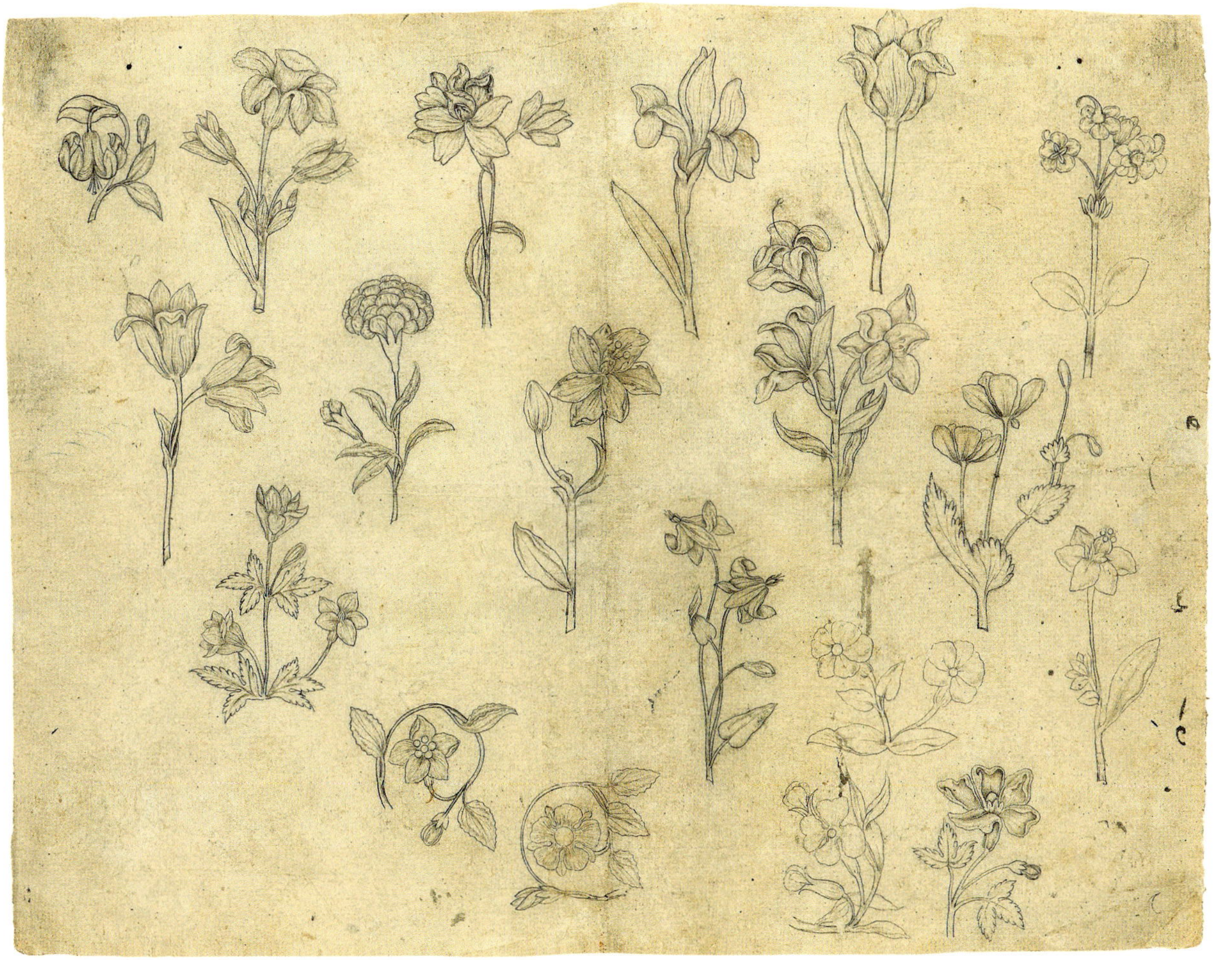

30 Two panels with flower designs

Mughal, *c.* 1650
Painted and lacquered wood
Top panel 8.1 × 22.7 cm, bottom panel 8 × 15.3 cm
Hodgkin Loan 117
Unpublished

These two fragmentary painted panels show the widespread use of Mughal floral motifs in the decorative arts of the period, in this case in what were probably furniture elements, possibly parts of a box. Both have symmetrically grouped compositions of flowering plants against rich gold grounds. In the upper panel, flowering rose plants stand on either side of a white lily (here shown with an incongruous, close-leaved stem), with a morning glory (Ipomoea) just below it. In the lowel panel, two hyacinths flank a dianthus or carnation.

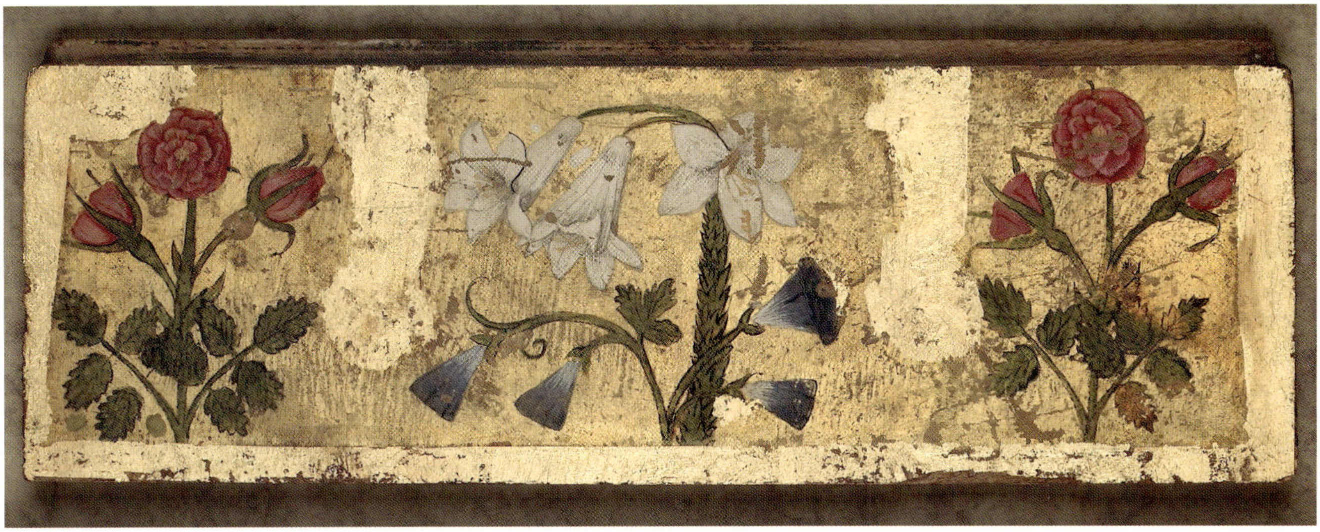

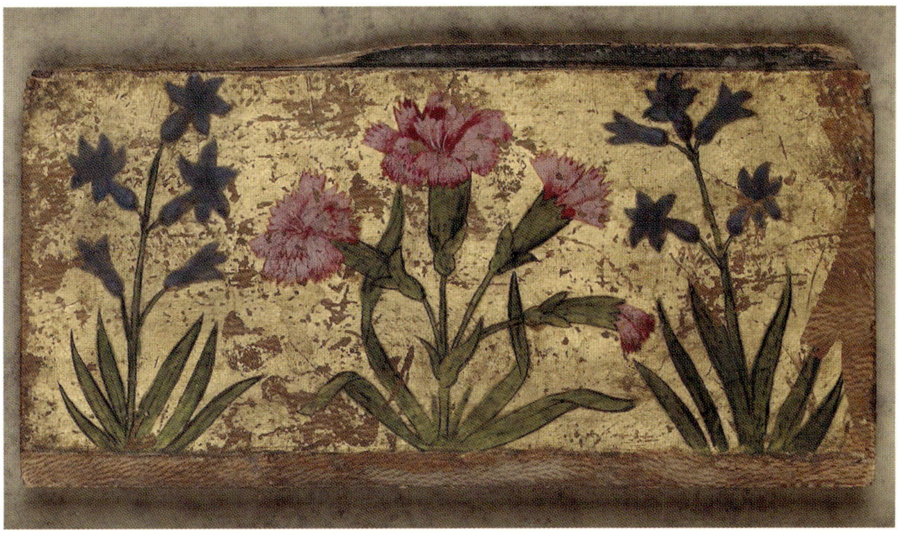

31 Prince Azam Shah enters Ahmedabad

Mughal, 1701. Attributed to Kalyan Das (Chitarman)
Brush drawing with colour and gold on paper,
35.9 × 61.9 cm
Hodgkin Loan 22
Published: Welch 1976, no. 22; Hodgkin and McInerney 1983, no. 39; Topsfield and Beach 1991, no. 17; Filippi 1997, no. 22; McInerney 2011, fig. 1

Prince Azam Shah (1653–1707) was the third son of Aurangzeb and served as Mughal governor of Gujarat from 1701–05. During this time, his "love of ease and aristocratic temperament made his tenure a period of peace, if also of supineness."[1] When Aurangzeb died two years later, the usual princely war of succession ensued. Azam Shah briefly laid claim to the throne but was killed soon after, with his two eldest sons, by Prince Muazzam who became the next emperor Bahadur Shah I.

Azam Shah's arrival in the Gujarati capital in 1701 is depicted here, as a Persian inscription above relates.[2] Evidently a study for a painting now lost or perhaps never executed, this large and remarkable drawing observes the Prince's progress though a city bazaar with unusual candour and detail. It has been plausibly attributed to Kalyan Das, later called Chitarman, and is his earliest known work.[3] He was to become the influential leading artist of the emperor Muhammad Shah (r.1719–48).[4]

There is a piquant contrast between its lower and upper halves. Below, Prince Azam is carried in a palanquin by his escort, his head and nimbus heightened with white pigment and colour. His son Prince Wala Jah follows on horseback with his own attendants, while to the right the procession's advance guard encounters a welcoming group of citizens (now mostly missing). The procession and its personages are well portrayed, but the upper half of the picture is much less conventional. A crowd of townspeople, shopkeepers, beggars and holy men line the street, while women and children look down from the rooftops. To the right, the spectators, held back by a line of soldiers, spill into the middle of the street. In the centre, disorder and quarrels break out as people scramble for the coins that were customarily thrown to the populace. Such earthy realism never appeared in the court scenes of Shah Jahan or his predecessors.

1 Sarkar 1924, V, p. 429.
2 'When he had become governor of Ahmedabad in Gujarat, the day he was [entering] the city: a depiction of that time, and he had dyed his beard red': (*waqti-ki subadar-i ahmadabad-i gujarat shuda budand, rozi-ki...shahr mishudand, taswir-i an waqt ast va rish khizab karda budand*).
3 McInerney 2011, for a study of this painter.
4 McInerney 2002.

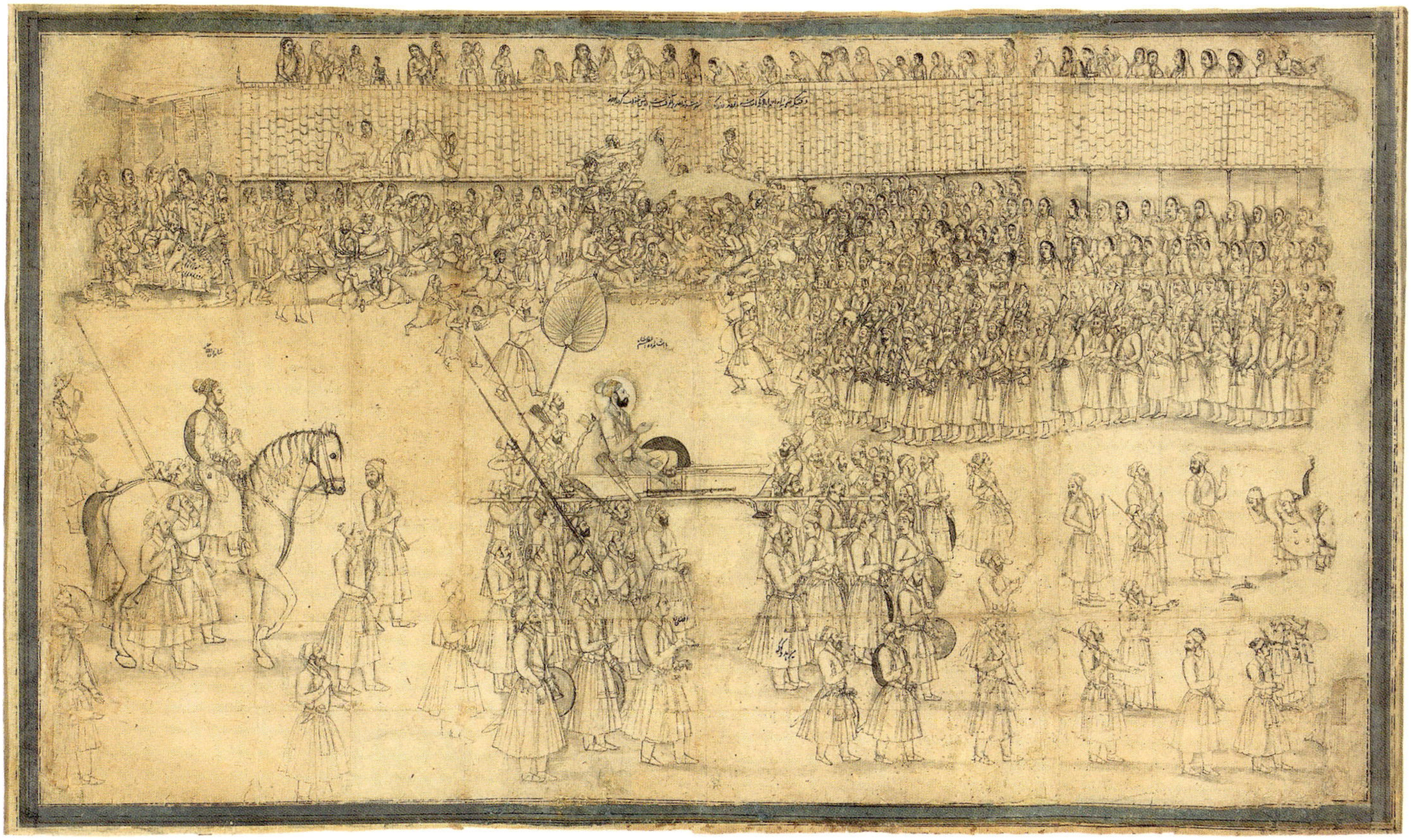

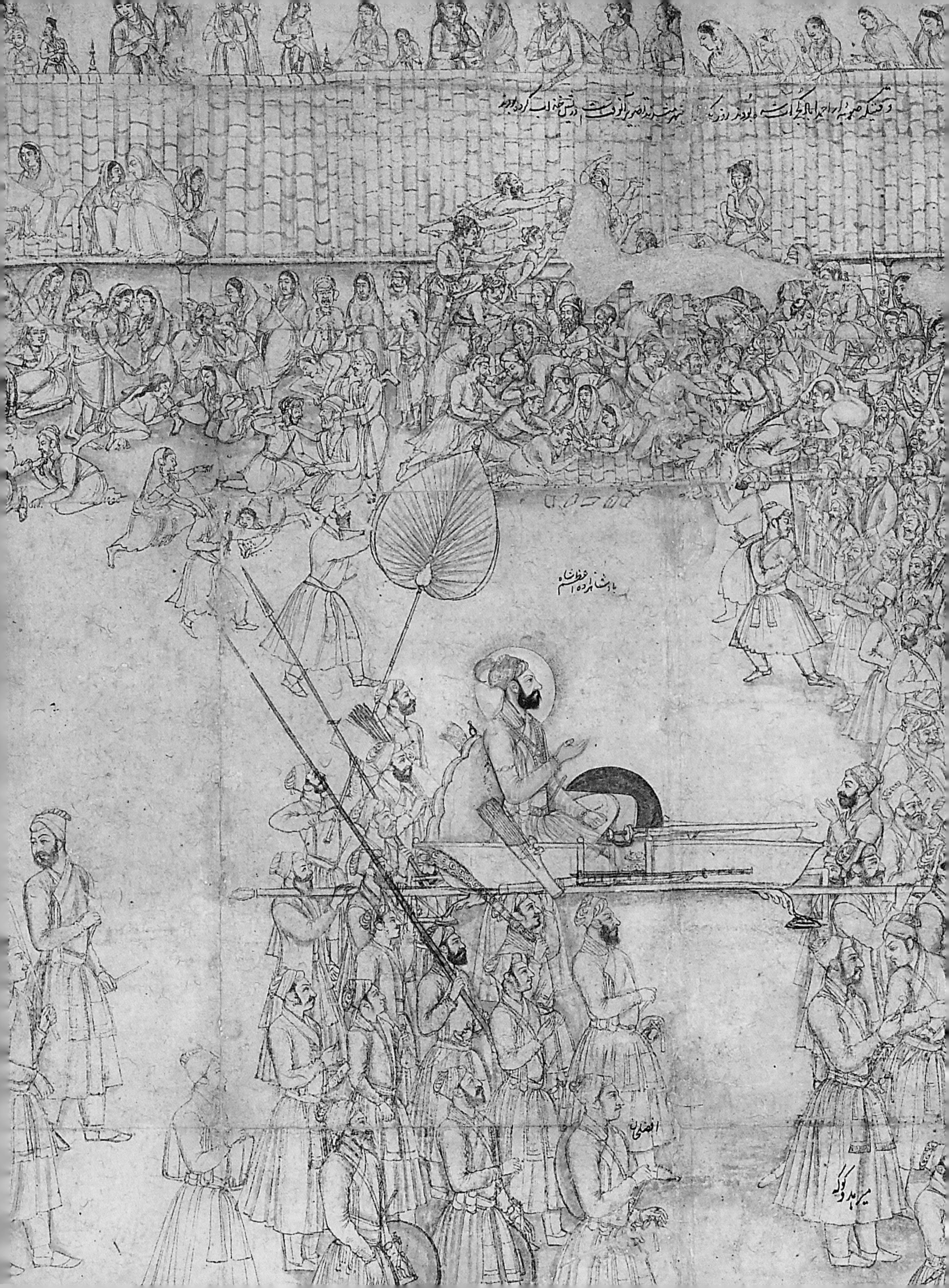

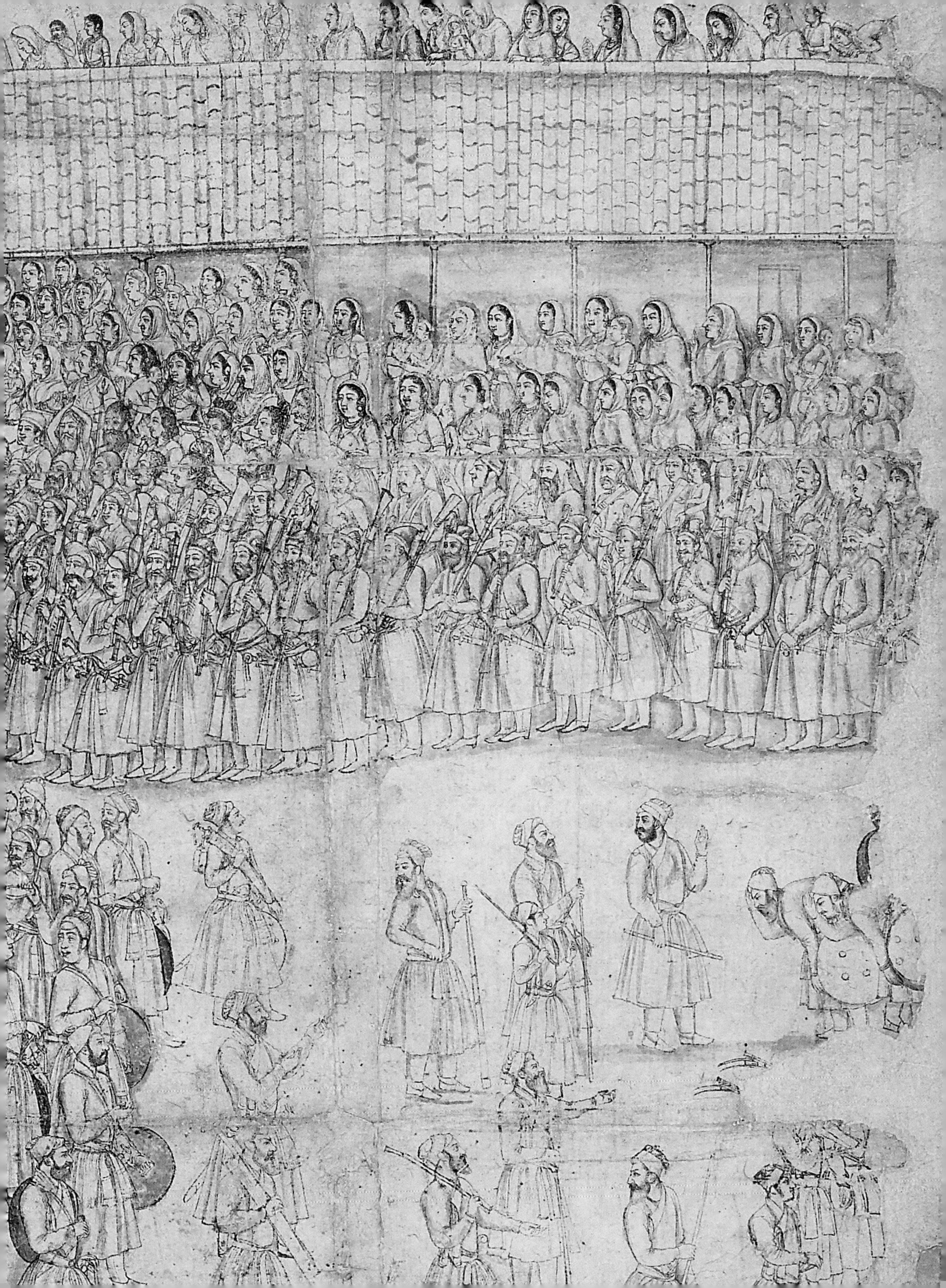

32 A Company officer receiving noblemen

Eastern India, Murshidabad or Patna, *c.* 1760–65
Gouache with gold on paper, 52 × 37.8 cm
Hodgkin Loan 27
Published: Filippi 1997, no. 27

Painted by a Mughal-trained artist working in eastern India, this is an unusually large and well observed depiction of an East India Company officer receiving two local noblemen or officials. The setting is a palatial audience-chamber with Mughal arches, columns and wall-niches, set on a garden terrace. Wearing a tricorne hat and braided green coat, this high-ranking officer sits in presiding place on a European chair, smoking a hookah placed on a tripod table. An attendant stands behind him with a yak-tail fan, and his dark-skinned boy servant stands nearby. His elder and younger guests, who are perhaps father and son, wear court dress and archer's thumb-rings. Also seated on European chairs, they converse easily with their host, the elder man resting his arm on a table with covered dishes and sprinkler-bottles. The attendants stand at respectful distances, some with weapons and one holding a back-scratcher in case it should be needed. Two *malis* tend the garden below, where cabbages and other vegetables grow in neat plots, while a *bhisti* with a water-skin lays the dust on the paths.

This Company officer is as yet unidentified,[1] though his evident seniority suggests he may be a British resident at Murshidabad or a Governor of Bengal, or even possibly a Director of the Dutch East India Company in Bengal.

1 He has been identified previously as William Fullerton, possibly receiving the Nawab Mir Qasim (Sotheby's sale cat., 26 April 1995, lot 133). But he does not much resemble Fullerton in face and figure, if the officer portrayed on a terrace by the artist Dip Chand in the V&A Museum is indeed him, as was first suggested by Skelton in 1956 (see e.g. Crill and Jariwala 2010, no. 49, with refs.).

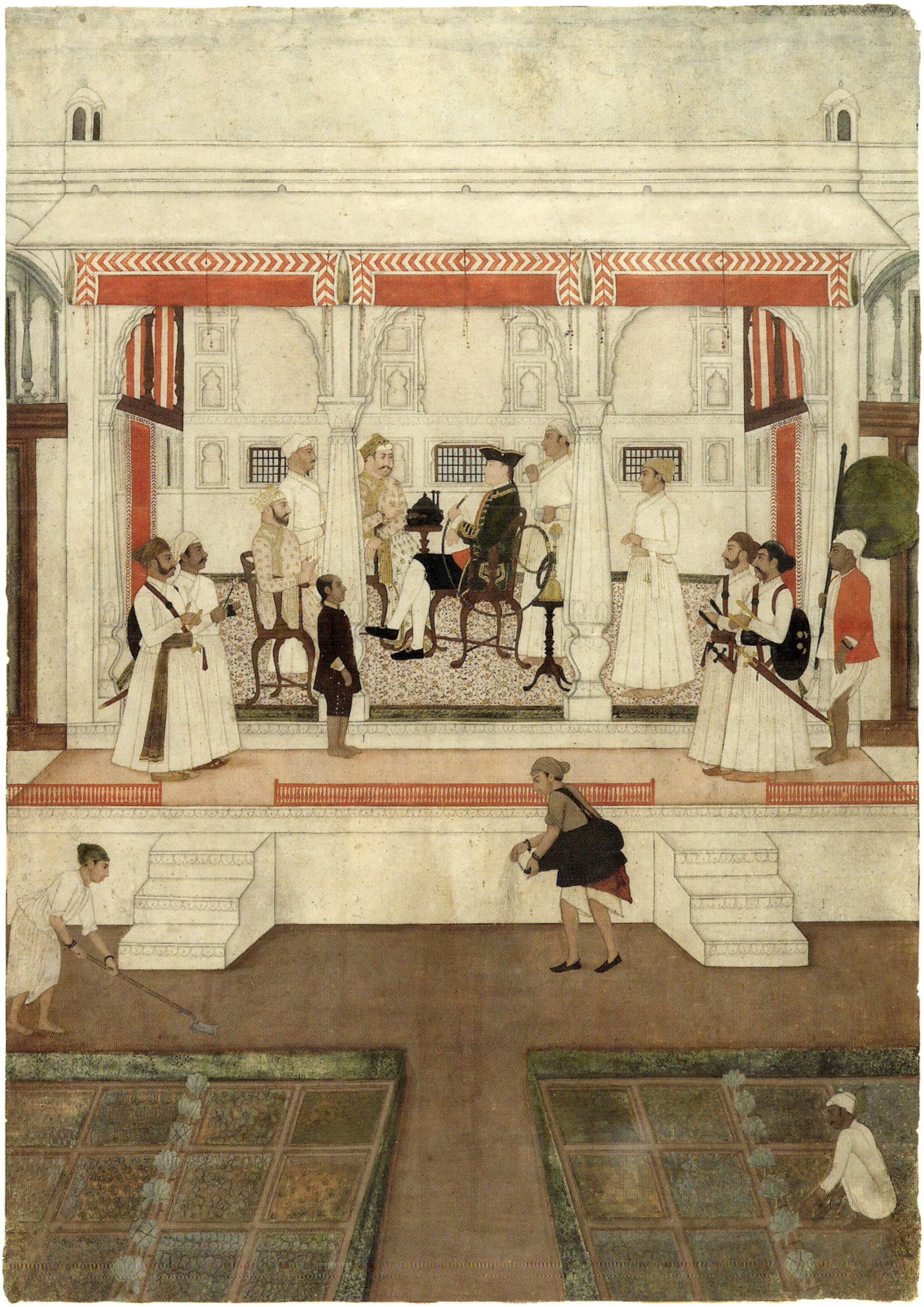

33 Durbar of Emperor Akbar Shah II

Mughal, *c.*1820–30
Gouache with gold on paper, 75.2 × 61.8 cm
Hodgkin Loan 93
Unpublished

'Lord of War-like Qualities and Spiritual Blessing, Sovereign of the Temporal World, Conqueror of Infidels', the penultimate emperor Akbar Shah II (r.1806–37)[1] presides at a durbar in the Red Fort at Delhi. Although bearing the same name as the most illustrious Mughal emperor, the elderly Akbar II was permitted few powers by the British other than to indulge in court ceremonial and public processions. According to Bishop Heber in 1824, he was reputedly "a very good-tempered, mild, old man, of moderate talents, but polished and pleasing manners",[2] who was dominated by his favourite wife Mumtaz Mahal. In this assembly her son, the long-haired Mirza Jahangir (who died of an excess of Hoffmann's cherry brandy in 1821), stands in the place of honour on the emperor's right, together with Prince Mirza Salim. Opposite them stand Prince Abu Zafar Siraj al-din Muhammad, the future Bahadur Shah II (no.34), with another prince.

This composition is known in a number of versions, with the same throne setting in the Diwan-i Khas or Hall of Private Audience and very similar assemblies of nobles and courtiers. Many of them are wrapped in winter shawls and lean on their ceremonial staffs, planted on the orange-red inner carpet or the red and green-striped outer carpet with its animated leaf and meander patterns. The British Resident, who sometimes appears in their midst, is absent on this occasion. There is however growing European influence in the modified recession of the durbar hall and the way many of the portraits are in three-quarter face rather than in profile. The emperor himself, and an elderly courtier standing at the near right, gaze directly at the viewer.

1 These Persian titles are inscribed on another version of this subject, in the British Library: M. Archer 1972, no.171, pl.57; see also Falk and Archer 1981, no.227(i), and Leach 1995, II, no.8.56, p.812, with references to further versions.

2 Heber 1828, II, p.302.

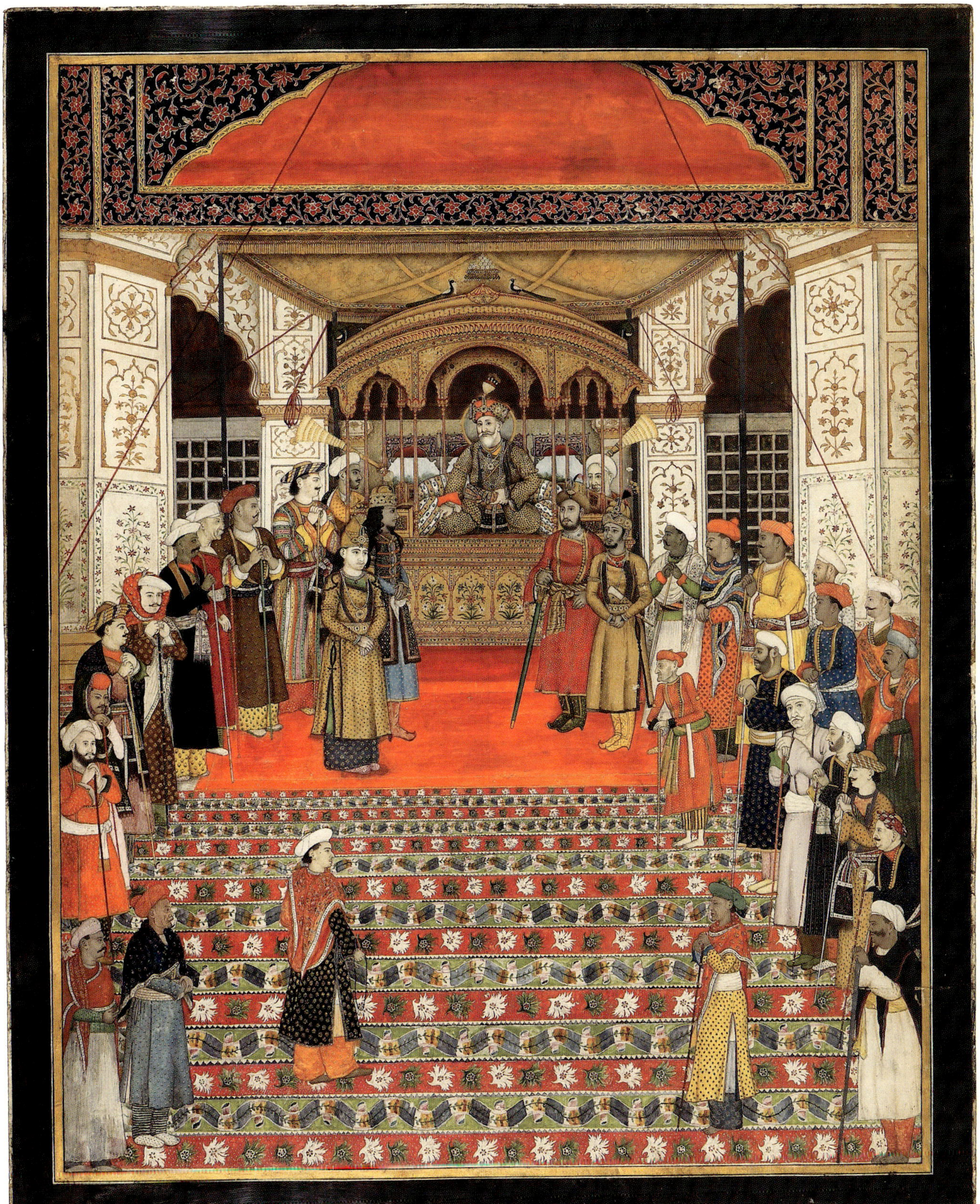

34 The emperor Bahadur Shah

Delhi, *c.*1855–58
Gouache and water-colour on paper, 36 × 24 cm
Hodgkin Loan 111
Unpublished

This unfinished study of a sadly gazing nobleman with jewelled turban, greying whiskers and a world-weary air is Europeanised in its full-face portraiture and painterly modelling of the face and eyes with highlights in the pupils. Its subject is the octogenarian last Mughal emperor Bahadur Shah II (r.1837–58). Although not modelled on August Schoefft's large oil portrait of the emperor of *c.*1853–54,[1] it perhaps shows a passing awareness of it. The artist captures with poignancy the unworldly character of this ageing prince cast into imperial trappings.

Like his father Akbar Shah II (no.33), Bahadur Shah ruled India in name only. He possessed neither army nor wealth and his domains hardly reached beyond the Red Fort. Already in his sixties when he came to the throne,[2] he had spent most of his life in the pursuit of Urdu poetry, of which he was a skilled exponent under the pen-name Zafar ('Victory'). Strongly drawn to Sufi mysticism, he had lived in a comparatively modest style. His principal weakness was for mangoes.

After his accession, he continued to devote himself to *mushairas* (poetical assemblies) and the patronage of poets such as Ghalib, until history overtook him in 1857. For his nominal leadership of the bloody and tragic Indian Rebellion of that year, Bahadur Shah was deposed by the British, so bringing the dynasty of Akbar, Jahangir and Shah Jahan to its pathetic close.

Most of Bahadur Shah's sons had already been shot. A famous photograph taken in May 1858 shows the elderly emperor reclining on a bed with a hookah beside him, shortly before his exile to Burma. He looks at the camera in complete despair.[3] A *ghazal* that has been popularly attributed to him at that time begins:

My heart has no repose in this despoiled land,
Who has ever felt fulfilled in this futile world?

1 Dalrymple 2006, illus. opp. p.313.
2 For accession portraits of Bahadur Shah of *c.*1837–38, see e.g. Soudavar 1992, no.142; Crill and Jariwala 2010, no.58; Welch 1978, no.52: in the last of these (now in the Doha Museum, Qatar) he is correctly shown white-bearded; also Seyller 2010, no.34, and Bautze 1998, no.61a, for contemporary miniature portraits.
3 E.g. Worswick and Embree 1976, illus. p.76.

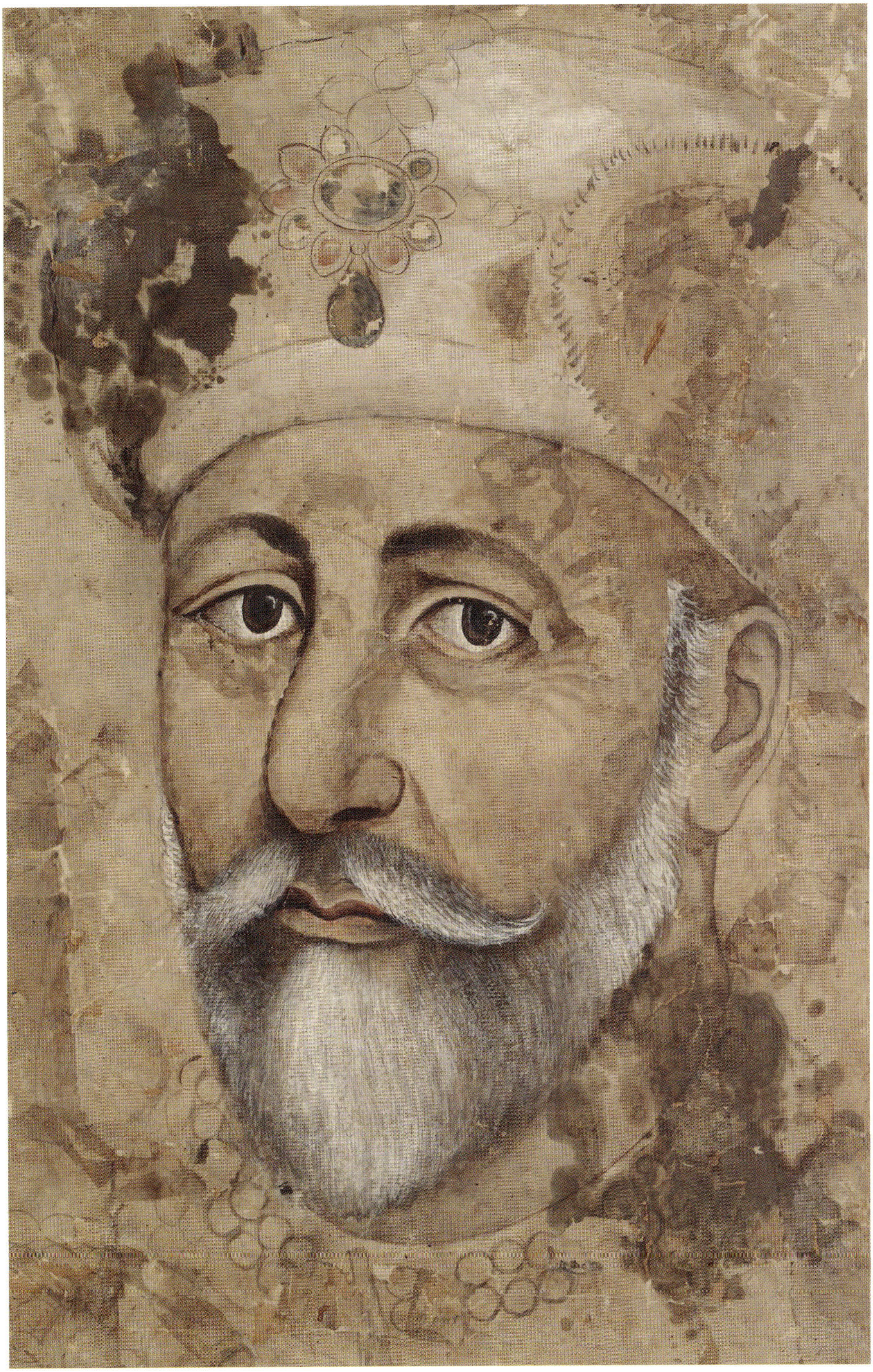

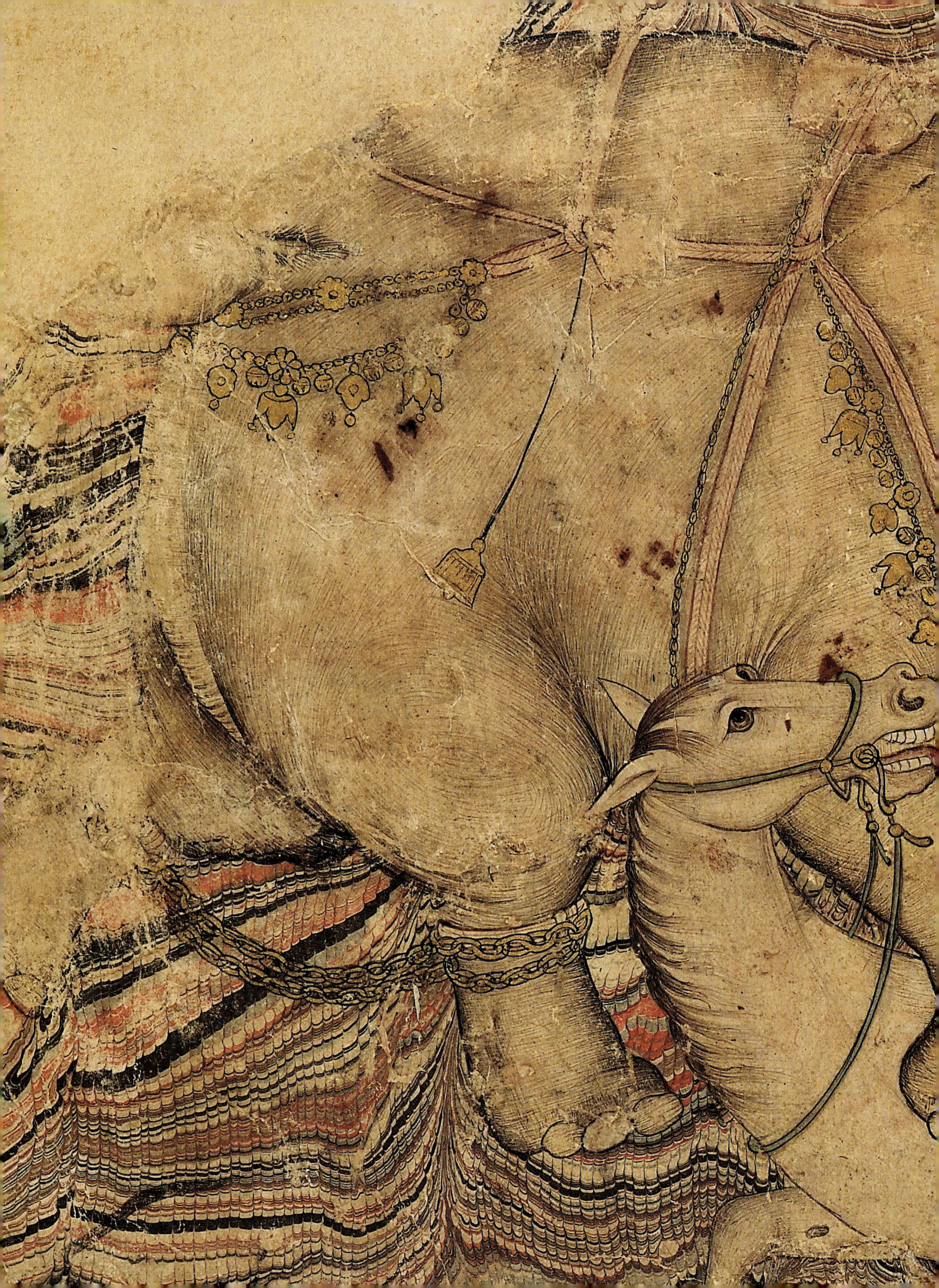

DECCANI

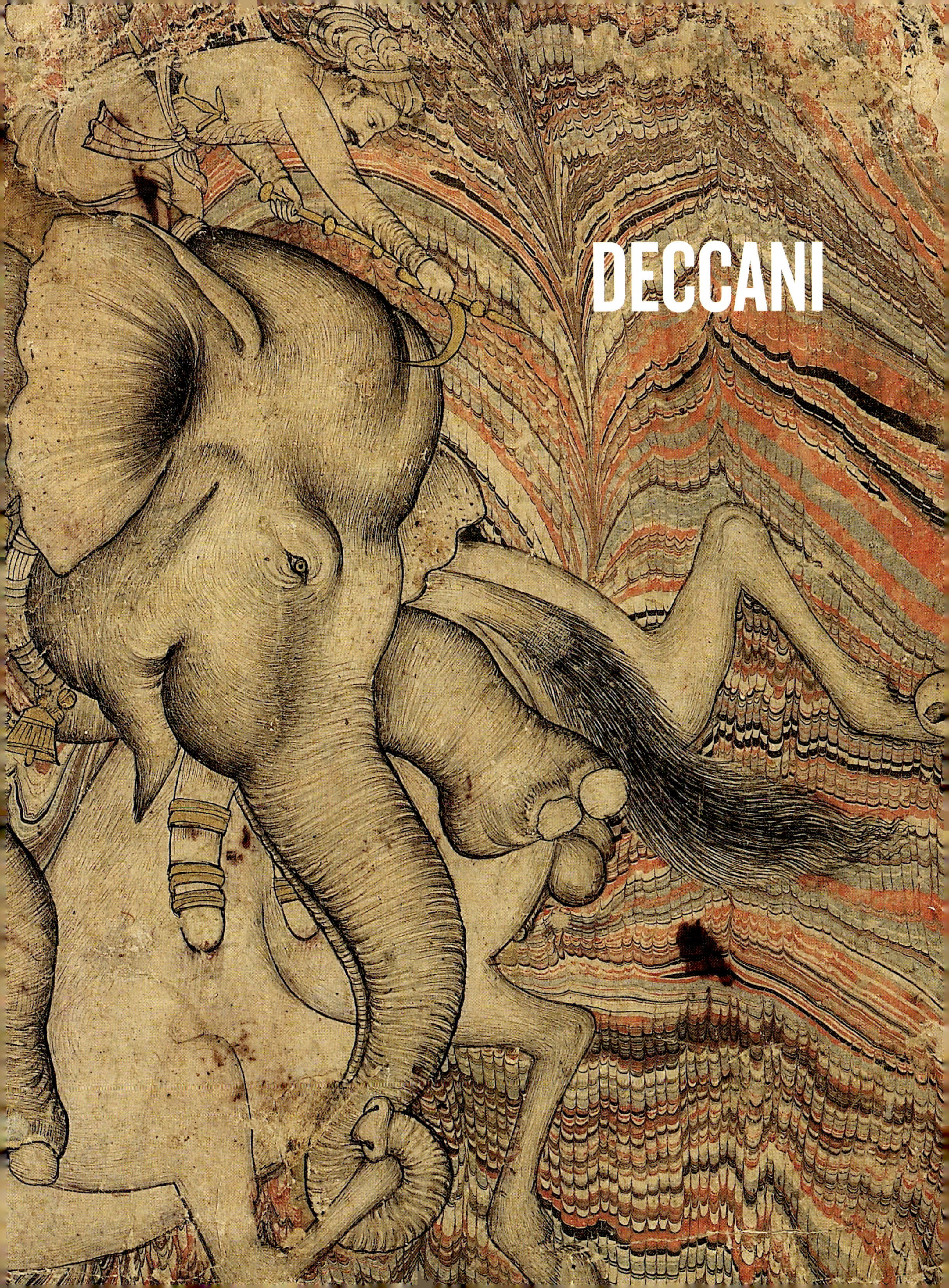

35 Three bamboo plants

From a *De Materia Medica* manuscript
Deccan, possibly Bijapur, *c.*1595
Gouache on paper, 40.2 × 27 cm
Hodgkin Loan 67
Published: Hodgkin and McInerney 1983, no.45; Topsfield and Beach 1991, no.7; van Alphen and Aris eds. 1995, illus. p.61; Filippi 1997, no.67

Written by the Greek physician and botanist Dioscorides in the first century AD, *De Materia Medica* is an extensive treatise on the medicinal properties of plants. In Latin, Greek, Arabic and Syriac versions, it was widely consulted in Europe and the Middle East for at least a millennium and a half. A number of important thirteenth century Arab illustrated manuscripts of this text are known, but Indian examples are extremely rare. The manuscript to which this page belonged was translated into Persian in 1595 (AH 1004), presumably from an Arabic version, and was possibly made for Sultan Ibrahim Adil Shah II of Bijapur (r.1579–1627), a renowned patron of art and learning.[1]

This illustration, without accompanying text, documents different types of bamboo. Scientific drawings of this kind traditionally depict plants in their most simplified characteristic forms on a plain ground, with roots, stems and leaves clearly indicated as an aid to identification by botanists or pharmacologists. Here, the upper and lower left plants are types of larger bamboo,[2] their bases showing a number of stems cut or broken off. The lower right plant, though evidently also of substantial size, may represent a small flowering bamboo, perhaps with some kind of tussock-forming grass behind it, or possibly a flowering sedge.[3] The healing properties of bamboo were known in India by this time, and in traditional Ayurvedic and Unani (Indo-Persian) medicine an extract from bamboo stems was used as a tonic for respiratory diseases.

Although this is a didactic and therefore schematic image, it is nonetheless painted with great verve and freedom and an abundant sense of natural energy. Howard Hodgkin comments, "Perhaps because the plant depicted is a bamboo and therefore familiar to the artist, he was inspired to make this memorable image, wholly Indian and yet curiously reminiscent of an ancient Egyptian wall painting."[4]

1 An attribution suggested by the late Simon Digby, on linguistic as well as pictorial grounds; see McInerney 1982, no.17, with further pages from this manuscript.
2 Though hard to identify by genus: I am indebted to Dr Stephen Harris for his botanical comments.
3 Probably genus *Cyperus* (family Cyperaceae), though *Cyperus* species generally do not get so substantial.
4 Hodgkin and McInerney 1983, no.45.

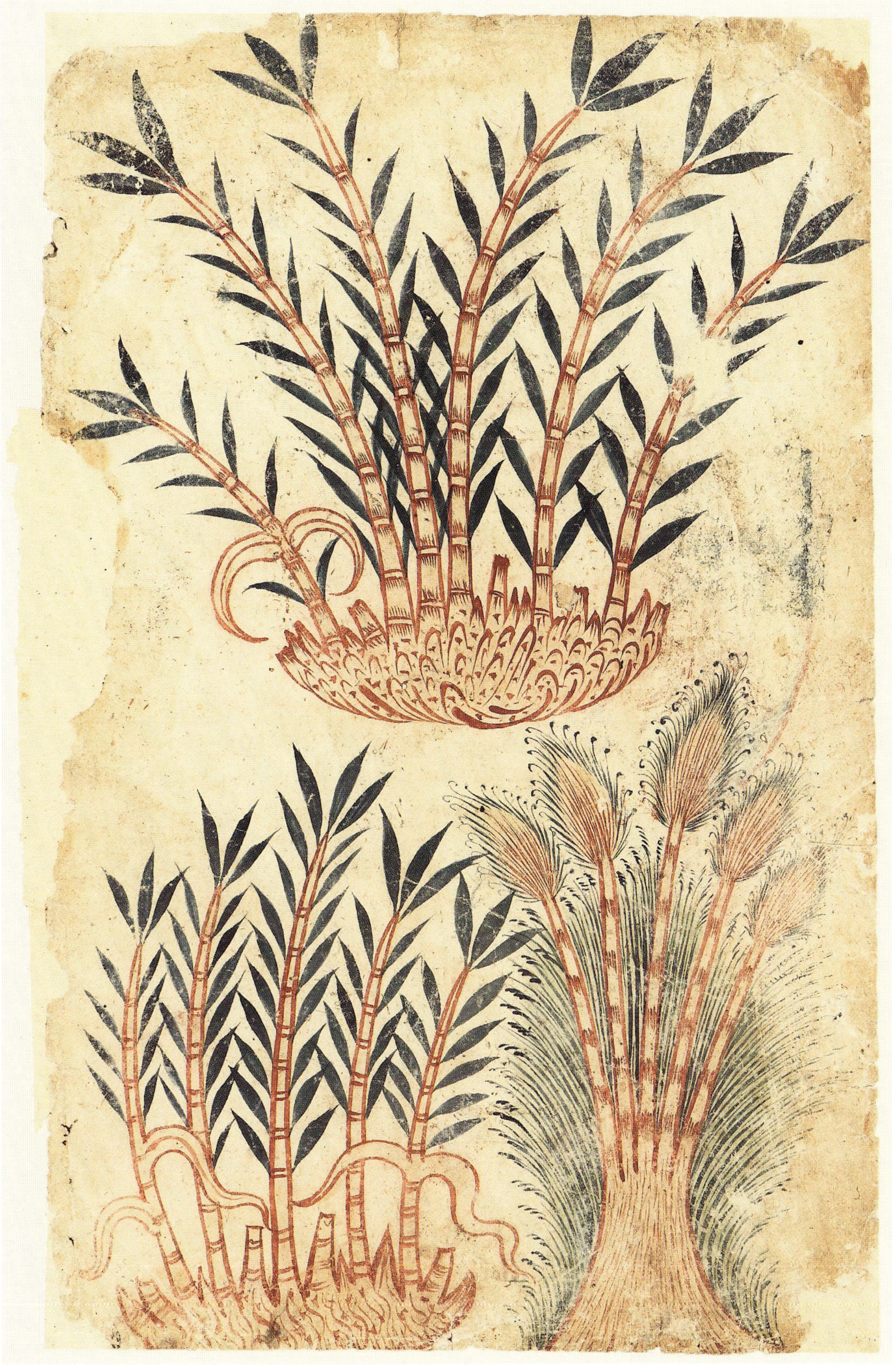

36 Sultan Muhammad Adil Shah and Ikhlas Khan riding an elephant

Bijapur, Deccan, *c.*1645. By Haidar Ali and Ibrahim Khan[1]
Gouache with gold on paper, 32 × 44.5 cm
Hodgkin Loan 54
Published: British Museum 1976, no.179; Zebrowski 1983, pp.131–33, fig.100; Topsfield 1984, pl.17; Welch 1985, no.200; Topsfield and Beach 1991, no.10; Filippi 1997, no.54; Michell and Zebrowski 1999, fig.132; Alderman 2006, fig.101; Crill and Jariwala 2010, no.32

Under Muhammad Adil Shah (r.1627–56) the Bijapur kingdom continued to enjoy relative independence from the Mughal empire, but its ties with the imperial court were both close and influential. Muhammad's sister had married Daniyal, the brother of Jahangir, and he was obliged to send regular tribute gifts of various kinds to the emperor. Often these took the form of "splendid elephants that looked like moving mountains",[2] which were always well received by the emperor. Bijapur indeed became an important source of elephants for the imperial stable.

At the same time Bijapur artists were becoming increasingly aware of Mughal pictorial models, particularly in the art of portraiture. One of the outstanding paintings of Muhammad Adil Shah's reign, this composition of an elephant in profile with two riders is borrowed directly from the contemporary Mughal repertoire (no.20). At the same time it has been transformed by its Deccani sensibility and palette. The elephant's volumes are less carefully differentiated by the artist, its dark grey mass fluidly outlined against the vivid blue ground, throwing into relief its splendid trappings, decorative pendants and bells. The regally attired Muhammad Adil Shah, holding the ankus, is a radiant figure with his gold nimbus and magnificent robe of gold minutely pricked to catch the light. Behind him rides his powerful African (*habshi*) minister Ikhlas Khan, in a flowered silver-grey robe. He had risen to high office under Muhammad's father Ibrahim Adil Shah and was often depicted by Bijapur painters. Here he holds a sword under his arm while waving a white cloth to guard the Sultan from flies. The two men ride the mighty animal with dignity and authority, like the ship of state itself.

1 Inscribed in Persian: *'amal-i haidar 'ali wa ibrahim khan.*
2 Inayat Khan 1990, p.189.

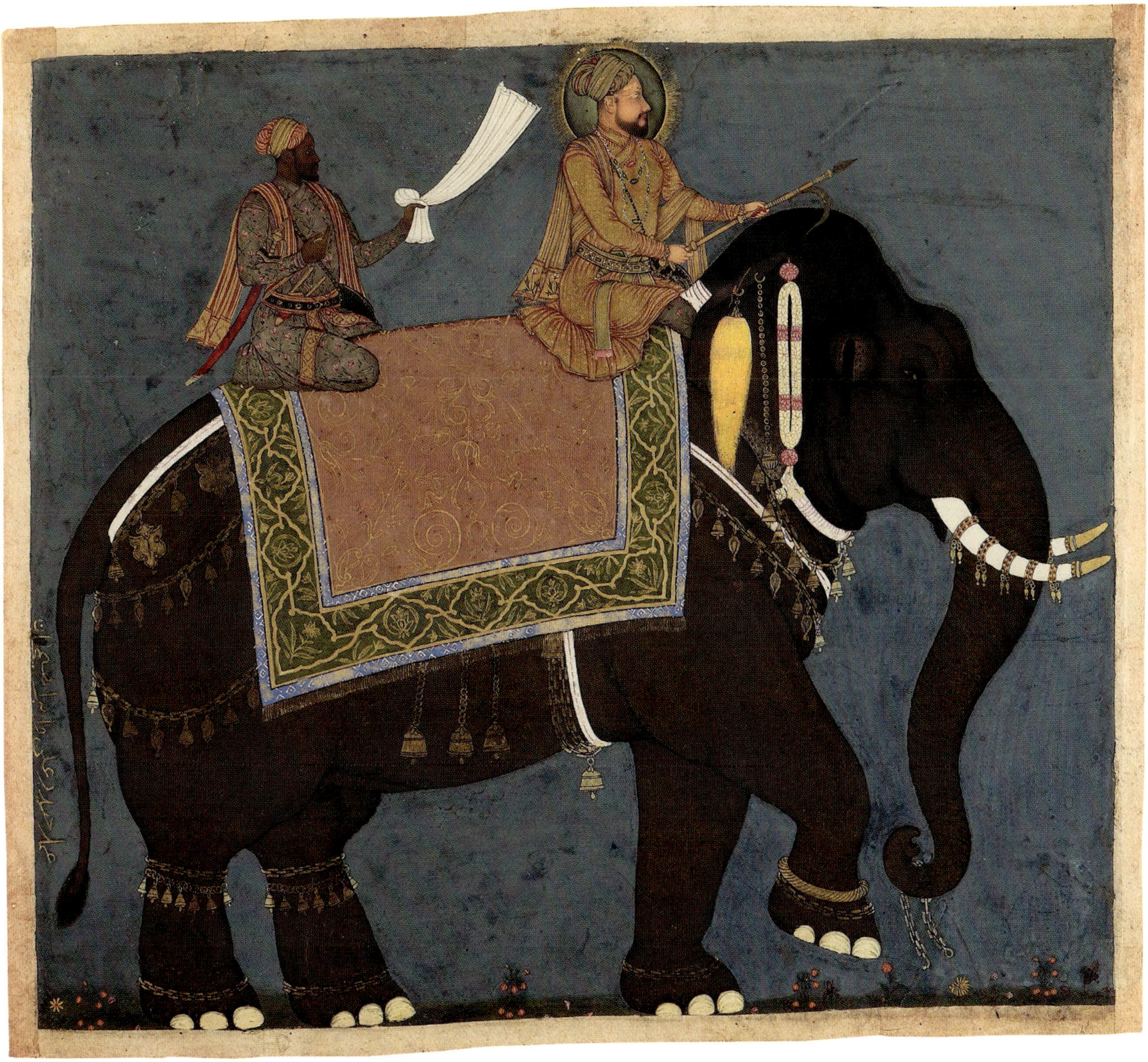

37 Sultan Ali Adil Shah shooting an arrow at a tiger

Bijapur, Deccan, *c.*1660
Gouache with gold on paper, 21.8 × 31.5 cm
Hodgkin Loan 98
Published: Zebrowski 1983, fig.110; Welch 1985, no.205; Michell and Zebroswki, fig.138, p.188[1]

In this superb fragment by a leading Bijapur master, Sultan Ali Adil Shah (r.1656–72) is radiant in his glowing gold robe and nimbus as he draws his bow and looses an arrow unerringly at a tiger. The dismayed animal stands at bay, clearly realising it has met its match. The Sultan stands in the supremely confident posture of the invincible ruler who displays his glory and might by slaying single-handed the fiercest of all beasts, the lion or tiger. This tiger-slaying pose is seen in India in Gupta gold coins of the fourth century, as also in Achaemenid and Sasanian lion-slaying scenes in Iran.

A muted grey ground sets off and intensifies the splendour of the Sultan's golden robe and deep lapis blue turban and bow. Landscape is suggested by trees to the left and right (the latter now almost missing) and a lightly coloured rocky outcrop. Peripheral areas of the painting were already missing when it was remounted in its album page. An enigmatic gold curlicue still rises from the missing area below, which has been interpreted as the tail of a mythological beast such as a griffin on which the Sultan stood,[2] or as the prow finial of a boat in which he rode.[3]

There was clearly an element of wish-fulfilment in the Sultan's symbolic triumph over the tiger. Like his predecessors, Ali Adil Shah was a gifted patron of art but no great statesman. He was moreover faced with continuing incursions by the expansionist Mughals and the energetic Maratha chief Shivaji. After ten years, he left state affairs in the hands of a minister, devoting himself to pleasure until his death in 1672. Fourteen years later Bijapur finally fell to the Mughals. This and other Bijapur works[4] appear to have been acquired by a Rajput chief serving with the Mughal forces, and later to have been preserved in the collection of the Maharajas of Kishangarh.

1 Also Sotheby's cat., 6 April 2011, lot 113.
2 Zebrowski 1983, p.140; Michell and Zebrowski 1999, p.189.
3 Welch 1985, p.307.
4 Haidar 1995.

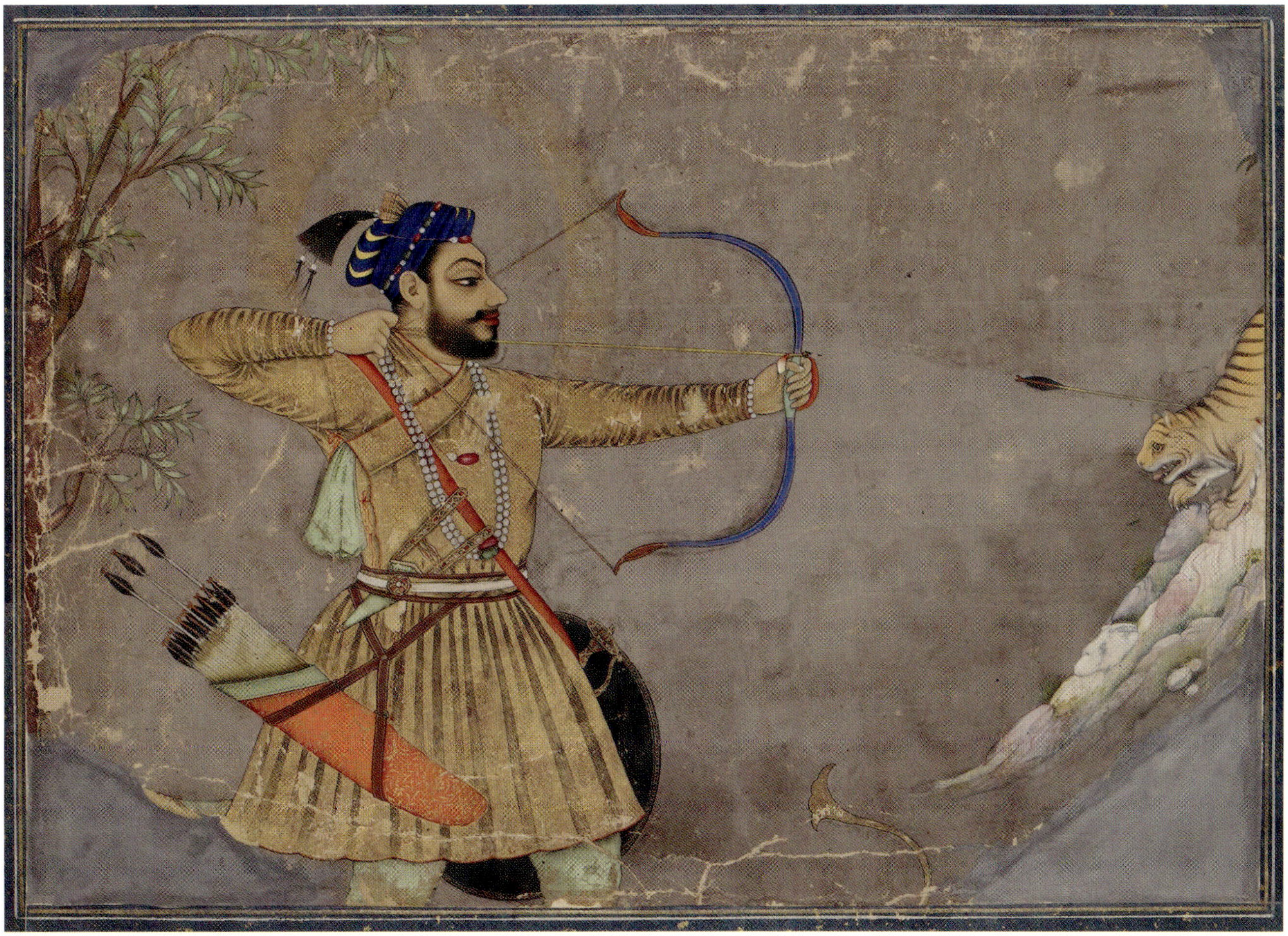

38 Sultan Ali Adil Shah in camp

Bijapur, Deccan, *c.*1656–59
Gouache with gold on paper, 20 × 16.7 cm
Hodgkin Loan 44
Published: Filippi 1997, no.44

Early in his reign, Sultan Ali Adil Shah (no.37) is seen seated on a low jewelled throne under a colourful canopy in his camp. He rests his right hand conventionally on his sword, while holding a small flower in his left. The companion kneeling before him may be his general Afzal Khan, perhaps reporting on the latest Mughal campaign against the kingdom, or some new incursion by the Maratha leader Shivaji. This scene combines courtly formality with a sense of easy intimacy. True to the ethos of Bijapur painting, neither man seems troubled by matters of state as they share in a tranquil enjoyment of the passing moment beside a well-laden mango tree, with ripening fruits hanging singly or in glowing clusters against a purplish ground.

Afzal Khan, who makes a conversational gesture with his right hand, was a redoubtable warrior of Afghan descent. In 1659 he was sent out to take the troublesome Shivaji dead or alive. When the two men eventually met, both came secretly armed. But it was Shivaji who prevailed, eviscerating Afzal Khan with his concealed *baghnakh* or steel 'tiger-claws', a murderous weapon worn on the hand.

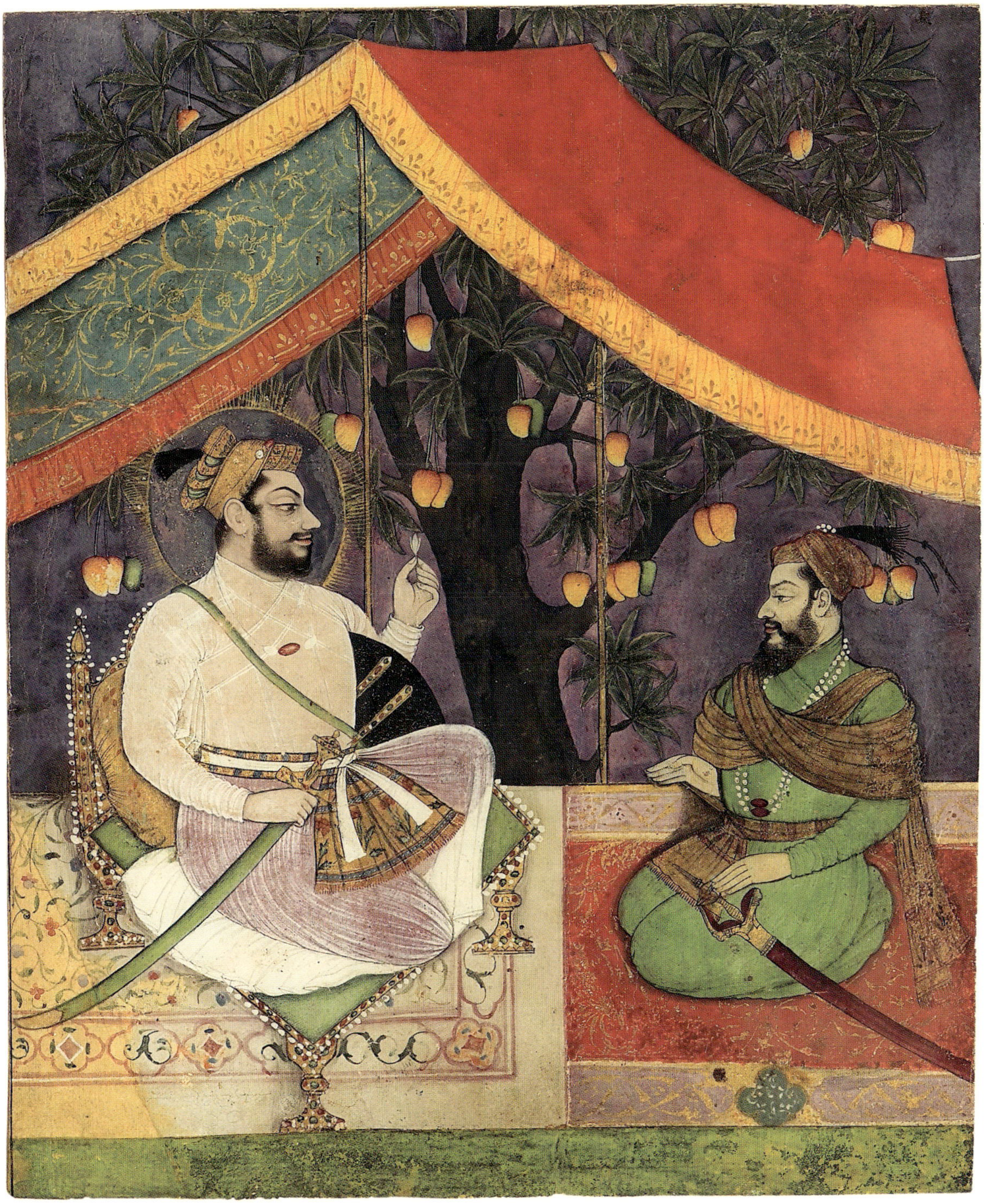

39 Wedding procession of Muhammad Quli Qutb Shah

Golconda, Deccan, *c.*1650
Gouache with gold on paper, 24 × 32.5 cm
Hodgkin Loan 15
Published: Filippi 1997, no.15; Michell and Zebrowski 1999, fig.148

A small wedding party travels home across a mysterious, dark blue nocturnal landscape. Only the flowers in the foreground and a distant village with temples and a tall slender pillar are clearly defined. A young prince holds his new bride close to him in the saddle as their horse is led homeward by a groom. Both are richly dressed and adorned with triple-pointed crowns, and the young woman has a Hindu tilak mark on her forehead. Attendants on other side hold royal umbrellas over their heads. Other youthful princes and attendants walk close behind, some making celebratory gestures, while two female attendants follow carrying trays with ritual vessels. In the deep blue void beyond, a bullock cart carrying four women passengers is driven briskly forward by its driver in a green turban.

Painted in the mid-seventeenth century for Sultan Abdullah Qutb Shah of Golconda (r.1626–72), this picture alludes to the legendary love of his grandfather Muhammad Quli Qutb Shah (r.1580–1612) for the beautiful Hindu dancing-girl Bhagmati. Although Muhammad Quli was a Shia Muslim, his own mother was a Telugu-speaking Hindu. As a young prince he would ride out to visit Bhagmati in her village a few miles from Golconda, fording the sometimes dangerous Musi river to do so. Soon afterwards, on his accession to the throne, he married her, and some years later he is said to have built his new capital on the site of her village, naming it Bhagnagar (subsequently Hyderabad) after her. With its evocation of the evening stillness and its atmosphere of calm fulfilment, this scene of the young couple's homeward return is a delicate and engaging work.

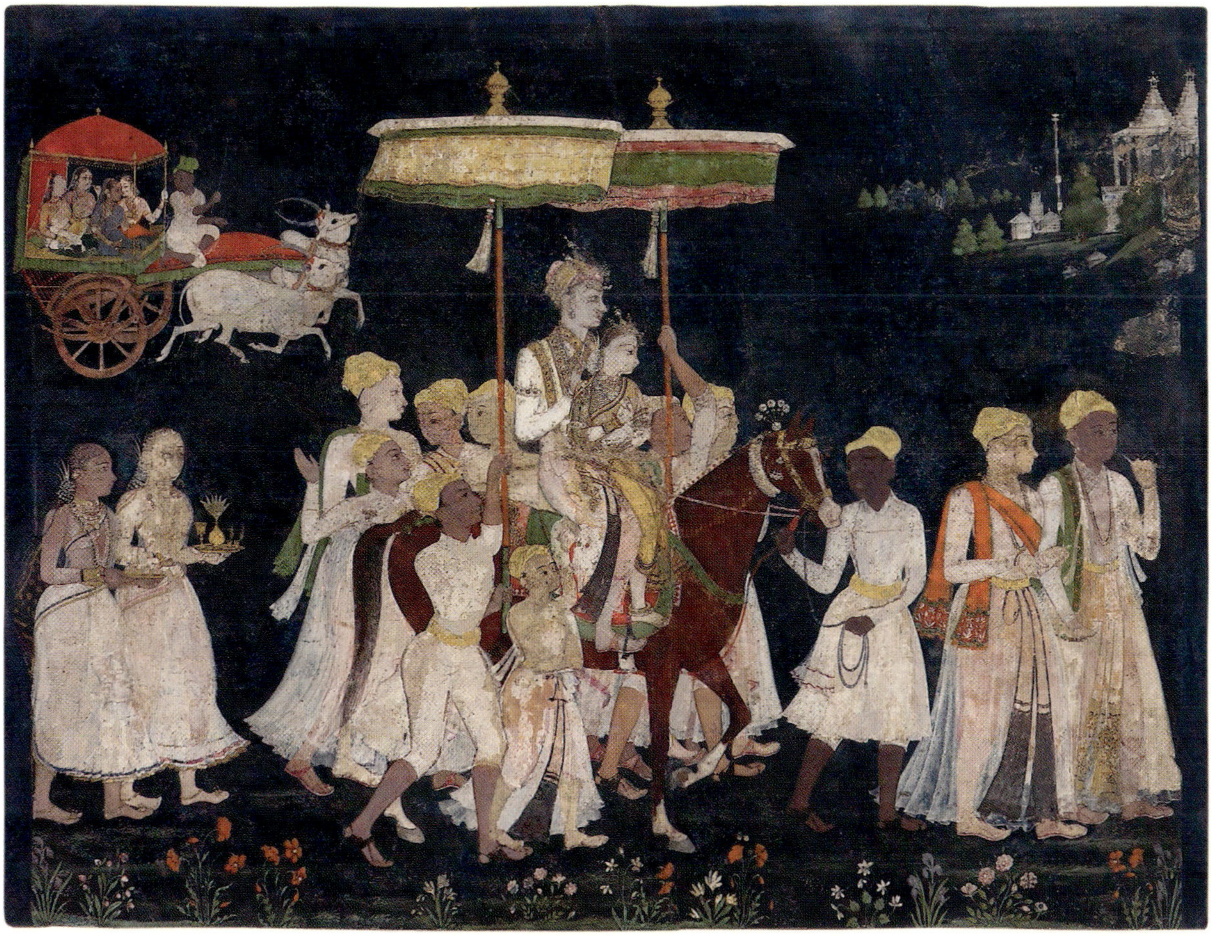

40 A marbled elephant

Bijapur, Deccan, *c.*1630–50
Brush drawing with marbling and gold and silver on paper, 12.7 × 21.6 cm
Hodgkin Loan 49
Published: Filippi 1997, no.49

A young prince, ankus in hand and a dagger at his waist, rides a briskly trotting elephant. His companion riding behind carries a flag, and the attendant running ahead has a long spear with a firecracker attachment used in controlling elephants. The caparisoned elephant is dexterously marbled in appropriate dark grey tones, shot with undulating lighter veins, some (at the shoulder and hind-quarters) almost callig-raphic in their staccato rhythms. The lighter-coloured tunics of the three men and the low hill in the right upper corner are also delicately marbled in varying patterns.

Called *kaghaz-i abri* or 'clouded paper' in Persian, the art of marbling flourished in Central Asia, Iran and Turkey. It had reached India by 1600 and became a speciality of the Deccan, particularly at Bijapur under Sultan Muhammad Adil Shah (1627–56).[1] Marbling effects are produced by swirling together pigments suspended in oil on a surface of water and skilfully transferring these ephemeral aqueous patterns to a paper surface. First the untreated areas in this picture, which remain the natural buff paper colour, would have been covered up with a prepared stencil or have been given a resistant coating. Pigments were then floated on water thickened with size and swirled or guided with a comb or stylus to form a design. Then the paper was brought into contact with the oiled water surface and the pattern fixed. Finally, outlining in black or gold and sparing touches of gold, silver and colour were applied. The background is relieved only by the little buildings, hill and trees to the right, although square seal marks have been added by the picture's later owners. This elegantly understated creation is the product of a refined pictorial taste and masterly skill in catching the subtle motions of oil on water.

1 E.g. Zebrowski 1983, pp.135–38; Welch 1985, no.198; Wolfe 1990, pp.8–12.

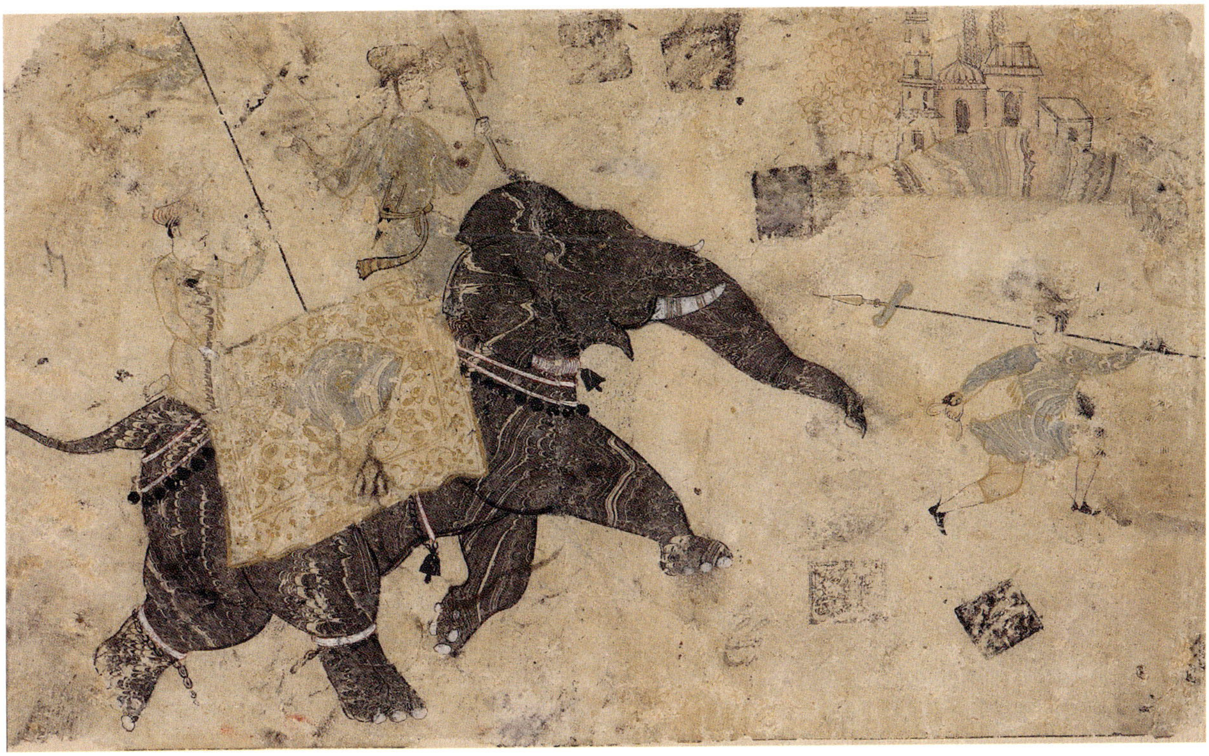

41 Elephant trampling a horse

Bijapur, Deccan, *c.* 1630–50
Brush drawing with gold and colour on marbled paper, 16.2 × 24.9 cm
Hodgkin Loan 91
Unpublished
See also detail, pp. 90–91

An enraged royal elephant, hung with chains and swinging bells, has charged an unfortunate stallion, trampling it and seizing it by the foreleg with its trunk. The mahout presses his ankus hard to the elephant's head to restrain it. The horse lifts its head in anguish, its hind-legs and genitals splayed by the force of the attack. The effect of this expressively drawn collision is amplified by the brilliantly executed marbling, with its multitudinous, semi-fortuitous yet artfully controlled bands of abstract patterning, also in turbulent motion. To the right of the mahout, these quivering seams of layered colours plunge and converge in a sudden cascade, following the contours of the elephant's head and the twisted rear leg of the stallion. Further below, the tighter and narrower bands swirl restlessly in fluted eddies and surges under and around the two striving animals.

Marbled studies of animals and other subjects were popular at Bijapur in the second quarter of the seventeenth century (no. 40), although relatively few now survive. In this powerful collaboration between artist and marbling master, the clashing animals and rider are drawn in reserve, as though superimposed on the vividly marbled paper.

This inventive mixed-media work may be compared with a contemporary Bijapur subject of an emaciated ascetic riding a starving nag, on a more sombre-toned marbled page, in which the nag is of similar generic type to the horse seen here.[1]

1 Pierpont Morgan Library, New York: Zebrowski 1983, fig. 106; Schmitz 1997, pl. 39, pp. 167–69.

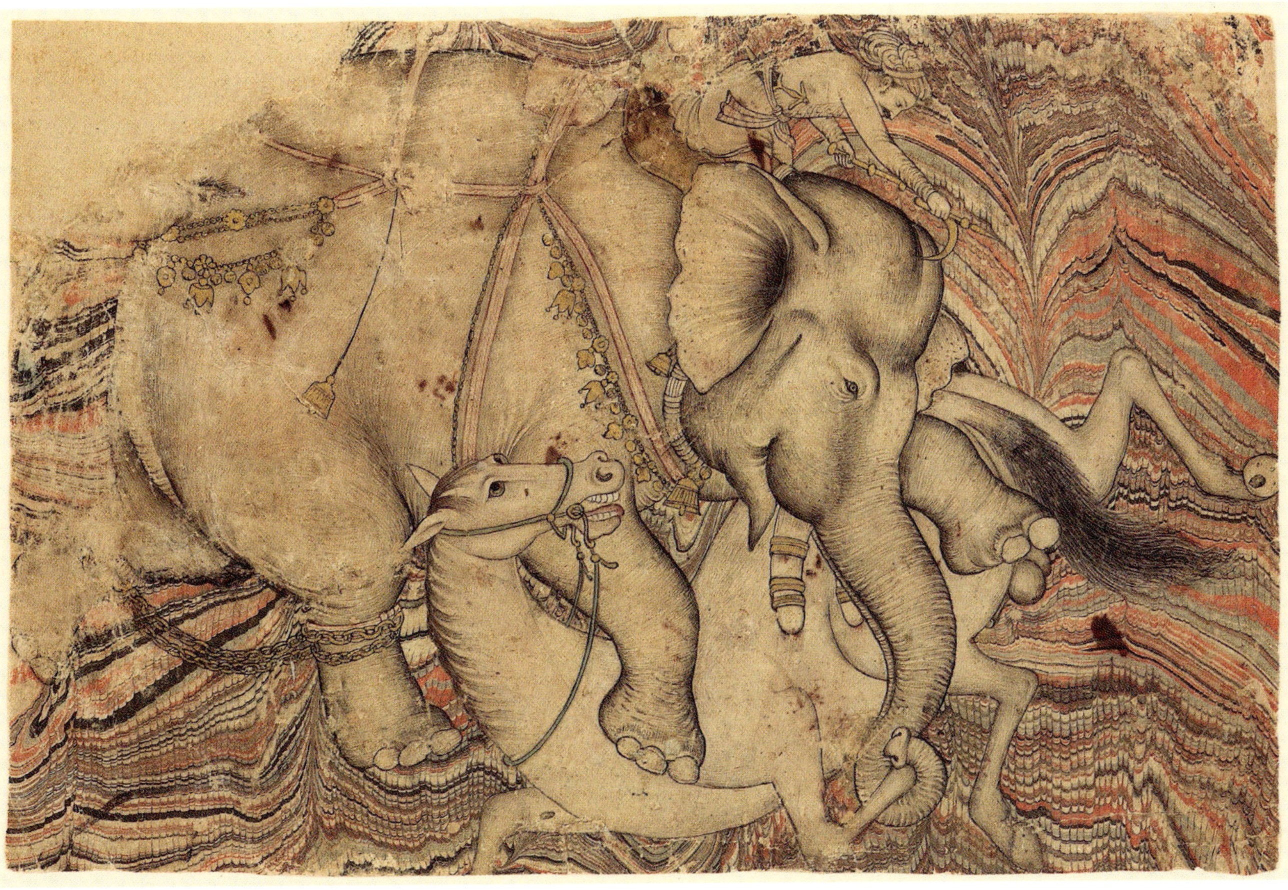

42 Album page with découpé calligraphy

Bijapur, Deccan, *c.* 1630–40
By the calligrapher Ali and the artist Muhammad Hasan
White cut-out paper and gouache on paper, 20 × 10 cm
Hodgkin Loan 99
Unpublished[1]

This type of découpé and appliqué paper design originated in Timurid Persia, later becoming popular in Ottoman Turkey. During the seventeenth century it was also practised in the Deccan, which had close cultural contacts with both these regions. However few Indian examples of this art now survive. Set against a near-black ground, the calligraphic text is an Arabic quatrain written in *nastaliq* script. It is addressed to Qanbar, the slave of the Imam 'Ali (cousin and son-in-law of the Prophet), who was put to death by the tyrant al-Hajjaj because of his loyalty to his master. Its first two verses read: "O Qanbar, you were mine yesterday, and today you have become like me." They reflect the strong currents of Shi'ite devotion and Sufi mysticism which prevailed at Bijapur, where this page was probably created in the royal library workshop of Sultan Muhammad Adil Shah (no. 36). The background to these elegantly written verses is a spiralling double scroll motif, with floral and foliate offshoots which fill the page to its corners. Unusually, this graceful and delicately detailed decorative design is accorded as much importance within the composition as the calligraphy itself.

1 But well catalogued in Bonham's sale cat., *Islamic and Indian Art*, 5 April 2011, lot 235 (on which the present entry is largely based); see also lot 236. Previously exhibited at the International Exhibition of Persian Art held at the Royal Academy, London, in 1931.

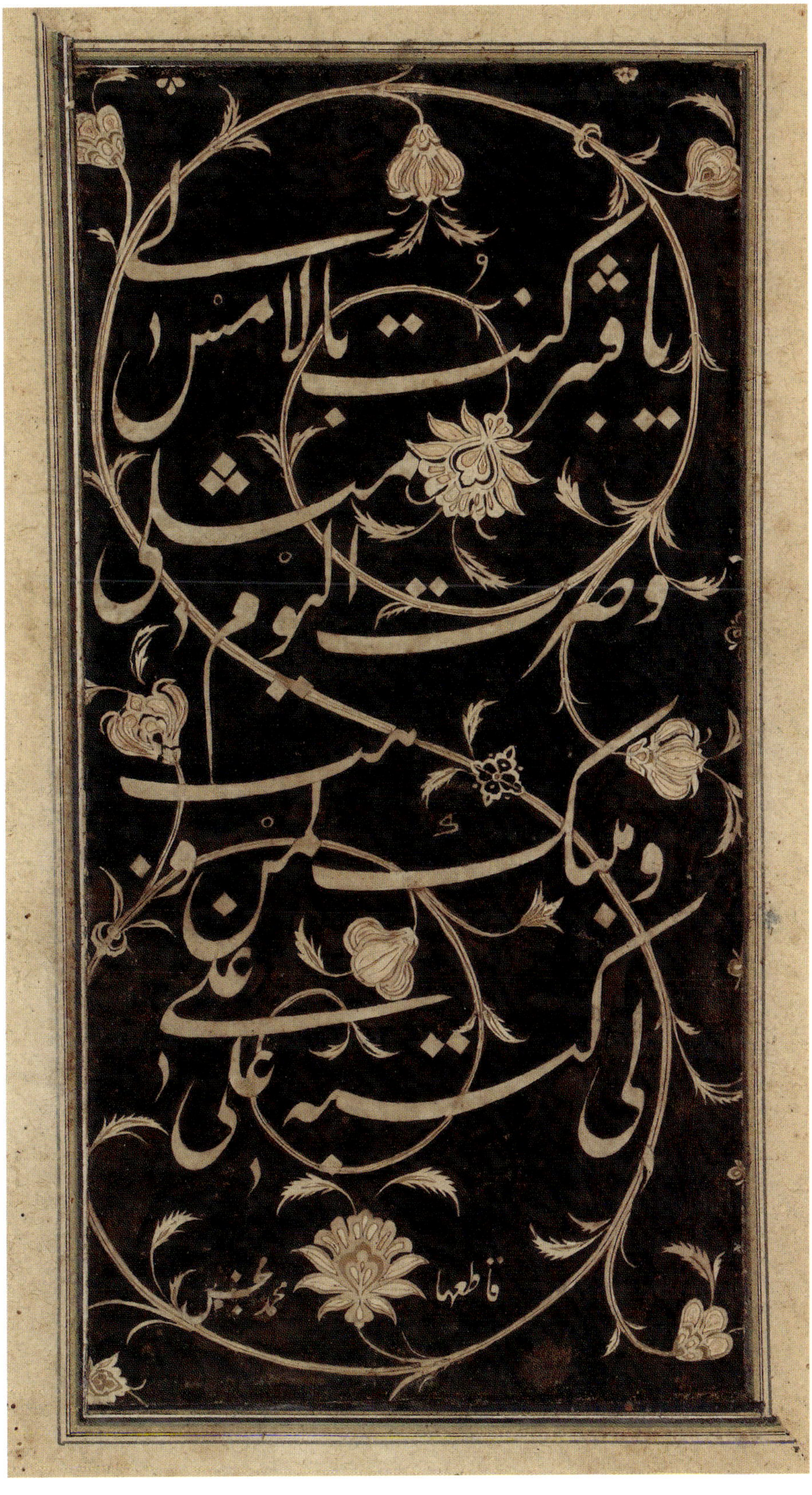
قاطعها
محمد محسن

43 Floral vase

Bijapur, Deccan, *c.*1650
Gouache with gold on paper, 25.5 × 16.7 cm[1]
Hodgkin Loan 66
Published: Topsfield and Beach 1991, no. 8; Filippi 1997, no. 66; Michell and Zebrowski 1999, fig. 135

This is a work of compelling, luxuriant fantasy. Perhaps originally placed as an independent illumination at the beginning or end of a manuscript or album, it was probably created for Sultan Muhammad Adil Shah of Bijapur (no. 36).[2] It makes lavish and effective use of gold, minutely tooled to catch the light, and here applied in subtly contrasting tones which combine with the brilliant colour pigments to sumptuous yet refined effect. While the decorative style follows earlier Islamic models, the motif of the vase of plenty is also an ancient one in Indian art, symbolising fertility and good fortune. It often appears in Islamic architectural decoration in the Deccan at this period, as for example in the seventeenth century painted plasterwork in gold and lapis in the Asar Mahal at Bijapur.[3] The maroon ground of the vase is almost concealed by the intricate and elaborately foliated central medallion, sundry trailing creepers and multi-coloured flower stems, and the bursting gold fronds, delineated with a calligraphic hand, that serve to outline the heart-shaped body of the vase. Emerging at the base of the vase's neck is the face of a *peri* (fairy) or angel, while the semi-abstract flaring neck again explodes with a climactic flourish of gold fronds and fantastical foliage. The trio of floral medallions which rise from the neck complete this exceptional composition.

1 Inscribed below in Persian script: *gul-i hazar gulha* ('Flower of 1000 flowers'), with further clerical annotations to the left.
2 Zebrowski also attributes to the present artist the border illumination on a portrait of Sultan Ali Adil Shah of *c.*1660 (Barber Institute, Birmingham: Zebrowski 1983, fig. 108).
3 E.g. Michell and Zebrowski 1999, col. pl. 12, p. 183; also Haidar 2011b, figs. 10, 21–23.

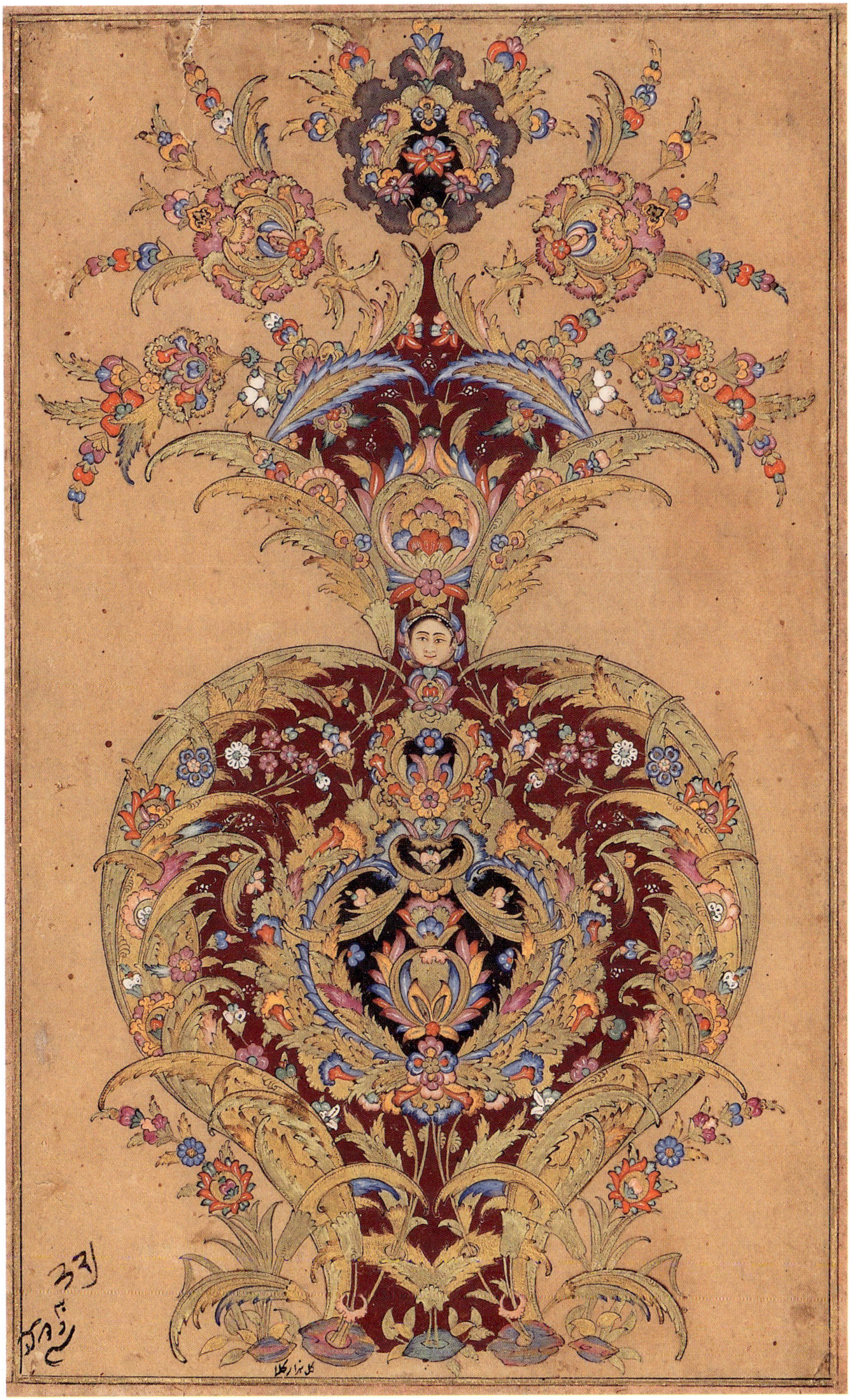

44–45 Pair of book covers

Golconda or Hyderabad, Deccan, *c.*1700 or later
Lacquered gouache with gold on leather, 23 × 16.5 cm
Hodgkin Loans 63–64
Published: Filippi 1997, nos.63–64; Michell and Zebrowski 1999, fig.155

These delightful painted and lacquered book covers were removed from an old European binding in recent times. Each is a variation on the theme of a chenar-like tree full of large birds and insects, flanked by auspicious, flower-filled vases of plenty (no.43). A horizontal band with a row of diverse flowering plants also appears below in each case. All these painted elements, including the dark viridian leaves of the trees, are vividly set off by the glowing gold backgrounds.

These abundant, bird-filled chenars (Oriental plane) recall Tree of Life designs in Golconda chintz textiles. In no.44, the opening out of the tree's central foliage through pruning allows a clearer view of the birds and butterflies within it. A pair of owls roost in the lower branches and a kingfisher plunges in flight to the left. The flanking polychrome vases with ornate handles are filled with arrangements of flowers. In no.45, the denser foliage tends to conceal the birds and winged insects within. The wide-bellied vessels standing on each side are jardinières heaped with a variety of flowering plants. The vessel on the right is flanked by an enormous butterfly and a smaller bird in flight. In their refined opulence and fantasy these designs are typically Deccani in execution and feeling.

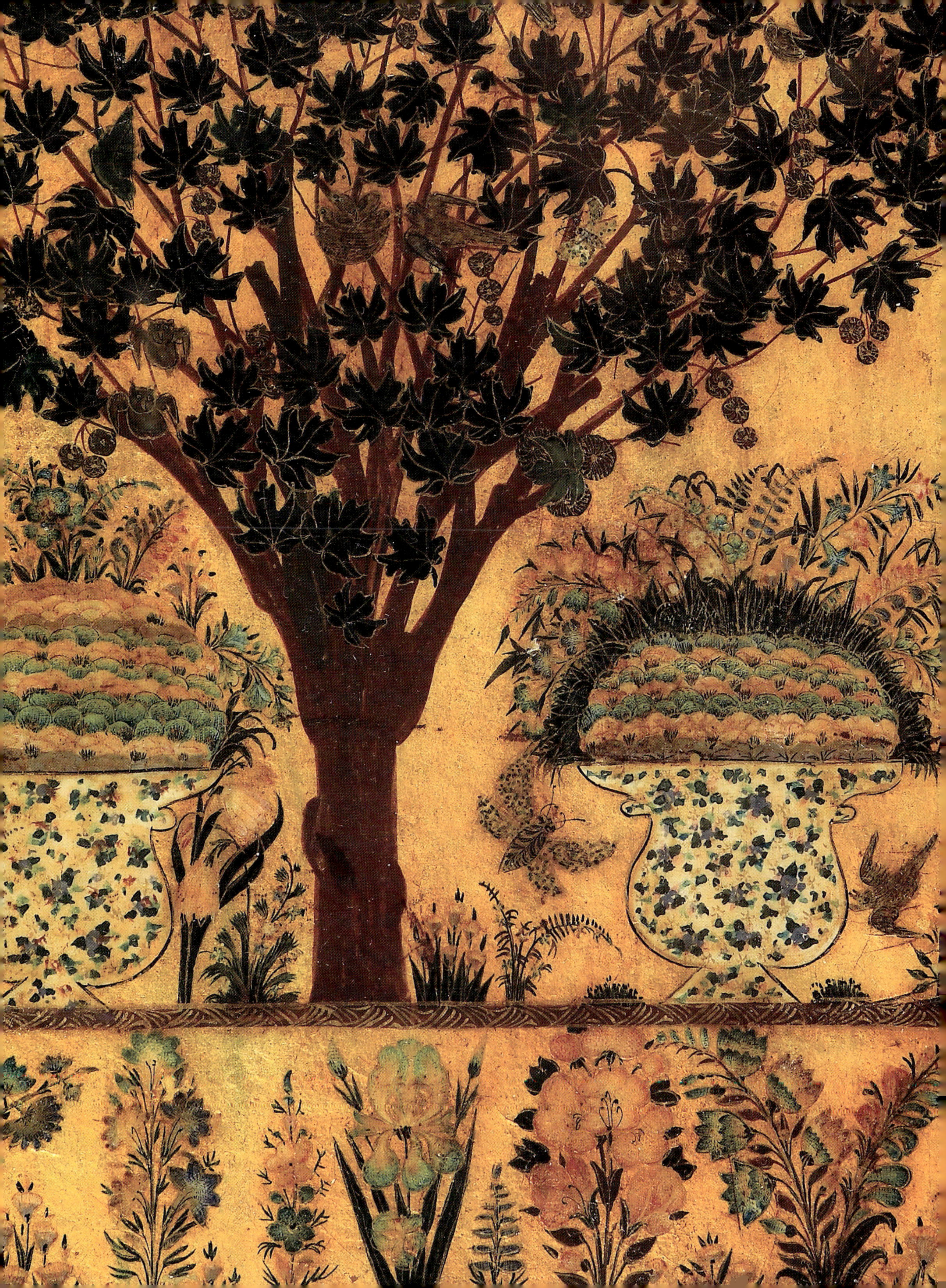

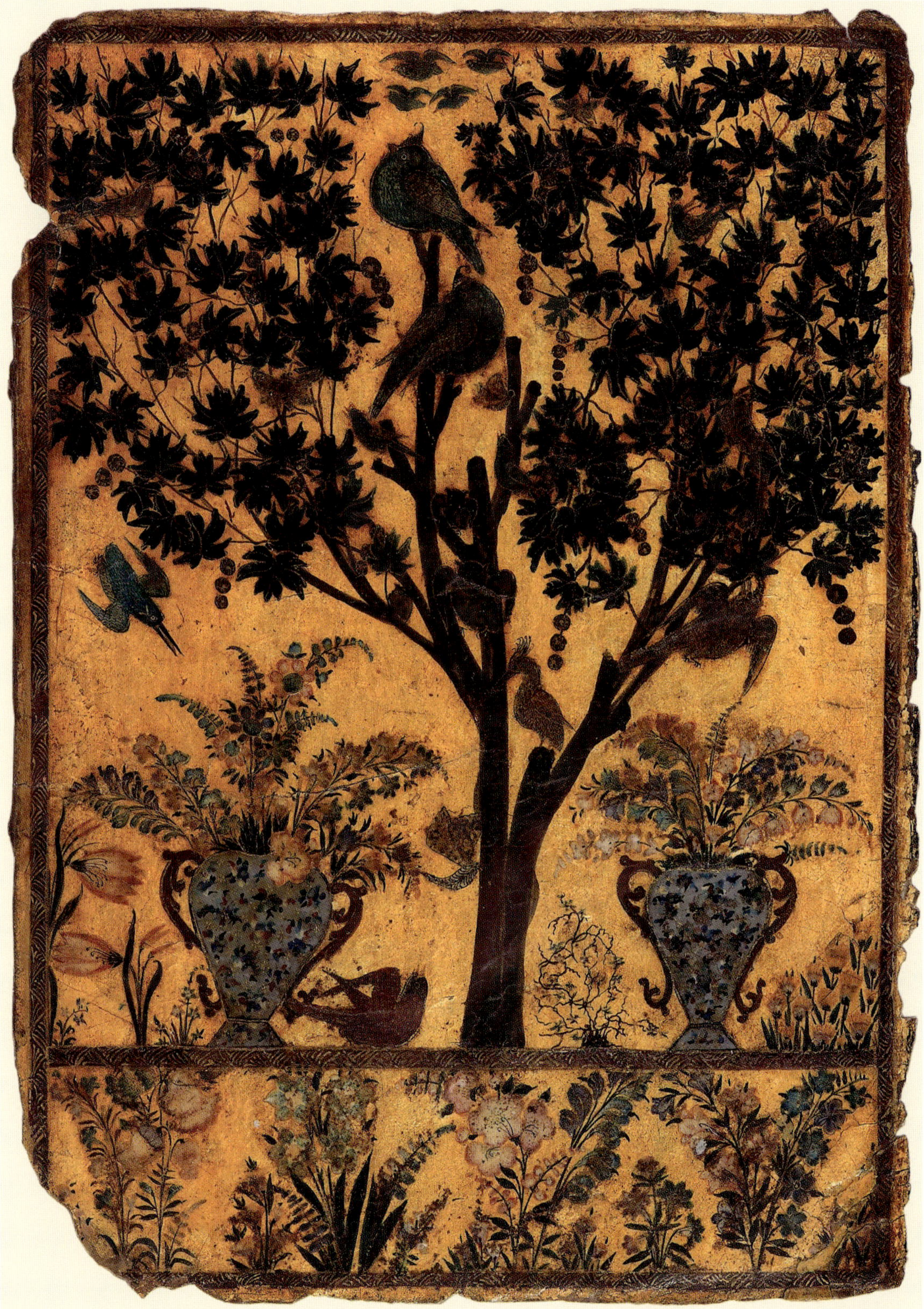

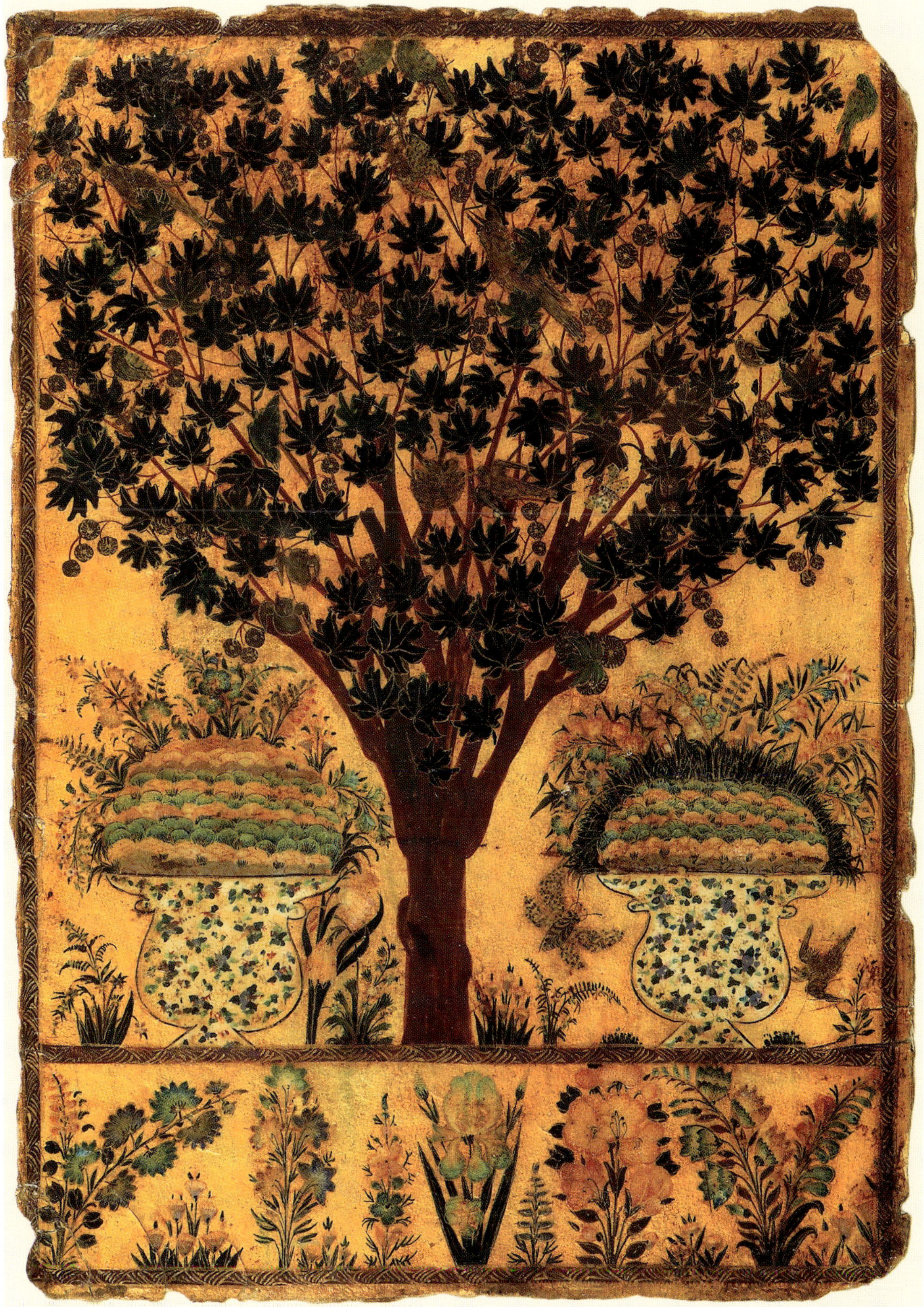

46 A hero wrestles a demon

Deccan or Rajasthan, late 17th century
Ink and gouache with gold on paper, 24.1 × 22.5 cm
Hodgkin Loan 113
Published: Welch ed. 1997, p.25, fig.14[1]

A stocky hero in a plumed cap, tunic and slippers has seized a fierce *div* (demon) by the thigh and collarband, so lifting and overturning him. The *div* meanwhile sinks fangs and claws into the hero's leg. Overthrowing demons was a speciality of Rustam, a mighty hero in the Persian *Shahnama* epic, but this more unassuming figure lacks his characteristic helmet and war-like accoutrements.[2]

This energetic coloured drawing is a striking example of the reception of a much earlier Turcoman subject into Indian painting. Possibly produced at a Deccani court, or conceivably at Kota in Rajasthan as suggested by Welch, it closely follows in reverse a fifteenth century composition found in one of the extraordinarily inventive Siyah Qalam album paintings in the Topkapi Saray Library in Istanbul.[3] This subject could have been brought to India in the form of a pounce or tracing carried by an itinerant artist from Central Asia or Iran. But in its lighter tone and calligraphic outline drawing the present version differs considerably from the sombre intensity of its Siyah Qalam prototype. Various incidental details differ also, as in the hero's simplified dress and the demon's clawed feet and leopard-spotted fur. The result is less a copy than a spirited reinterpretation.

1 Also Sotheby's catalogue, *The Stuart Cary Welch Collection*, 31 May 2011, lot 8. The inscription at lower left is there plausibly read as *rustum wa div*, though the first two letters [*rus*] are far from clear.
2 Compare Mason ed. 2001, no.14, for an earlier Mughal subject of Rustam toppling a demon.
3 Album Hazine 2153, fol.64r.: Ipsiroglu 1976, pl.32; also *Islamic Art*, I, 1981, fig.275; Welch ed. 1997a, fig.15.

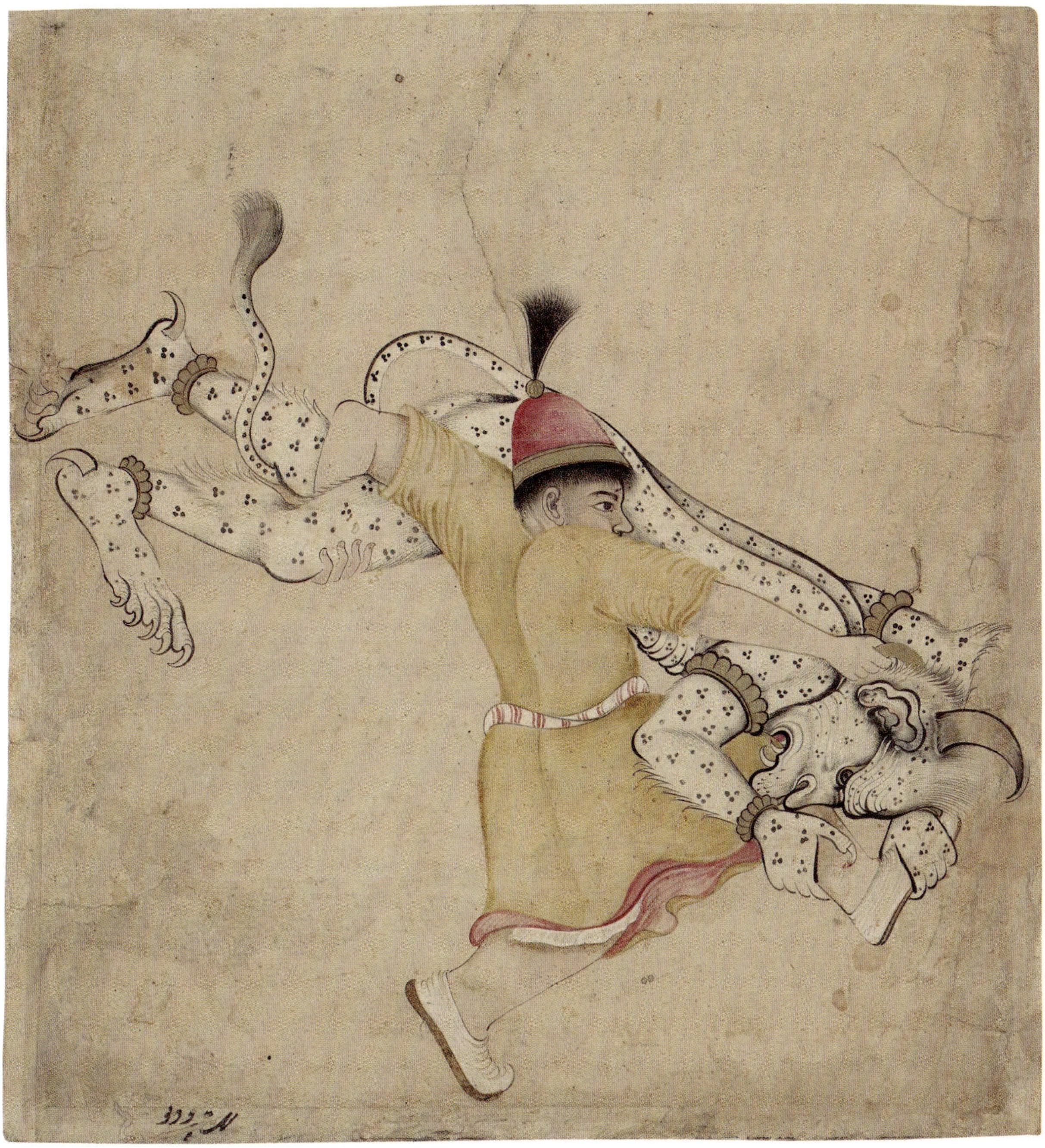

47 Sidi Masud Khan

Golconda, Deccan, *c.* 1680
Gouache with gold and silver on paper, 20.3 × 17 cm
Hodgkin Loan 103
Published: Robbins and McLeod eds., 2006, fig. 330, p. 257[1]

Africans, many of them Abyssinians (*habshi*) or Ethiopians, were well known in Mughal India, not least in the Deccan. Some came originally as traders, most as slaves. However a number of gifted individuals among them later rose to great prominence, especially at the court of the Bijapur Sultans, where Ikhlas Khan (no. 36) was the first and most famous of several African *wazirs* or prime ministers.

This painting belonged to a Golconda series of portraits of eminent men and seems to depict a later Bijapur *habshi* minister, Sidi Masud Khan.[2] He held sway under Sikandar Adil Shah until 1683, not long before Bijapur fell to the Mughals. He then moved to Adoni, the principal fort of the Kurnool district, where he governed independently for a short time and built a notable mosque. Soon he too had to capitulate to Aurangzeb's forces. Maharana Anup Singh of Bikaner, the Mughal general who took over Adoni, discovered in Masud's possession a notable collection of Bijapur paintings. A connoisseur himself, he carried them back to his desert capital in Rajasthan.

Set against a pale green ground within an oval cartouche, this painting is of a type produced in considerable numbers by Golconda artists, mainly for European patrons. Masud Khan's portrait, with a rich gold turban outlined in red, evidently follows an earlier Bijapur model. Wearing a flowered surcoat over a pink robe, the *habshi* minister holds his sword hilt and a flower, testifying to his worldly power and his refined taste.

1 Also Maggs Bros. Bulletin no. 34, *Oriental miniatures and illuminations*, London, 1981, no. 6.

2 A portrait of Ikhlas Khan in the San Diego Museum (Zebrowski 1983, fig. 96; Alderman 2006, pl. 100) is wrongly inscribed below as depicting Masud Khan. Alderman 2006, pl. 107, n. 24, describes another *habshi* figure in a later Bijapur picture (clearly a different man from the present subject) as 'possibly Sidi Masud'.

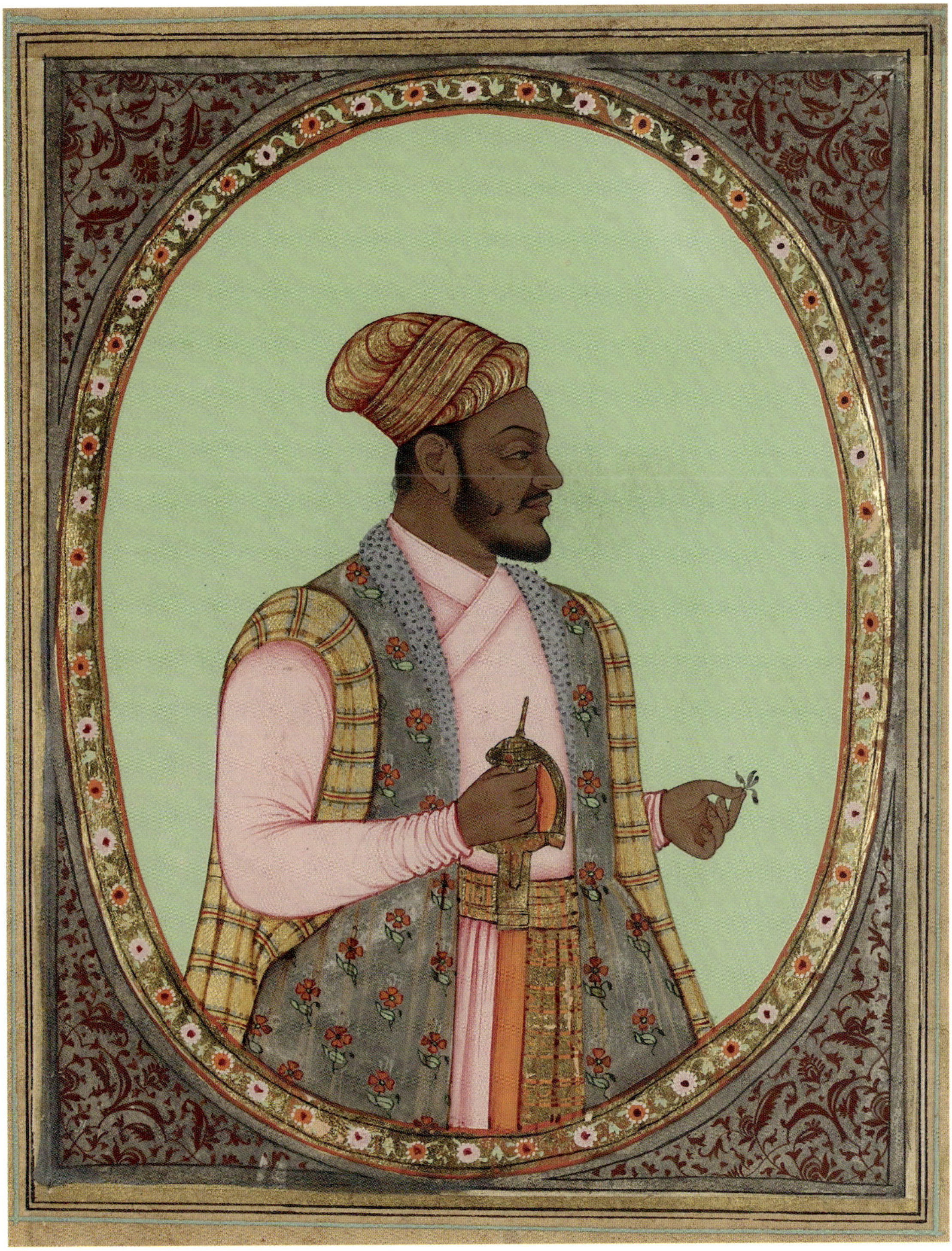

48 Maharaja Krishnaraja Wodeyar III

Mysore, Karnataka, *c.*1870
Gouache on paper, 58.5 × 47.5 cm
Hodgkin Loan 42
Published: Filippi 1997, no.42; Topsfield ed. 2006, illus. p.154

A Mysore Raja with coloured sectarian markings on his forehead sits for his portrait in an ivory chair of European style, his slippered feet resting on a footstool. Seen in three-quarter face, he directs a level gaze at the viewer as though at a camera lens. One hand hangs from the arm-rest with thumb and finger joined as if in a demonstrative gesture. His attendant makes a respectful gesture of salutation, standing barefoot on a carpet boldly patterned with flowery octagons. The wall behind is an intense green hue of European origin. At the centre is a Victorian double wall lamp with cut glass pendants and an elaborate brass bracket.

This portrait appears to represent Maharaja Krishnaraja III (r.1799–1868), but as he had appeared in middle age some thirty years before. A scion of the ancient Wodeyar dynasty, Krishnaraja had been restored to the throne by the British at the age of five, following the defeat of Tipu Sultan in 1799. At sixteen, he assumed ruling powers but then came under the sway of dubious hangers-on. In 1831 the British relieved Krishnaraja of his ruling powers. Retaining his large royal income, this cultivated and intelligent Raja then devoted himself to his interests in religious philosophy, mathematics, astrology and games and puzzles. Until his death in 1868 he devised many ingenious board and card games of complex symbolic kinds, as well as mathematical puzzles of the chessboard knight's tour type.[1]

1 Topsfield ed. 2006, articles by V. Rangachar and A. Topsfield.

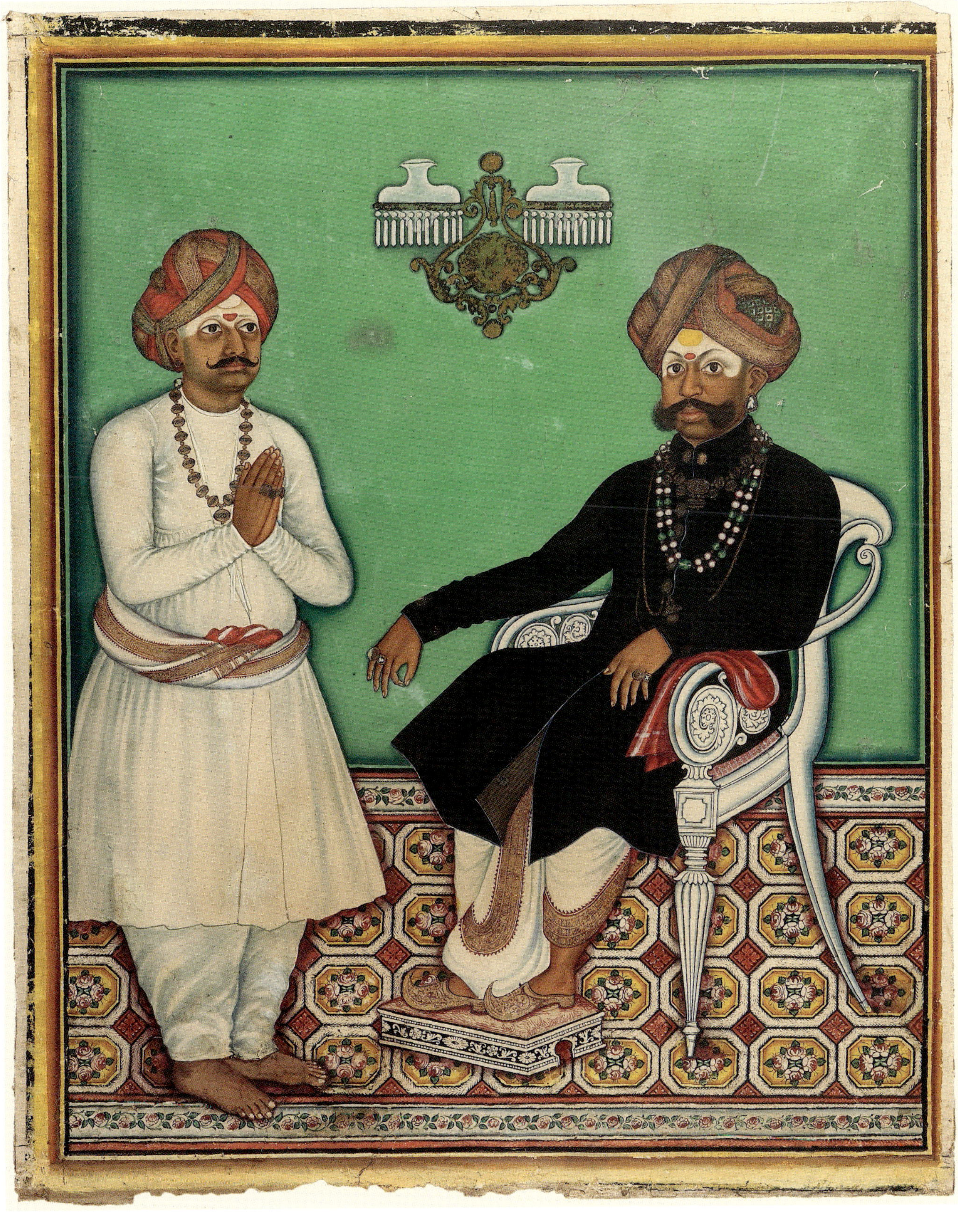

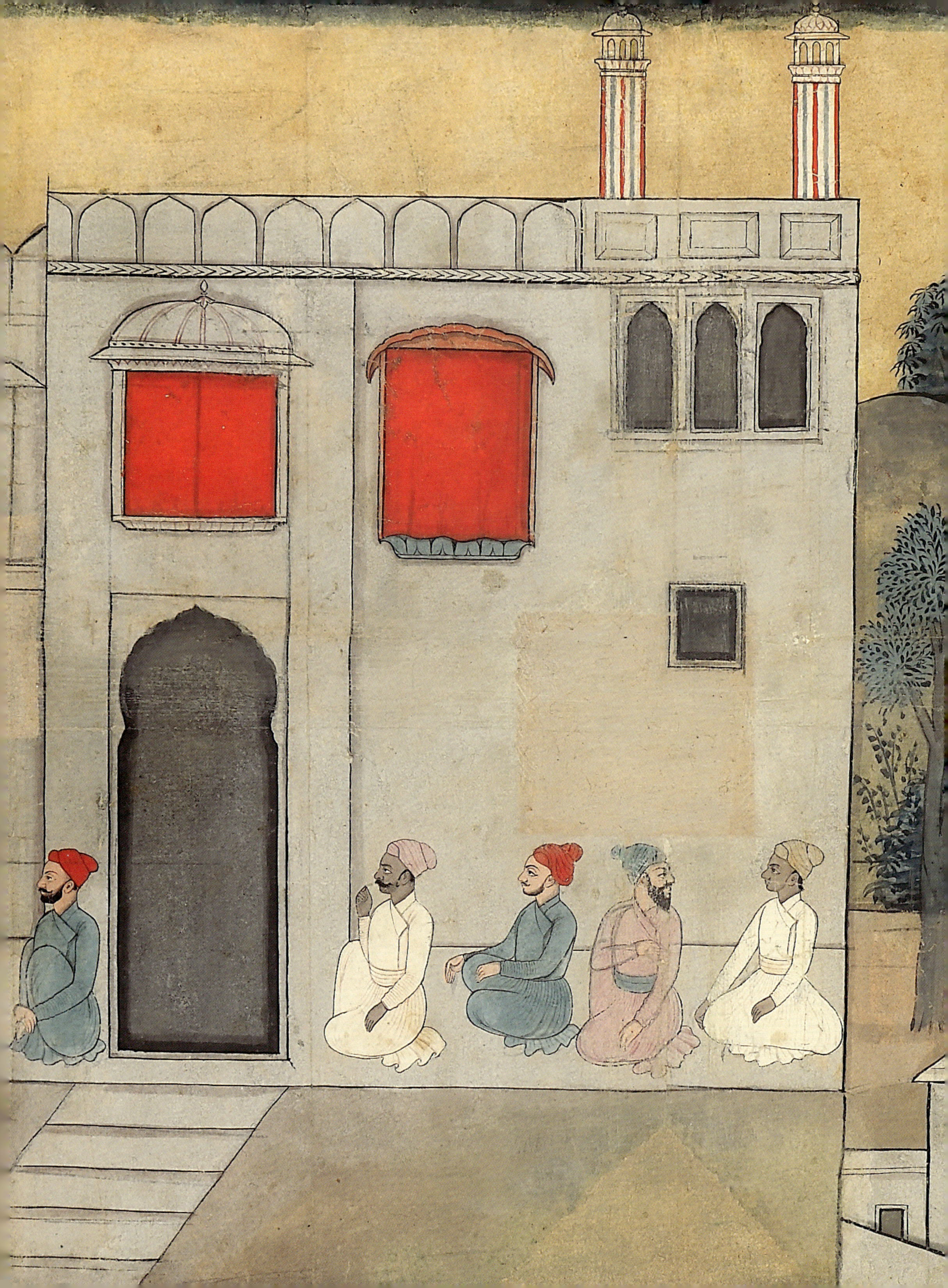

PAHARI

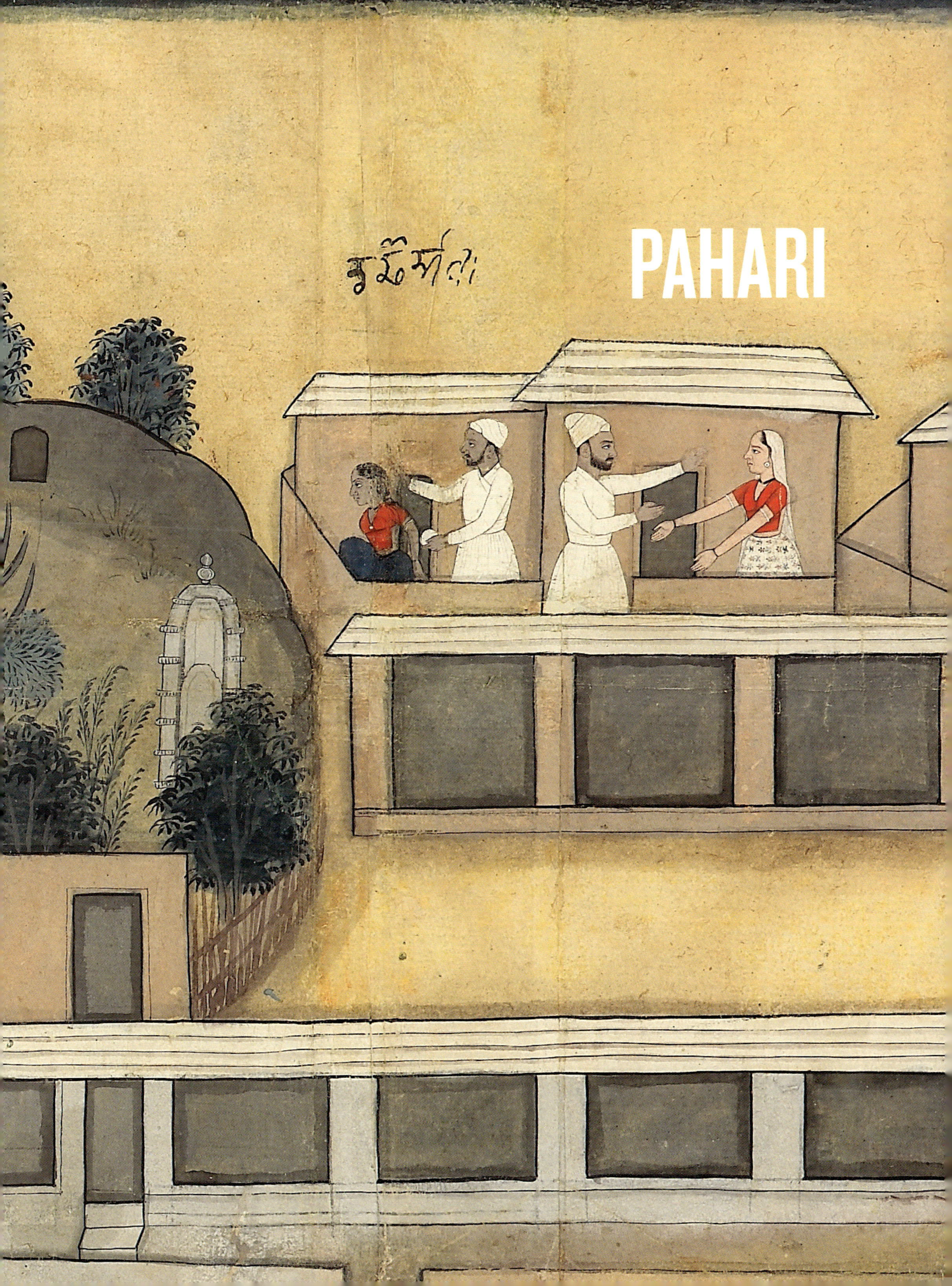

49 Marriage procession in a bazaar

Mandi, Punjab Hills, *c.*1640–50
Gouache with gold on paper, 32 × 49 cm
Hodgkin Loan 28
Published: Digby 1973, pl.III (detail); Victoria & Albert Museum 1982, no.160, col. pl.4; Glynn 1983, fig.13; Bayly 1990, no.26; Topsfield and Beach 1991, no.15; Kossak 1997, no.19; Filippi 1997, no.28; Glynn 2011a, fig.6

See also detail, p. 2

Painted by a Mughal-trained master working at the Punjab Hill court of Mandi, this procession scene provides an unusually vivid view of contemporary life in an Indian bazaar. In the main street a princely bridegroom on a horse is escorted to his wedding by a cavalcade of nobles, attendants and musicians wearing saffron-stained clothes. An elephant with a royal banner precedes them and *naqqara* drummers on camels bring up the rear. The procession is set against a strong apple-green ground. The populace look on from the street and rooftops, and the open-fronted bazaar shops are busy and well-stocked. The merchandise in each is clearly shown: from the left, brass *lotas* and other vessels; *pan* (betel-leaf); sweet-meats; glass and ceramic flasks and vases; knives, daggers and sword-hilts; textiles; and grains and pulses. All the figures, including the diverse bystanders in the foreground, some of whom seem perturbed or agitated, are sensitively observed and painted by the same hand.

This picture is the first in a sequence of three narrative scenes. The two that follow depict the groom's arrival at a palace, followed by the wedding ceremonies.[1] It is difficult to say which story they illustrate, although they have been associated both with the *Ramayana*[2] and *Mahabharata*[3] epics. They are however by the same master as a dispersed group of similarly large illustrations to the *Bhagavata Purana* and the *Ramayana*, which form the first known phase of painting at the court of Mandi. Strongly based in the Mughal style, these works are among the most impressive narrative paintings from the Punjab Hills.

1 Catherine and Ralph Benkaim collection: Glynn 1983, figs.14–15.
2 Glynn 1983, pp.52–54; Glynn 2011a, p.415.
3 Topsfield and Beach 1997, no.15, n.4, a suggestion made by Francis G. Hutchins.

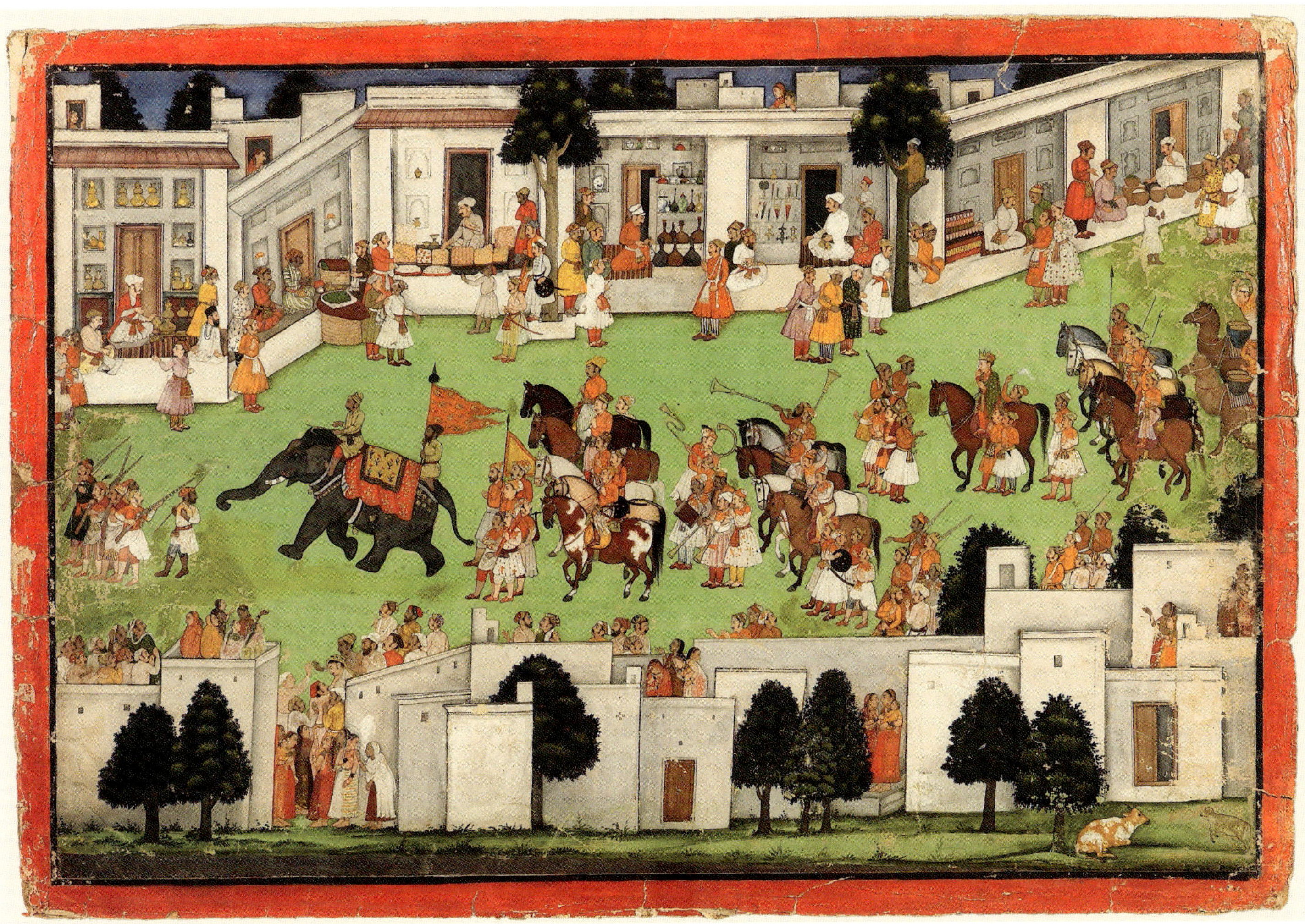

50 Bhadrakali, destroyer of the universe

From a 'Tantric Devi' series
Basohli, Punjab Hills, *c.*1660–70
Gouache with gold, silver and green
beetle-wing case on paper, 23 × 21 cm
Hodgkin Loan 82
Published: Filippi 1997, no. 82; Dehejia ed. 1999,
no. 38 and frontispiece, and McInerney 1999;
Menzies 2006, no. 74

Devi, the Great Goddess, assumes myriad forms, both benign and wrathful, from gentle youthful beauty to fearsome fiendish hag. To the devotee all these manifestations of her divine nature are equally venerable and true. "She is the one who gives him birth and loves him in the flesh, also the one who destroys him in the flesh."[1] These dramatically varying forms of the Goddess were represented with extraordinary verve by a master-painter of Basohli in the 1660s, in a series of at least seventy images accompanied by Sanskrit verses. Commonly known as the 'Tantric Devi' series, it was probably commissioned by a princely devotee for his personal *darshan* or contemplation. Less than half of its pages now survive. This page, numbered 47, shows Bhadrakali ('Auspicious Kali'), one of the most powerful and terrifying iconic visualisations of the Goddess, in which the full destructive ferocity of her darker nature is distilled:

> In her lotus-like hand she holds
> the severed head of the creator of the world
> She smiles and sounds satisfied
> She devours the mover of the entire universe
> Like limp darbha grass she holds the bodies
> of eternally dark Vishnu and Shiva
> I meditate upon Bhadrakali
> glowing like new clouds
> standing upon a corpse[2]

Blue-skinned, glaring, with lolling tongue and electrified hair yet still carefully bejewelled, Kali's darkly looming, stocky figure astride the corpse dominates the picture space, against the glowing primary colours of the yellow ground, red border and narrow band of cloud-flecked sky. In her bloody lower hands she holds the four severed heads of Brahma and the limp corpses of Vishnu and Shiva, the three main gods in the Hindu triad. With her upper hands she flourishes her broad sword aloft, while feeding corpses into her gaping mouth. Severed hands hang from her belt. To the Tantric initiate, the Goddess's cosmic power is seen to be supreme, absorbing the powers of all the other gods, and transcending the illusory bonds of Time, Karma and Death.

1 Goswamy and Fischer 1992, p. 36, also nos. 7–12.
2 Tr. V. Dehejia: Dehejia ed. 1999, p. 269.

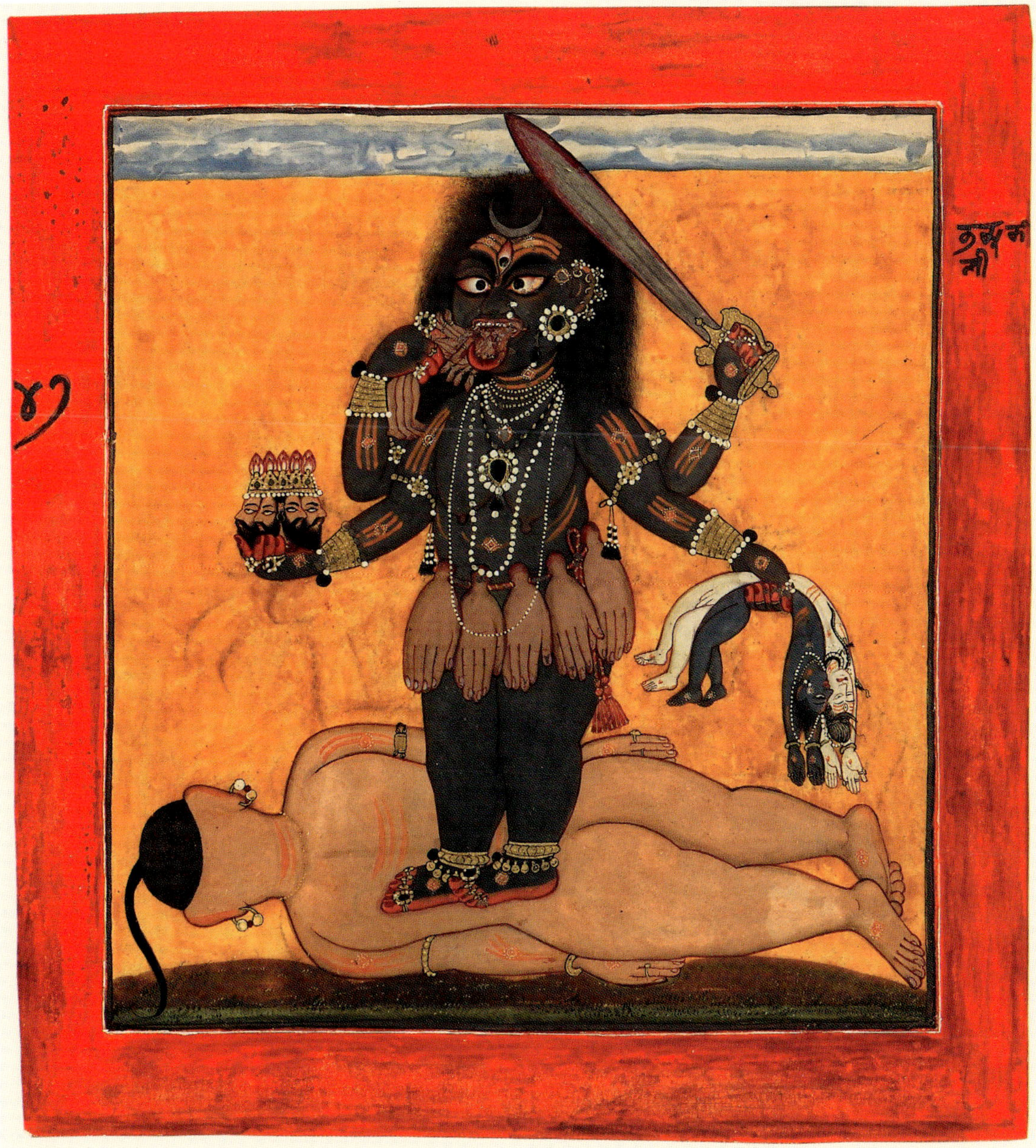

51 Harihara Sadashiva

Mandi, Punjab Hills, *c.*1710–20
Brush drawing, gouache on paper, 33 × 27 cm
Hodgkin Loan 4
Published: Topsfield and Beach 1991, no.30; Filippi 1997, no.4

Sadashiva, the Eternal form of Shiva, whose five heads face the cardinal points and the zenith, is here shown in the form of Harihara, bearing the combined attributes of Shiva and Vishnu. In his five right hands he holds the trident, hand-drum, skull-cup, sword and cobra of Shiva, and in his left hands, the mace, conch, discus and lotus of Vishnu as well as a shield. As the divine ascetic, Shiva sits cross-legged with long matted locks, wearing a leopard-skin dhoti, disc-shaped earrings and a necklace of human heads. He also wears items of princely jewellery, such as thumb-rings used in archery. His eyes are turned upwards in yogic trance and his foreheads bear the third eye of insight. His heads and arms are festooned with garlands of the sacred (and hallucinogenic) datura plant.

This powerfully simplified image of the meditating god is related to a more fully coloured version in the Victoria and Albert Museum.[1] Both can be attributed to an anonymous master working at Mandi in the early eighteenth century. This sparingly coloured drawing on a plain ground is perhaps even more starkly impressive than the V&A painting. The modelling of the god's massive hairy chest and belly recalls that of certain portraits of Raja Sidh Sen of Mandi (r.1684–1727),[2] for whom this picture would have been painted. Sidh Sen is remembered as of a ruler of great physical stature and military prowess, who lived for nearly a hundred years. As a devotee of Shiva he had also acquired yogic powers whereby, according to legend, he would fly to the source of the Ganges each morning to bathe, or would levitate while meditating before the image of Shiva in the palace. Sidh Sen's self-identification with the god is reflected in a number of apotheosizing portraits,[3] showing him in ascetic guise or holding divine attributes in his multiple arms.

1 E.g. Archer 1973, 'Mandi' no.15; Kramrisch 1981, no.P-9; Goswamy and Fischer 1992, no. 84, also pp.190–93 for a study of this master.
2 E.g. Archer 1973, 'Mandi' nos.18 and 21; Goswamy and Fischer 1992, no.76; Khandalavala n.d., fig.44, p.109.
3 E.g. Kramrisch 1981, no.P-16; Glynn 1979, figs.1–4; Goswamy 1986, no.138.

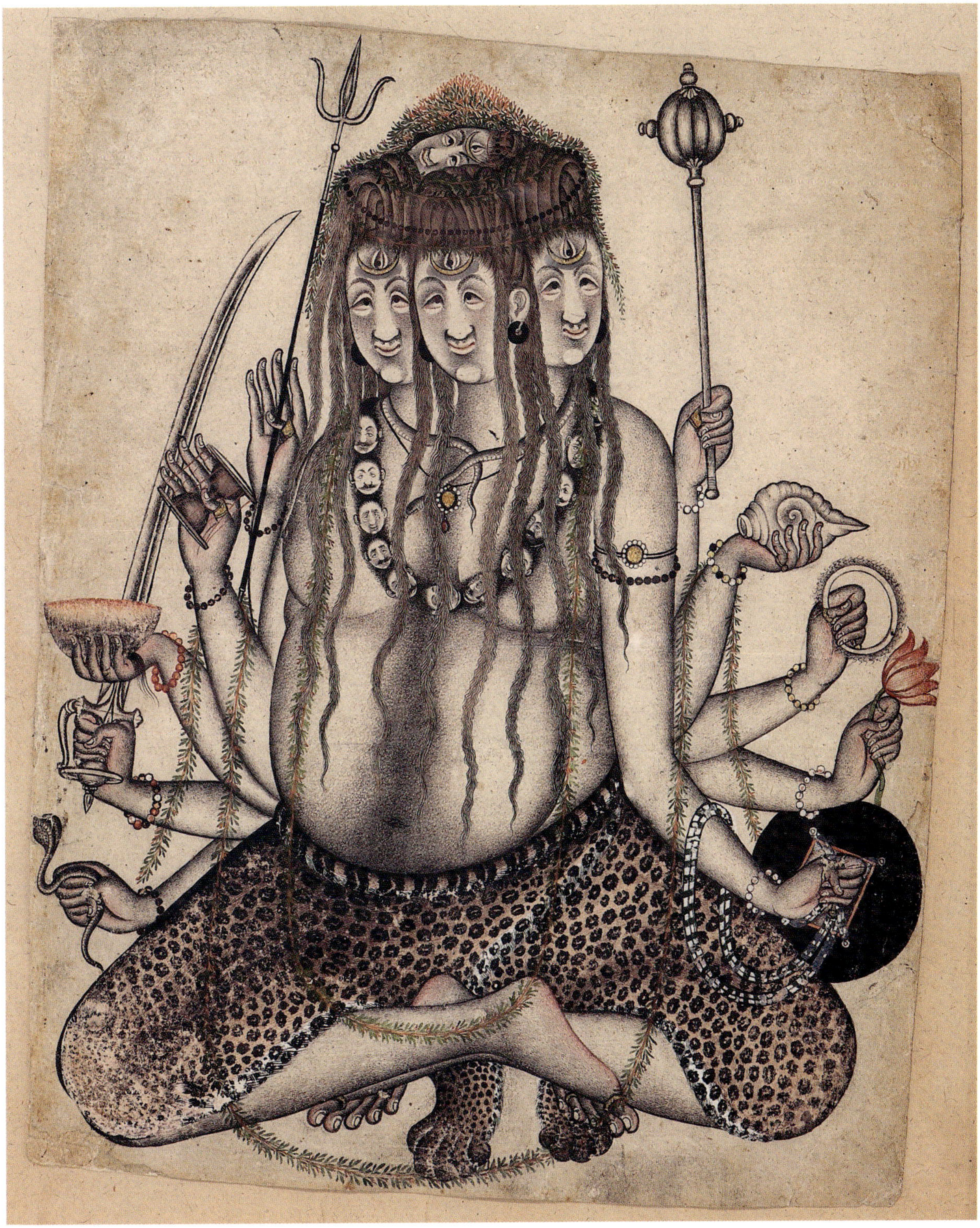

52 Brahma, creator of the universe

Mankot, Punjab Hills, *c.*1720
Gouache on paper, 16.5 × 12.5 cm
Hodgkin Loan 6
Published: Filippi 1997, no.6

Four-headed and four-armed, the creator god Brahma holds in his upper hands a manuscript of the Vedas, the earliest Hindu scriptures, and sacred *kusa* grass used in ritual. In his lower hands he holds prayer beads and a jewelled water vessel or *kamandalu*, representing the earth. Wearing a yellow dhoti, Brahma sits astride his *vahana* or personal vehicle, the *hamsa* or goose or white swan. Standing on a grassy rise, this auspicious bird is shown with raised head, its long neck curving elegantly forward. The artist has set Brahma and his mount in iconic fashion against a plain red ground, conveying with simple power the impassive majesty of the god. The painting may have belonged to a series painted for a prince's private *darshan* or contemplation, or else, like a comparable subject in the Boston Museum,[1] it may have belonged to a series of images relating to divination or the interpretation of dreams.

Known as a creator deity from late Vedic times, Brahma was never widely venerated in later ages like Shiva and Vishnu yet became linked with them in a triad of major Hindu gods. As first member of this classic triad, he represents spiritual power and maintains the cosmic equilibrium between the opposing principles of Vishnu as preserver of the world and Shiva as its destroyer.

1 Museum of Fine Arts, Boston, acc. no.17.2766: Coomaraswamy 1926, no.XXXVI, pl.XVII: one of sixteen pages from a series, depicting gods, epic heroes and other subjects.

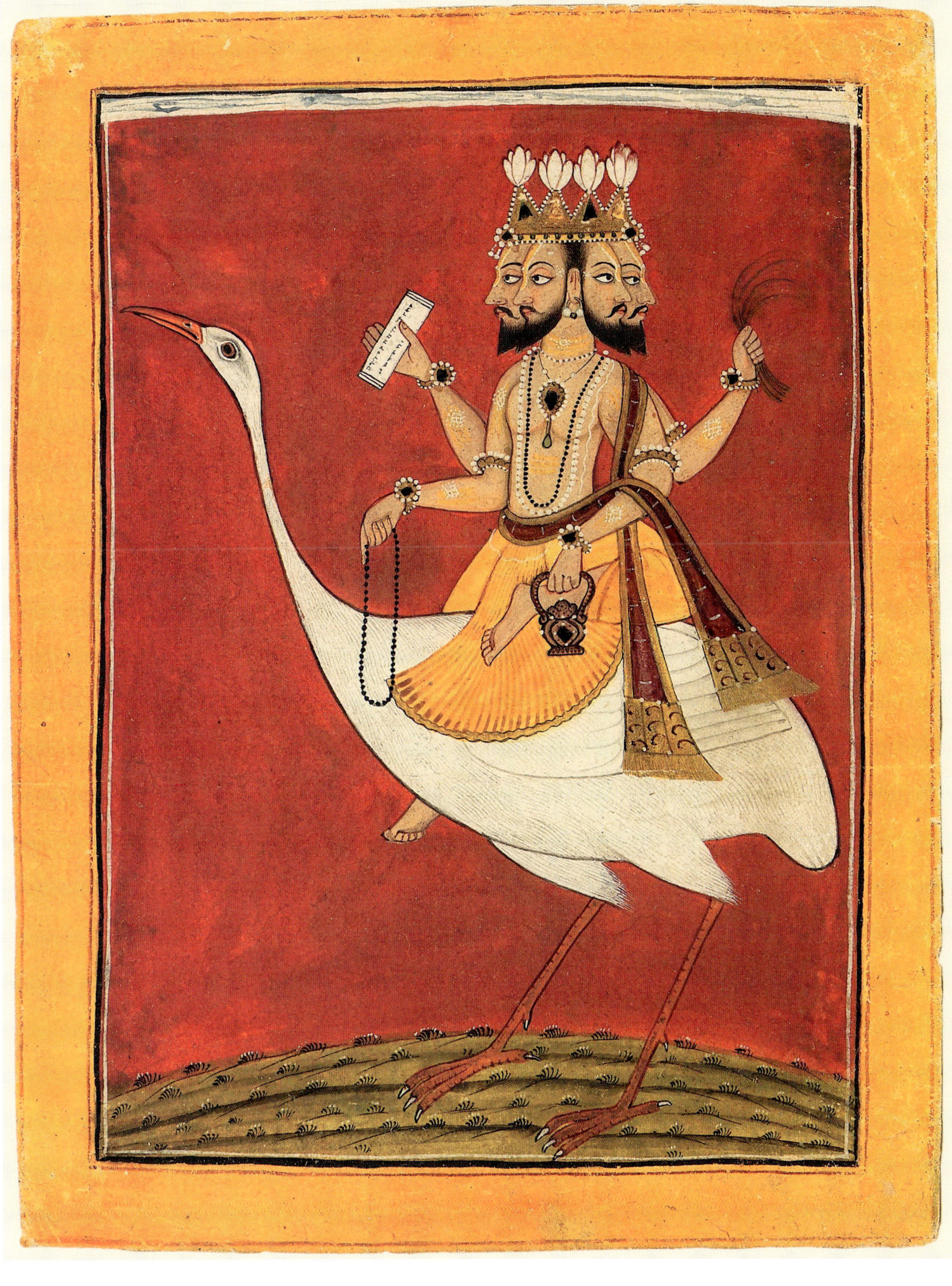

53 Raga Chandra, the moon god

Basohli or Nurpur, Punjab Hills, *c.*1680
Gouache on paper, 20.5 × 21.2 cm[1]
Hodgkin Loan 84
Published: Filippi 1997, no.84

One of the most popular subjects in later Indian painting, *Ragamala* ('Garland of Ragas') paintings were conceived as depicting the essential qualities of the ragas or musical modes, according to scenes prescribed by poetical texts. The principal ragas were grouped with their *raginis* or 'wives' in series of 36 or more paintings. In the Punjab Hills extended series of 84 pictures were current which also included the 'sons' of ragas (*ragaputra*). These small, highly concentrated and vibrantly coloured scenes employ a changing cast of gods, nobles, ladies, ascetics and animals, seen in varying combinations and settings.

In this painting, one of five pages from the same *ragamala* in the Hodgkin collection (nos. 53–57),[2] the moon god Chandra rides a blackbuck, silhouetted by the white disc of the full moon within a radiant field of yellow. Attenuated bands of cloudy sky and grassy landscape appear above and below. Chandra holds a lotus bloom in his left hand and his triple-pointed crown is also trimmed with lotuses. He wears pearl bands and necklaces as well as yellow sectarian *tilak* markings on his upper body. His tame blackbuck is neatly caparisoned, with a bell at its neck. Together they process serenely like the moon across the sky.

Raga Chandra is appropriately a musical mode sung in the depth of the night, in the period after midnight.[3] In Kshemakarna's treatise, Chandra (or Chandrabimba) is the second son (*ragaputra*) of the family of Hindola Raga.[4] It was represented by Pahari artists, who were generally not conversant with Kshemakarna's descriptive verses, in varying ways, though generally as here with a prominent full moon.[5]

1 Inscribed above in takri script: *rag chandra hindole sut* (Raga Chandra son of Hindola).
2 Another page from this dispersed series is in the Custodia Collection, Paris, and others have appeared on the art market at various times. It has usually been assigned to Basohli, but recently Catherine Glynn has argued for a Nurpur origin: Glynn, Skelton and Dallapiccola 2011, pp. 33–34
3 Randhawa 1971, p. 63.
4 Waldschmidt 1967, p. 114, fig. 3; Ebeling 1973, p. 74.
5 E.g. Tandan 1983, fig. 31; Glynn, Skelton and Dallapiccola 2011, no. 3.

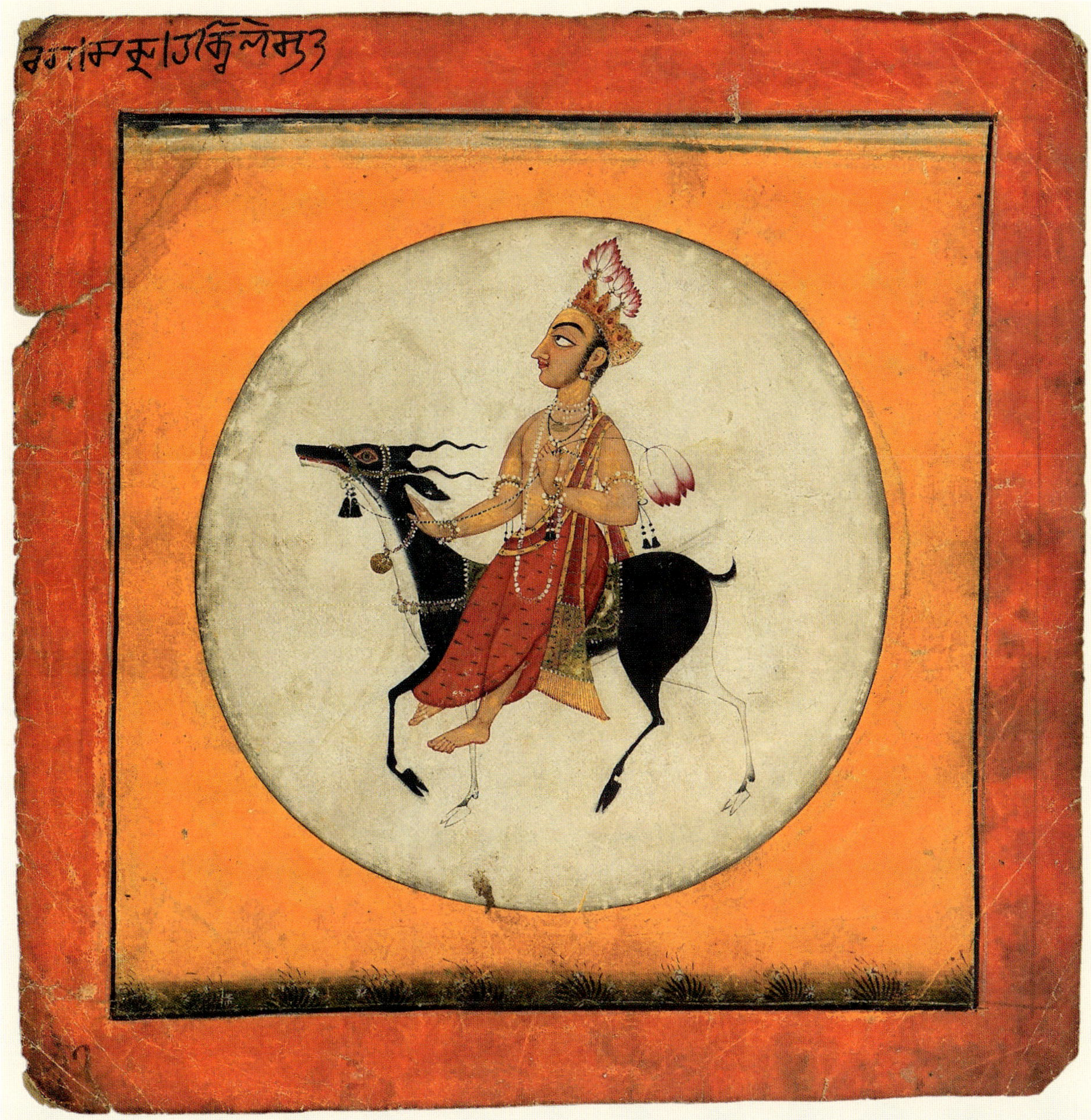

54 Raga Madhava: A prince and lady meeting

Basohli or Nurpur, Punjab Hills, *c.*1680
Gouache on paper, 21.1 × 21.1 cm[1]
Hodgkin Loan 83
Published: Filippi 1997, no.83

In this page from the same *ragamala* series as no.53, the musical mode Madhava is visualised as a nobleman in court dress, seated at his ease within a pavilion chamber, who turns towards a lady standing at its threshold. Their eyes meet as he holds up a small flower as an offering. She extends her hands towards him in a complaisant gesture, one hand passing behind the pillar and into the chamber. There is a sense of imminent erotic possibility. In a moment she will no doubt enter the chamber, its rich and deeper tones contrasting with the hot yellow background.

In Pahari *ragamala* series, Madhava, a son (*ragaputra*) of Raga Bhairava, is a not very common raga and has a varying iconography. It is shown most often as an encounter between a prince and lady in a chamber of some kind, though seldom with the immediacy and power seen here.[2]

1 Inscribed above in takri script: *rag madhava bhairava sut* (Raga Madhava son of Bhairava).
2 Compare e.g. Skelton 1961, no.35 (also Goswamy and Fischer 1992, no.35); Ebeling 1973, fig.364; Tandan 1983 fig.13; Randhawa 1971, p.71, fig.13; Waldschmidt 1967, fig.26, pp.148–49, showing a differing iconography.

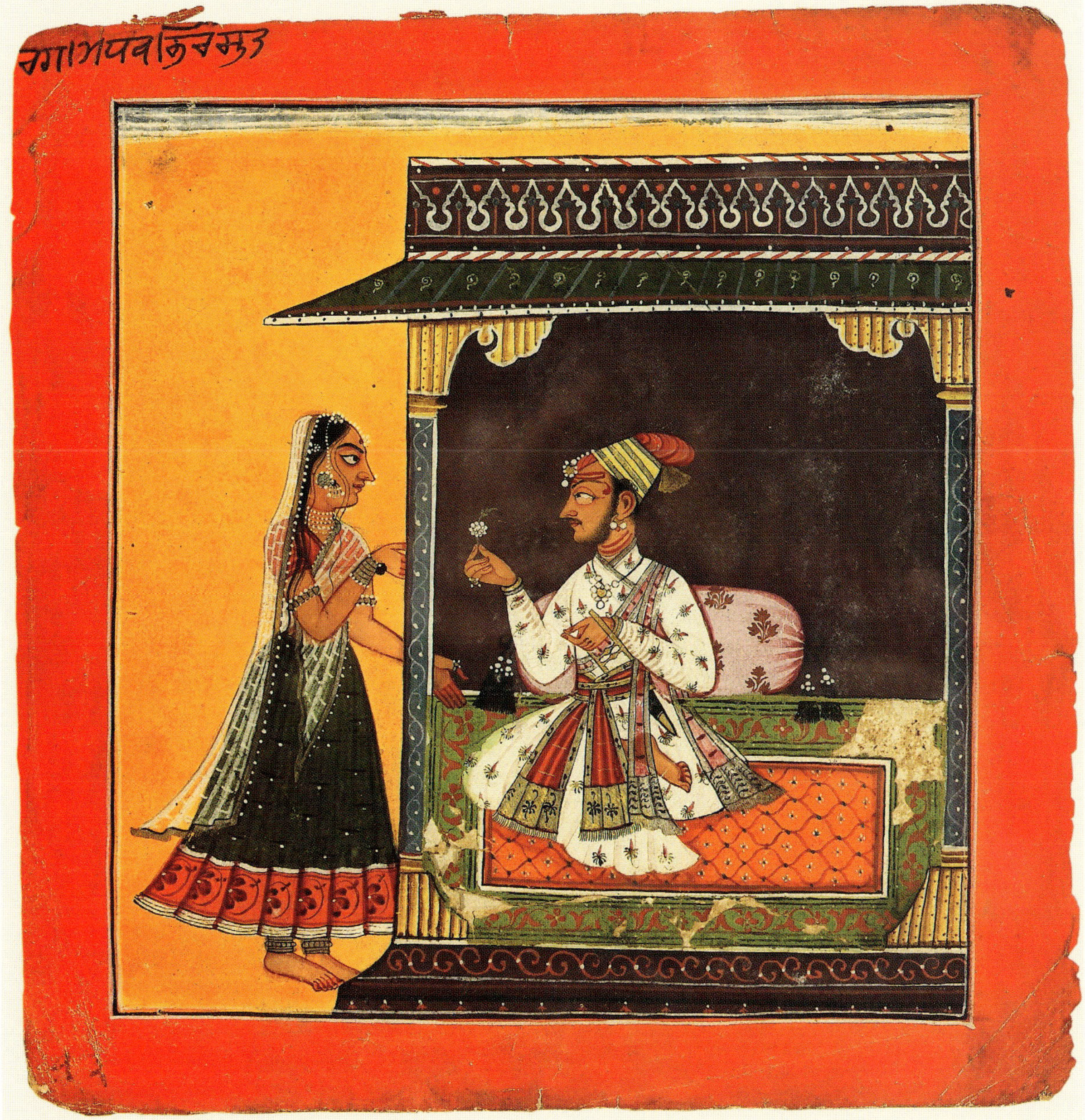

55 Bhairavi Ragini: A lady and a bull

Basohli or Nurpur, Punjab Hills, *c.*1680
Gouache on paper, 20.5 × 20.5 cm[1]
Hodgkin Loan 86
Published: Filippi 1997, no.86

The mode Bhairavi, from the same *ragamala* as no.53, is visualised as a noble lady seated in a palace chamber who nonchalantly caresses the muzzle of a white brahman bull with her hennaed hand. Silhouetted against the yellow ground and red border, the captivated bull stares the lady fixedly in the eye, its expression suggesting wry astonishment. The maid standing in the half-open doorway behind makes a gesture of wonderment at this sight.

The bull has been associated in India since ancient times with fertility and virile power. Here there may be a reference also to Nandi, the bull vehicle of Shiva, sometimes known as Bhairava (the Terrible), to whose raga family Bhairavi ragini belongs. Although submitting docilely to the lady's caress, the brahman bull shown here appears a more mettlesome, moody beast than the sweetly amiable animals found in most later versions of this ragini subject.[2]

1 Inscribed above in takri script: *rag... bhairavi bhaireda bharaj* (Bhairavi ragini wife of Bhairava).
2 E.g. Tandan 1983, fig.3; Goswamy and Fischer 1992, no.34; Ebeling 1973, fig.310; Waldschmidt 1967, fig.45, pp.109–10; Mehta 1926, pl.54, p.118.

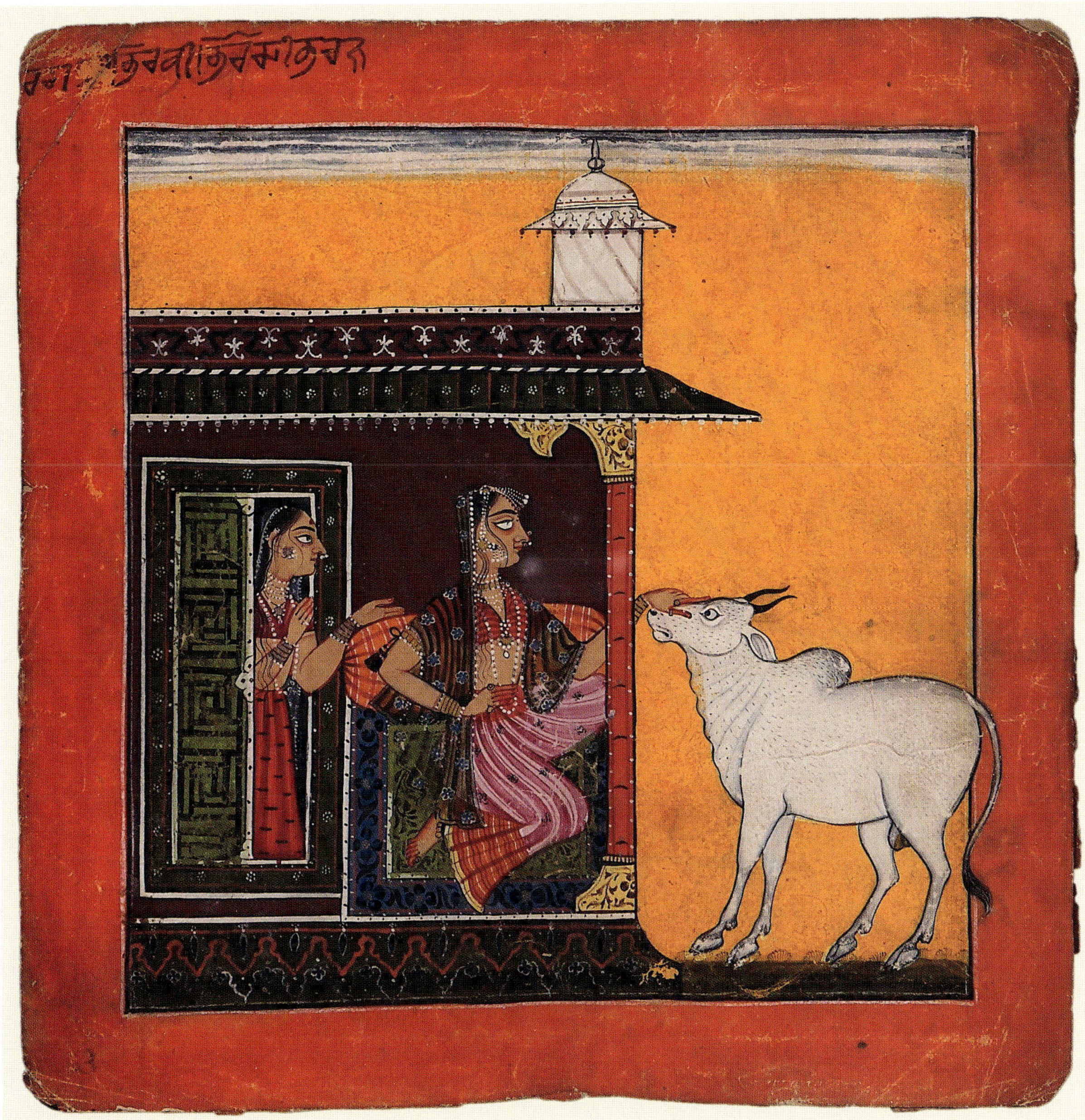

56 Raga Malava: Wrestlers

Basohli or Nurpur, Punjab Hills, *c.*1680
Gouache on paper, 21.5 × 21 cm[1]
Hodgkin Loan 85
Published: Filippi 1997, no.85

Against the intense yellow ground generally found in this *ragamala* series (nos.53–55, 57), two wrestlers grapple vigorously as they strive for ascendancy. The fairer-skinned wrestler in the striped green trunks, who reaches down to seize the arm of his darker-skinned adversary, has multiple yellow *tilak* marks on his face and torso. Somewhat improbably in a wrestling bout, he also wears more in the way of pearl necklaces, earrings, arm-bands and anklets than the other two figures. It is likely that he is of noble birth, as a third wrestler seems to stand by holding his turban for him. Wrestling was a popular sport among the nobility, and many Rajput courts also maintained corps of professional wrestlers (*Jethi*) to provide entertainment and to engage in challenge matches against other courts.

Malava raga belongs to the family of Shri Raga. This treatment of its normal iconography has an unusual power in its intense colouring and strong and fluent line drawing.[2]

1 Inscribed above in takri script: *raga malava sri rage sut* (Malava Raga son of Shri Raga).
2 For later Pahari versions, see Tandan 1983, fig. 51; Archer 1973, Kulu 13 (xxiii); Topsfield ed. 2004, no.171; Waldschmidt 1967, fig.8, p.152

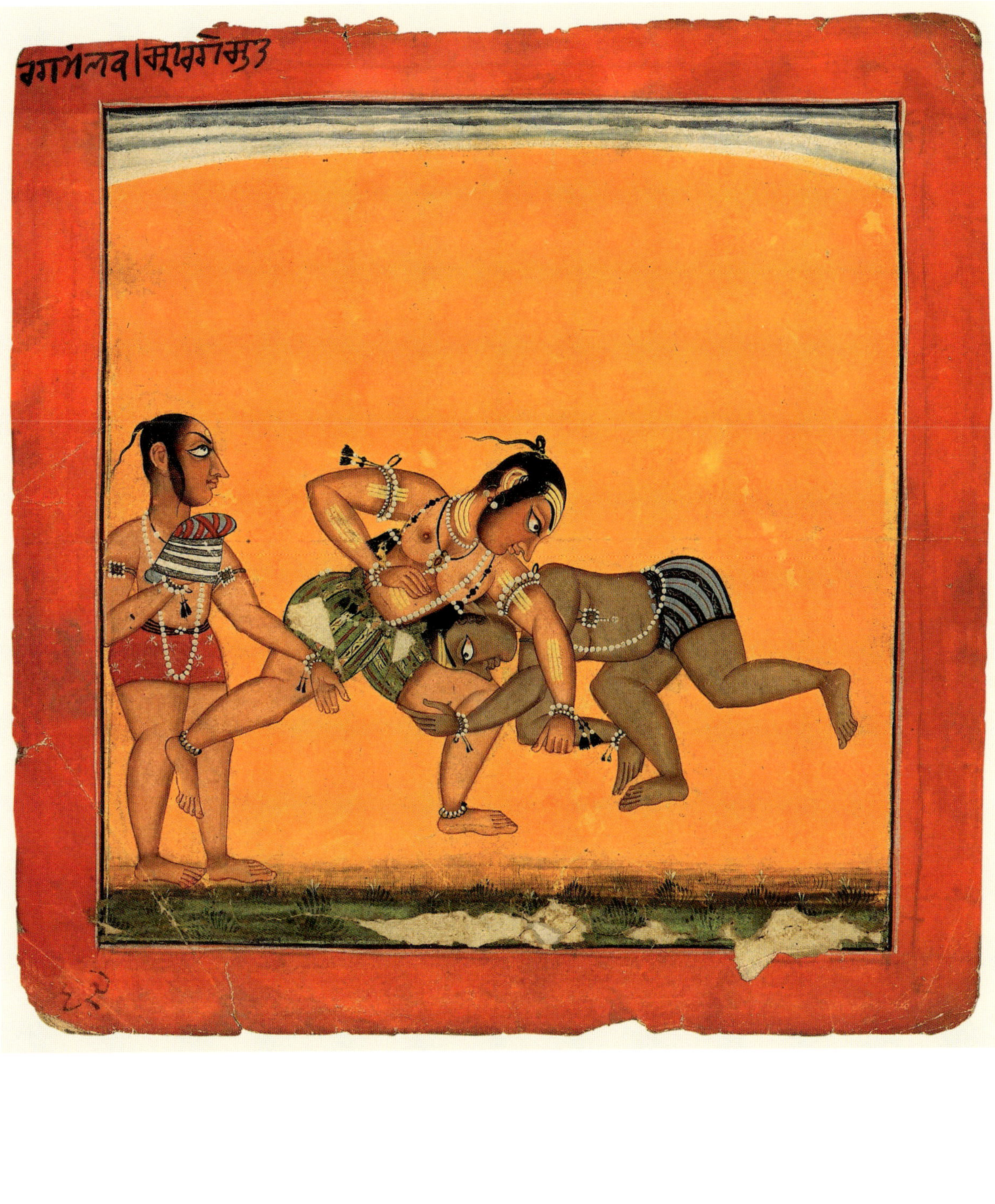

57 Raga Kumbha: A meeting at a well

Basohli or Nurpur, Punjab Hills, *c.*1680
Gouache with gold and silver on paper,
21.2 x 21.2 cm[1]
Hodgkin Loan 114
Unpublished

In a further page from the same *ragamala* (nos. 53–56), a young woman who has come to draw water rests her foot on the cross-bar laid over the mouth of a well, while she lowers her metal pitcher by a cord tied round its neck. The ring support for the pitcher lies nearby. Although ostensibly a village girl, she wears the pearls and jewellery of a court lady, and a slender tree with three stylised lobes of foliage appears to arch over her in sympathy or attraction. A nobleman on a hunting expedition has arrived in search of water, a bow over his arm and sword at his shoulder. He gestures as if requesting a drink from the lady, who gazes demurely downward at her pitcher in the well. This chance meeting is imbued with nascent romance.

Deriving originally from folk-tales, such emotionally charged encounters at well-heads between passing princes on horseback and beautiful village girls drawing water became a common subject in eighteenth century Mughal painting.[2] This popular convention, with an additional emphasis on the water-pot (*kumbha*), has been adapted in the present iconography for this raga. Kumbha is a *ragaputra* (son) of Shri Raga, and its characteristic sound is compared by the theorist Kshemakarna to that of a stream of water running from a pitcher.[3]

1 Inscribed above in takri script: *raga kubha sri rage sut* (Raga Kumbha son of Shri Raga).
2 E.g. Hurel 2010, no. 140.
3 Waldschmidt 1967, pp. 46, 143–44; Ebeling 1973, pp. 76, 288.

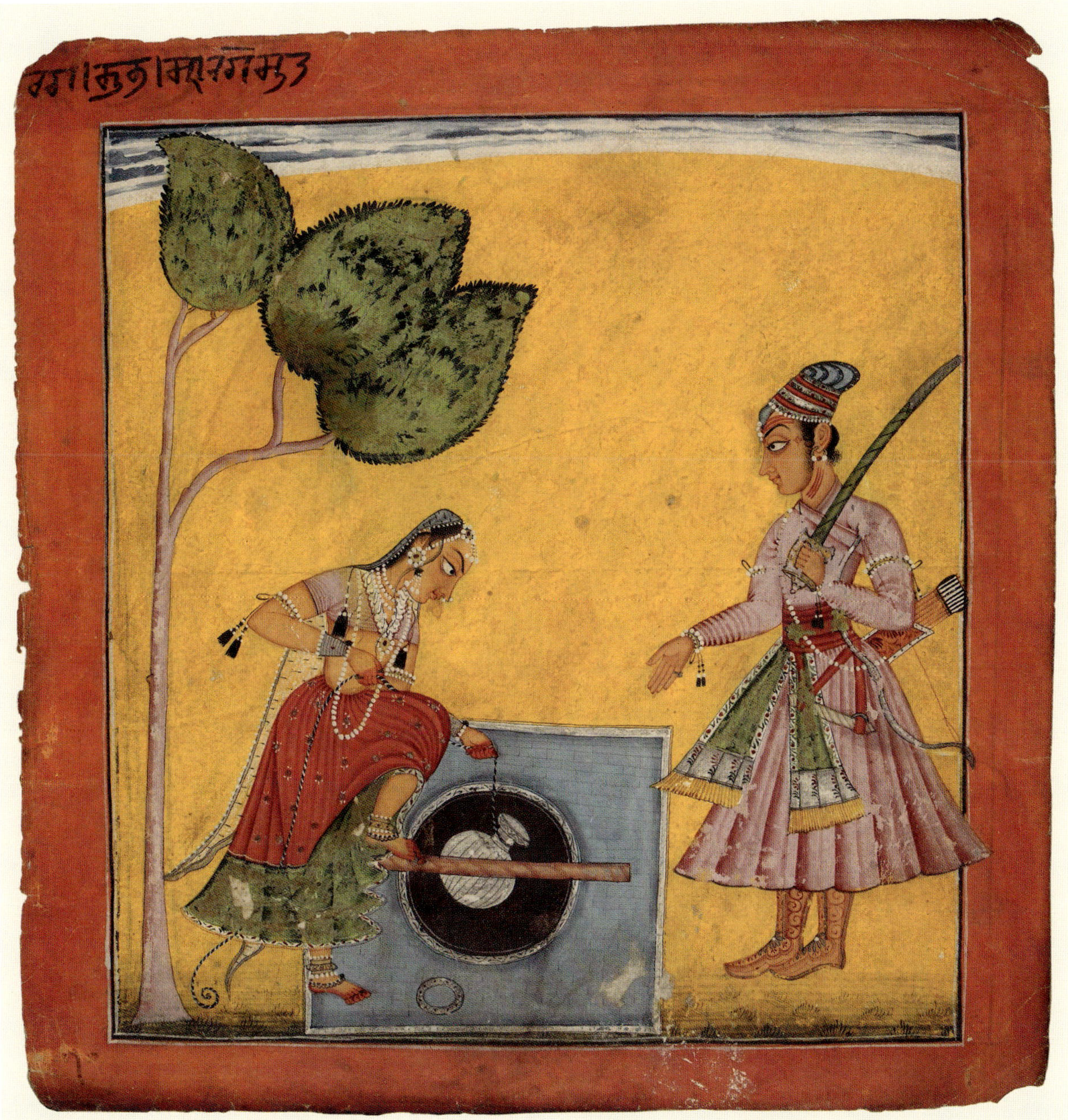

58 Ramakali ragini: A lady offers milk to a snake

Basohli, Punjab Hills, *c.*1690–95
Gouache on paper, 19.5 × 19.5 cm[1]
Hodgkin Loan 105
Unpublished

The musical mode Ramakali is here depicted as a lady seated under a slender sapling who offers a small cup of milk to a snake. This lengthy cobra has coiled itself in corkscrew fashion around the trunk and branches of a tree. Snakes are both feared and revered in India, and snake (*naga*) cults are found throughout the subcontinent. Often their propitiatory rites include offerings of milk which are left at a tree that is considered the snake deity's abode. Here the noble lady calmly pays her respects to the resident *naga* while seated comfortably on a carpet beside a stream. She is well adorned with jewellery, as the Sanskrit verses for this subject describe:

> As a woman wearing a dark bodice, a string of pearls round the neck and a garment shining like gold, having excellent bracelets round each wrist and rings round both ankles, having a moon-like face, excited with the lust of love and frequently speaking tender words...[2]

This page belongs to a dispersed early Pahari series, often called the 'second' Basohli *ragamala*,[3] now represented in many private collections as well as the Rietberg Museum, Zurich, and San Diego Museum. In later versions of this subject the lady was more often shown as standing between two cobra-filled trees, holding up a cup in one or both hands for the snakes to drink from.

1 Inscribed above in takri script: *ragani ramkali sri (di) raga di bharaj* (Ramakali ragini wife of Shri Raga).
2 Waldschmidt 1967, s.v. 'Ramagiri', pp.166–67 and fig.41; the names Ramagiri and Ramakali were to some extent interchangeable. See also Coomaraswamy 1926, no.LXX, pl.XXXII; Ebeling 1973, fig.336; Archer 1960, pl.67.
3 Archer 1973, Basohli no.14 (1–2).

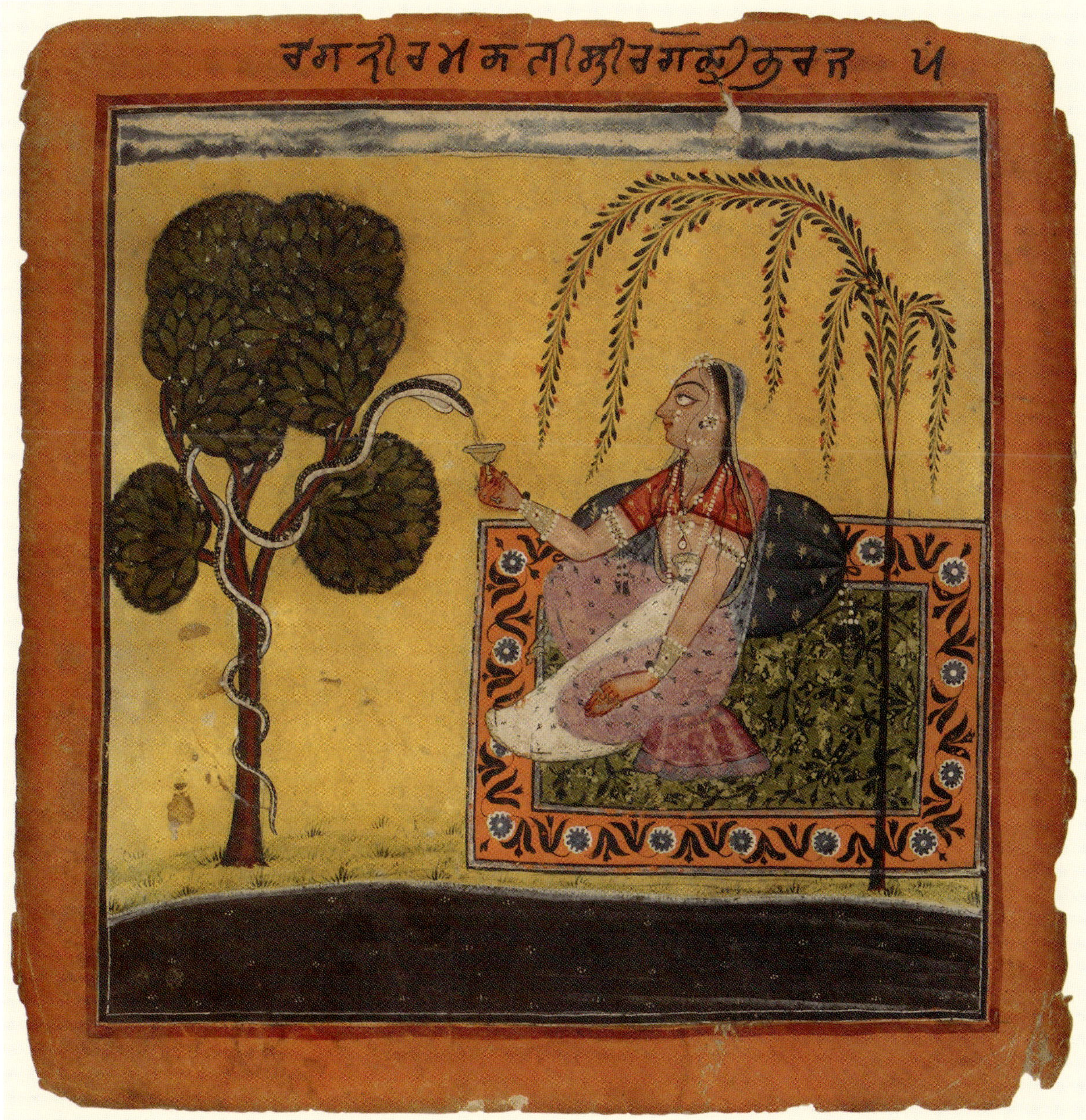

59 Kedara Raga: Ascetics making music

Arki, Punjab Hills, late 17th century
Gouache on paper, 21 × 18.5 cm
Hodgkin Loan 87
Published: Topsfield and Beach 1991, no.29; Filippi 1997, no.87; Pal ed. 1997, no.187

The musical mode Kedara is visualised here as two yogis or Hindu ascetics making music within a small pavilion.[1] Seated on a leopard skin, a traditional seat of yogis who have mastered the temptations of the sensual world, the vina player improvises a raga in a devotional or contemplative mood, gazing with rapt concentration towards his kneeling companion or disciple, who beats the *tala* or rhythmic cycle with a pair of cymbals. The ascetics' ash-smeared skin is grey while their orange and yellow dhotis, together with the strong red ground and yellow border, complement the muted colouring of the pavilion interior with its pale wall and brown striped durree. Behind, at the centre of composition, a half-open door leads to a darkened chamber.

This painting of Kedara, a *ragaputra* or son of Megha Raga, belongs to a series which has been attributed to Arki, capital of the small southern Hill kingdom of Baghal, not far from Simla. Other pages from the series employ variations of the same pavilion setting.[2]

1 Compare Ebeling 1973, fig.379.
2 Archer 1973, 'Baghal (Arki)', nos.2 (1–3); Archer 1976, nos.2–3; also Khandalavala 1958, supp. fig.27; Pal 1978, no.57; Tandan 1983, p.96.

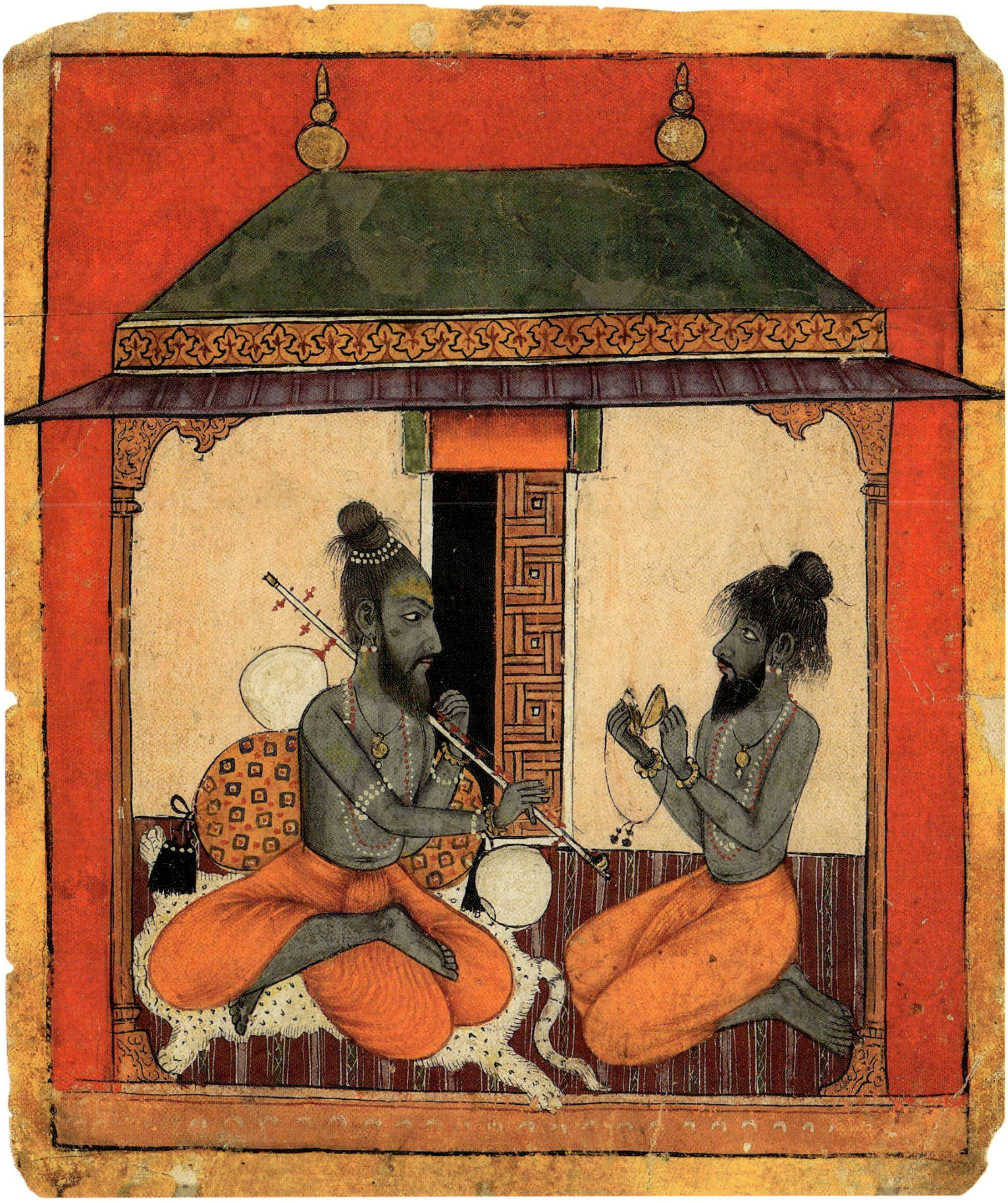

60 Kusuma Raga: A prince and lady

Nurpur, Punjab Hills, *c.*1700–20
Gouache with gold on paper, 22.5 × 19.6 cm
Hodgkin Loan 104
Unpublished

The musical mode Kusuma, of the family of Dipak Raga, is visualised as a prince and lady sitting together in a form of amorous encounter. Seated at his ease on their shared rug, the mustachioed and *tilak*-marked prince stares keenly at the lady, while directing at her his floral bow and arrow, like those traditionally held by the love-god Kama. Looking modestly down, she half-draws her veil over her face. The blue foliate patterns of the yellow rug swirl around them. Two stylised trees with branches outlined in blue echo the human figures in the highly simplified background.

The characteristic sound of the mode Kusuma ('Flower') is compared by Kshemakarna to the sound of anklets in motion.[1] According to his description, Kusuma wears a red garment while seated on a lotus and holding lotus blossoms in his hand. In Pahari paintings of this subject, the blossoms are transmuted into the potent floral bow and arrows of Kama, the Indian Cupid.[2]

1 Waldschmidt 1967, pp.42, 45 fn.42,145–46, fig.55; also Ebeling 1973, fig.354.
2 See Archer 1976, no.70, for another page from this Nurpur series.

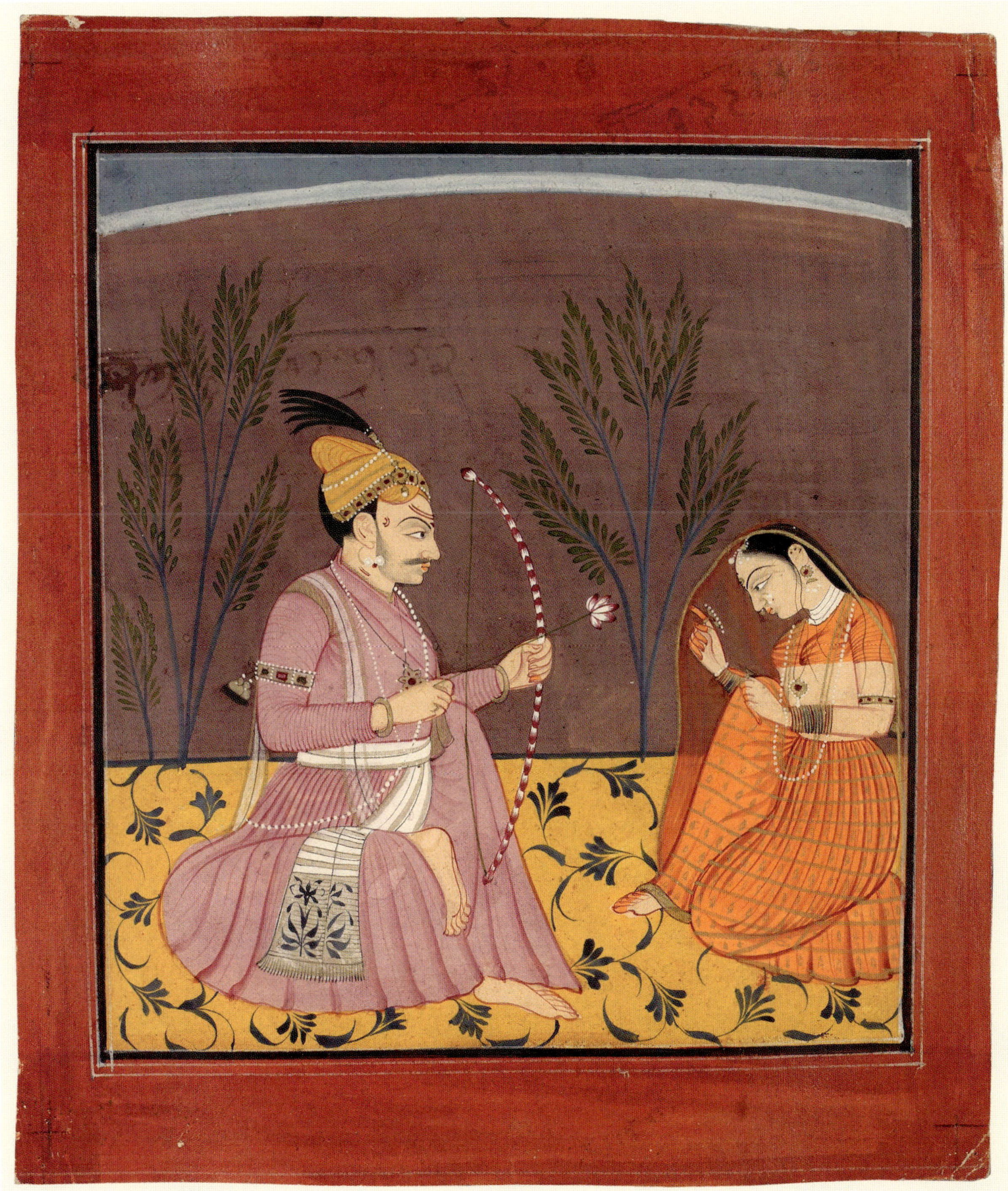

61 Maharaja Kirpal Pal of Basohli smoking

Mankot, Punjab Hills, *c.*1690
Gouache with gold and silver on paper, 22.5 × 33 cm
Hodgkin Loan 37
Published: Topsfield and Beach 1991, no.27;
Filippi 1997, no.37

At several Pahari courts in the late seventeenth century a tradition of royal portraiture developed, deriving from Mughal models but transforming them entirely with a characteristically Rajput spatial freedom, strength of line and controlled intensity of colour. The convention of a Raja smoking a hookah with one or two attendants allowed potent conjunctions and variations of colour and pattern in costumes, floor coverings and backgrounds. In this portrait of a Basohli ruler by an artist from neighbouring Mankot, Maharaja Kirpal Pal (r.*c.*1678–93) sits resplendent in a red robe against a contrasting green cushion and glowing yellow ground. The lesser figures of the attendant with a fly-whisk and cloth and the kneeling hookah-bearer wear more muted tones. A durree with reverberant green and orange stripes provides the ground-notes, along with the strong red of the picture border (now largely missing).

Hawk-eyed and mustachioed, Kirpal Pal dominates the composition. He is known to history as a devotee of Vishnu and Shiva, a successful warrior and an active patron of art and learning.[1] The jewelled pendant worn at his chest was a family heirloom which may have been given to his forebear Bhupat Pal (no.62) by the emperor Shah Jahan. Kirpal Pal holds the hookah's mouth-piece lightly between two fingers, his other hand resting on his heel. A *pan*-box and small spittoon stand before him. The fan-bearer recedes politely into the left margin, and a respectful distance separates the Raja from the hookah-bearer who keeps his chilum alight. The yellow void between the two men is elegantly bridged by the undulating hookah tube. There is a tacit communion between the three figures, a shared participation in the tranquil moment.

1 Archer, 1973, I, p.17, and e.g. 'Basohli' no.11 (1).

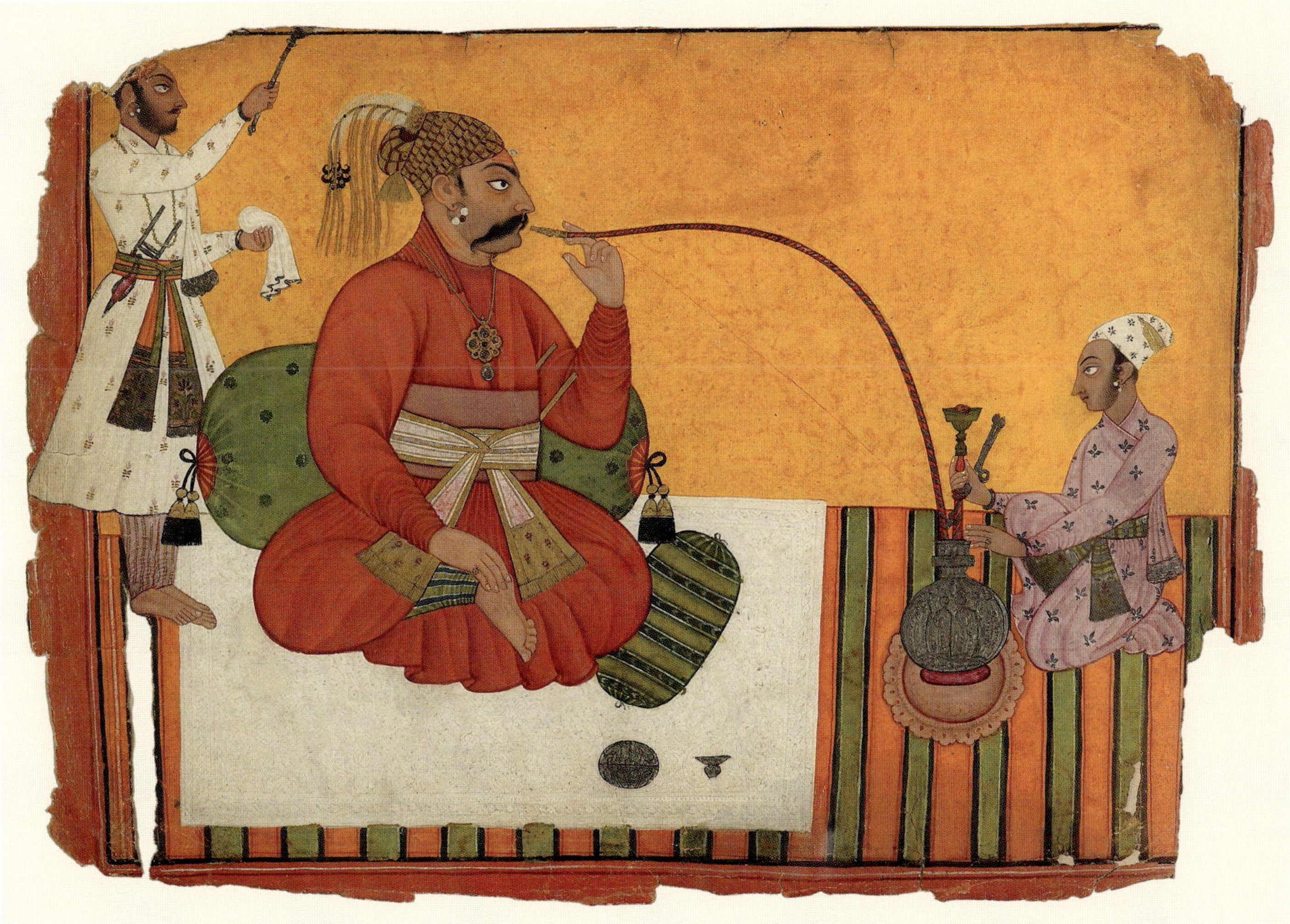

62 Maharaja Bhupat Pal of Basohli smoking

Mankot, Punjab Hills, *c.*1685
Gouache with gold and silver on paper, 21 × 26.5 cm
Hodgkin Loan 38
Published: Topsfield and Beach 1991, no.28;
Filippi 1997, no.38; Crill and Jariwala 2010, no.43

This portrait of Maharaja Bhupat Pal (r.1598–1635), who founded Basohli town as the state capital, was painted half a century after his death.[1] Like other early seventeenth century Rajput rulers, he spent much of his time in attendance at the Mughal court. As a result of intrigues by a rival Hill Raja, Jagat Singh of Nurpur, he was imprisoned for many years by Jahangir. He was released in 1627 by Shah Jahan, with whom he became friends, but in 1635 he was murdered at Delhi by the ever scheming Jagat Singh.[2] Bhupat Pal is said to have been a man of mighty physique, who would daily consume a goat and a small mountain of rice, and could erase the inscription on a rupee coin with his thumb and fingers.

In this powerful portrait by a Mankot painter the composition is tauter and more highly charged than in *Maharaja Kirpal Pal smoking* (no.61), particularly with the loss of the upper part of the picture. Bhupat Pal looms commandingly over the smaller kneeling servant who holds the hookah and a pair of tongs. But the two figures are dynamically linked by the diagonal hookah tube, with the royal sword in a green and gold scabbard lying parallel to it. Although this is a scene of relaxation, the artist creates an intense and turbulent interplay of pure colour areas with the striped cushion and patterned carpet, the Raja's striped turban, *patka* sash and *paijama* trousers, and the answering stripes of the hookah-bearer's robe.

1 For inscribed and other portraits of Bhupat Pal, see Archer 1973, I, p.17 and Mankot, no.12; Topsfield and Beach 1991, p.76, fig.4; also Goswamy 1986c, fig.7.
2 Hutchison and Vogel 1929, II, pp.600–02.

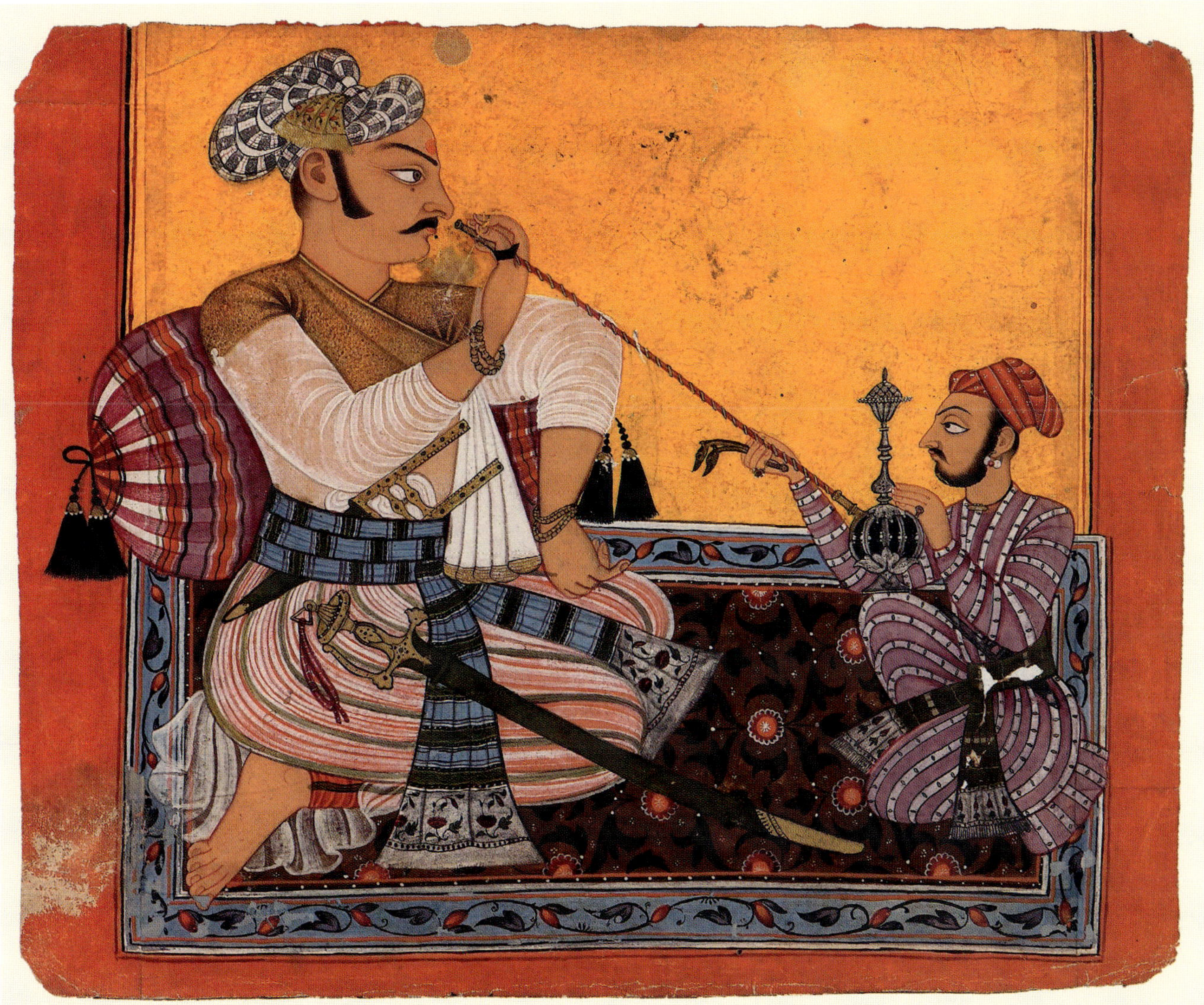

63 Maharaja Medini Pal smoking

Basohli, Punjab Hills, *c.*1730–35
Gouache with gold, silver and beetle-wing case on paper, 33.2 × 24.3 cm[1]
Hodgkin Loan 90
Unpublished

The youthful Basohli ruler Medini Pal (r.1722–36) sits smoking on a garden terrace, while a young female attendant or concubine tends his hookah, her foot and scarf ends trailing into the red border. Holding a flower, the Raja rests against a red cushion set on a blue trellis-patterned rug, which is laid over a vibrant durree in yellow, green and candy pink stripes. Trees and trailing blossoms with pairs of birds appear against the dark green ground. Monsoon clouds above crackle with gold serpentine lightning, enhancing the amorous tension in the air.

Medini Pal had become ruler at the age of eight and was only twenty-two when he died in 1736.[2] He is seen here as a young adult, with wispy moustache and side-whiskers, elongated slender body, and a large and staring leaf-shaped eye in the Basohli manner. His white robe is boldly saffron-checked across the shoulders, and his jewelled pendant with a suspended emerald is the same Mughal heirloom that his grandfather Kirpal Pal wore (no.61). The young girl wears a fine veil and transparent muslin robe over her bare torso and striped *paijama*. She is heavily bejewelled and wears a dancer's anklets with bells. She adjusts the water-pipe's coals with one hennaed hand, while holding in the other a quid of *pan* (betel leaf) which she will presently offer to the keen-eyed Raja.

1 Traces of a mutilated inscription appear on the upper border.
2 Archer 1973, I, p.18, listing further portraits of Medini Pal; also Glynn 1979.

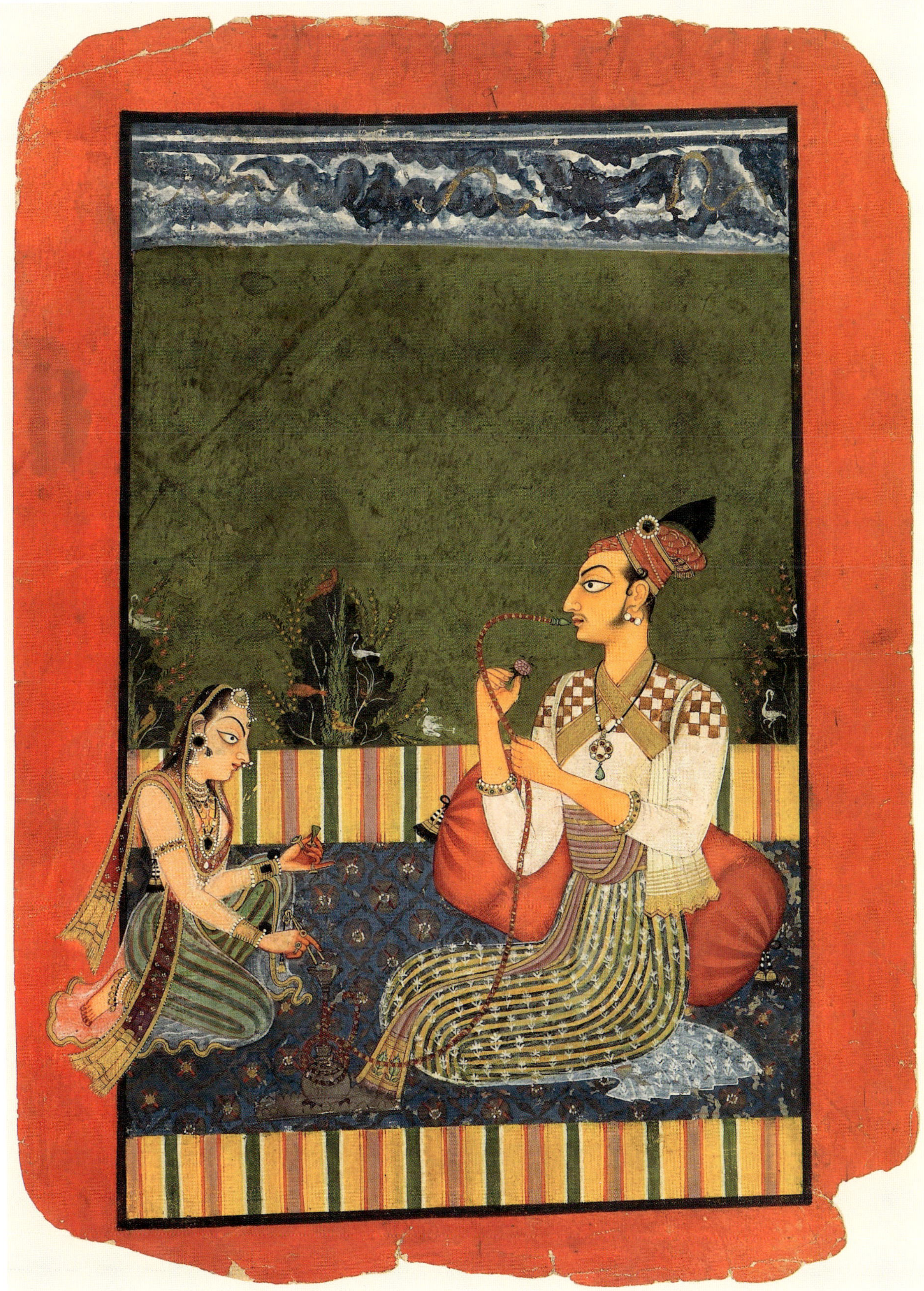

64 Maharaja Suraj Mal with a hawk

Nurpur, Punjab Hills, *c.*1730–40
Gouache with gold on paper, 19.6 × 13.6 cm
Hodgkin Loan 89
Unpublished

This is a posthumous portrait of Suraj Mal (r.1613–18), an early Nurpur ruler who rebelled heroically but unsuccessfully against the emperor Jahangir, leading to his death in exile soon after.[1] He was succeeded by his younger brother Jagat Singh, who was more a collaborationist and devious intriguer than martial hero.

In this formal portrait of the *jharoka* window type, Suraj Mal appears dark-skinned in an orange robe against a deep reddish-brown ground. With his craggy features, sweeping moustache and keen eye, he is every inch the veteran Rajput hero. Resting one hand on the balcony coverlet, he caresses the breast of his prize hawk with the other. Hunting with hawks was a widespread tradition among the Hill Rajas (no.65), as at other courts in Mughal India. Suraj Mal's hawk, with fiercely curving beak and bells on its feet, stands bolt upright and eye to eye with its master. There is a close rapport between Raja and raptor.

1 Archer 1973, I, p.383; ibid., 'Nurpur' no.37, and Archer 1976, no.76, for later versions of the present subject.

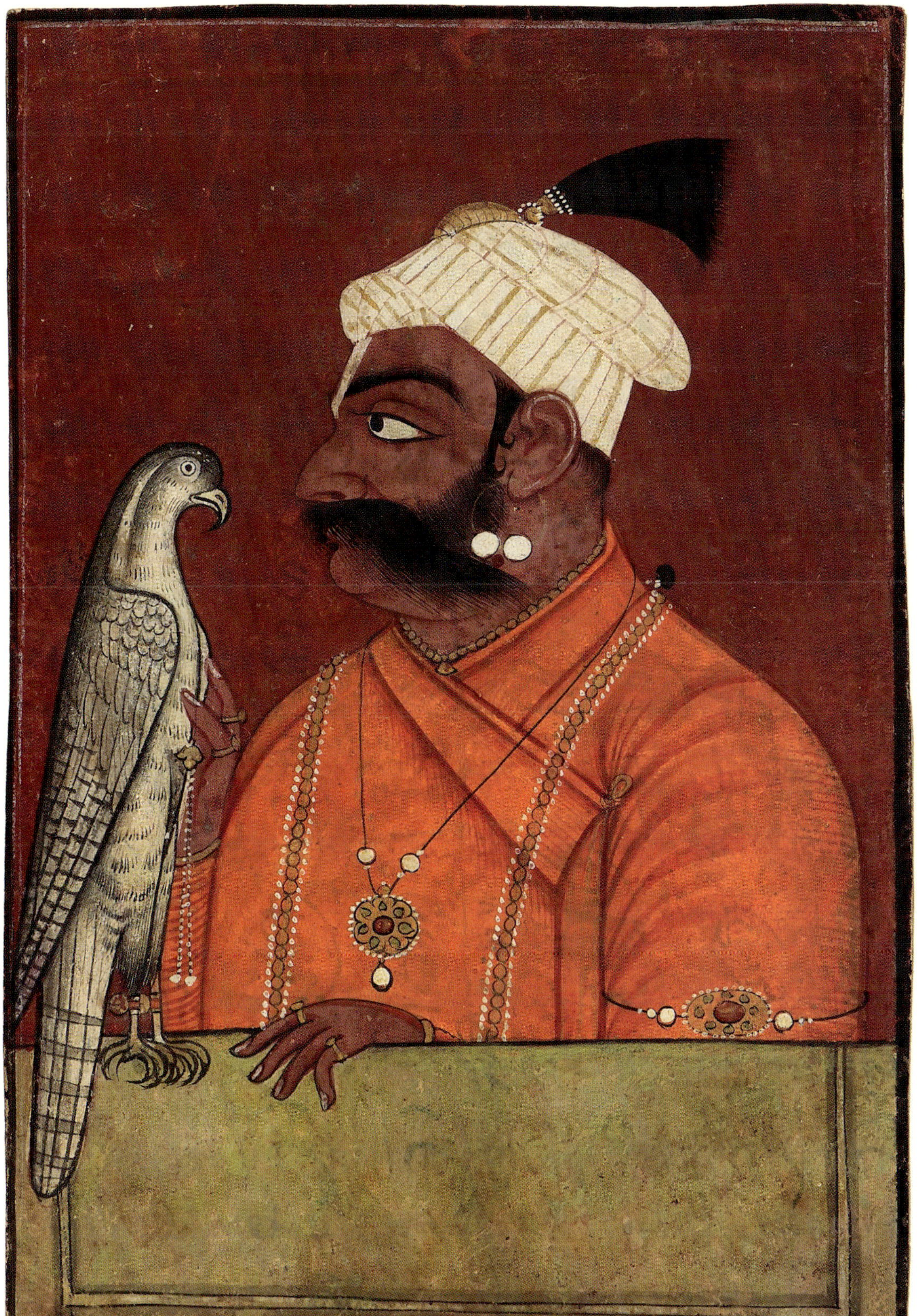

65 Goshawk drinking

Mandi, Punjab Hills, *c.*1730

Gouache with gold and silver on paper, 12.1 × 17.8 cm

Hodgkin Loan 106

Unpublished

Painted in the Punjab Hills about a century later than the three Mughal bird studies in the Hodgkin collection (nos.12–14), this is a strong and original image of a Northern Goshawk (*Accipiter gentilis*), a large and powerful predatory bird often used in falconry.

Set against a deep chestnut ground and almost filling the picture space diagonally, this prized royal bird with bells at its feet has left the painted perch to which it is lightly tethered. Alighting on the rim of its waterbowl, an exotic blue and white jardinière or plantpot, it leans down to drink. Of Chinese origin, the jardinière is seen in a slightly flattened perspective, its base extending into the red border.

The goshawk was the emperor Akbar's favourite hunting bird, a preference which seems to have been shared by the Rajas of Mandi. As at many other Rajput courts, hawking became a strong tradition there, and an earlier Mandi ruler, Raja Hari Sen (r.1623-67), is chiefly remembered by history as a passionate hawker.[1] Pahari rulers were often portrayed with a hawk or falcon on their wrist, as a mark of their hunting zeal and perhaps also to complement their own aquiline features or heroic demeanour (no.64). This unusual Pahari hawk portrait seems to have no clear prototype among earlier Mughal studies of hawks at rest on their perches, or falcons on their blocks.

1 Hutchison and Vogel 1933, II, p.382; Archer 1973, I–II, Mandi no.2.

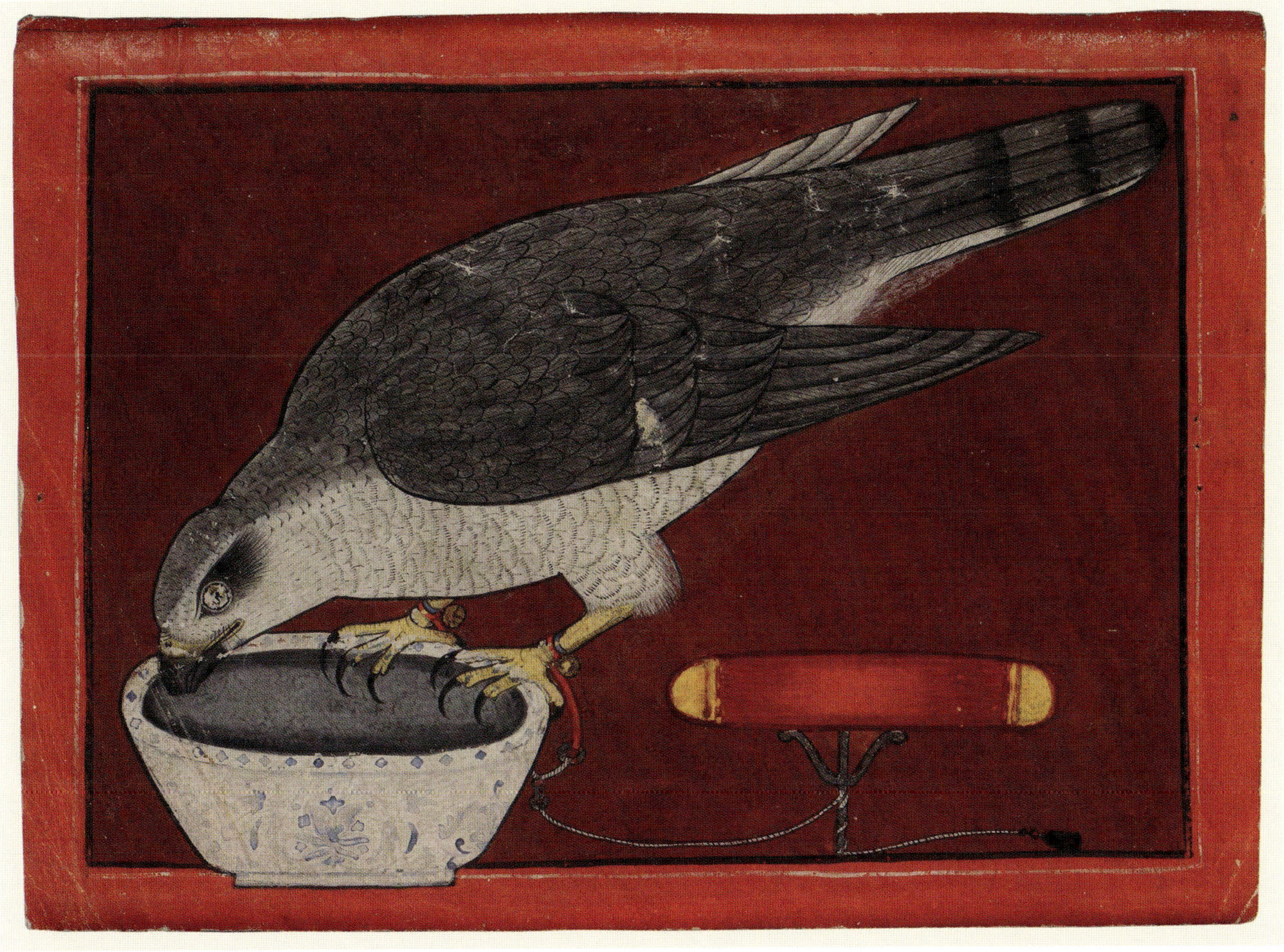

66 Elephant eating a tree

Mankot, Punjab Hills, *c.* 1700
Brush drawing, partially coloured, 36.8 × 38.1 cm
Hodgkin Loan 59
Published: Hodgkin and McInerney 1983, no. 30; Topsfield and Beach 1991, no. 31; Filippi 1997, no. 59

His tethering chains loosened, a caparisoned royal elephant enjoys a respite from state duties as he feeds happily from an available tree. Breaking off a branch with his trunk, he holds it down with one foot while stripping off the foliage. The bearded mahout directs the operation with a commanding gesture, while his two juvenile assistants carrying spears or goads look on with interest or even surprise.

In this unusual brush drawing, freely sketched with a sparing use of colour and wash, the artist captures a common scene of court life with freshness and wit. Nevertheless his composition may derive more from earlier pictorial models than from direct observation. The subject shows general affinities with both Mughal[1] and Deccani[2] antecedents, but it is based more directly on a contemporary, Deccani-inspired Pahari painting depicting an elephant attacking a tree in which a man is hiding:[3] the treatments of the elephant's head and body are particularly close. Both elephants also are spirited beasts, but similar aspects of their anatomy show curious inaccuracies. Of the present painting, Howard Hodgkin has even suggested that "certain details, such as the drawing of the feet, suggest that the artist had never actually seen an elephant."[4] This might perhaps be possible. While elephants were known at the Punjab Hill courts, for practical reasons they were more rarely used in the rugged Pahari terrain than in the Mughal and Rajput domains in the north Indian plains.

1 E.g. Hickmann and Enderlein 1979, pl. 5.
2 Falk and Archer 1981, no. 403; Seyller 2011, fig. 7.
3 Museum Rietberg, Zurich: Seyller 2011, fig. 8; also Boner, Fischer and Goswamy 1994, fig. 24.
4 Hodgkin and McInerney 1983, no. 30.

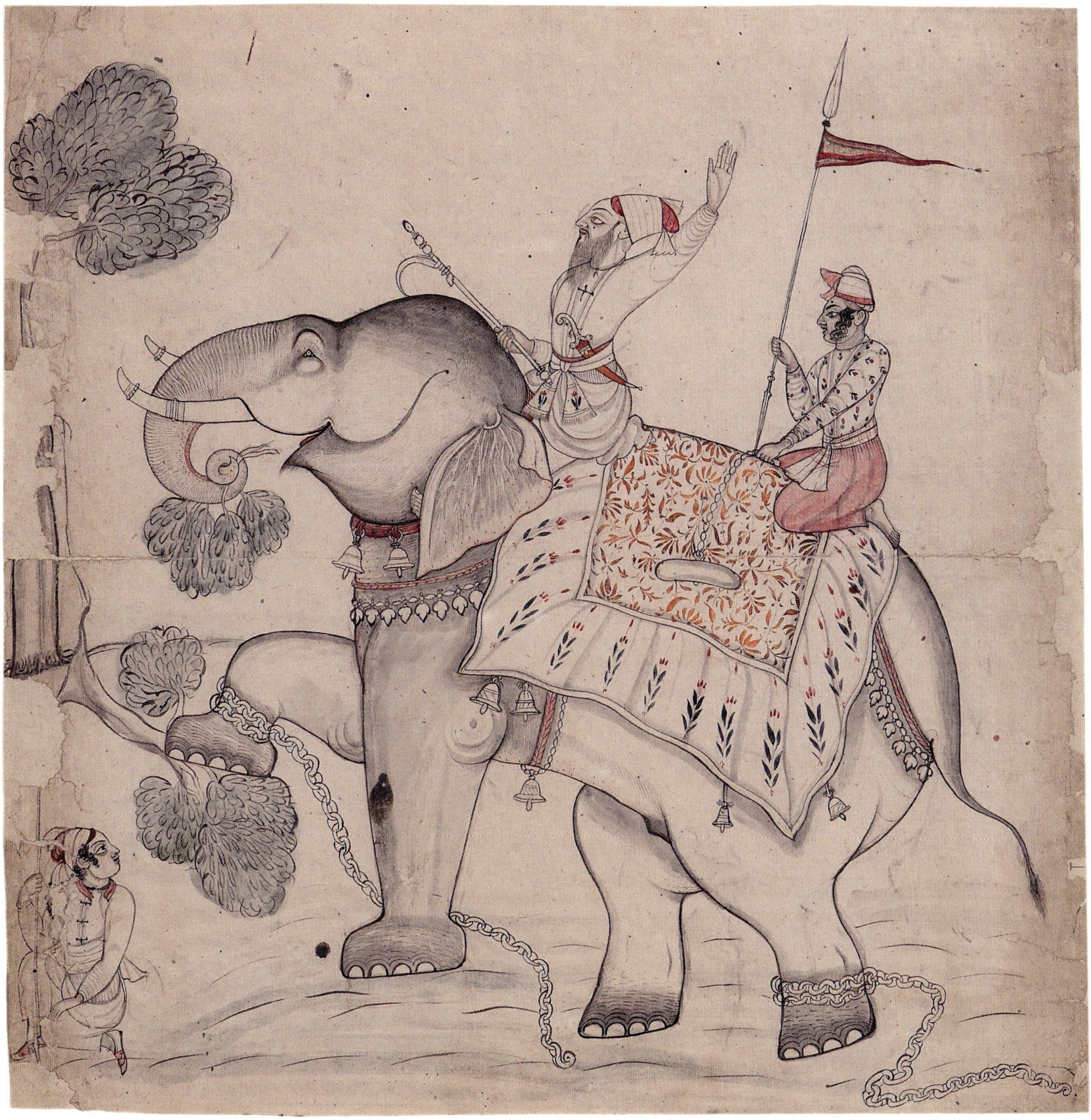

67 Angada delivers Rama's message to Ravana

Illustration to the 'Siege of Lanka' *Ramayana* series
Guler, Punjab Hills, *c.*1725
Gouache with gold on paper, 60 × 82.5 cm
Hodgkin Loan 8
Published: Jain-Neubauer 1981, figs. 31–33; McInerney 1982, no. 34; Craven 1990, no. 10, pp. 40–41; Topsfield and Beach 1991, no. 32; Filippi 1997, no. 8

This unfinished picture belongs to a famous group of Pahari paintings, generally known as the Siege of Lanka series. Probably painted for Raja Dalip Singh of Guler (r.1695–1741), this ambitious series of unusually large scale illustrations was never completed.[1] Its subject, from the *Yuddhakanda* or sixth book of the *Ramayana*, is Rama's siege of the fortress of Lanka, where his wife Sita had been imprisoned by the demon king Ravana. Here Rama, his half-brother Lakshmana, their new ally Vibhishana and the monkey and bear armies are camped on the mountain-side facing Ravana's golden fortress, with its rooftop pavilions with sloping *bangla* eaves.

Rama's companions remind him of the need to enter into diplomacy with an enemy before committing oneself to battle. He therefore sends the monkey prince Angada to tell Ravana to yield Sita or be destroyed. Silhouetted in mid-air and bridging the two halves of the composition, Angada crosses over to the enemy fort with a flying leap. He then delivers his message to the many-headed Ravana in an audience-chamber, while leering demon attendants look on. Ravana of course does not heed Rama's ultimatum. In the next painting in the series Angada escapes from the palace with Ravana's crown,[2] and after that the battles begin.

While the left side of the composition, including the figures of Angada, Ravana and the two groups of demons, is partly finished, Rama and his forces on the right remain in the preliminary stages of painting. The threateningly grouped armies of monkeys and bears appear as barely delineated grey and black masses. The fish and aquatic beasts in the foreground are similarly unfinished. This uneven distribution of surface detail accentuates the formal qualities of the dramatically simplified composition, comprising sky, ocean, hillside and golden fort, which recurs with variations in other pages from the series.

1 Forty pages survive, only eight of them fully finished; see e.g. Coomaraswamy 1926, V, pp. 78–84; Archer 1973, I, pp. 146–47; Jain-Neubauer 1981, pp. 14–21, 37–49; Craven 1990, pp. 2–66; Goswamy and Fischer 1992, no. 99 and pp. 243f., attributing this series to the painter Manaku; and more recently the same authors' 'Manaku', Goswamy and Fischer 2011a.

2 Metropolitan Museum, New York: Jain-Neubauer 1981, fig. 34; Craven 1990, pl. 11.

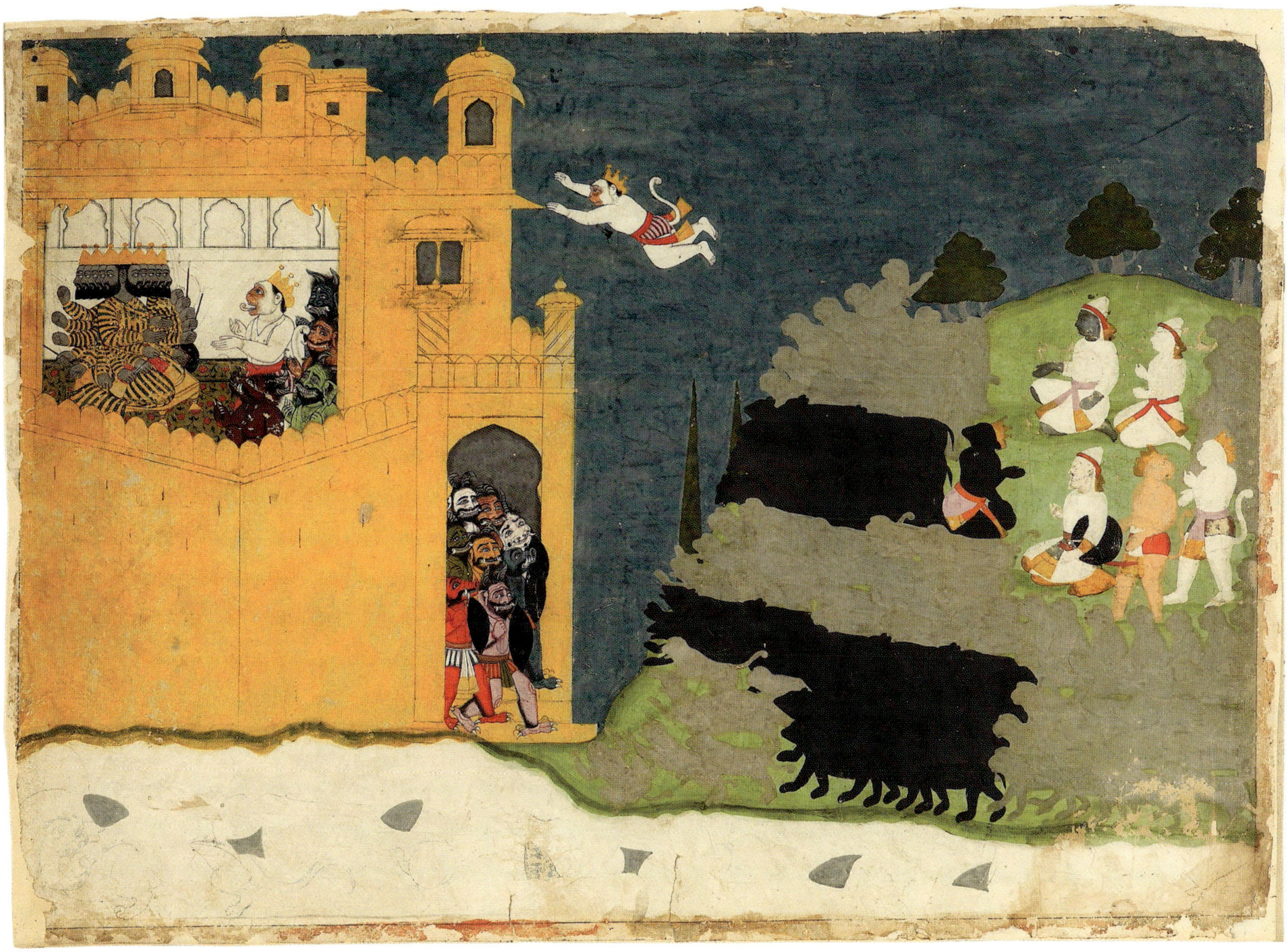

68 A Krishna shrine

Chamba, Punjab Hills, about 1740
Gouache on paper, 61 × 44.5 cm
Hodgkin Loan 3
Published: Hodgkin and McInerney 1983, no.41; Filippi 1997, no.3

In this large and highly assured coloured drawing, a priest and devotee stand on either side of a towering Krishna shrine. The officiating *pujari*, wearing a sacred thread over his shoulder, is named above as Baliram, while the devotee or acolyte holding a *mala* or prayer-beads is called Jangu. Conch shells and cymbals used in temple ritual lie before them, as well as brass lamps and ritual offering vessels on a low altar table.

High above, the principal icon of Krishna is entirely covered by flower garlands suspended from the neck of a magnificent peacock, emblematic of the god. This peacock finial's tail-feathers radiate in a nimbus-like circle, with further garlands hanging from it. Just below stand ritual vessels and implements, including an offering-stand in the form of an adoring cow which gazes up at the obscured cowherd god. One level further down stands a row of *arati* lamps and hand-bells, several with finials depicting Garuda, the man-bird vehicle (*vahana*) of Vishnu, of whom Krishna is a manifestation. Known for their piety, the seventeenth and eighteenth century Chamba rulers were principally devotees of Vishnu. They particularly favoured his incarnation as the princely epic hero Rama,[1] though latterly venerating his Krishna incarnation also.

This is a unique portrayal of a fully installed Pahari shrine and its priestly staff. The mainly red, blue and white colouring is sparing but effective, giving due emphasis to the lavish adornment of the deity and peacock. Howard Hodgkin has commented: "A remarkably formal drawing, thought to have been a study for a wall painting but the elaborate execution particularly noticeable in the peacock's tail and the garland, suggests it was made for its own sake."[2]

1 Archer 1973, I, 'Chamba' no. 2, also pp.64 et seq.
2 Hodgkin and McInerney 1983, no.41.

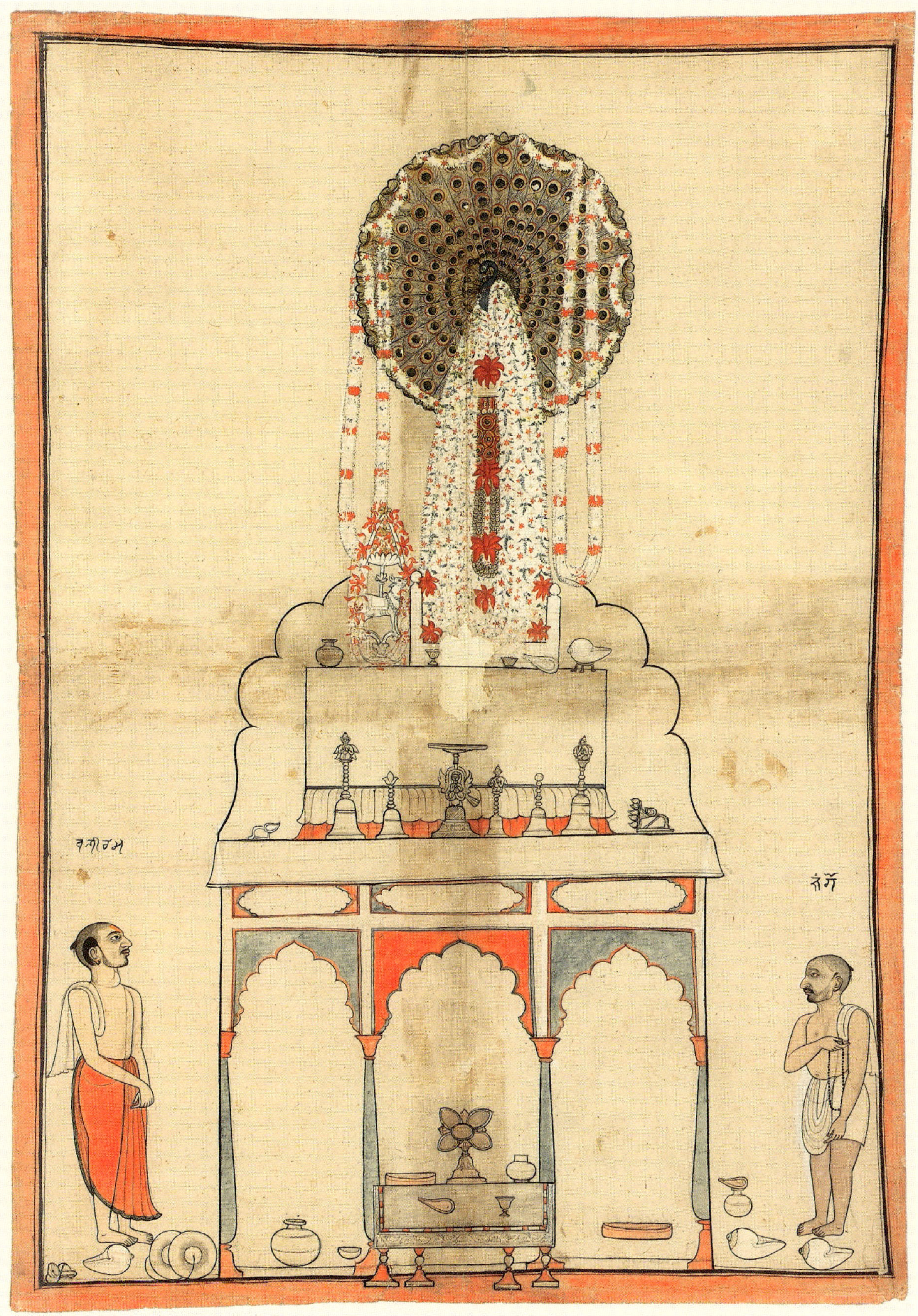

69 A fly-infested feast

Chamba, Punjab Hills, *c.*1740–50
Brush drawing with colour on paper, 41 × 59 cm
Hodgkin Loan 13
Published: Welch 1976, no. 75; Hodgkin and McInerney 1983, no. 44; Topsfield and Beach 1991, no. 33; Filippi 1997, no. 13

This drily observed scene of a communal meal in a fly-infested enclosure is a very unusual work. A prince and his retinue are entertained by a group of Brahmins in an open air refectory. Beneath a grass-roofed shelter, the head priest and his acolyte in pink dhotis and the prince, in white robe and turban, sit glumly on their separate mats. They eat off silver trays, while the rest of the company have leaf plates. Vigorous swatting by their attendants only partly clears the air around them of the flies which elsewhere envelop the proceedings.

These remorseless red-headed insects swarm thickest near the feasters, waiters and the cook with his pots. Yet they are stoically ignored by the portly Brahmins munching their rice at the far right, by their junior colleagues eating in the foreground and by the courtiers and young princely relatives to the left. However one or two of the standing waiters have a slightly depressed air. Meanwhile, in a fly-free zone beyond the rustic fence, the unfed royal attendants look on with severe expressions and mild gestures of wonder; the artist's pentimenti or earlier drawing marks are clearly seen here and elsewhere in the picture.

The meaning of this curious scene remains unclear, but some satire is perhaps intended on the venal complacency of the priestly class[1] and on the prince's efforts to ingratiate himself with them.

1 Compare e.g. Goswamy 1986b, nos. 78–79, for similar themes.

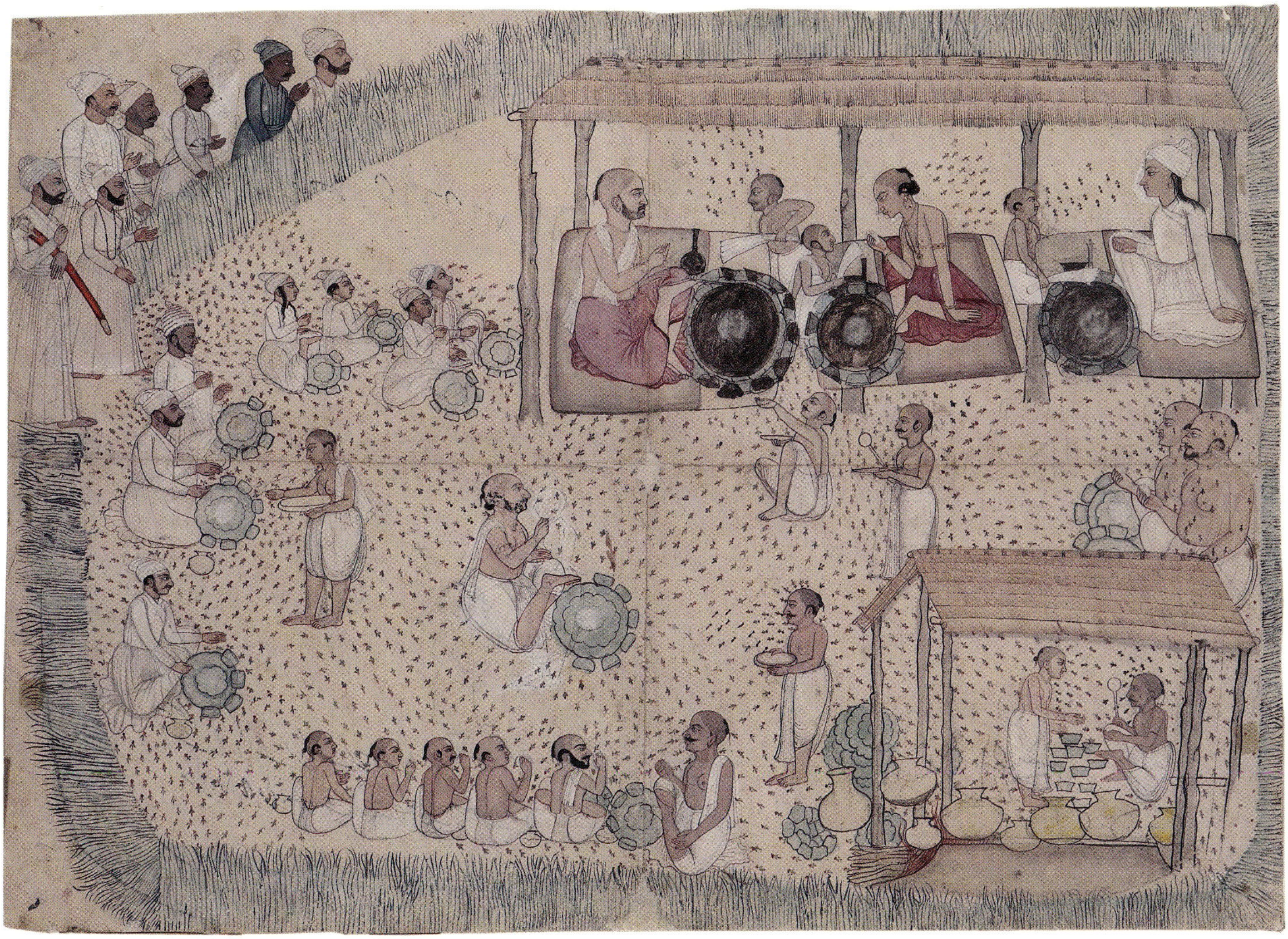

70 A wife seeks justice or mercy

Guler style, Punjab Hills, *c.* 1740–50
Gouache on paper, 38 × 78 cm
Hodgkin Loan 7
Published: Filippi 1997, no. 7

See also detail, pp. 120–21

This unique large narrative scene represents an unidentified family drama, perhaps concerning infidelity or theft. Its setting is a Pahari town with a small palace next to a hill with a temple and an adjoining bazaar and houses, all seen under a tawny evening light.

The story appears to derive not from a literary narrative but from some oral tradition, perhaps relating to a famous scandal that lived on in local memory. It has been suggested that it may relate to the small Hill state of Dada-Siba, as the word *dadhwal* inscribed in takri script on the right of the picture is a designation given to Rajputs from that place.[1]

The palace is a low, asymmetrical structure with little candy-striped turrets and the two main windows filled with bright red blinds. The artist's palette is otherwise restrained, with a judicious use of grey, white, red, blue and ochre tones. In a house to the right a husband is chastising his wife, while in the next room an older woman either remonstrates on her behalf or calls for her punishment. Then, in front of the palace, the husband and wife stand before a waist-high plinth, possibly an oath-stone or place where punishments were delivered. The husband stands accusingly while his wife looks up to supplicate for mercy or justice from the local ruler in the balcony who will judge their case, perhaps with the help of his companions. Several attendants watch these proceedings with interest, one of them gazing down from the palace roof. Both the nature of the misdeed and the outcome of the drama remain unclear. Perhaps other pictures may have shown these events, making a short series.

1 I am grateful to B.N. Goswamy for this and other suggestions concerning this picture, as well as to Vijay Sharma.

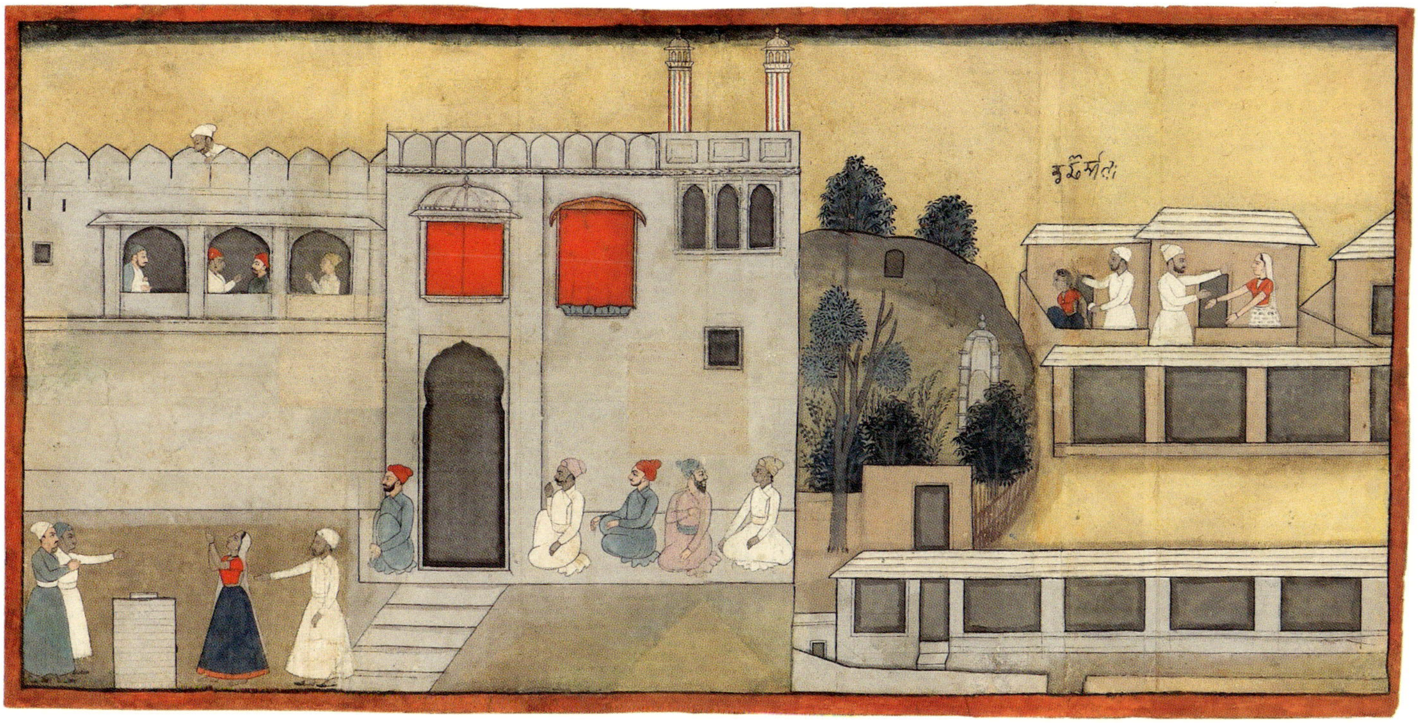

71 Balwant Singh hunts a tiger

Guler, Punjab Hills, *c.*1750. Attributed to Nainsukh
Gouache with gold on paper, 20 × 42.9 cm
Hodgkin Loan 109
Published: Goswamy and Fischer 2011, fig. 9, p. 676

A cultured but otherwise obscure Pahari nobleman, Raja Balwant Singh (1723–63) is known above all for his patronage of Nainsukh ('Delight of the Eye'), one of the most gifted Indian artists of the eighteenth century. An unusually close understanding developed between the two men, allowing Nainsukh an intimate understanding of his patron. Well versed in Mughal technique, Nainsukh's drawings and paintings interpret with insight, originality and elegance his master's daily doings or pursuits, and his dreams or inner concerns. Even in this scene of a hunting-field, at first sight a conventional Mughal period subject, something more complicated may be going on.

In Nainsukh's scroll-like coloured drawing, a tiger of enormous proportions has been encircled by Raja Balwant Singh and his mounted companions and hunting dogs. Yet it continues to walk calmly forward, only turning its head to gaze and perhaps roar at Balwant Singh, who gallops in from the right. Dressed in hunting green, he aims his arrow. He is followed by two companions who make gestures of surprise or wonderment. Four more horsemen with swords or spears surround the tiger in a symmetrical group. The setting is in open grassland, suggested by sparse painted tufts and wash streaks on the uncoloured paper ground. In places white under-painting marks show the artist's discarded first ideas about forming a dog's tail, or giving a horseman a bow not a sword.

Assembled with care from its individual constituent figures, this is an artfully composed scene and possibly not one that Nainsukh had witnessed. The tiger's unearthly, even portentous size suggests this may be an imaginary hunt, perhaps one that Balwant Singh had dreamt about and wished to see visualised by his court painter and confidant.

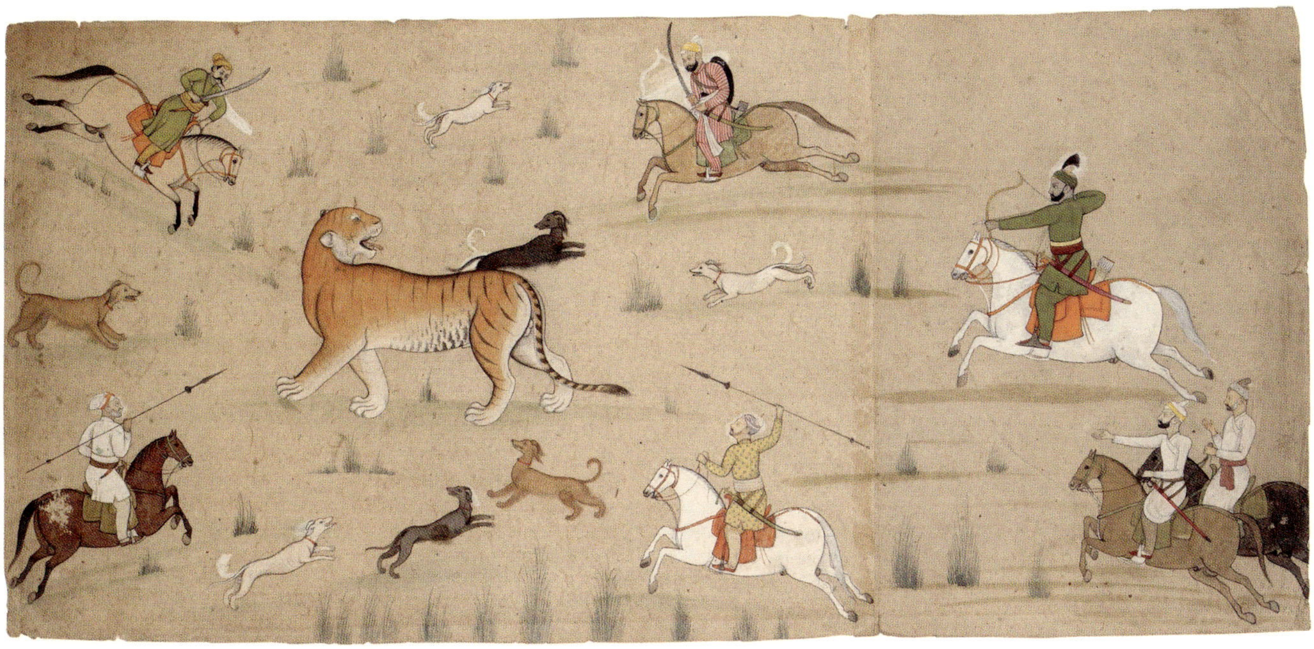

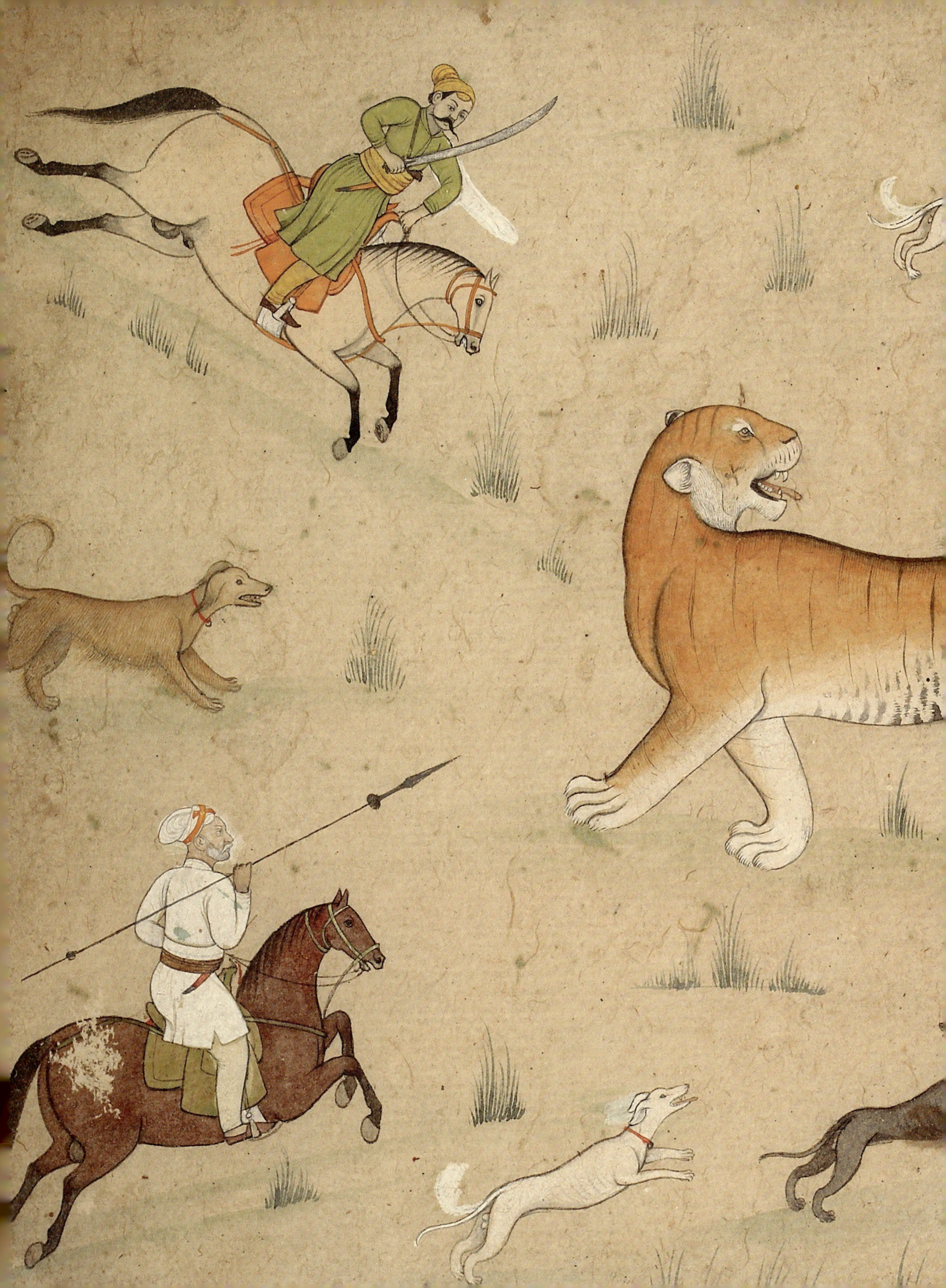

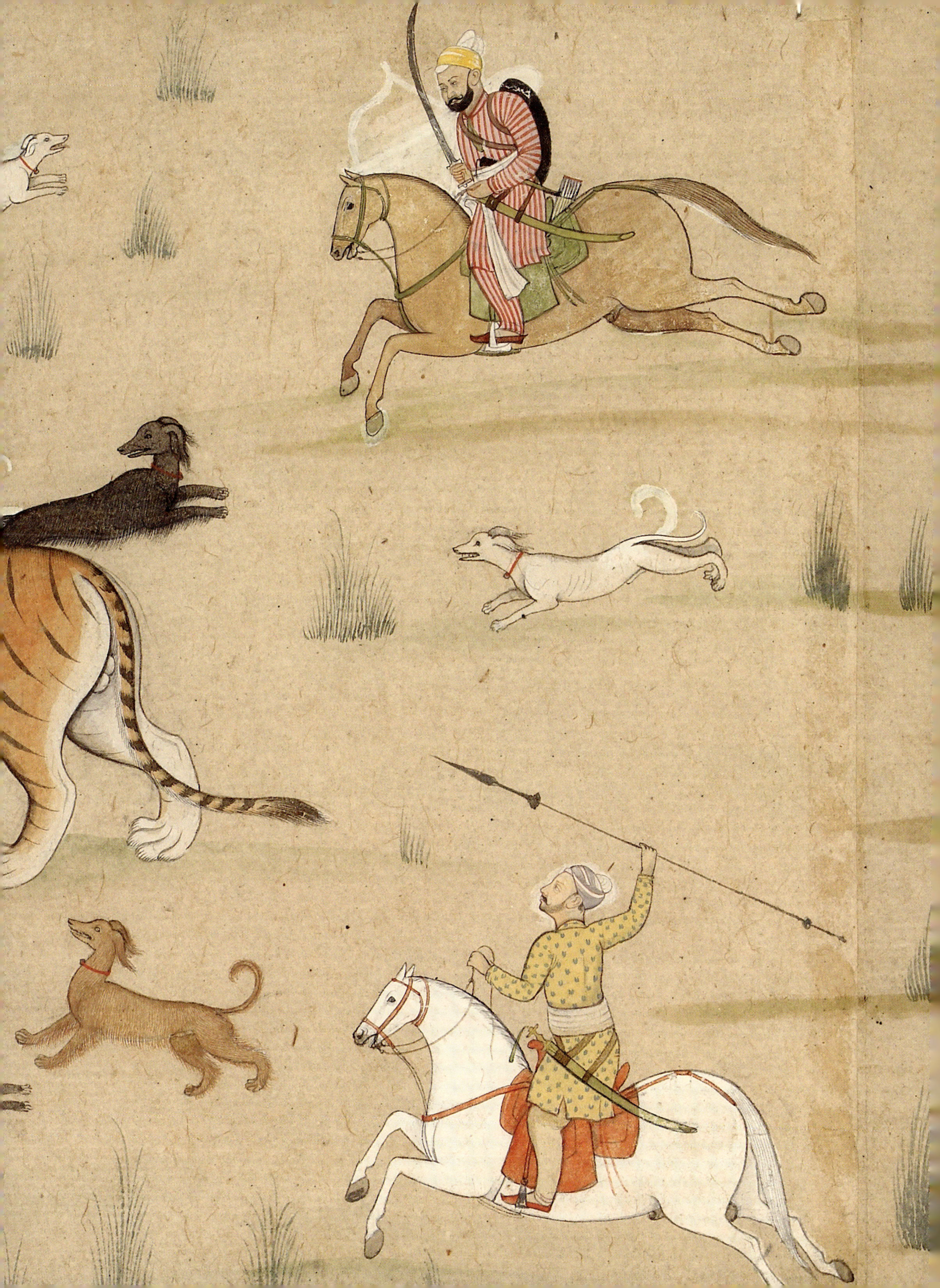

72 Balwant Singh and a goose

Guler, Punjab Hills, *c.*1750–60.
Attributed to Nainsukh
Brush drawing with light pigment
on uncoloured paper, 28 × 39.4 cm
Hodgkin Loan 108
Unpublished[1]

In this superbly spare drawing, Raja Balwant Singh stands in a walled courtyard, shown in flattened plan form, with a low pavilion behind him. He rests one hand on his sword hilt, his other hand grasps his *patka* sash end. His expression is pensive, even concerned. He is gazing at a small goose, the only other occupant of the courtyard. The goose looks back at him. It is an enigmatic encounter, to which no further clue is given.

Is the goose a passing migrant that has dropped in at Balwant Singh's palace, and does he perhaps take its unexpected appearance as an omen or portent of some kind? Or did he dream of meeting such a goose, and taking it as an omen, ask his painter to depict the scene? Or is it a familiar and friendly goose, which he might greet on his daily round? Or does it remind him of some recent hunting expedition? Balwant Singh often hunted waterfowl, either with a hawk or by stalking;[2] might this goose be one that had got away? It is at any rate a real goose,[3] not a mythological *hamsa*, a traditional Indian symbol of purity and spiritual knowledge.

The drawing is executed on the natural paper ground in dark line with sparing pale grey washes and only the slightest touches of white pigment or colour, notably on the Raja's pale pink slippers and striped *paijama* hems. It can be attributed to the great Guler artist Nainsukh, who enjoyed an unusually close rapport with his patron Balwant Singh (no.71). He frequently depicted the Raja in novel or surprising attitudes observed directly from life, and often also shown deep in introspective thought.[4] Meeting the goose has prompted in Balwant Singh a similar mood of reflection or disquiet.

1 Christie's New York cat., 16 Sept. 2008, lot 451, with notes on provenance.
2 E.g. Goswamy 1997, pls.11, 49, 70.
3 It is of *anser* species; the hint of barring on the flanks may indicate it is a White-fronted Goose.
4 Goswamy 1997; Goswamy and Fischer 2011b.

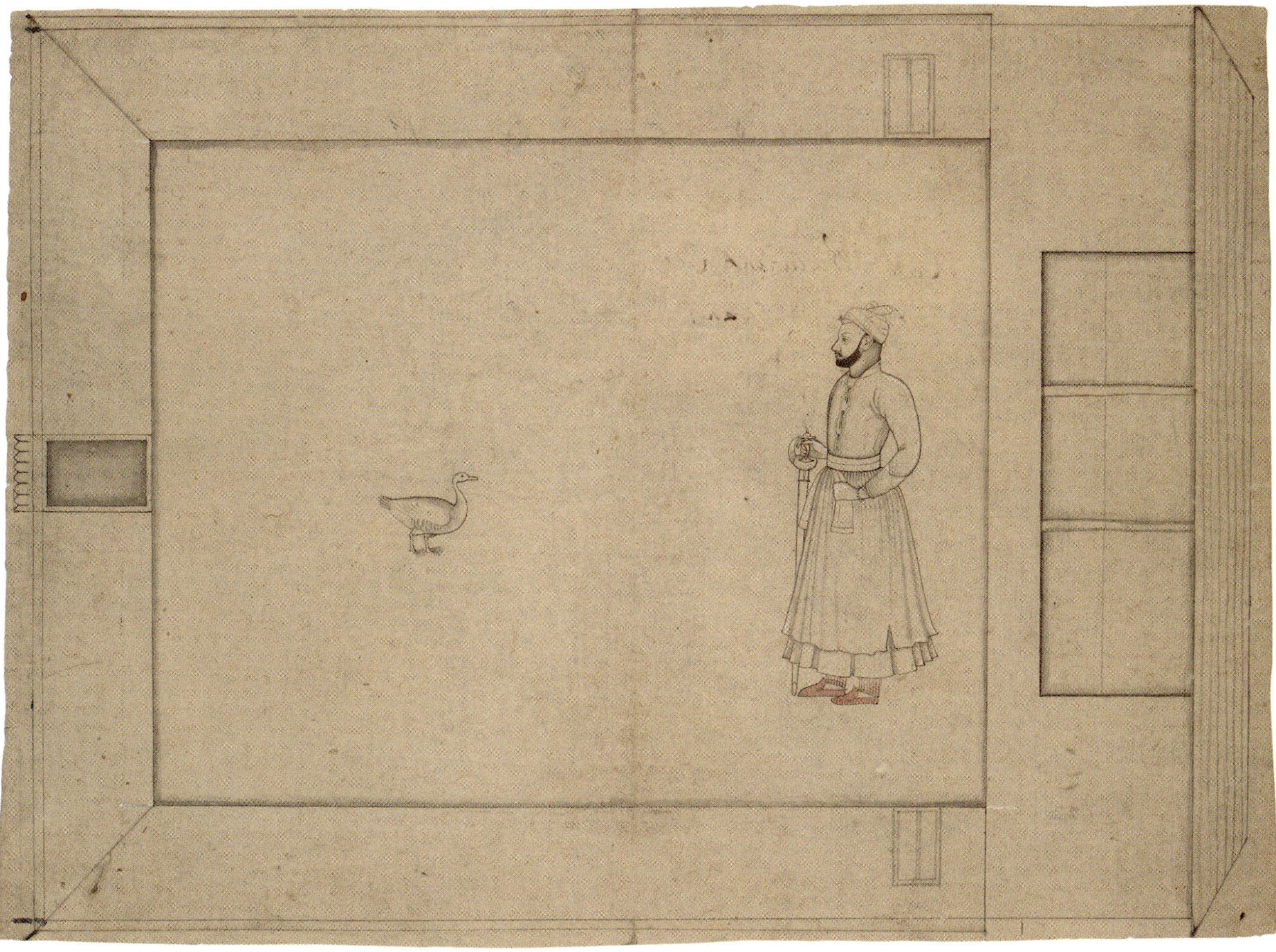

73 The disrobing of Draupadi

Guler, Punjab Hills, *c.*1760–65. Attributed to Nainsukh or a close follower
Gouache with gold on paper, 24.6 × 34.2 cm[1]
Hodgkin Loan 9
Published: Topsfield and Beach 1991, no. 34; Filippi 1997, no. 9

In this episode from the *Mahabharata*, the five Pandava brothers and their joint wife Draupadi are dispossessed and humiliated by their cousins and rivals, the Kauravas. The virtuous Yudhishthira, eldest of the Pandavas, has rashly gambled away their wealth, their liberty and even their wife in a disastrous dice game which will lead to their exile. Duhshasana, one of the Kaurava princes, drags the virtuous Draupadi into the audience hall and attempts to strip her naked before the assembly. Yet her honour is miraculously preserved:

> But when her skirt was being stripped off, another similar skirt appeared every time. A terrible roar went up from all the kings, a shout of approval, as they watched that greatest wonder on earth... A pile of clothes was heaped up in the middle of the hall, when Duhshasana, tired and ashamed, at last desisted and sat down.[2]

As Duhshasana drags veil after veil from Draupadi's head, she stands with proud contempt amid a growing heap of clothing. The Pandava brothers sit nearby in a dejected group. The dumbfounded Yudhishthira lays a restraining hand on the knee of the mace-bearing Bhima. Nakula and Sahadeva commiserate, Arjuna sits slumped forward. The cloth chaupar board on which the fatal game was played is now only indistinctly seen against the bold verticals of the striped durree, though its three oblong ivory dice are more visible. The blind Kaurava king Dhritarashtra presides above, while his eldest son Duryodhana gesticulates towards Draupadi.

Composed with power and finesse, this painting may be a late work by Nainsukh or a close follower. Nainsukh is best known for his highly original portraits of Balwant Singh of Jasrota (nos. 71–72). After his patron's death in 1763, he worked for Raja Amrit Pal of Basohli for a few years, mainly on illustrations to mythological series.[3] The facial types and the poised figure drawing, the tripartite durbar hall with its furled blinds with hanging ties, and the red and brown-striped durree all recall his work.

1 Inscribed in the takri and devanagari scripts with the characters' names.
2 van Buitenen tr., *Mahabharata*, II, p. 146.
3 For accounts of Nainsukh's career, see Archer 1973, 'Jammu', *passim*; Goswamy and Fischer 1992, pp. 268–77, nos. 112–29; Goswamy 1997; Goswamy and Fischer 2011b.

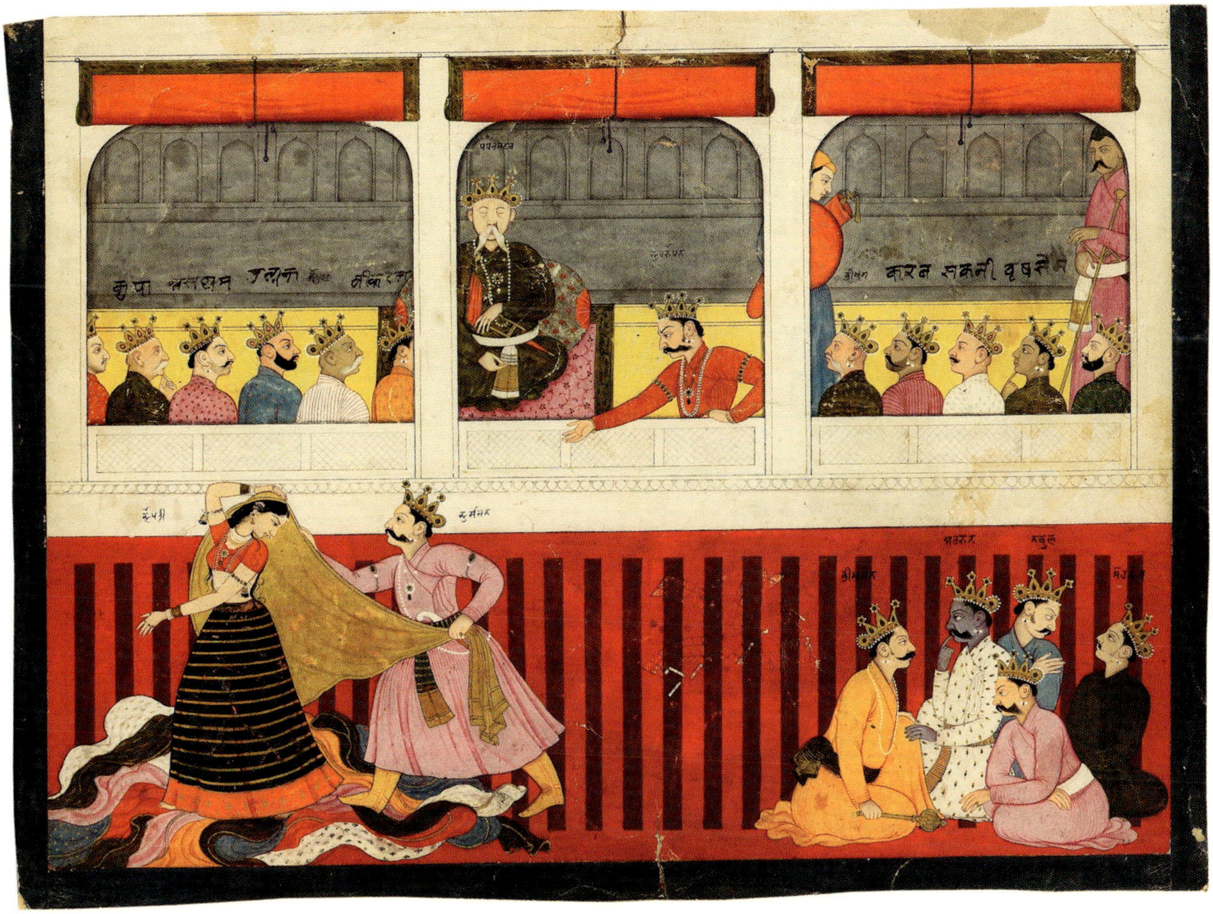

74 Travellers making music

Guler, Punjab Hills, *c.*1760–70. Style of Nainsukh
Gouache on paper, 17.1 × 23.2 cm
Hodgkin Loan 107
Unpublished

A group of Hill travellers take a rest from their journey, laying aside staffs and cloth bundles beside a tree and a narrow stream. They sing together with gusto, perhaps performing some folk tune or devotional song. One man beats the *tala* rhythm on a clay pot, while others clap in time or snap their fingers. Another man is moved to dance on the spot while singing, one slippered foot raised and a hand tucked back inside his waist-sash. To the right, an older man leans back and listens to the performance.

A few peripheral details are now lost through scorching at the edges of the page and trimming by an earlier owner, who may also have added the pencilled inscriptions in English. Comparison with a closely related drawing, possibly a preparatory study,[1] suggests that the lightly clad figure now half-seen at upper right was either also dancing or returning from his ablutions with water-pot in hand, pursued by a barking dog. Rich in human sympathy and observation, this lively study of everyday Hill life recalls the work of the great Pahari artist Nainsukh (nos. 71–73). It can be attributed either to him in his late period, or else to a close follower.

1 Jagdish and Kamla Mittal Museum, Hyderabad: Mittal 2007, pl. 48.

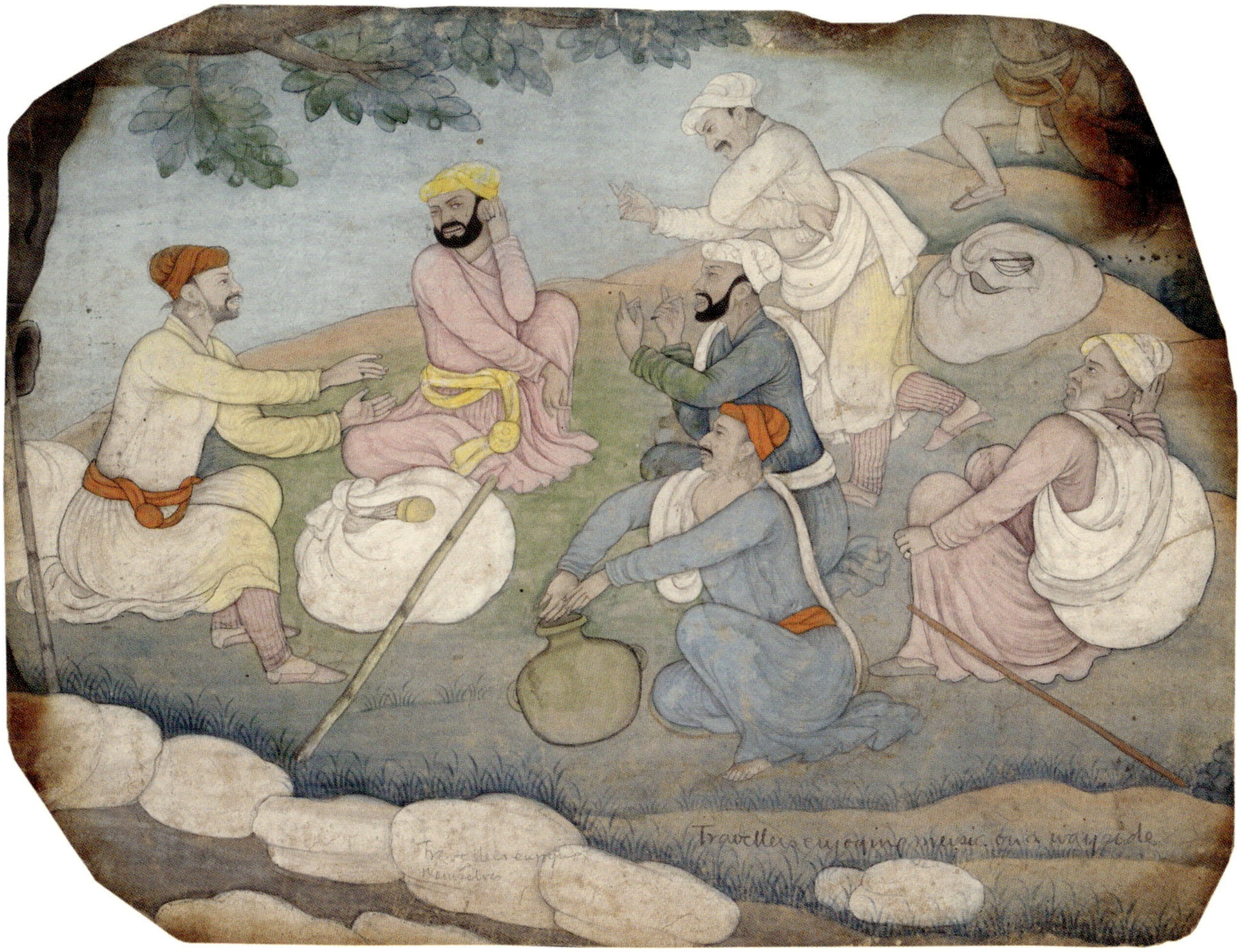
Travellers enjoying music on a wayside

75 Pavilion with Krishna paintings

Kangra, Punjab Hills, about 1800
Gouache on paper, 18 × 23 cm
Hodgkin Loan 5
Published: Filippi 1997, no. 5

In this unusual composition a small palace pavilion is outlined and detailed with formal clarity. It stands alone against a blue ground, with no human or other presence. No windows are visible. Much is going on however in the nine painted panels on its facade, grouped around the dark central doorway with its furled cloth hanging. These lively vignettes depict the superhuman or amorous exploits of the god Krishna in his childhood and youth spent among the cowherds and milkmaids (*gopas* and *gopis*) in the Braj country near Mathura. This little painted pavilion was perhaps set on a terrace or in a garden, and may have been a favoured retreat of a ruler such as Sansar Chand of Kangra, (r.1775–1823), who was a particular devotee of the god.

From the lower right, Krishna appears in the form of Vishnu reclining on the snake Shesha amid the primordial cosmic waters, then receiving the obeisance of the god Brahma. To the left of the door, the infant Krishna suckles the demoness Putana to death, and in later youth be saves the cowherds from a forest fire by swallowing its flames.

From upper right, he slays the buffalo and horse demons; as an infant (above the door)he drags a heavy mortar to which his foster-mother had tethered him and uproots two trees; and as a young adult, he playfully steals the *gopis*' clothes while they bathe in the river; and finally he is shown at a forest tryst with his favourite *gopi* Radha. Such scenes were common subjects in palace mural decoration, and a contemporary Kangra picture[1] shows an artist at work on painted niche-panels of a similar kind.

1 Museum of Fine Arts, Boston: e.g. Cummins 2006, pl. 107.

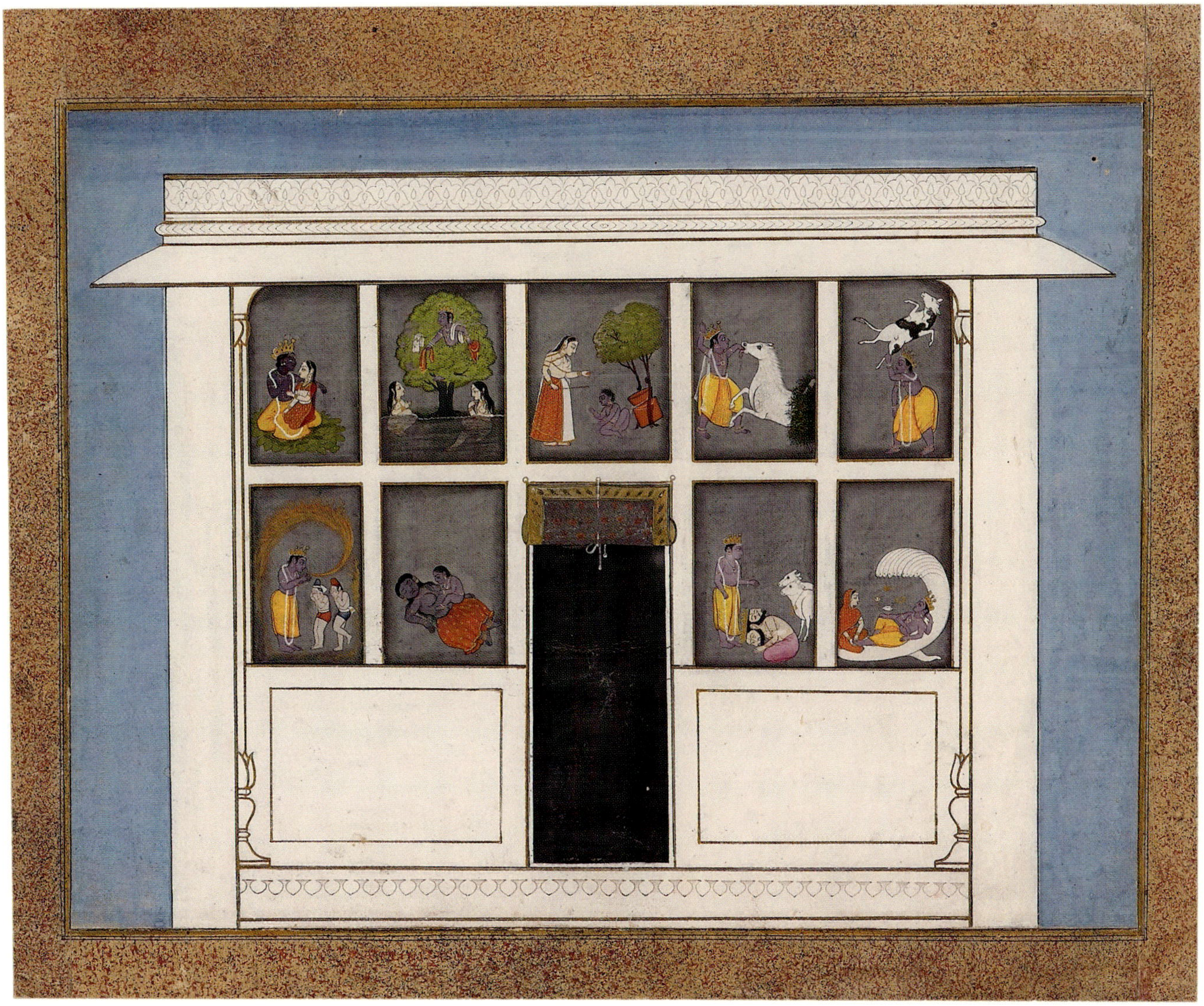

76 A lady in an interior

Kangra, Punjab Hills, *c.*1810–20
Gouache with gold and silver on paper, 20 × 13 cm
Hodgkin Loan 118
Unpublished

This intimate vignette of palace life is framed within an arched window surround, its raised cloth blind allowing us to see within the chamber. Well wrapped in a red quilted shawl, a lady of classic Kangra charm and elongated eye gazes into the glowing coals of a brazier on wheels that warms her room on a chilly evening. She raises her hand to enjoy its heat, while holding the hookah tube with her other hand beneath her shawl, its jade mouth-piece resting close to her lips. She has evidently been singing, as a green tanpura, her accompanying instrument, lies beside her on a cushion. A bed under a flowered coverlet is glimpsed through the doorway behind her. More unusually, the candle under its protective shade in the left foreground is throwing dark flickering shadows of the lady and her maid onto the wall behind. Such naturalistic effects after European models were not often attempted by Pahari court painters, and this deployment of shadow enhances what would otherwise be a largely conventional scene.

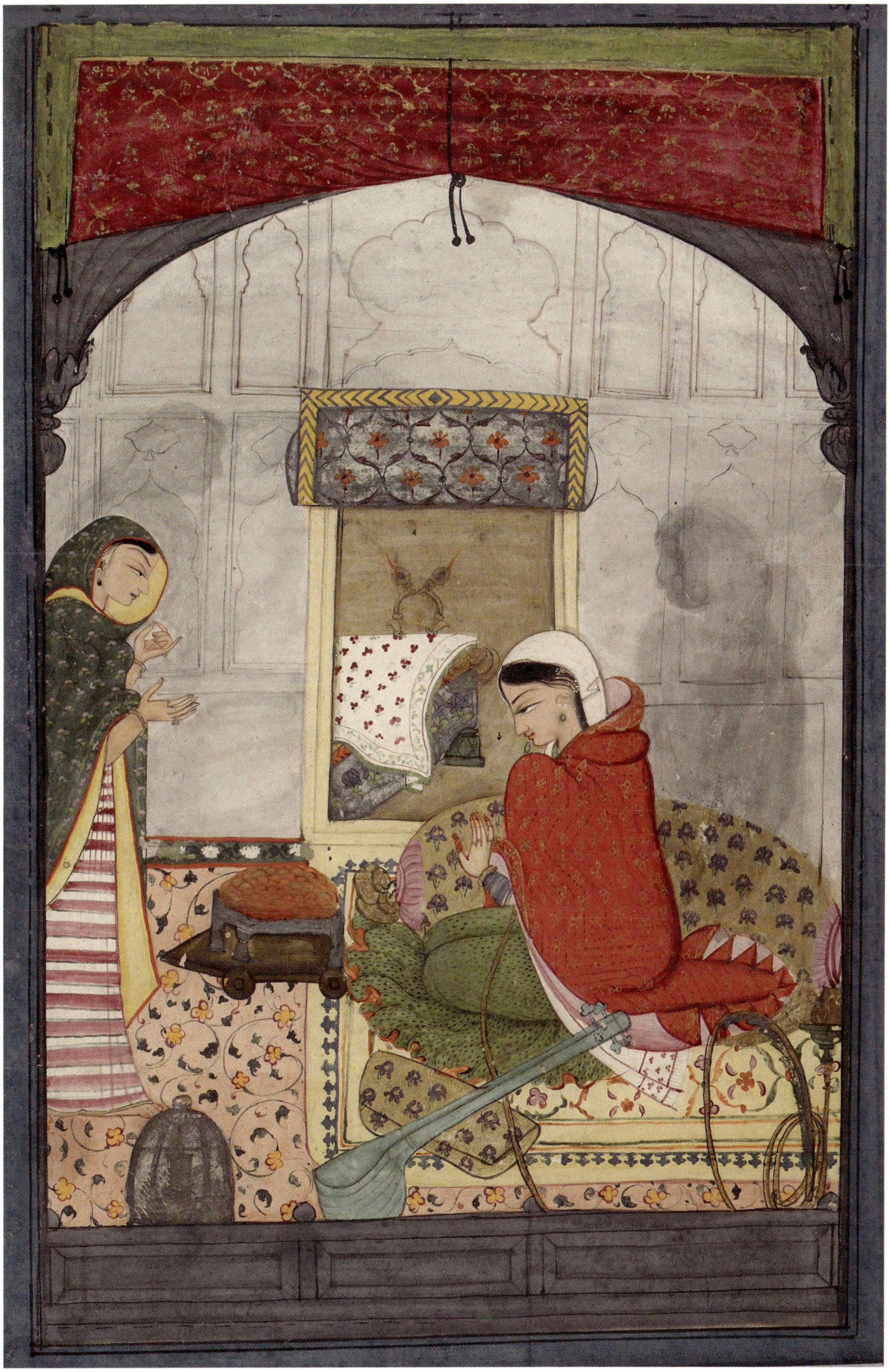

77 Maharaja Ranjit Singh in a bazaar

Lahore, Punjab, *c.*1840–45
Gouache on paper, 18 × 21 cm
Hodgkin Loan 110
Unpublished

Maharaja Ranjit Singh (r.1801–39), the one-eyed Lion of the Punjab and charismatic leader of the Sikhs, rides in his elephant howdah through a bazaar in Lahore. Preceded by a horseman and an attendant carrying his cloth-wrapped sword, he goes on his way strangely disregarded by the populace. In the foreground a picturesque group of Hindu ascetics, one smoking a pipe, converse with a yellow-clad Akali Sikh and a passing Jain monk, who wears a white mouth-cloth to protect any insects from accidental harm. In the bazaar shops behind, two craftsmen are fashioning gold and silver thread, while next door in a kite-seller's shop a father and his small sons admire the kites and balls of twine.

Probably painted a few years after Ranjit Singh's death, this slice of bazaar life recalls in its human variety Kipling's descriptions of Lahore in his great novel *Kim* half a century later. A fragmentary inscription below ("*Souvenir à* ...") suggests this picture was probably painted for one of the French officers serving at the Sikh court at this period.

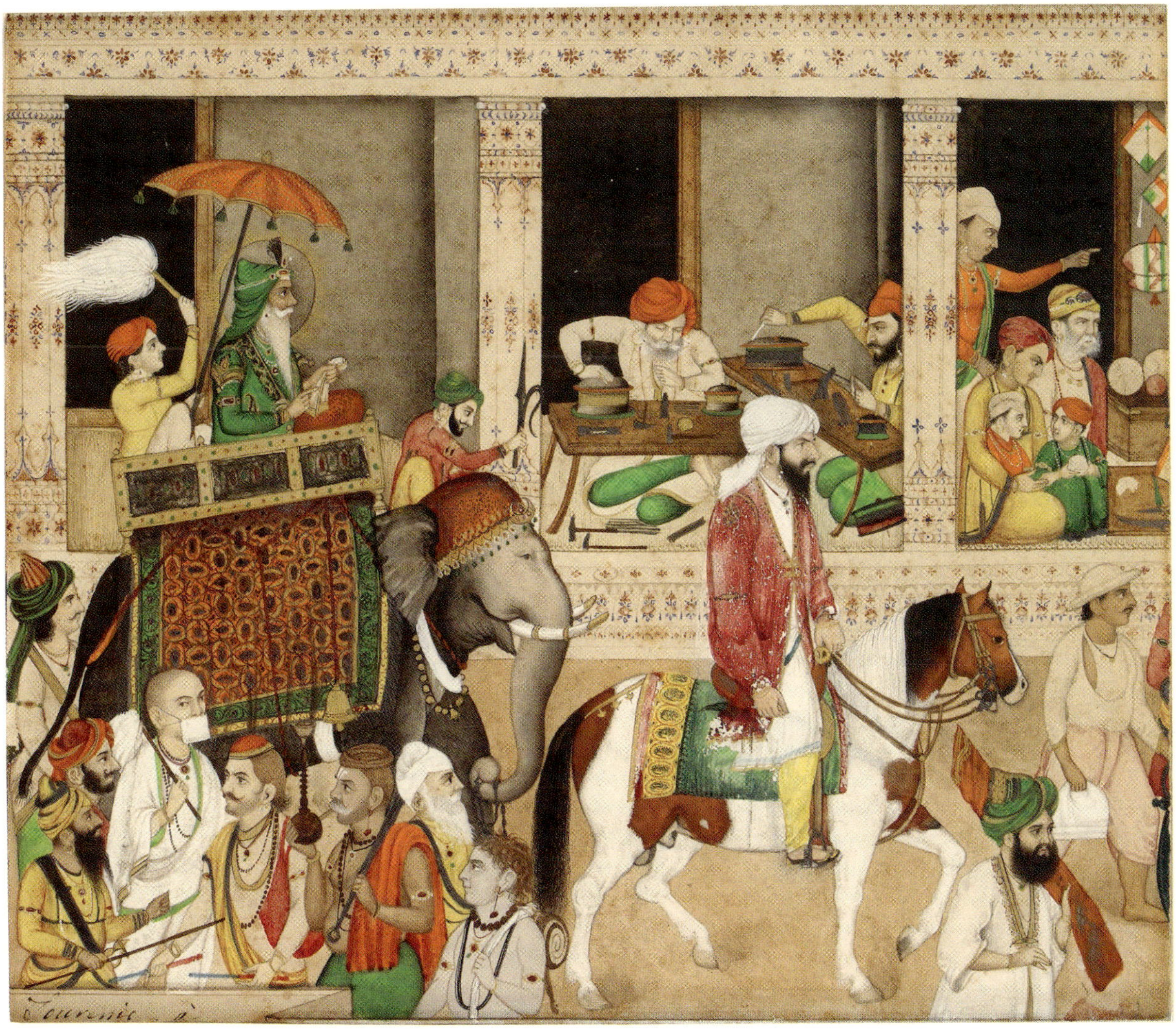

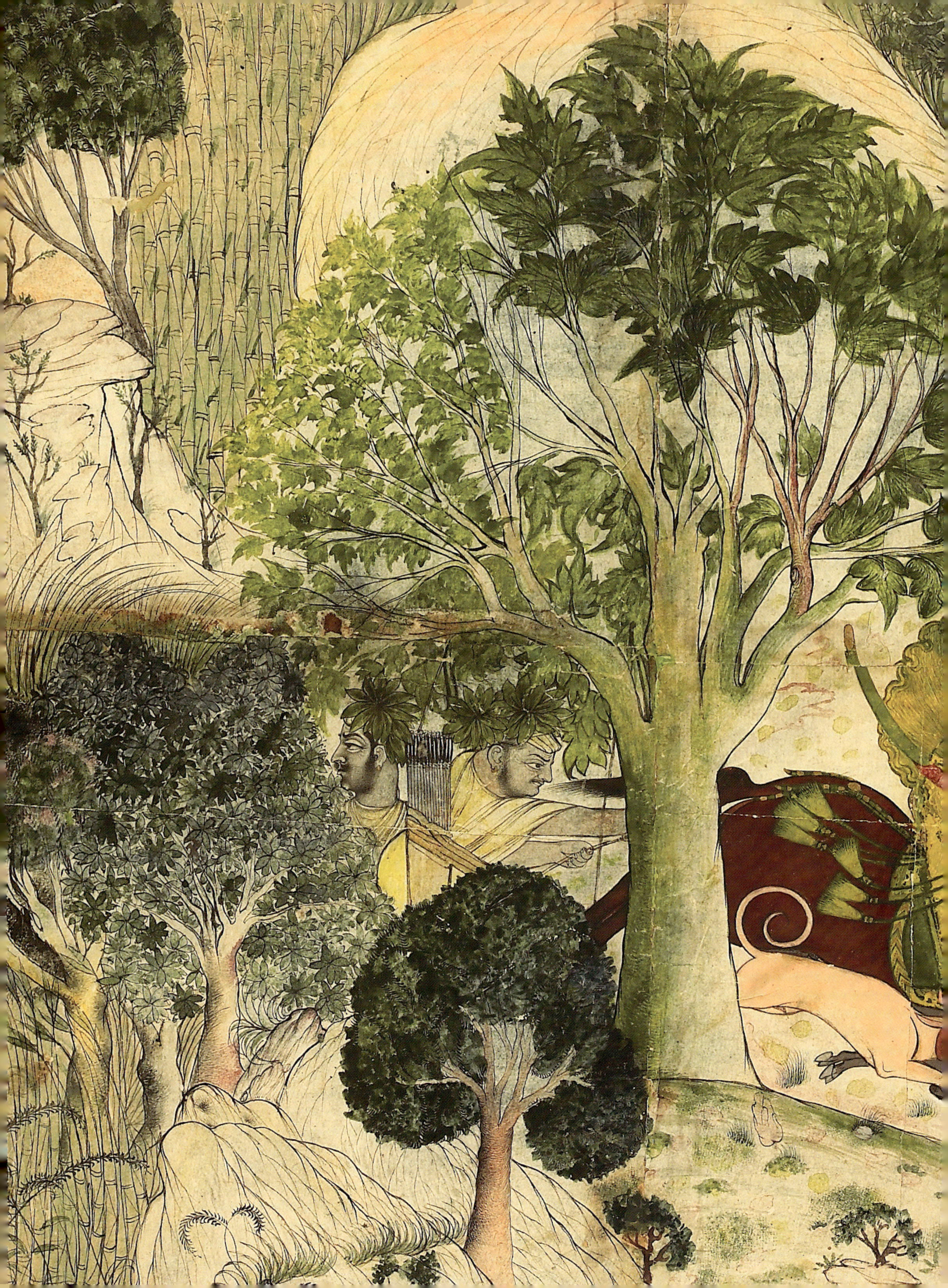

RAJASTHANI

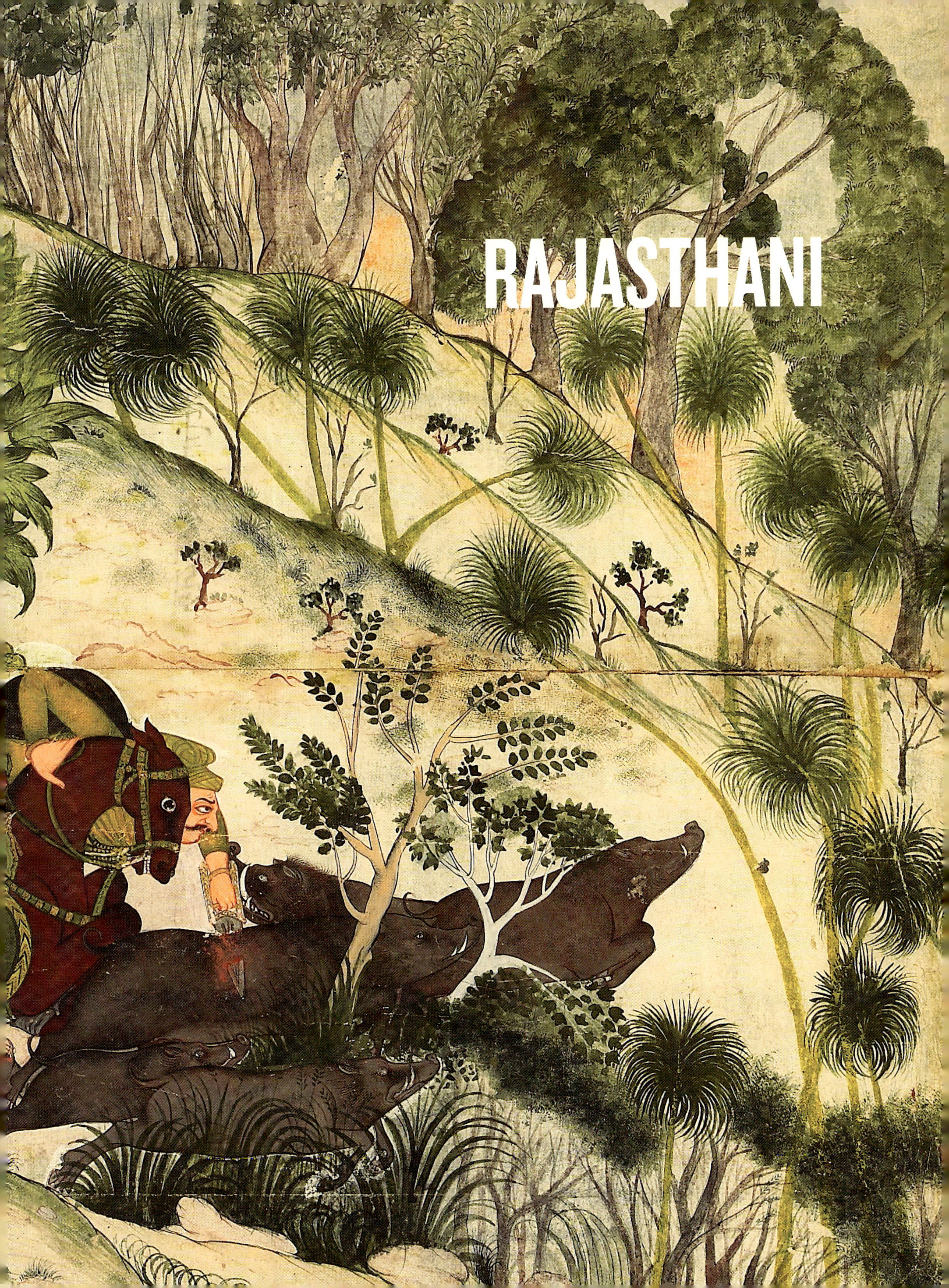

78 A royal lion hunt

Bundi, Rajasthan, *c.*1640
Gouache on paper, 37.5 × 102.7 cm
Hodgkin Loan 75
Published: Arts Council 1982, no.207; Hodgkin and McInerney 1983, no.38; Topsfield and Beach 1991, no.13; Beach 1992, fig.92; Filippi 1997, no.75

At the centre of this fragmentary coloured drawing, a prince riding a charging elephant assails a lion with his arrows, the frilled hem of his muslin robe flying behind him. Other nobles on elephants ride hither and thither in support. Emerging from a bamboo thicket, the lion has seized the elephant's foreleg, while the lioness and cubs stand at bay in the rocks nearby. In a motif deriving from Persian painting, a bear perching on a rock heaves a boulder at the royal escort stationed to the left of the picture. This and other conventions have been adapted by the Rajasthani artist from imperial Mughal painting, but his interpretation of the hunt is wholly Rajput in its fluid treatment of space, abrupt shifts of scale in the human figures and elephants, and boldly adumbrated landscape forms. The elephants in particular have a power and intensity not found in the more polished Mughal models from which they derive.

The vigour and breadth of scale of this work show strong affinities with earlier, free-flowing hunting scenes, from the reign of Rao Ratan Singh (1607–31),[1] that form part of the mural decoration of the Badal Mahal apartment of the Bundi palace. The charging elephant in particular is already found there.[2] This figure would recur in the later work of artists at the adjoining Hara Rajput court of Kota,[3] where from the mid-seventeenth century the genre of elephant paintings was developed with greater verve and imagination than at any other Indian court (nos.80–85). It is difficult to say whether this painting was made at Bundi or at Kota by a Bundi-trained painter.[4] The main figure does not seem to be a specific prince but represents a Rajput heroic ideal of the ruler who can both ride a charging elephant and slay a lion, the pre-eminent prey of kings.

1 See Bautze 1986b; Bautze 2000, figs.5–10; Beach 2008, pp.139–40, figs.20–21.
2 Beach 2011a, fig.11.
3 E.g. Beach 2011b, fig.4; first published in Lee 1960, no.36.
4 Beach 1992, pp.124 and 165–66 (suggesting Kota); more recently Beach 2011a, p.304, n.28, argues for Bundi.

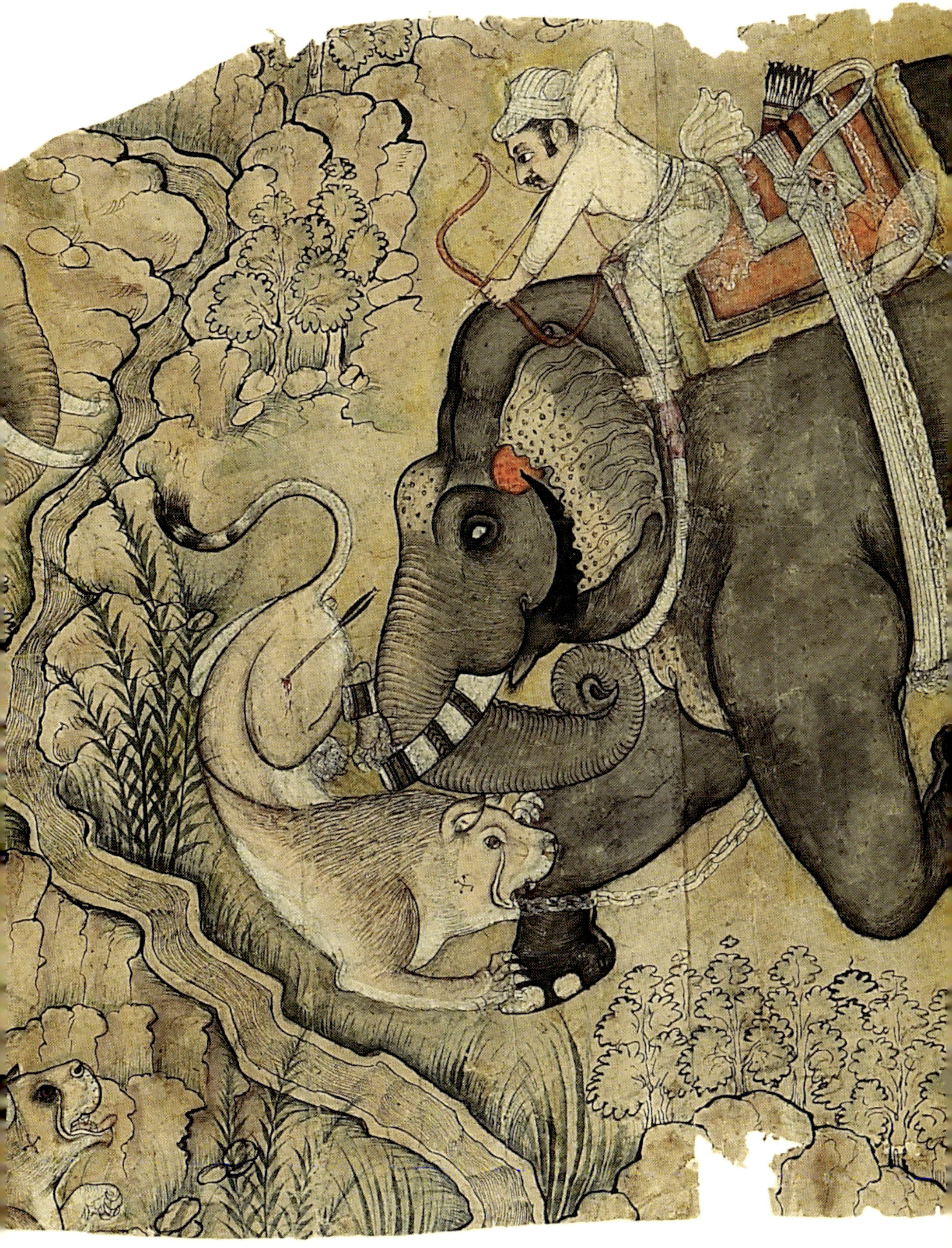

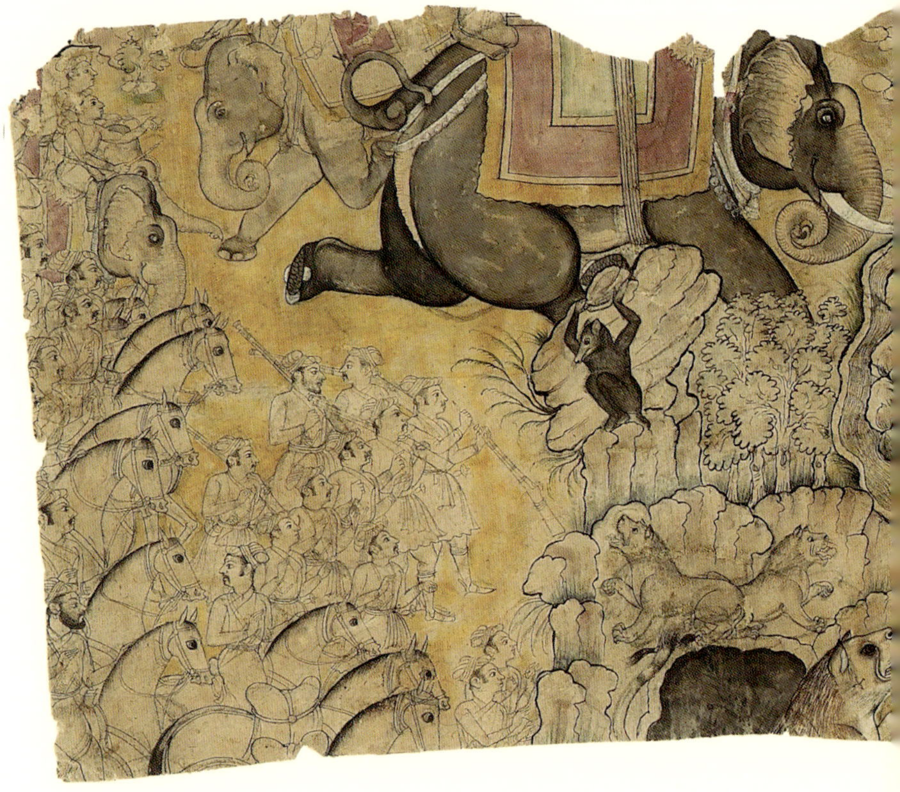

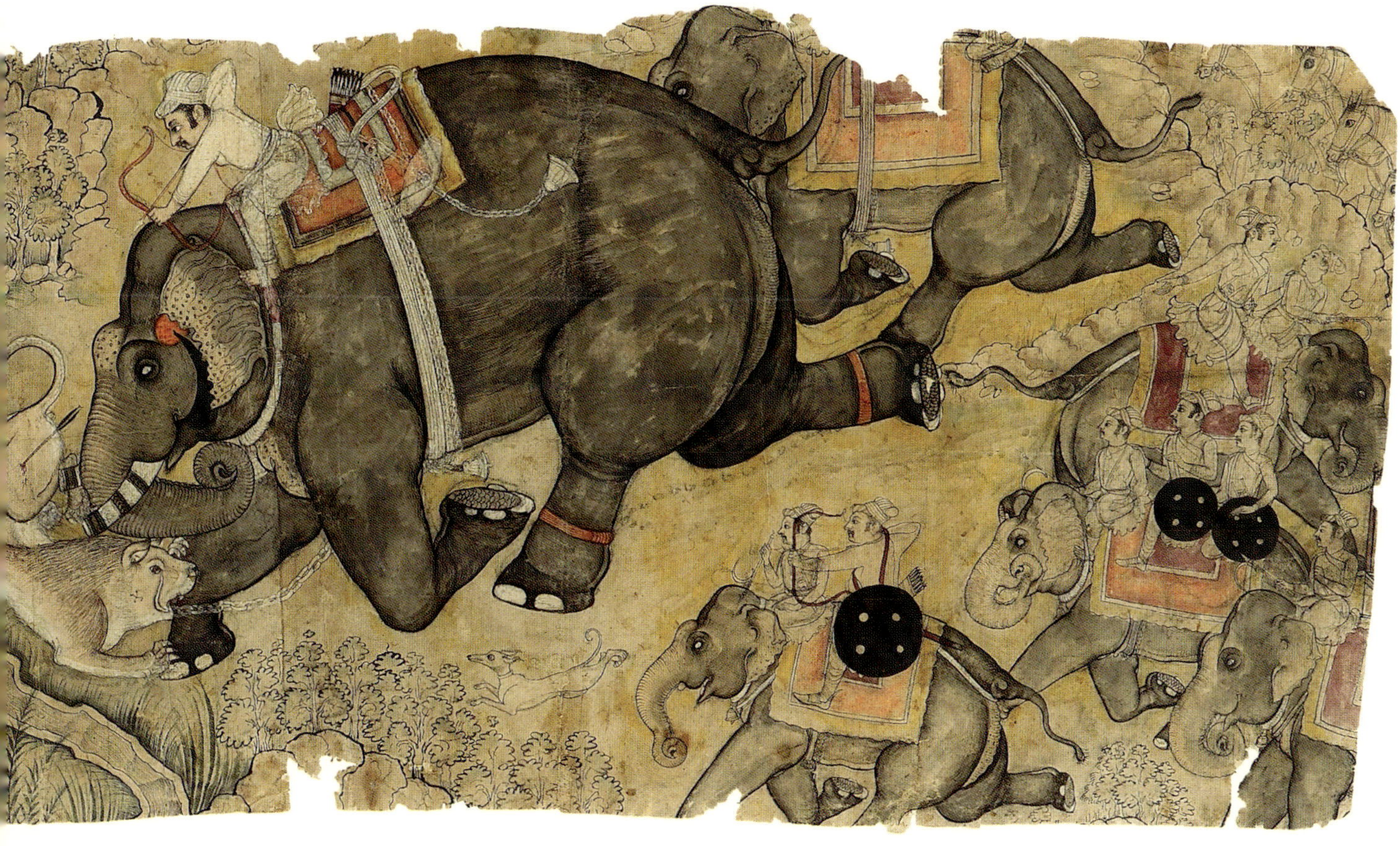

79 Rao Bhao Singh riding an elephant

Bundi, Rajasthan, *c.* 1675
Gouache with gold and silver on paper, 29.5 × 40 cm
Hodgkin Loan 57
Published: Filippi 1997, no. 57

Ankus in hand, the Bundi ruler Bhao Singh (r. 1658–81) sits astride a royal elephant of great size. The artist has followed a contemporary Mughal convention whereby the elephant's stature is magnified in relation to its rider or mahout (nos. 24–25). Here also the elephant has an inverted crescent mark painted around his temporal gland, two keepers walk in front with a restraining spear and *charkhi*, while a row of flowers lines the foreground. In other ways the treatment is much more in keeping with the Rajput tradition. The muted pale green often found as a background in Mughal works becomes a strong dark green, and the elephant's linear contours are more strongly and rhythmically drawn. His colouring is also more sharply contrasted between dark grey and the bright speckled pink of the trunk, ear, belly and loins. While the subtler effects of the Mughal technique are missing, a more powerful and immediate visual impact is created. As in many Bundi and Kota elephant subjects, the animal's keenly staring and red-rimmed eye is shown enlarged and boldly outlined and accentuated by swirling linear modelling around it. Conveying the latent energy and wild spirit of the beast, it has a life of its own.

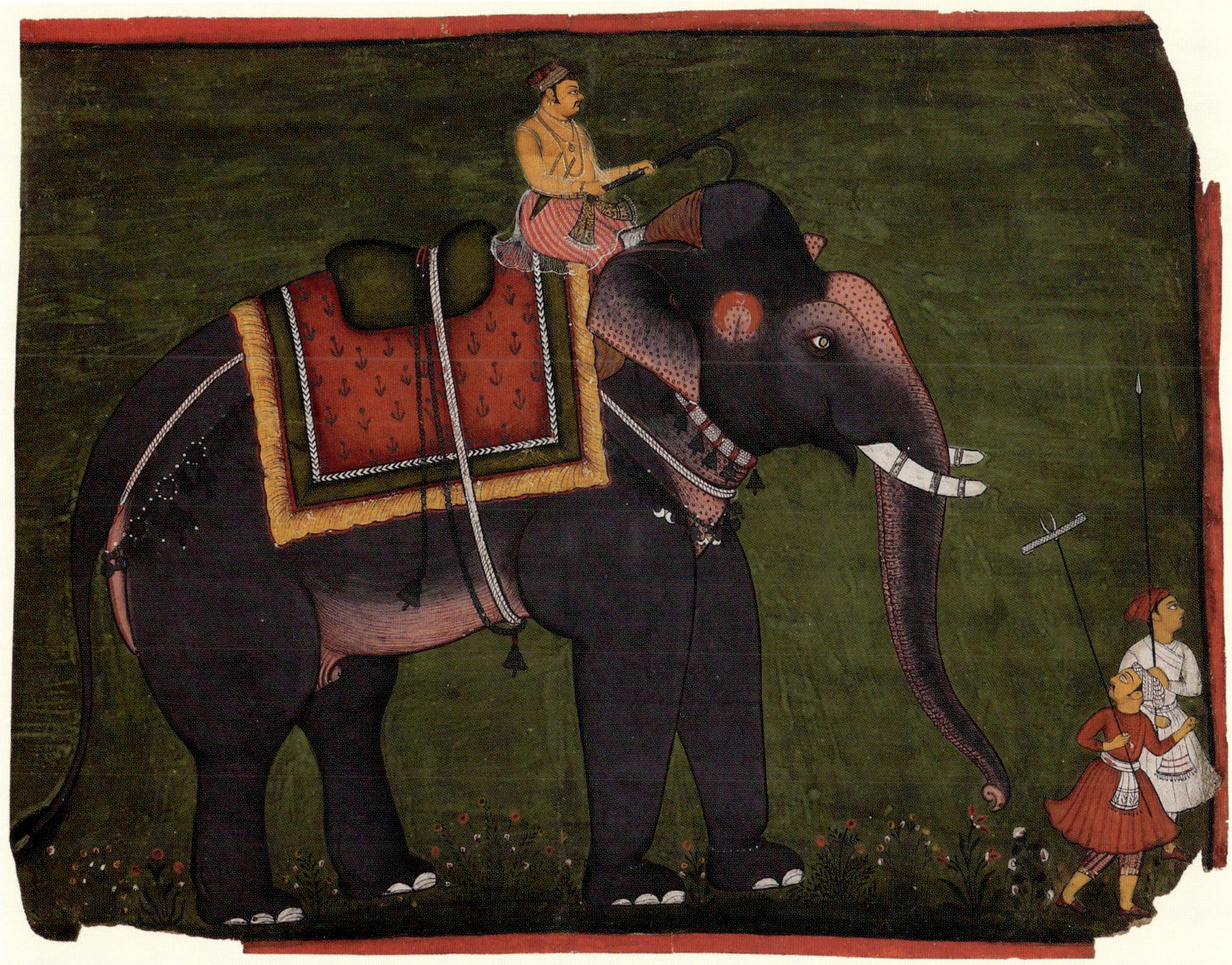

80 Elephants fighting

Kota, Rajasthan, *c.*1655–60
Brush drawing, gouache on paper, 34.2 × 69 cm
Hodgkin loan 62
Published: Ashton ed. 1950, no. 484; Beach 1974, fig. 75; Welch 1976, no. 44; Hodgkin and McInerney 1983, no. 20; Topsfield 1984, fig. 24; Cimino 1985, no. 90; Topsfield and Beach 1991, no. 14; Filippi 1997, no. 62; Welch ed. 1997a, fig. 6; Beach 2011a, fig. 13.

The Rajput rulers shared the Mughal emperors' taste for elephant fights. These dramatic spectacles were held regularly as part of the weekly routine at the major courts, with additional combats on festival days. The most impressive fights between outstanding animals were also often recorded by artists at several courts, and portraits or studies of the royal elephants were constantly made. No Rajasthani school excelled Kota in this respect, largely through the achievement of an unnamed mid-seventeenth century master,[1] whose example continued to influence local artists for a century or more.[2] This exceptionally dynamic drawing is one of his greatest works.

The composition with the fighting elephants barely controlled by their mahouts and an assistant on foot, derives from earlier seventeenth century models both in Mughal painting, such as a spirited drawing in Paris also on a plain paper ground,[3] and the palace mural paintings at Bundi.[4] But this tumultuous clash of mighty beasts is the work of a painter who had studied the forms and movements in action of the court elephants with the greatest attention and empathy. He deploys an extraordinary linear energy and dramatic use of shading, with densely swirling passages of line and dramatic distortions of anatomical form. The attendant's *charkhi* spear points to the impact between the heads of the colliding animals. One mahout leans forward over his elephant's head, the other sits further back making a gesture of command, his ankus tucked under a rope. He wears a string of pearls and it has been suggested that he could be a princely figure, perhaps Rao Jagat Singh (r.1657–84),[5] who was also probably the patron for whom this work was made.

Howard Hodgkin has commented, "The design of the two conjoined heads and trunks is an extraordinary invention which speaks for itself. It is worth noting that though the sheet is damaged (fragments of the border exist on all four sides) the dramatic composition, with the figure cut off in the foreground, follows the original intentions of the artist and is not the result of cutting."[6]

1 Beach 2011a, for a reappraisal of this much discussed painter.
2 E.g. a later version of the present composition of *c.*1725 is in the Jagdish and Kamla Mittal Museum, Hyderabad: Mittal 1989, no. 29.
3 Hurel 2010, no. 26; Bibliothèque Nationale 1986, no. 59.
4 E.g. Welch ed. 1997a, fig. 5.
5 Beach 2011a, p. 301.
6 Hodgkin and McInerney 1983, no. 20.

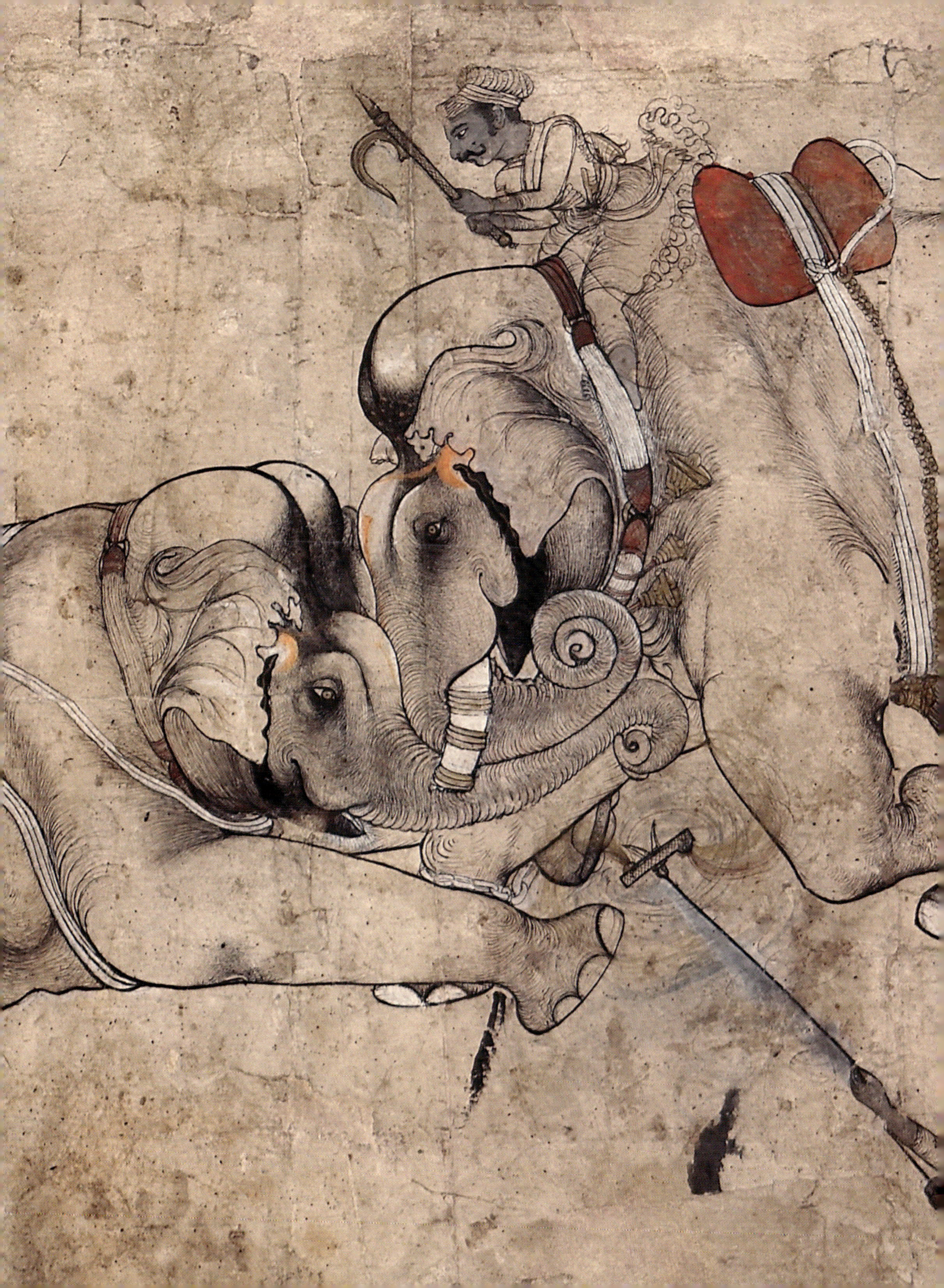

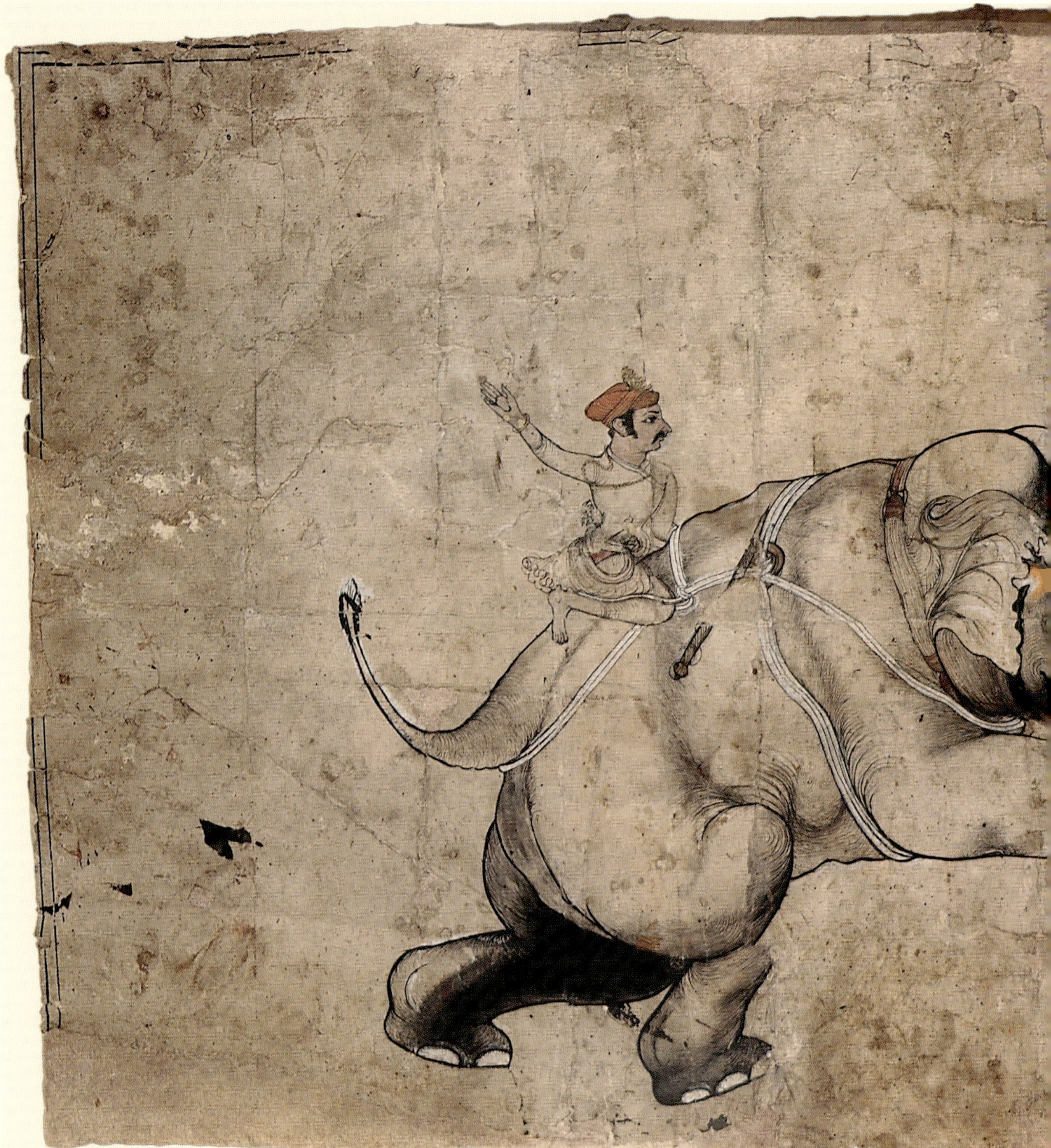

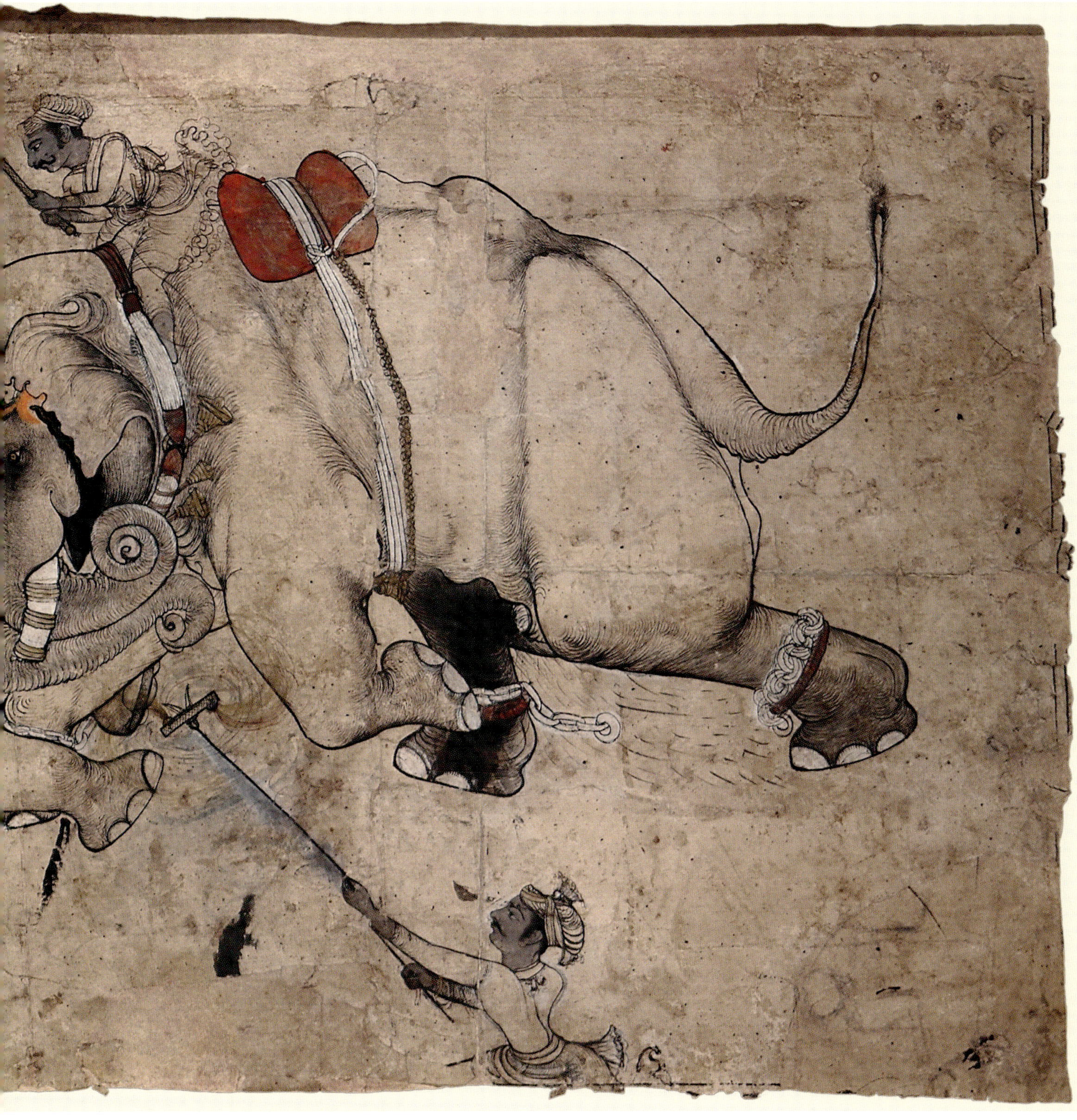

81 Enraged elephant

Kota, Rajasthan, *c.*1690
Brush drawing with gouache and silver on paper, 23.5 × 38.1 cm[1]
Hodgkin Loan 45
Published: Hodgkin and McInerney 1983, no. 23; Filippi 1997, no. 45

Bull elephants periodically become frenzied and aggressive during their *mast* ('drunken, intoxicated') season. This condition is marked by a thick discharge from glands in the animal's temples and by unpredictable, often violent, behaviour. Wild-eyed and enraged by *mast*, this elephant tears at his heavy restraining chains while his mahout and two keepers struggle to control him with a spear and *charkhi* with fizzing Catherine wheel. The tips of two further spears appear at far left, probably held by further attendant figures now missing. The vital surging contours and densely modelled volumes of this elephant, as well as the intent figure of the mahout, are indebted to the example of the master of *Elephants fighting* (no. 80), a generation or more before. In the present work, the mahout, keepers and the paddock foreground are more fully coloured, and the elephant's chains were painted silver, now oxidized to dark grey.

1 Inscription in devanagari above, now partly damaged: *hathi mast ?daya haruji? ma.*

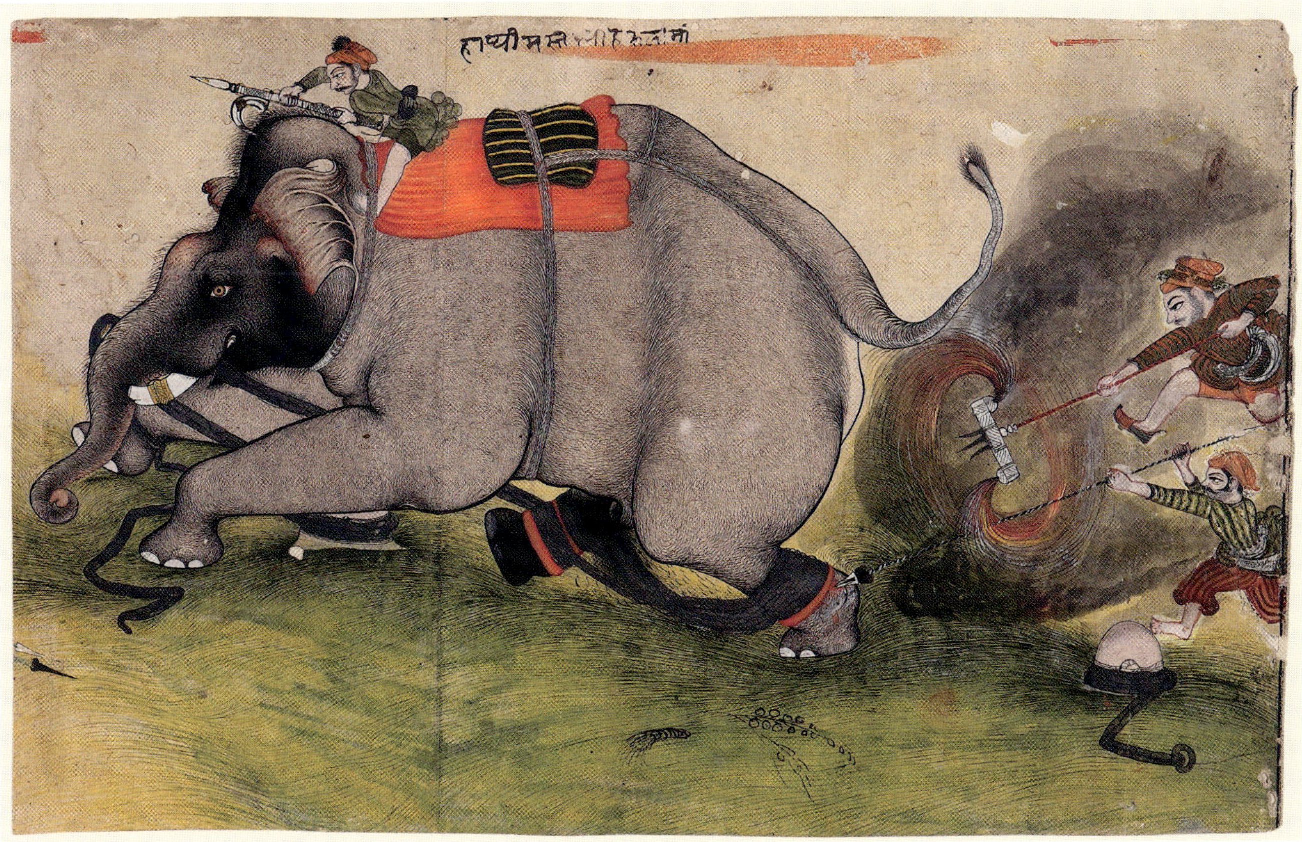

82 Elephant's head

Kota, Rajasthan, *c.*1700–10
Brush drawing on paper, 23.5 × 23.5 cm
Hodgkin Loan 51
Published: Pal 1981, fig.2; Filippi 1997, no.51

Elephants in their *mast* season (no.81), which had become excited or violent and were thus at the formidable height of their vitality, became a favourite subject for drawing studies at the Kota court. This powerful fragmentary drawing shows the head and forequarters of a court elephant in *mast*, with his fixedly staring eye, his flexing and curling trunk and a stream of dark secretion seeping from his crescent-shaped temporal gland. The elephant's wide open and animated eye seems to swim in a vortex of fluid eddying lines and hatchings. Similar dynamic linear swirls appear around the mouth and ear. Such passages are typical of the Kota elephant drawing style established by the great seventeenth century master (no.80). In contrast, the shoulders, neck and rope collar with bells are more summarily sketched.

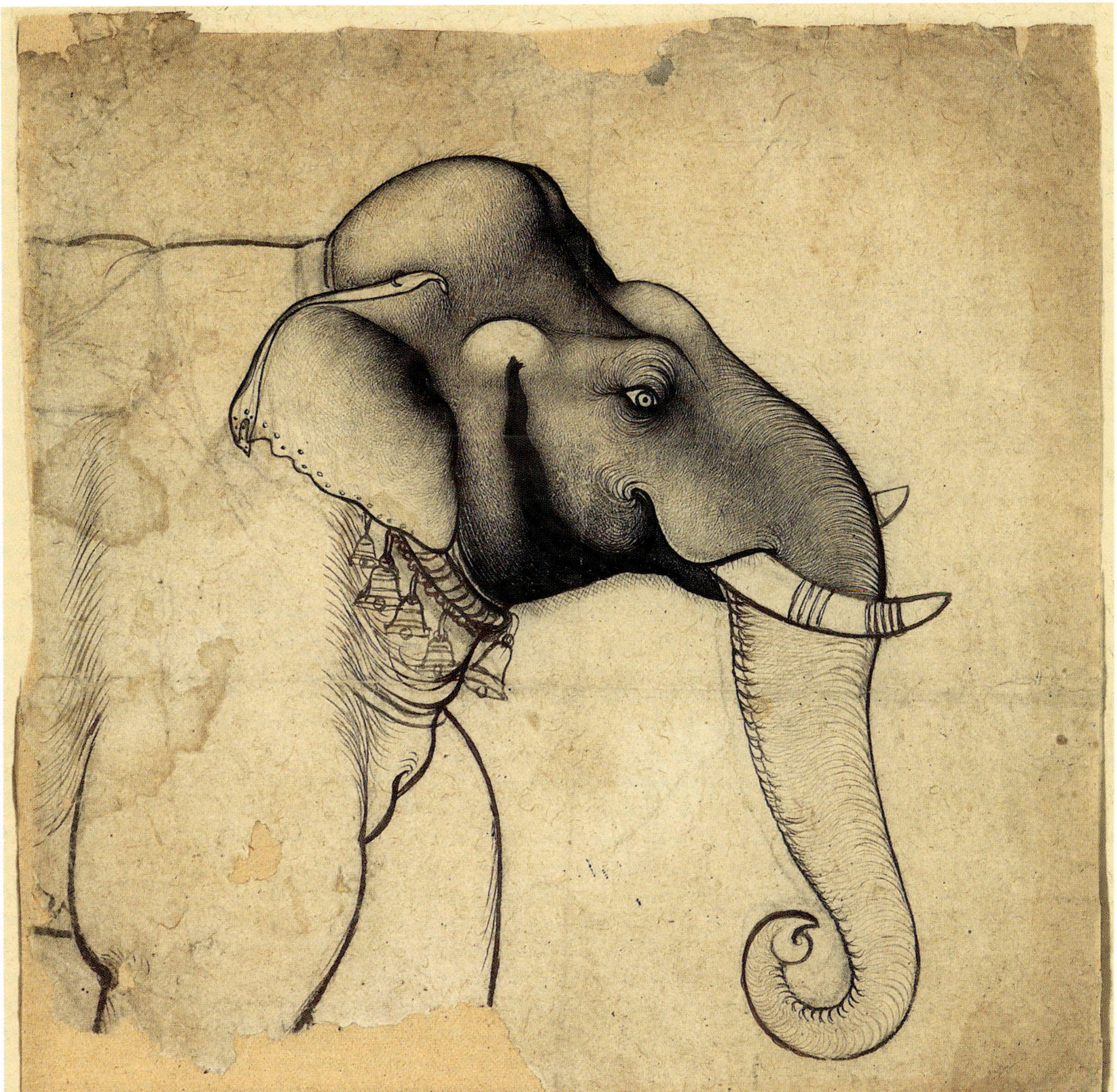

83 Fallen elephant

Kota, Rajasthan, *c.*1700
Brush drawing on plain paper, 22 × 25 cm
Hodgkin Loan 52
Published: Filippi 1997, no. 52

In this rapid and lively sketch, the artist experiments unusually with the fluid dorsal contortions of a tethered elephant that has either lost his footing, or is lying down briefly to rest, or is perhaps having a playful roll on the ground in his paddock, as far as his heavy chain allows. From his spirally coiling trunk to his looping tufted tail, the massive fluid volumes of his twisting body and legs splaying at different angles are fluently drawn with heavy outlines and rapid linear modelling. With its rough pentimenti and marginal squiggles, this forceful study of a prostrate elephant still suggests the animal's innate power and capacity for turbulent motion. It may have served as a preliminary study for an elephant figure in a later finished painting of larger scale.

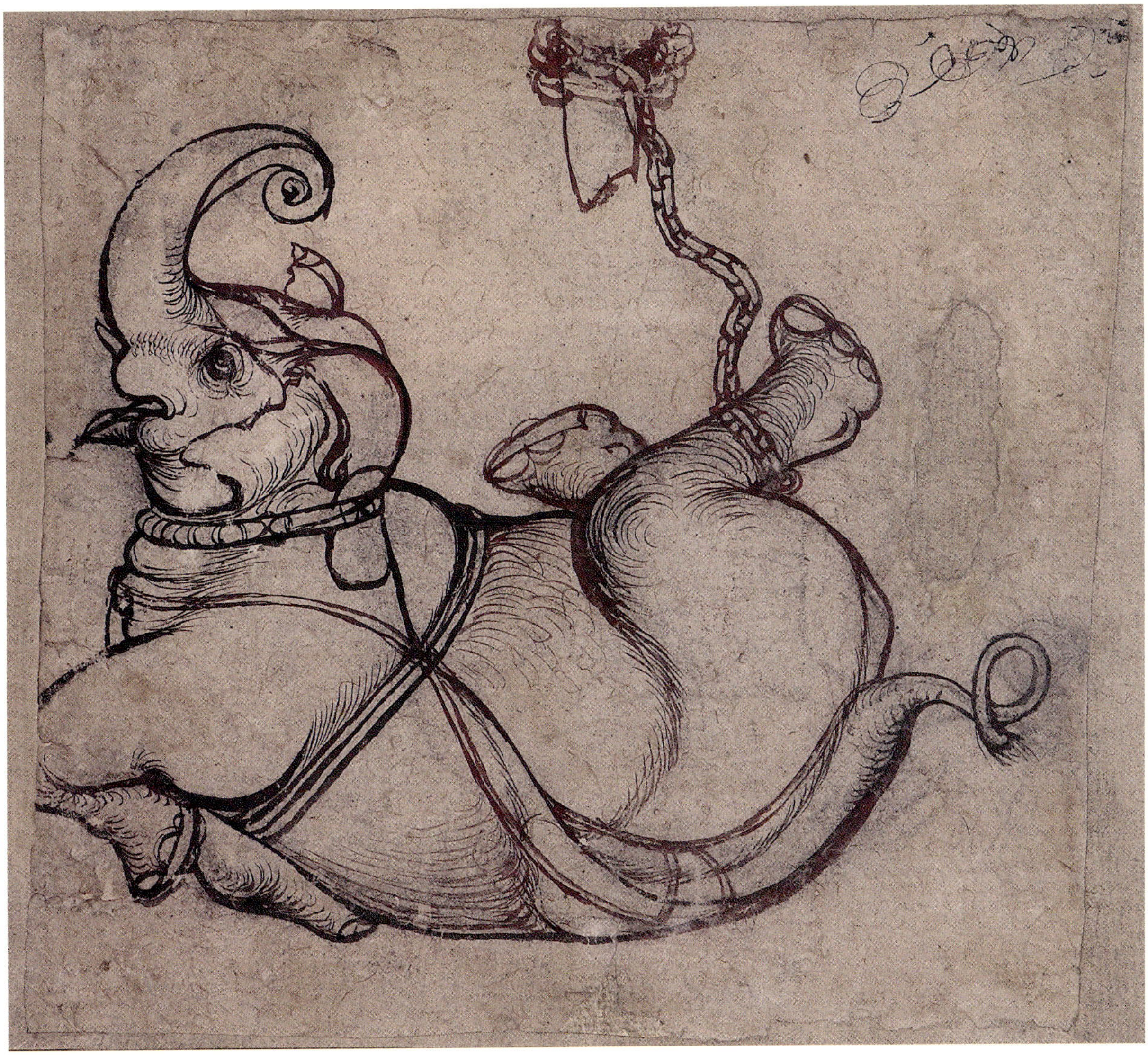

84 Elephant at a gallop

Kota, Rajasthan, *c.*1710–20
Gouache on paper, 35.6 × 41.9 cm[1]
Hodgkin Loan 53
Published: Filippi 1997, no. 53

Guided by the touch of the mahout's ankus, this vigorous young elephant advances speedily in spite of the heavy metal chains still attached to his ankles or partially gathered up on his back. He carries another short length of chain in his mouth. He is perhaps at the beginning or end of his aggressive *mast* period (no. 81), as a trail of dark secretion has streamed from his temple. His eye too is red-rimmed, with a blazing orange pupil fixed on the yellow space ahead of him. The surging power of an elephant gathering speed is well conveyed. In this more fully coloured work on a partially coloured ground, the elephant's grey skin still has quite a high degree of linear modelling and an effective use of shading around the head and rear leg.

1 Visible through the paper near the mahout's head, a devanagari inscription on the reverse is as yet unread.

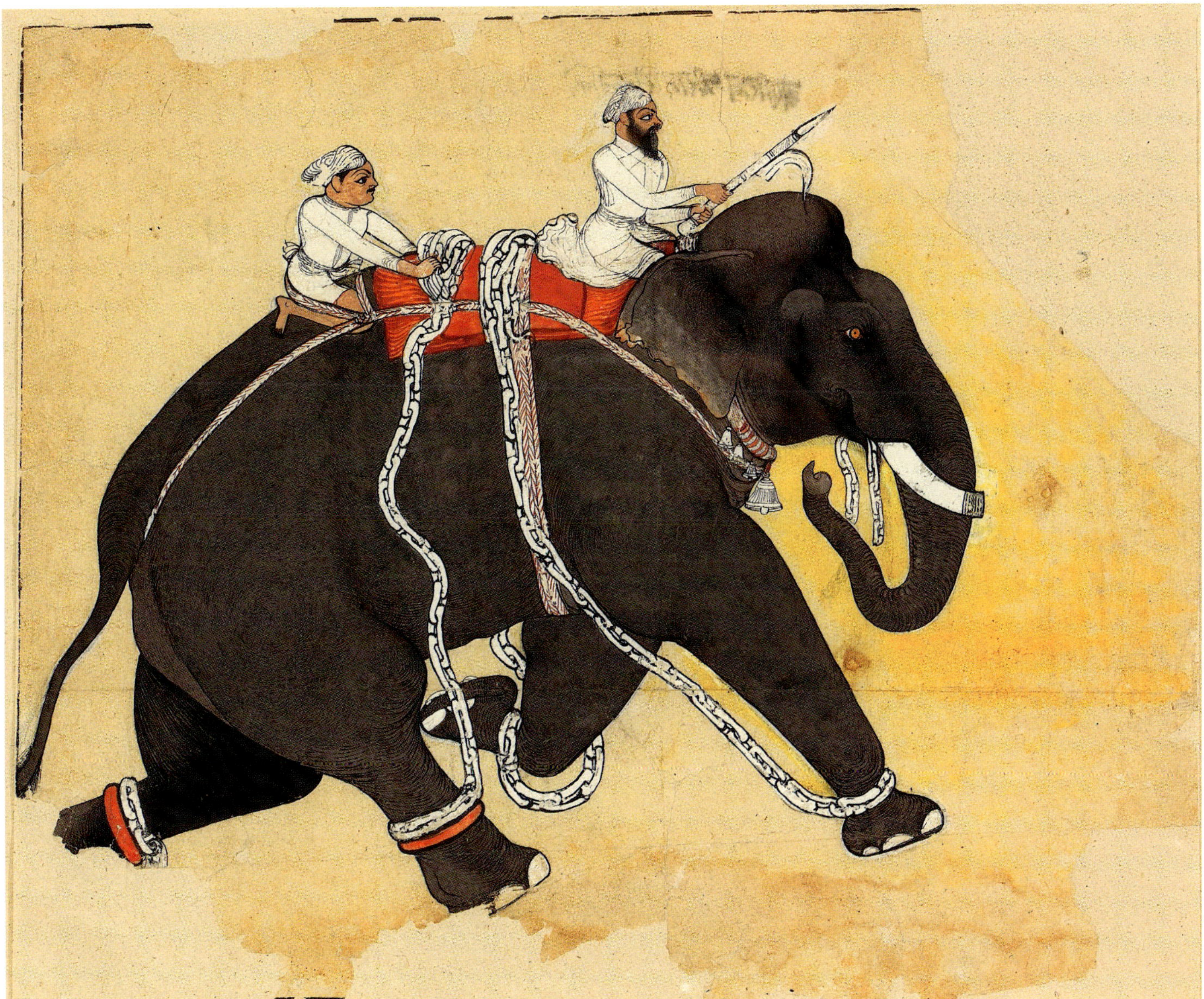

85 Elephant with howdah

Kota, Rajasthan, *c.* 1680
Charcoal on paper, 40.8 × 51.4 cm
Hodgkin Loan 50
Published: Hodgkin and McInerney 1983, no. 28; Filippi 1997, no. 50

Charcoal was mainly used for broad preparatory under-drawing, and surviving Indian drawings and sketches in this medium are rare. Here the artist has freely sketched a caparisoned elephant with a saddle-cloth and howdah, in which a royal person would ride in cushioned comfort, perhaps with a companion or with his hookah. Howard Hodgkin remarks, "In spite of the looseness of execution, this is probably not drawn from life. More likely it is an under-drawing, which would then be over-painted in black with the point of a brush and the charcoal then finally erased."[1] As so often, the elephant's head is rendered with particular sensitivity. The figure of the mahout holding his raised ankus is less distinct and was attempted by the artist more than once.

1 Hodgkin and McInerney 1983, no. 28.

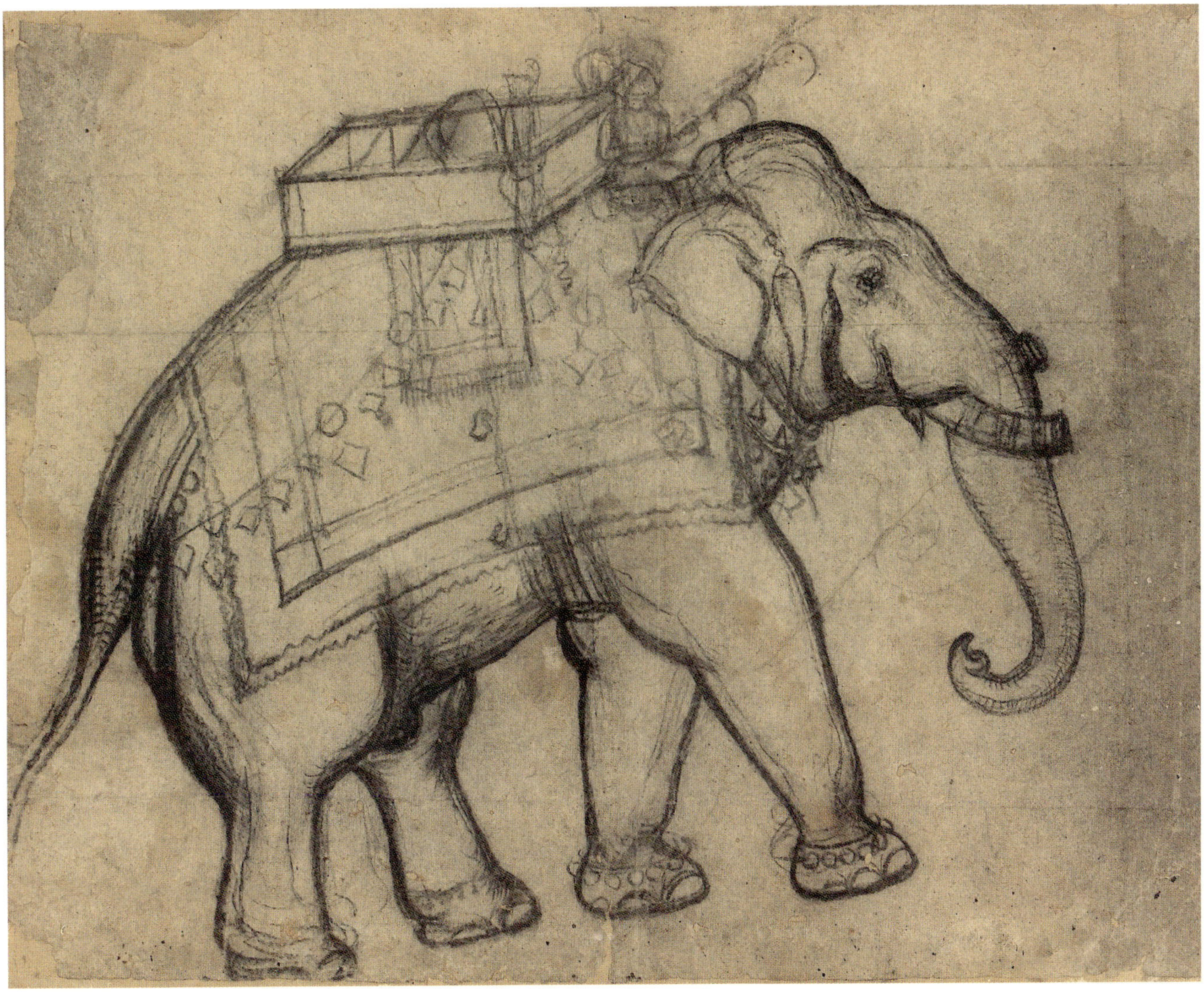

86 Muslim nobleman

Kishangarh, Rajasthan, early 18th century
Gouache with gold on paper, 30 × 25 cm
Hodgkin Loan 39
Published: Filippi 1997, no. 39

A young Muslim gentleman is seen at his ease, holding a flower in his hand as a mark of refinement. His only jewellery is an archer's thumb-ring, an allusion to his prowess as a huntsman. His green turban with a plume would also have been appropriate for the hunting-field. It is complemented by a pale yellow robe with green trefoil sprig pattern, tied on the right side in the Muslim fashion.

This sensitive bust portrait clearly follows earlier Mughal models (no. 16), though its outline drawing artfully simplifies and enhances the subtle curves of the lips, nostril, ear, eye and brow. While remaining close to life, the facial features are to this extent idealised and refined by the Rajasthani court artist. This painter probably worked at a court such as Kishangarh, where strong Mughal influences were assimilated during the eighteenth century, giving rise to a highly expressive local style which took such enhancements of the human features to ever advancing degrees of stylisation (no. 97).

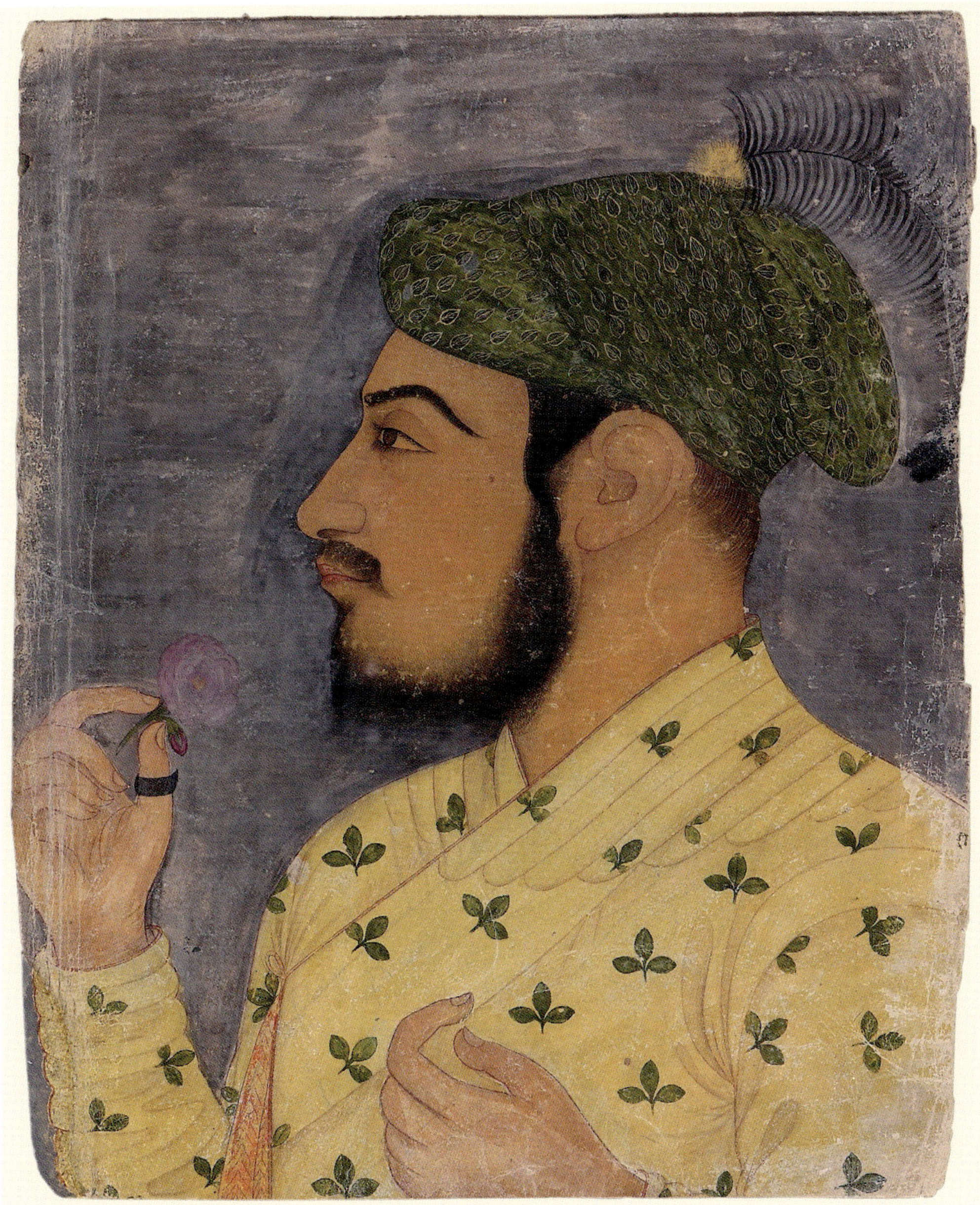

87 Maharaja Raj Singh of Junia

Junia, Rajasthan, *c.* 1698. Attributed to Chand
Brush drawing with colour, 56 × 35 cm
Hodgkin Loan 33
Published: Topsfield and Beach 1991, no. 5; Filippi 1997, no. 33

Raj Singh, ruler of a small state in the Ajmer region, appears framed within a roughly sketched *jharoka* window, of the kind used by the Mughal emperors and other rulers to show themselves to the people. Wearing the tall turban of the Rathor clan, Raj Singh holds a rose, which like his lips and jewellery has been sparingly heightened with colour. In this large scale portrait study, the artist shows his mastery of fluent and expressive outline, together with his spare but effective modelling of the ruler's face and costume. It can be attributed to the artist Chand,[1] whose works are related in style to the leading Rathor court of Jodhpur, as well as the small court of Sawar, twenty miles south of Junia (nos. 89–92).

This portrait study is closely related to a larger, fully coloured painting by Chand of Raj Singh with attendants in a flowering garden.[2] Raj Singh is depicted there in similar pose and attire and again behind a low balustrade, though holding a wine-cup instead of a flower.

1 A portfolio of Chand's work, bearing the seal of Raj Singh and the date 1698, was formerly in the collection of the late Kumar Sangram Singh of Nawalgarh: Singh 1965, pp. 39–40. It included a self-portrait by Chand, as yet unpublished.

2 Late Kumar Sangram Singh Collection, Jaipur: illus. Topsfield ed. 2000, p. 8, fig. 8; Topsfield and Beach 1991, p. 70, fig. 3.

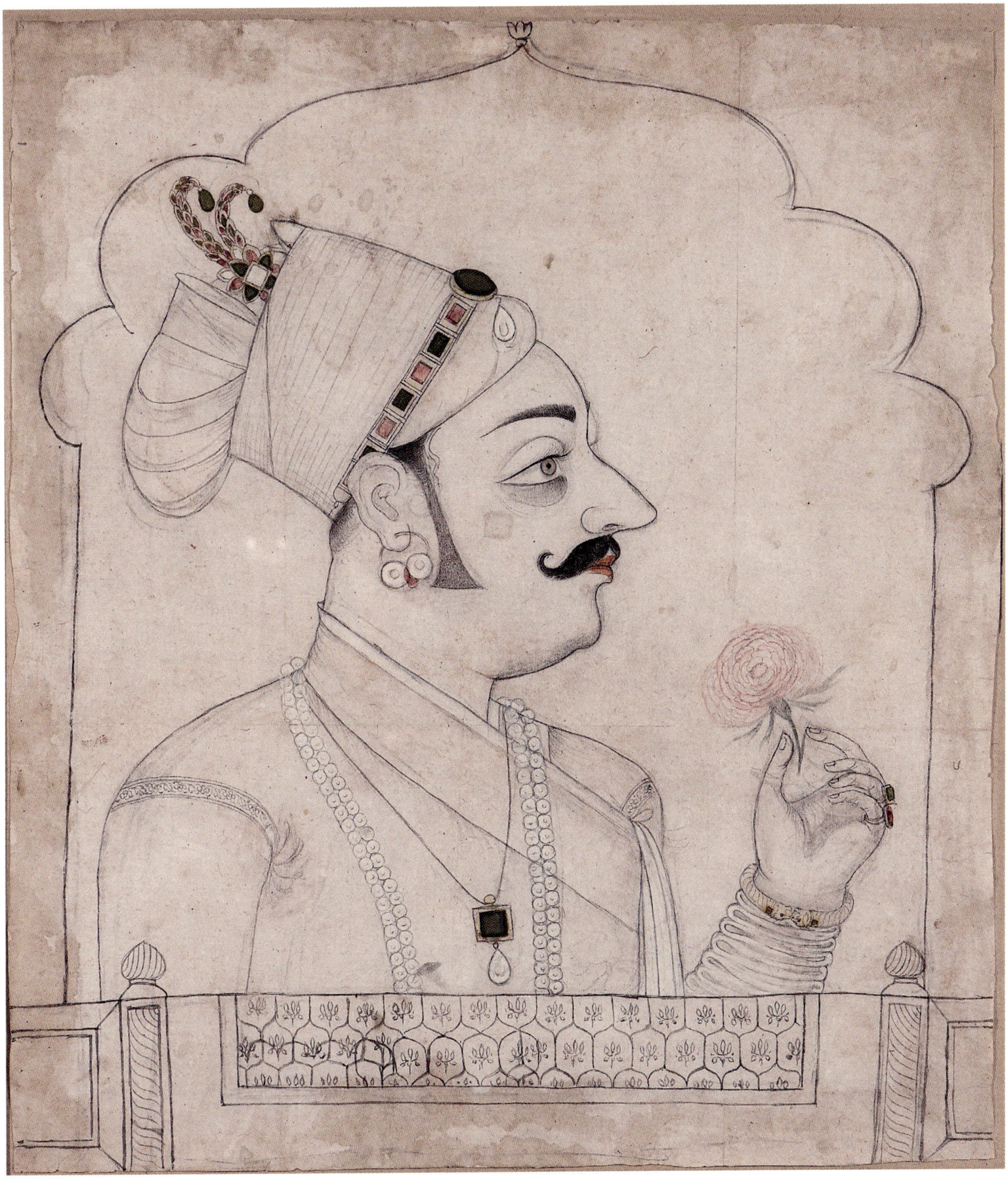

88 Maharaja Bakhat Singh

Nagaur, Rajasthan, *c.*1735
Gouache with gold on paper, 43.5 × 30.5 cm[1]
Hodgkin Loan 36
Published: Heeramaneck 1984, pl.81; Topsfield and Beach 1991, no.26; Filippi 1997, no.36

In this *jharoka* window portrait of Maharaja Bakhat Singh (1706–52), the strong profile depiction of the Rathor prince with his flamboyant moustache and side-whiskers is complemented by a rich interplay of floral patterned textiles and architectural ornament. Bakhat Singh appears against a pale green ground, holding a rose sprig and wearing a turban with pink floral motifs on a green ground and a white robe with a bold iris pattern, as well as pearls and jewels. A finely detailed Mughal floral textile is draped over the balcony. The arch above has delicately painted spandrels and prominent foliated scrolls and lotus pendants. This painting and a companion piece[2] are among the finest eighteenth century portraits from the Marwar region.

The younger son of Maharaja Ajit Singh of Jodhpur, Bakhat Singh murdered his father in 1724 in circumstances that remain obscure.[3] His brother Abhai Singh, who may have connived at the parricide, awarded him the territory of Nagaur soon after. At Nagaur, a desert city north-east of Jodhpur, Bakhat Singh distinguished himself as a patron of architecture and painting. He built a pleasure palace with white stucco walls elegantly painted with floral designs, and for twenty years he commissioned a series of remarkable large paintings showing him engaged in pleasurable pursuits in his new palace and its extensive gardens. In two such scenes he appears at a *jharoka* window.[4]

Bakhat Singh is otherwise remembered as a cultivated prince, having

> a joyousness of soul ... which, united to an intrepidity and a liberality alike unbounded, made him the very model of a Rajput. To these qualifications were superadded a majestic mien and Herculean frame, with a mind well versed in all the literature of his country, besides poetic talent of no mean order...[5]

He eventually succeeded to the Jodhpur throne in 1751, but died soon after from the effects of a poisoned robe given to him by a vengeful niece.[6]

1 Mutilated devanagari inscription on the reverse: *...sri 108 sri... vakhat singhji.*
2 National Gallery of Canada, Ottawa: Heeramaneck 1984, pl.82; Diamond and Glynn 2008, no.9: Glynn suggests these large *jharoka* portraits may have been made as presentation gifts to fellow clansmen or other Rajput nobles. For another *jharokha* portrait of Bakhat Singh, see Crill 1999, pl.67; Topsfield and Beach 1991, p.72, fig.4.
3 Diamond and Glynn 2008, p.14 and refs.
4 Mehrangarh Fort Museum, Jodhpur: ibid., nos.10–20 (nos.15 and 17 show *jharoka* scenes).
5 Tod 1971, II, p.1057.
6 Ibid., pp.866–67.

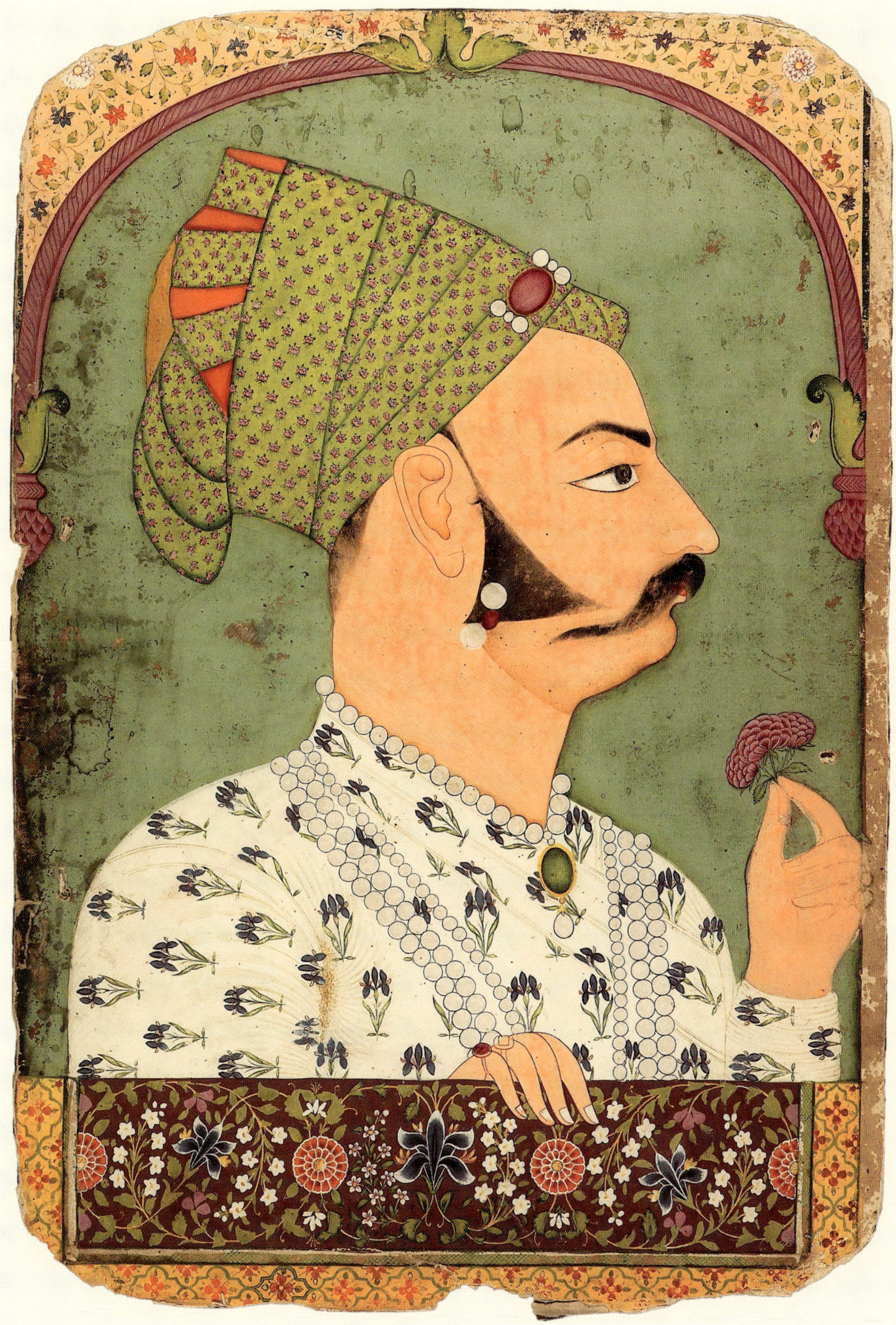

89 Maharaja Raj Singh in a garden arcade

Sawar, Rajasthan, *c.*1710–15
Gouache with gold on paper, 29 × 39.2 cm
Hodgkin Loan 41
Published: Filippi 1997, no.41

In this unusual portrait, the imposing figure of Raj Singh of Sawar (r.1705–30) appears, flower in hand, against a strong pale green ground, as if he is displaying himself ceremonially at a palace *jharoka* window. Yet the decorative cusped arch which frames him is no public viewing balcony, but part of an arcade set in a secluded pleasure garden. The gold-embroidered cloth on which he rests his hand covers a low garden wall, with flowering plants, a fountain and water-course in front of it and a row of flowering shrubs behind. In this agreeable retreat he is waited on by female attendants, who are depicted as half his size. One bears porcelain wine-flasks on a tray, the other waves a peacock-feather fan. Raj Singh seems to have delighted both in gardens (no.90) and in the company of women.[1]

Established in the time of Jahangir, Sawar was a small Sisodia Rajput kingdom in the Ajmer region of central Rajasthan, virtually on the borders of Amber, Mewar, Bundi and Kota. The local style of painting that flourished there, above all in the time of Raj Singh, shows some affinities to the court styles of those neighbouring kingdoms, but retained its own distinctive, often freely improvisational vision.

1 E.g. Welch 1997b, illus p.21; Weber 1982, Abb.110; Topsfield ed. 2004, no.148.

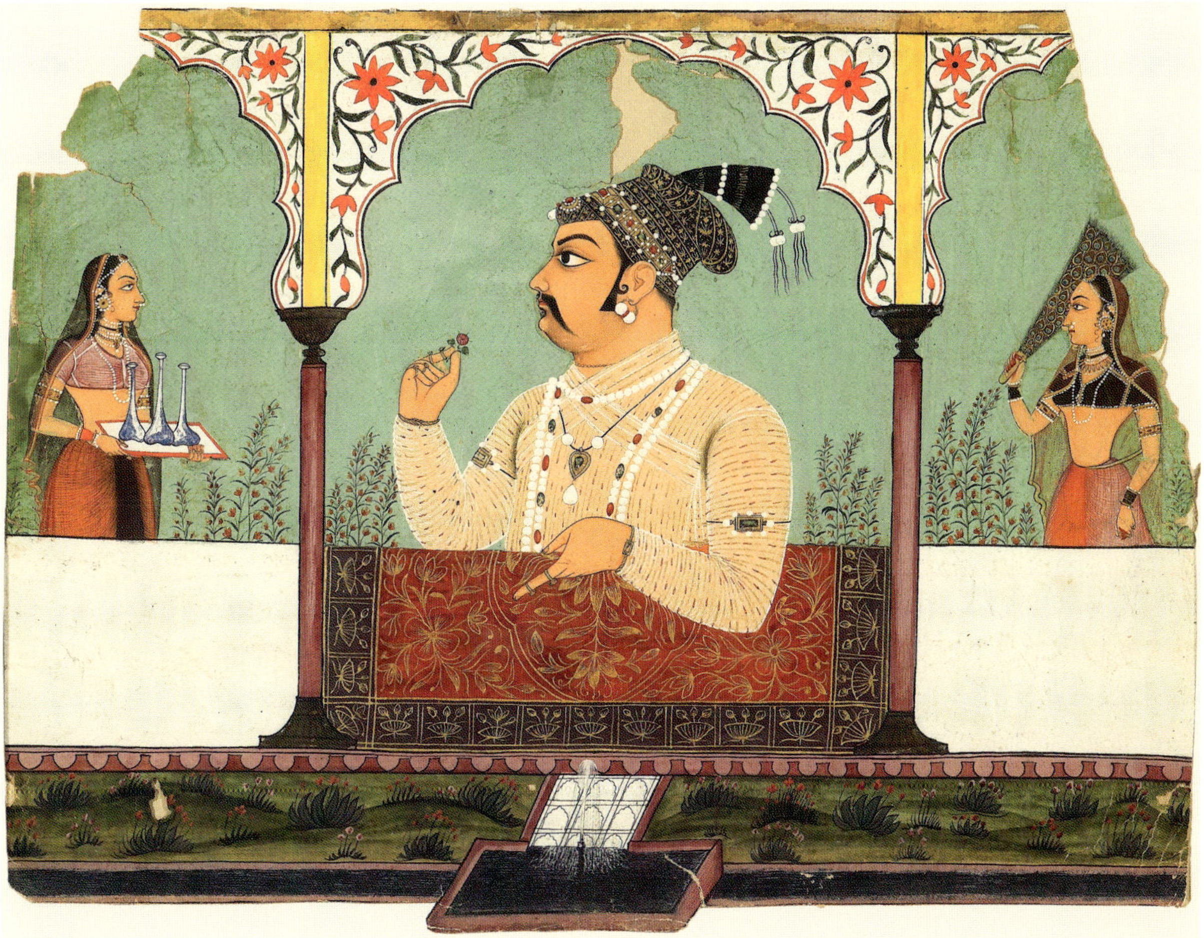

90 Maharaja Raj Singh receives a yogi in a garden

Sawar, Rajasthan, *c.*1714

Gouache on paper, 48 × 53 cm[1]

Hodgkin Loan 25

Published: Singh 1965, no.88 (not illus.); Hodgkin and McInerney 1983, no.42; Topsfield and Beach 1991, no.24; Filippi 1997, no.25

Using the uncoloured buff paper as its ground, this is a picture of exceptional charm, combining court painting conventions with the decorative freedoms of Rajasthani folk art. As Howard Hodgkin has remarked, "it has a peculiar combination of the naïve and sophisticated, particularly in terms of scale."[2]

Maharaja Raj Singh, the largest figure, is receiving an important yogi on the terrace of his royal garden. Seated on a low throne and smoking his hookah, he converses with his guest, a smaller figure, long of beard and finger-nail, who also smokes, seated within a creeper-festooned pavilion. Between them, pigeons strut and a small royal child waves a rattle. On either side are the usual courtiers and attendants. Below, on the far side of the formal garden with its square plots, fountain, cypresses and flowering trees, bands of male and female musicians are playing, and between them, completing the symmetry of the composition, is a pair of tiny fighting elephants, presumably ornamental sculpted figures.[3] The garden meanwhile teems with multicoloured birds, including peacocks, doves, parrots, hoopoes and others more naïve and indistinguishable. The birds which flock to the pigeon roost at upper left include one or two shown frontally and foreshortened. Both birds and music seem to have been important to Raj Singh. His idea of felicity, as shown in another painting,[4] was to sit with his hookah in a bird-filled garden and be serenaded by his girl musicians.

1 A devanagari inscription on the reverse is partly obscured by repairs: *maharaja sri raj s[?inhaji]* (in another hand:) *[raja]sthan savar ka chhe;* (below:) *sam 1771 chhabi divali par najar ki di*: 'Maharaja Raj Singh...It is from Savar in [Raja]sthan...The picture was presented at the Diwali festival, V.S. 1771'.

2 Hodgkin and McInerney 1983, no.42.

3 They appear in an earlier, less schematic view of the same garden: Weber 1982, Abb. 110, pp.535–40; Cimino 1985, no.69.

4 Welch, 1997b, illus. p.21; also Lee 1960, no.52; Patnaik 1985, pl.27.

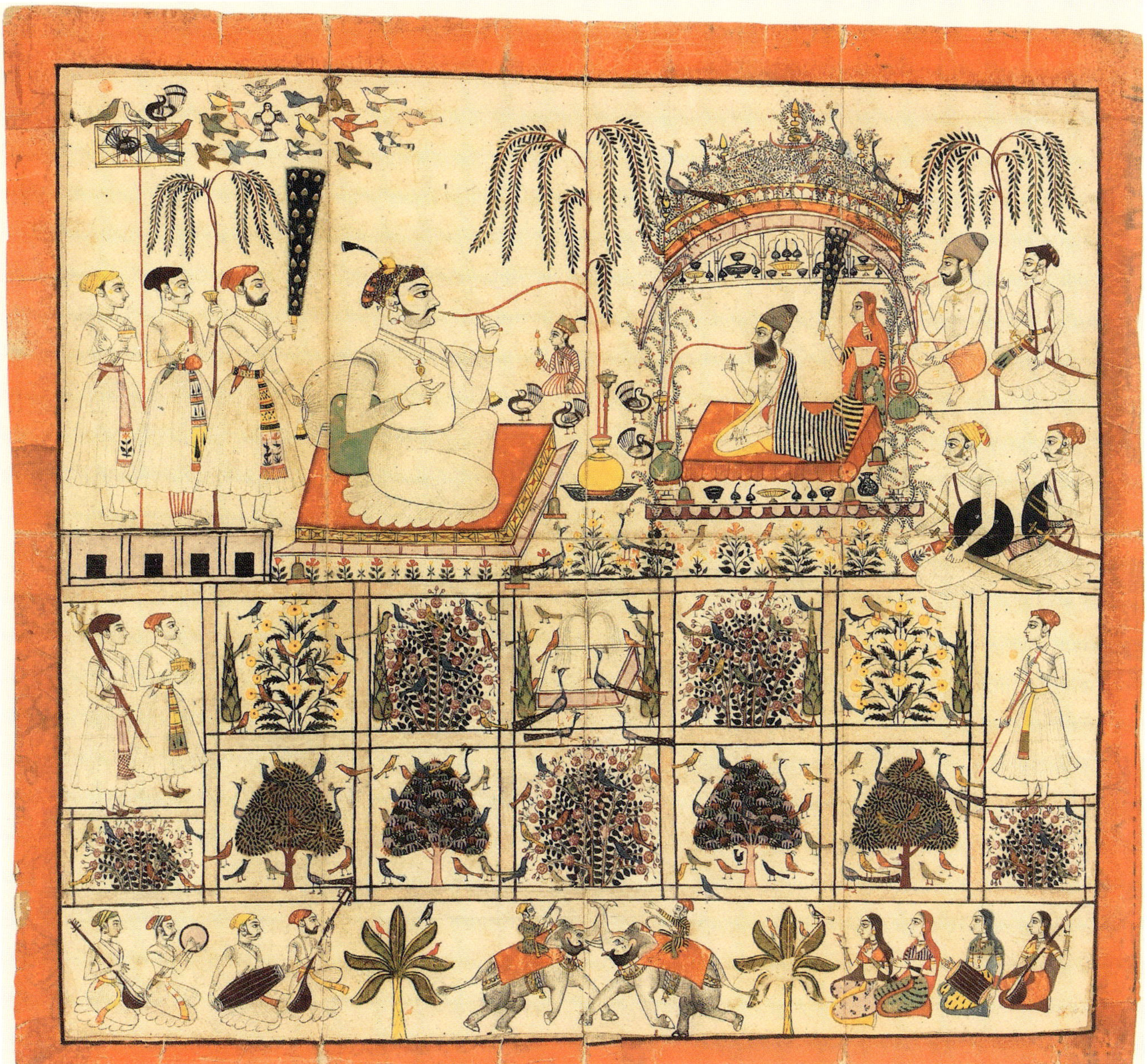

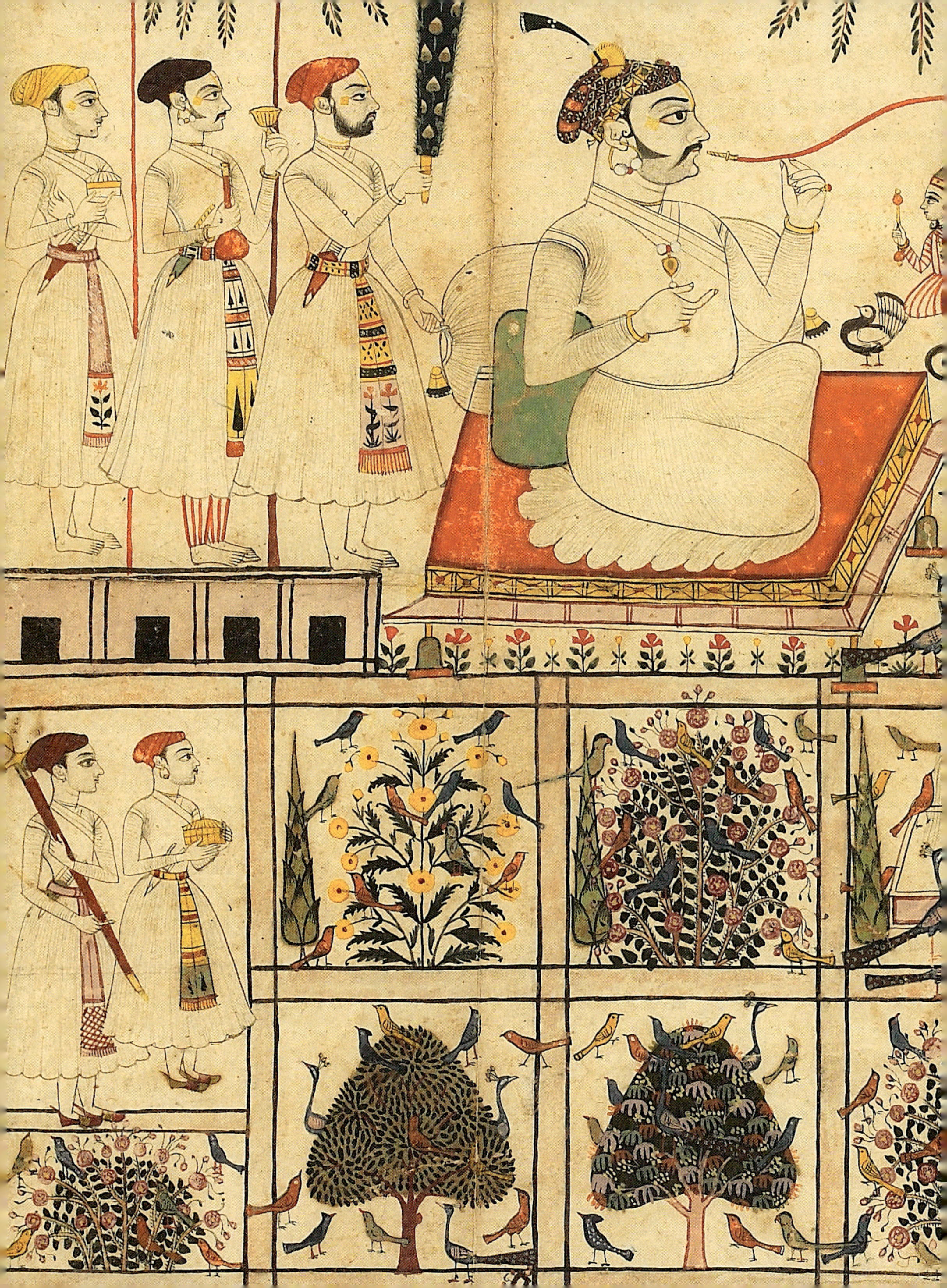

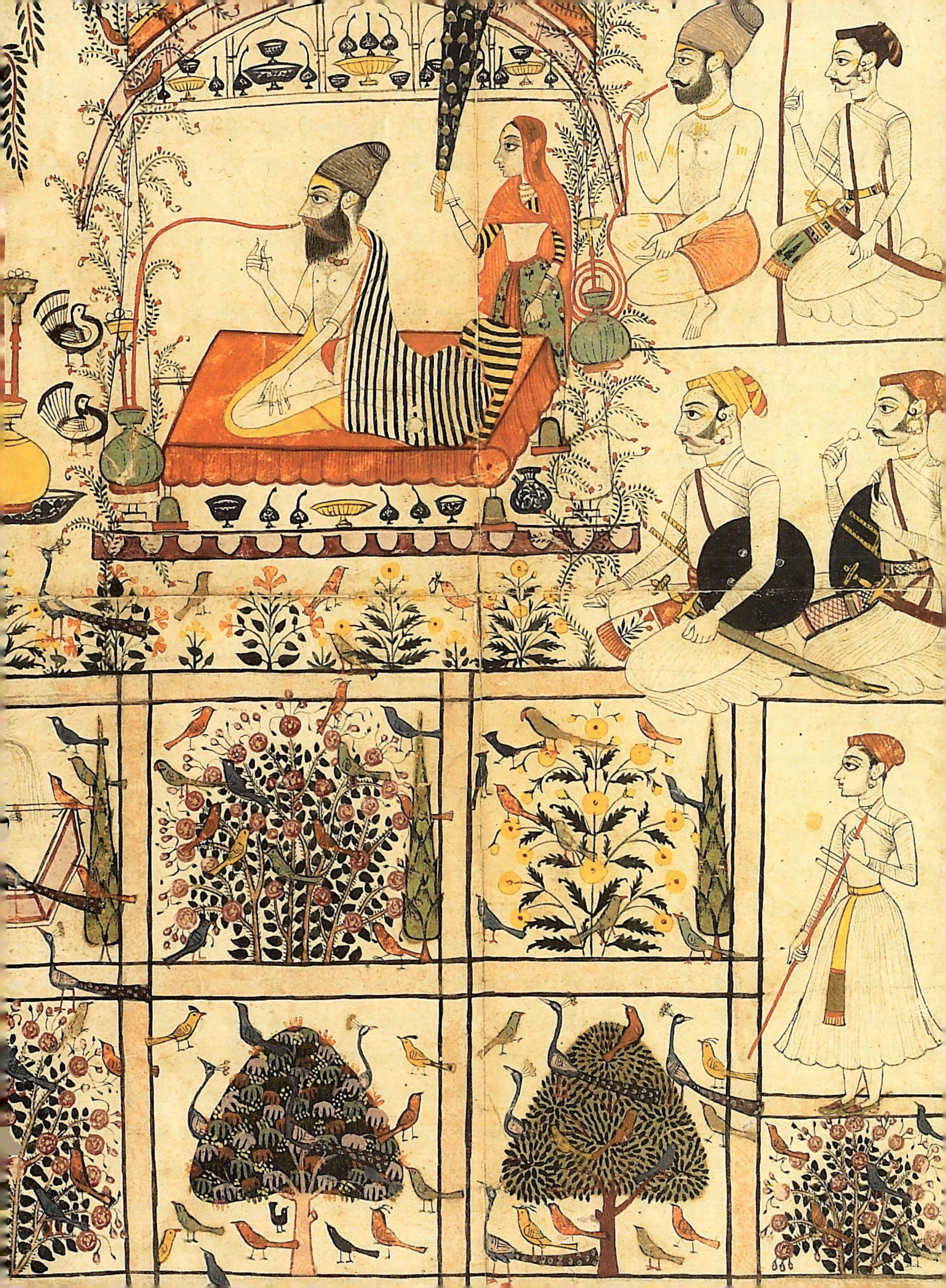

91 Maharaja Raj Singh and his elephants

Sawar, Rajasthan, *c.*1710–15
Brush drawing with gouache on paper, 52 × 61 cm[1]
Hodgkin Loan 73
Published: Hodgkin and McInerney 1983, no.32; Topsfield and Beach 1991, no.23; Filippi 1997, no.73

See also detail, p. 8

Maharaja Raj Singh (r.1705–30) rides in procession with his elephants, attendants and huntsmen with hawks. There are many more elephants, young and old, than a hunting trip would require, and it likely that the royal stable is being taken out into the country for exercise and recreation. Raj Singh rides on the largest elephant, with a boy mahout and the attendant Sevo with a peacock-feather fan. Other attendants carry the royal parasol, the Raja's *pandan* (betel-leaf box) and hookah. The human figures in the foreground are of widely varying scale, and some seem to have been improvised afterthoughts. As Howard Hodgkin remarks, "The technical elaboration of the drawing itself suggests that it must have been made as a work of art in its own right rather than as a study for something else."[2]

This is a picture of much élan and it is above all an elephant picture. From the skittish calves to the powerful veteran bearing the royal howdah, the fourteen elephants are drawn with a fluent and vigorous line and minimal colouring. Their progress is matched by that of the huntsmen and royal escort with the Raja's horse beyond the hill. Overhead, the royal hawks make their kills in a swooping sequence adapted from contemporary Mewar works (nos.99–100). Sawar lies virtually on the borders of Mewar, among other kingdoms. While its chiefs had close ties with the Mewar ruling family at Udaipur, Bundi and Kota lay even closer, and there is an affinity also between Sawar elephant drawings and those of Kota.

1 Inscribed on the front in devanagari script: *kuvas sevo* ('the personal attendant Sevo'). A damaged inscription on the reverse appears to identify Maharaja Raj Singh. An unreliable later inscription on paper attached to the back of the picture reads: *maharaja sri rajai sinhaji chhabi sakar ki 1713.*

2 Hodgkin and McInerney 1983, no.32.

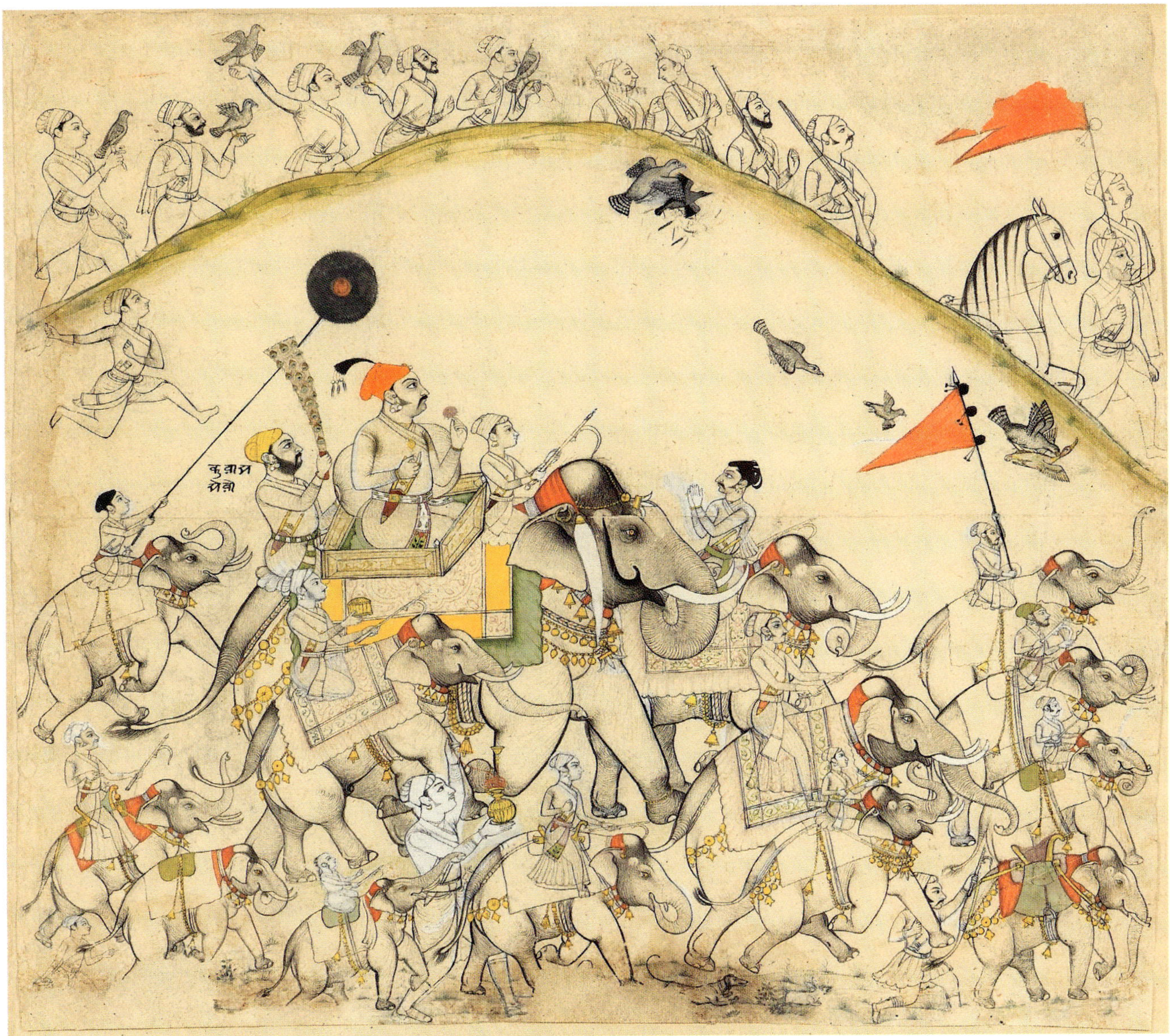

92 Page of sketches and figure studies

Sawar, Rajasthan, early 18th century
Brush drawing on paper with pigment, 40.6 × 62.9 cm
Hodgkin Loan 16
Published: Hodgkin and McInerney 1983, no.33; Filippi 1997, no.16[1]

See also detail, p. 282

This sheet of half a dozen sketches or preparatory studies for various subjects, mainly mythological, was compiled by a painter at the court of Sawar. Howard Hodgkin has called it "a random collection of figure studies and designs for pictures".[2] Some of the subjects are more developed than others. Several are spontaneous sketches adumbrating ideas for compositions, with a number of pentimenti or false starts visible.

At upper left, the artist has sketched a kind of compartmented shrine, containing two standing images of Krishna playing the flute and, more unusually, a horn. Various images of deities, swathed and otherwise, as well as ritual vessels, a bell and conch appear in its left side. Krishna appears again towards the centre of this sheet, standing in passionate embrace with his consort Radha within a forest bower, a conventional image that is treated more elaborately in a Sawar painting in an American collection.[3] At upper right is a more elaborate scene of Rama and Sita enthroned at the conclusion of the *Ramayana* epic, attended by Lakshmana, Rama's monkey allies, rishis (sages) and the large figure of Vibhishana (no.93). Rapidly sketched deities shower flowers from the sky.

Below this at lower right, Rama and Sita appear again with Lakshmana, in their exile in a mountainous forest earlier in the epic narrative. Adjacent to this is a small scene of a lady visiting a holy man in a forest grove. Finally at lower left is a sketch, no doubt observed from life, of Maharaja Raj Singh of Sawar (nos.89–91) seated informally with courtiers and clerical staff. His dagger lying beside him, he is perhaps discussing court business, although three of the figures hold *malas* or prayer beads.

This sheet of artist's studies is a fortunate survival, perhaps rescued from the vicissitudes of the Rajasthani paper trade in the 1950s and 60s, when many old drawings from defunct artists' studios were sold for scrap by weight. Some at least were rescued from recycling by the more discerning local art dealers and connoisseurs.

1 Also exhibited and published in D. Petherbridge, *The primacy of drawing*, London, 1991, p.23, no.14; and M. Craig-Martin, *Drawing the line*, London, 1996, p.19, no.169.
2 Hodgkin and McInerney, no.33.
3 Spink 1971, fig.68.

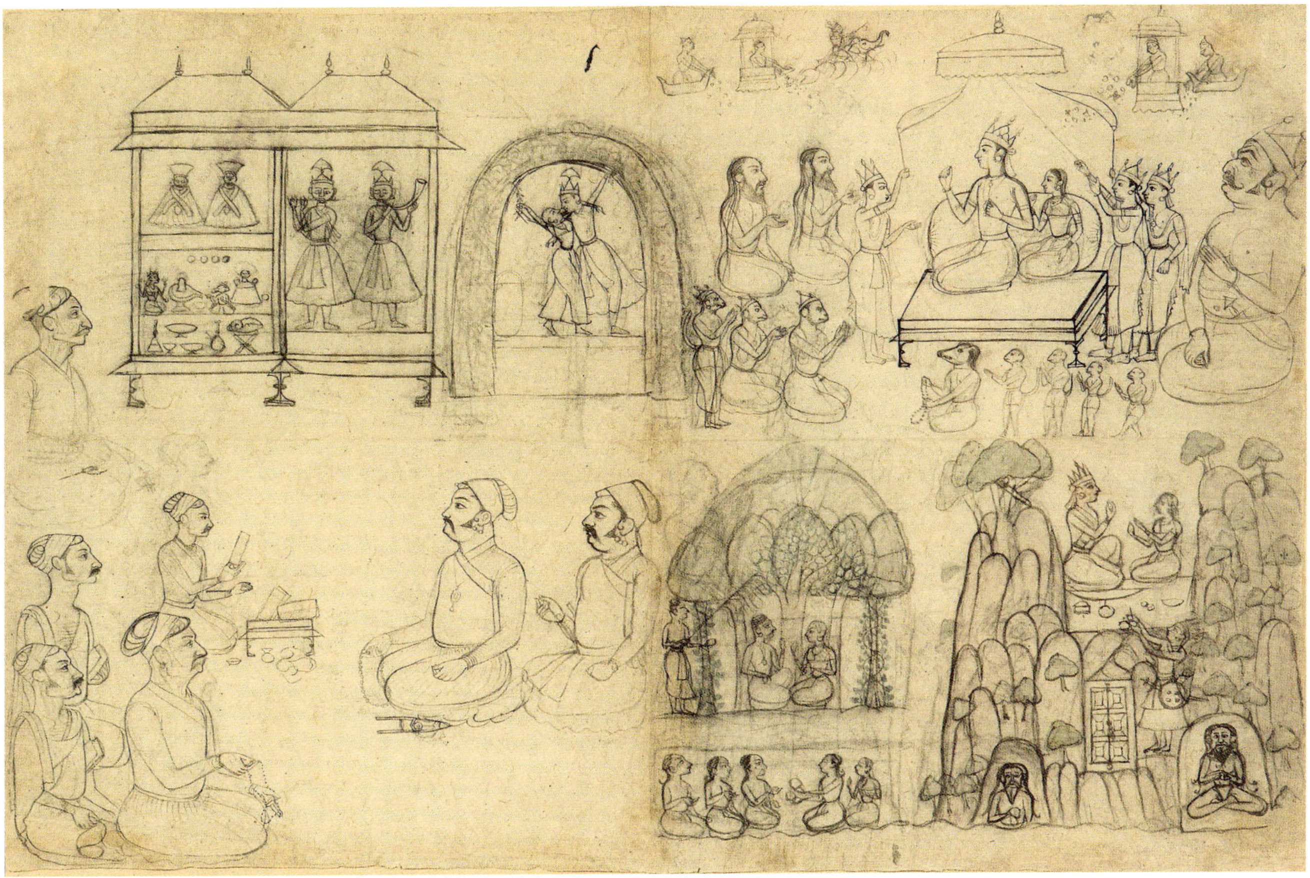

93 Vibhishana in the camp of Rama

Illustration to the *Ramayana*
Sawar, Rajasthan, *c.*1700
Gouache on paper, 67 × 45 cm
Hodgkin Loan 11
Published: Arts Council 1982, no.383 (not illus.); Topsfield and Beach 1991, no.21; Filippi 1997, no.11

Vibhishana ('the Terrifying') was the more righteous brother of Ravana, the demon king of Lanka in the *Ramayana* epic. Ravana had abducted Rama's wife Sita and brought her to his palace at Lanka, but ultimately he would be defeated by Rama, Lakshman and their monkey and bear allies. When Rama and his allies lay siege to Lanka, Vibhishana tries unsuccessfully to dissuade Ravana from fighting against Rama. He then goes over to Rama's side,[1] as shown here. Later, after Ravana's death, Vibhishana will succeed to the throne of Lanka.

In Rama's camp under a starry sky, the mustachioed Vibhishana kneels respectfully before the divine hero, who reclines regally on a deer-skin rug at the centre of the composition, holding arrows at the ready in his hand. His head rests on the monkey king Sugriva's lap, while Hanuman massages his feet. His half-brother Lakshmana is seated behind. Rama, Lakshmana and Hanuman wear leaf and flower-patterned dhotis which recall the simple leaf skirts they had adopted during their earlier exile in the forest. Meanwhile Shuka, a demon emissary from Lanka, is led into Rama's presence by two monkeys. He has been sent by Ravana in a vain attempt to undermine Sugriva's loyalty. Rama then saves Shuka from a beating by the outraged monkeys and returns him to his master. Meanwhile the monkey and bear warriors look on, groom themselves or sleep. They vary greatly in scale, from the huge mace-bearing monkey guards at the corners of the picture to smaller and less anthropomorphic figures, which are more animated and closely observed from life.

Only a few pages survive from this ambitious *Ramayana* series,[2] which shows great vigour and freshness in its figure painting, especially of animals and birds, and in its compositional groupings and bold shifts of scale. Here the artist unusually adopts a vertical rather than horizontal format, aligning the composition on the recumbent central figure of Rama.

1 Shastri tr. 1957, III, chs.14–20.
2 Other pages are in the Kanoria collection, Patna, and J.P. Goenka collection, Bombay.

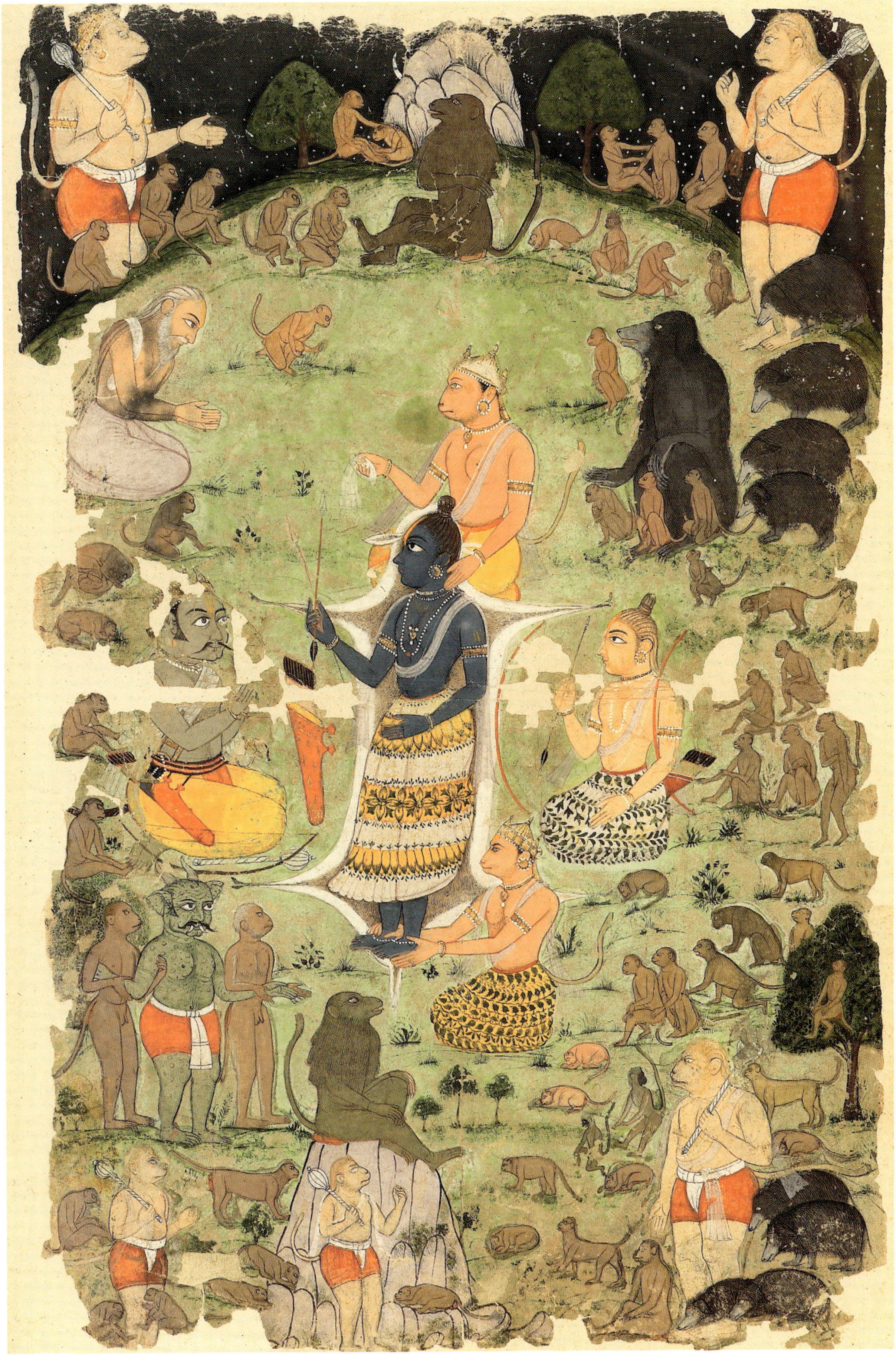

94 Maharaja Dhiraj Singh riding

Raghugarh, Central India, *c.*1700
Gouache on paper, 56 × 35 cm[1]
Hodgkin Loan 34
Published: Arts Council 1982, no.136 (not illus.); Topsfield and Beach 1991, no.18; Filippi 1997, no.34.

In an inspired variation on the equestrian portrait genre, Dhiraj Singh sits in calm self-possession astride his rearing horse, as if floating in an undifferentiated sea of pale green, the ground colour typically employed in Mughal portraiture. He holds a sword over his shoulder, while another hangs ready at his waist. With its flowing curves and dappled cheek, his majestic grey stallion is finely delineated and detailed. The only other figures are a pair of absurdly tiny attendants, a groom and fan-bearer in green, who trot gamely alongside their gigantic master and his mount. With his strong profile and powerful bearing, his curling moustache and suggestion of a smile, Dhiraj Singh is as always the focus of our attention (no.95).[2]

Lying just inside Madhya Pradesh, south-east of Bundi and Kota, Raghugarh maintained a vigorous local pictorial tradition from the late seventeenth century. Its rulers were the heads of the Khichi branch of the once-mighty Chauhan Rajputs. Dhiraj Singh (r.1697–1726) was as active a warrior as he appears here. Sir John Malcolm records that he waged successful campaigns against neighbouring kingdoms, and was of sufficiently high standing to receive the rulers of Udaipur and Jaipur and marry their daughters. Eventually he "was slain in an affray with the Aheer tribe, whom he had been long engaged in reducing to order."[3]

1 Inscribed above in devanagari script: *maharaja sri dhiraj singhji.*
2 E.g. also Welch 1985, no.251 (entry by J. Mittal); Fondation Custodia 2002, no.34, for further portraits of Raj Singh.
3 Malcolm 1972, I, p.464.

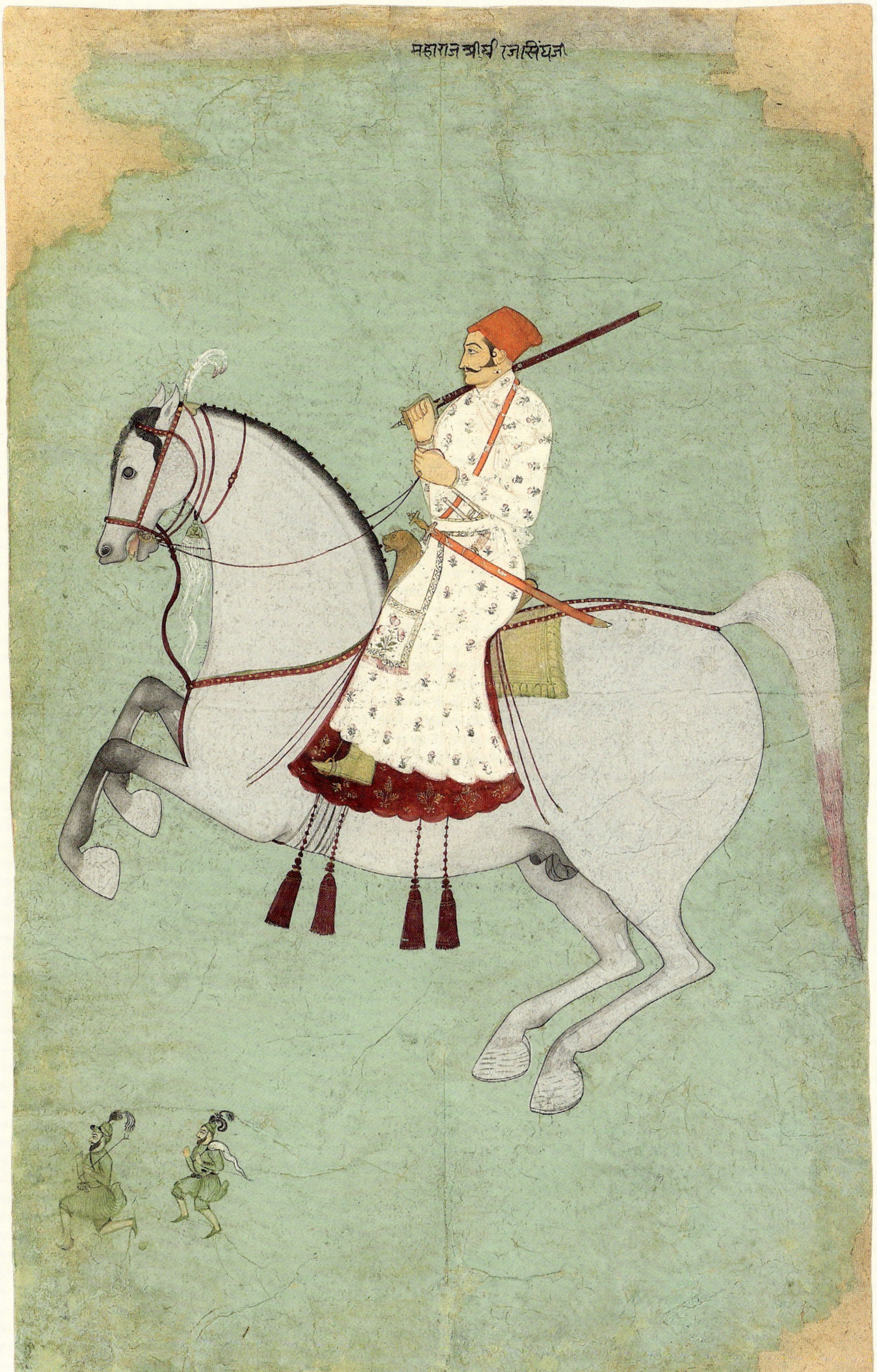

95 Maharaja Dhiraj Singh watches a nautch

Raghugarh, Central India, *c.*1700
Gouache with gold on paper, 27 × 19.4 cm
Hodgkin Loan 40
Published: Filippi 1997, no.40

The Raghugarh ruler Dhiraj Singh enjoys an evening nautch or dance performance on a palace terrace. Set against a warm, greyish ground, his powerful figure appears as always in profile, keen-eyed and with moustache impeccably curled. His duties for the day are over, so he holds a flower rather than a sword (no.94), and wears a rich crimson robe with gold floral trellis pattern. A crimson and yellow canopy hangs above him.

Seated in dignified self-possession, Dhiraj Singh appears wholly absorbed in the animated soirée of music and dance. Close to the Raja, the dark-skinned nautch girl half-kneels in a *kathak* dance pose, her hands raised with thumb and forefinger joined in an expressive gesture. Verging into the picture border, her companion with hand-cymbals and a male *pakhavaj* drummer beat out the rapid rhythms of the dance with rapt attention. All four figures, though perhaps not the absently gazing fan-bearer, participate in this dramatic moment of the dance.

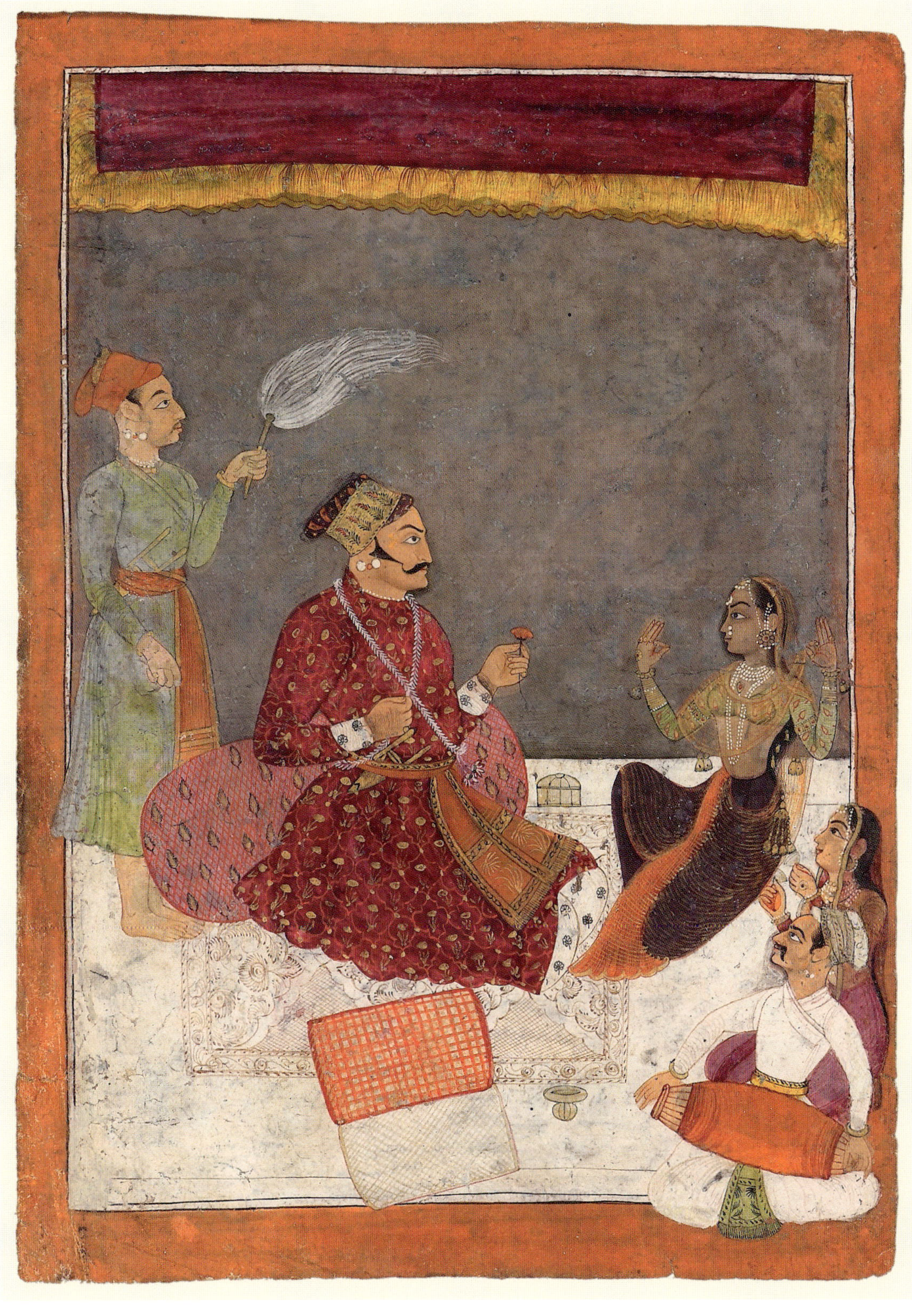

96 Sarat Purnima: The *gopis* dance in the forest

Kishangarh, Rajasthan, *c.*1720–25
Gouache on cotton cloth, 185 × 167 cm
Hodgkin Loan 30
Published: Filippi 1997, no.30; Pal ed. 1997, no.90a

This large temple hanging (*picchavai*) of the Vallabhacharya sect depicts four *gopis* (milkmaids) performing a joyful dance. It would have hung to the right of an image of Krishna playing his flute, with a matching hanging on the other side. Bejewelled and garlanded, the *gopis* hold hands as they dance before the cowherd god. The leading figure raises her free hand and gazes up at Krishna in adoration, while her companions look modestly downward. This subject is associated with the festival of Sarat Purnima, the full moon night of the autumn month of Ashvin, when Krishna took part in a round dance (*Rasmandala*) with the *gopis*, in which each felt herself to be dancing blissfully alone with the young god.[1]

Beneath the clear starlit sky which follows the passing of the monsoon, the sacred forest of Vrindavan is represented by three trees with trunks entwined by flowering creepers. In the central tree between two plantains, many of the perching birds also turn towards Krishna, as do the fish and waterfowl in the Jumna river below. Among the orb-like silver stars, celestial sky-boats (*vimana*) float overhead, carrying gods and heavenly beings (*gandharva*) who shower down lotus flowers. This procession is led by Indra in the first sky-vehicle, followed by a prince who bends to scatter flowers, then a further deity and a group of heavenly court musicians playing a horn, shehnai, cymbals and *naqqara* drum.

This early and refined *picchavai* by a Kishangarh court artist is highly charged with devotional and amorous feeling. Its figures and facial types with a characteristic elongated eye are typical of the earlier phase of Kishangarh painting, while the sky-boats and the forest with birds recall the painting style of Sawar, not far to the south. The prince shown scattering flowers above may be Savant Singh (b.1699), eldest son of Maharaja Raj Singh (r.1706–48), who became famous as a devotee of Krishna and as a devotional poet writing under the name Nagari Das.

1 As often shown in later *picchavai* iconography: e.g. Emerson, 1987, no.1, for a 19th century hanging showing the compositional ensemble as a whole, with the fluting Krishna flanked by the dancing gopis; also Skelton 1973, p.93 and nos.6–10.

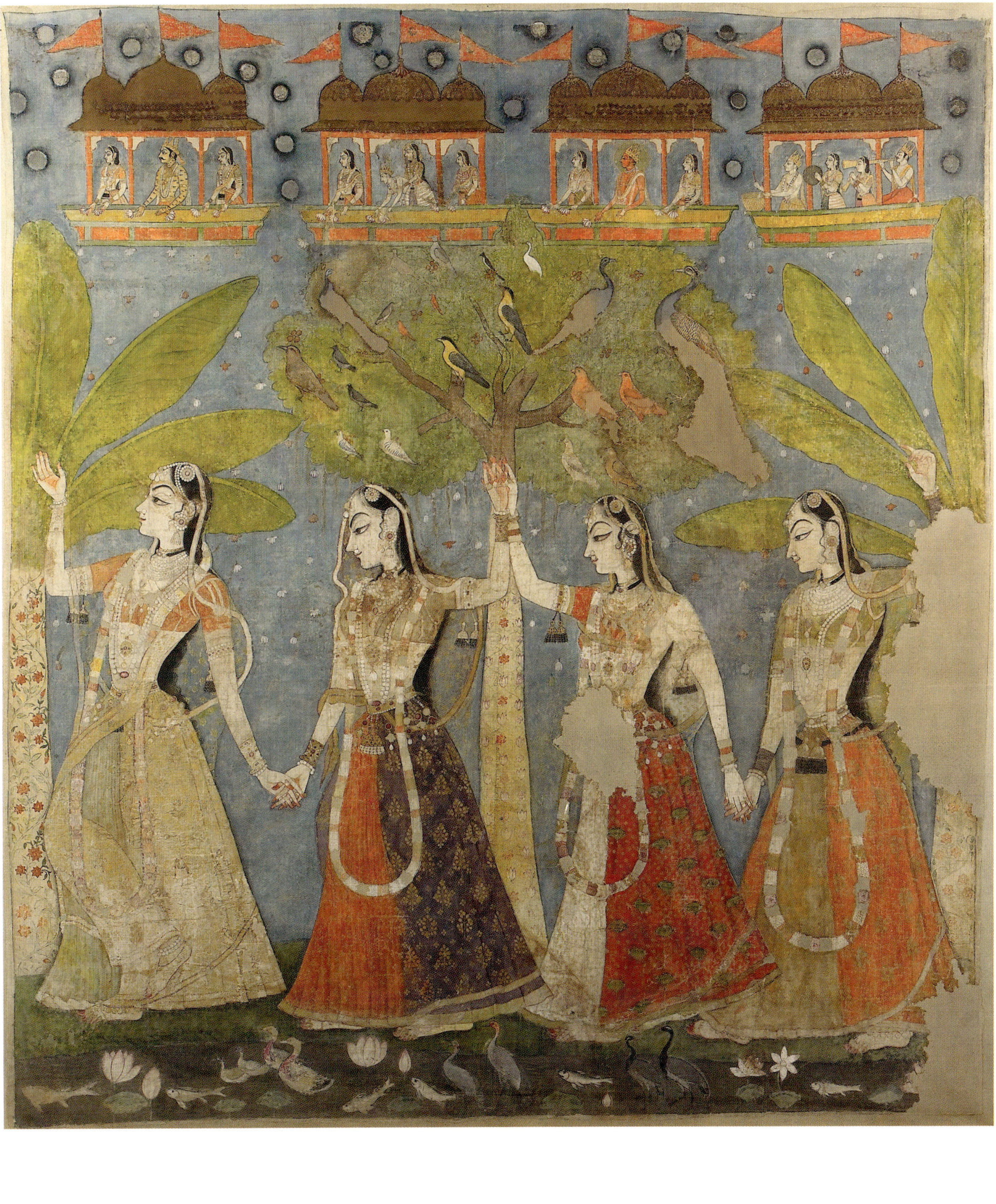

97 A lady singing

Kishangarh, Rajasthan, *c.*1740–45.
Possibly by Bhavani Das
Gouache with gold on paper, 37 × 25.5 cm[1]
Hodgkin Loan 31
Published: Topsfield and Beach 1991, no.38;
Brand 1995, no.105; Haidar 1995, fig.163;
Filippi 1997, no.31

Because of the seclusion of women in court society, authentic portraits of women are rare in traditional Indian painting. Court artists however could observe and record more accessible figures, such as the dancers and musicians who attended court gatherings. One such singer is depicted here as a *nayika*, a type of ideal heroine according to Indian poetical theory. Her lips slightly parted in song, she plucks a tanpura to provide a drone accompaniment. This elegant green and gilt instrument bisects the page diagonally. She opens her other, hennaed hand wide in an expressive gesture. Her upper body and long serpentine tresses are overlaid by a fine transparent shawl, freely rendered in broad washes and bold strokes of thin colour. This painterly style suggests the artist had received Mughal training, and it appears that this genre of idealised female portraits was introduced to Kishangarh by the master-painter Bhavani Das, to whom – or else to a close follower – this work can be attributed.[2]

The lady's pronounced profile, arching eyebrow and elongated, lotus-like eye typify the ideal of physical beauty developed by Kishangarh painters under Maharajas Raj Singh (r.1706–48) and Savant Singh (r.1748–64). Both were followers of the Vallabhacarya sect of Krishna worship and Savant Singh was a well-known devotional poet. The local painting style evolved into a lyrical and ultimately mannered expression of Vaishnava poetic feeling, in which the divine consorts Krishna and Radha were depicted together in idyllic palace and landscape settings. Such scenes may also have reflected Savant Singh's inseparability from the singer and poetess Bani Thani, who became his consort by the late 1730s and later accompanied him into retirement at holy Vrindavan in 1757.[3] The idealised lady in this picture[4] may not be Bani Thani, but represents a court singer of her kind.

1 Inscribed in devanagari on the back: *sabi nayaka gati hui* ('Picture of a *nayika* singing'); numbered 40, and a Kishangarh court stamp.
2 Haidar 1995, pp.175–76, fig.164; Haidar 2011a, p.545.
3 Dickinson and Khandalavala 1959, pp.8–12; Haidar 1995, pp.124–29.
4 Also e.g. Ehnbom 1985, no.72 (and Haidar 1995, fig.162), attributable to the same artist.

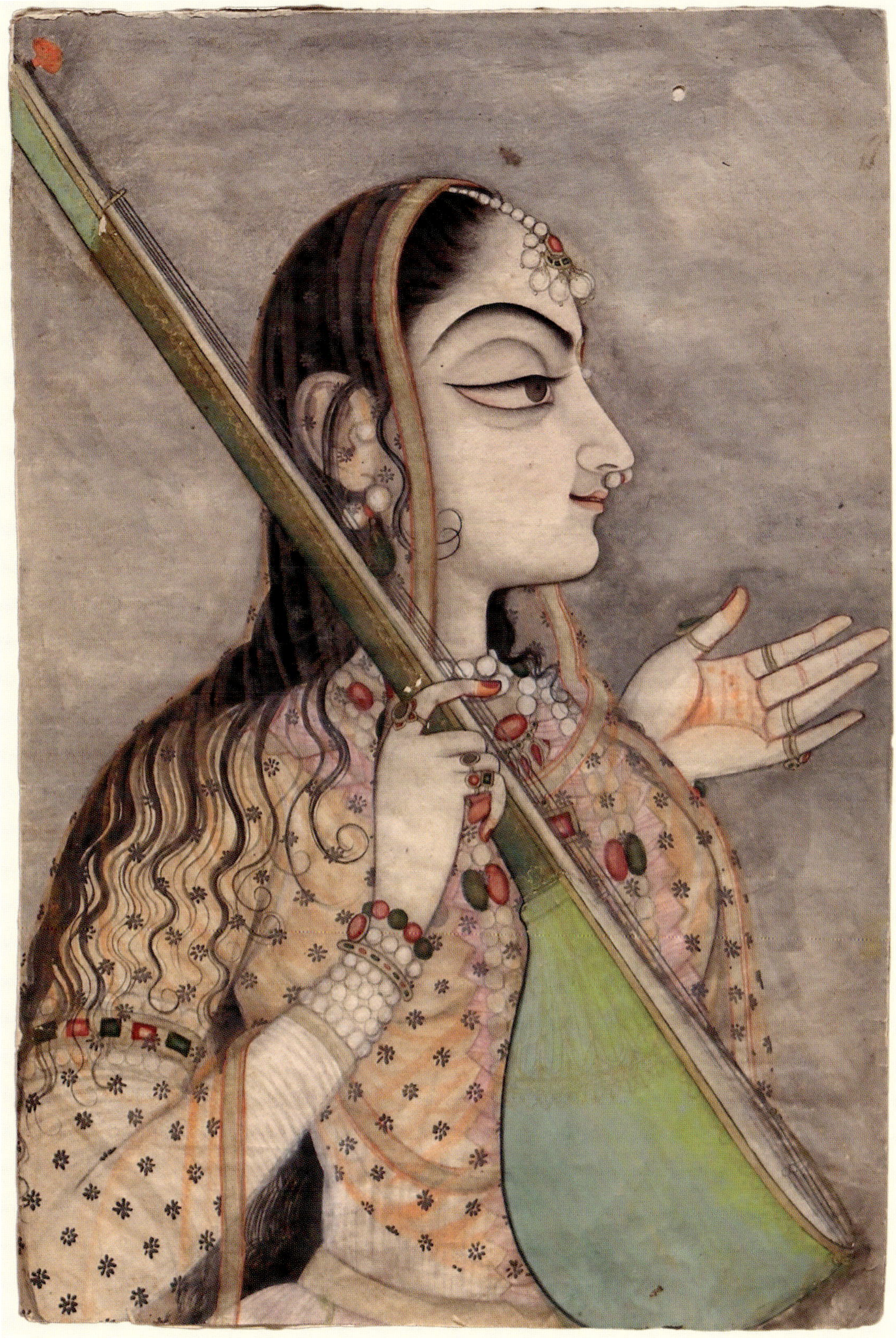

98 Maharana Amar Singh with his ladies

Udaipur, Rajasthan, *c.*1708–10
Gouache with gold on paper, 40 × 21 cm[1]
Hodgkin Loan 23
Published: Topsfield and Beach 1991, no.20; Filippi 1997, no.23; Williams 2007, no.13

As is evident from the paintings of his reign,[2] Amar Singh II of Mewar (r.1698–1710) greatly enjoyed the company of his zenana ladies – wives, concubines, maidservants, dancers and musicians. In this unusually pared down composition, the Rana and his ladies disport themselves decorously in three successive scenes which may represent the pastimes of a particular festive day. The Rana appears with the full beard which he adopted in the last three years before his death at the age of thirty-eight.

Above, the Maharana watches a nautch girl dancing in an arcaded hall, here coloured a strong blue, while female musicians and attendants stand at either side. In the central section, the party has moved to a bathing-pool with water stained red with saffron colouring, according to the inscription. While the women play or swim fully clothed in the water around him, the bare-chested Amar Singh stands waist deep and calmly smokes his hookah. Finally, in the Gulab Bari rose-garden, the ladies move among the bushes and heap rose-petals on gold trays, against a dark chocolate ground colour. The petals were used to make rose-water (*gulab*) or the strong liquor known as *gulabi*. Amar Singh stands as ever with hookah tube in hand, sampling petals offered by a lady. Because of topographical disjunctions between these episodes, the painter adopts a traditional narrative scheme of successive registers, each with its own distinguishing ground colour.

1 Inscribed in devanagari on the reverse: *maharana sri amar sanhaji vetha 1 / eka jaga kesar ko cevaco navai / eka jaga gulab badi ludavai*: 'Maharana Amar Singh is seated; in one place he bathes in a bath of saffron; in another he immerses himself (?) in the Gulab Bari (Rosewater Garden)'. This inscription has been reattached to the backing of the picture following conservation work. Besides losing its borders and being trimmed at the edges, the painting has at some time been divided and rejoined along a line between its first and second registers.

2 E.g. Topsfield 2002, figs.88, 105–8.

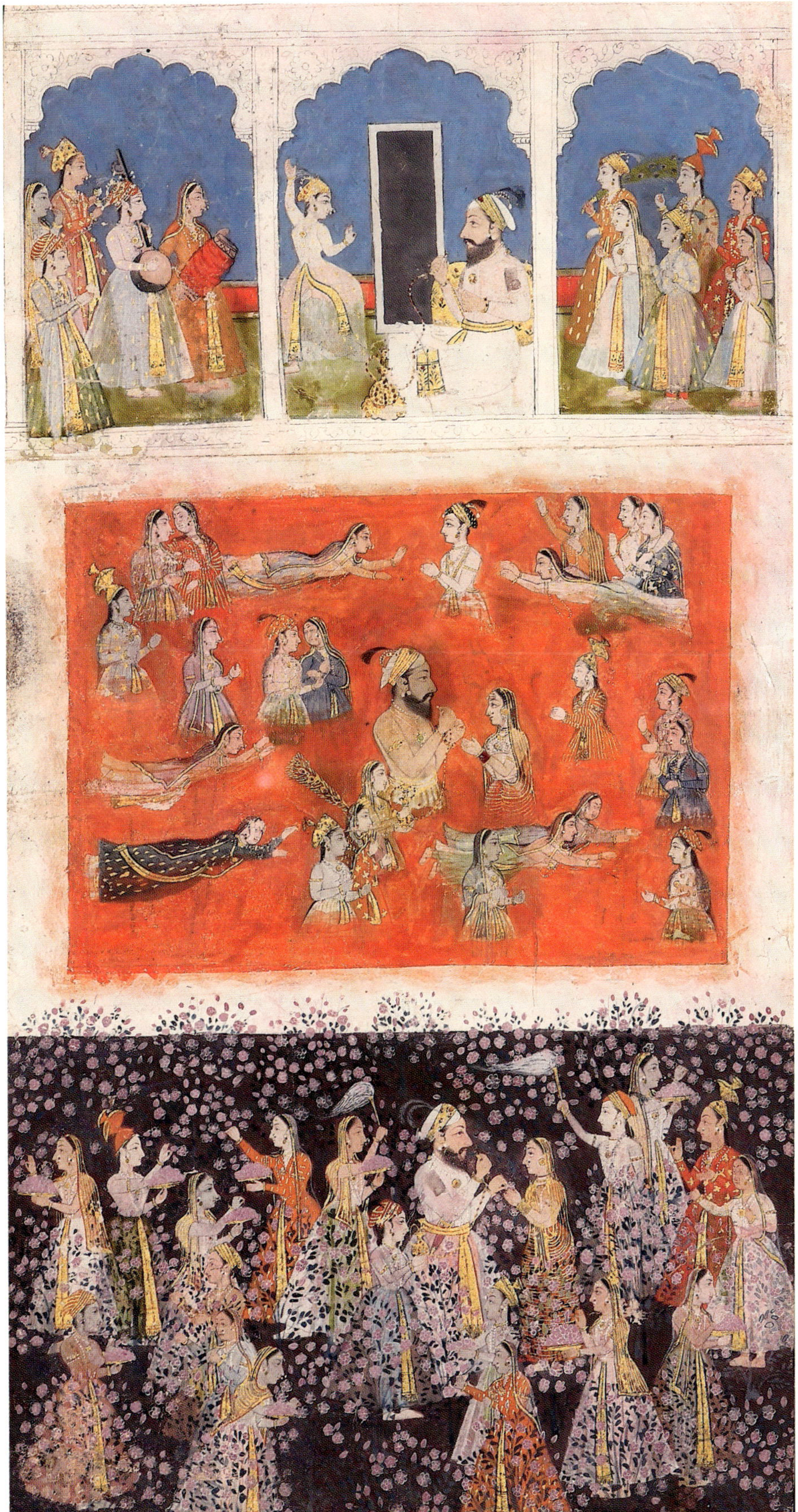

99 Maharana Amar Singh hunting sarus crane

Udaipur, Rajasthan, *c.*1700
Gouache on paper, 31 × 43.5 cm
Hodgkin Loan 76
Published: Falk et al. 1978, no.56 (not illus.); Topsfield and Beach 1991, no.19; Filippi 1997, no.76; Williams 2007, no.11

In this engaging picture painted not long after his accession, Maharana Amar Singh II of Mewar (r.1698–1710) is seen on a hawking expedition in open country. In an old-fashioned convention deriving from manuscript painting, he appears twice, outlined against a schematic blue hill, in consecutive scenes punctuated by the central tree. On the left, his shikaris (huntsmen) point out a group of sarus cranes that have gathered near a river. The royal hawk is then released. It pursues the frightened flock, finally bringing down a crane in the (damaged) far right corner. There the shikaris congratulate the Maharana as he inspects the kill while smoking his hookah. In the landscape beyond, also divided into separate colour areas, villagers and their animals are seen in the fields and marshes, a lady fetches water and another rocks her baby under a tree.

An innovative patron, Amar Singh did much to introduce the Mughal-inspired genre of portraiture at Udaipur. He had working for him a gifted and versatile but unnamed master artist, to whom this picture can attributed.[1] An original and freshly observed work, it is the earliest example of a royal hawking portrait in Mewar, predating by a few years a comparable subject by the same painter in the stippled, grisaille style that he frequently adopted.[2]

1 For a recent study of this master see Glynn 2011b; also Topsfield 2002, pp.117–37.
2 National Gallery of Victoria, Melbourne: Topsfield 1980, no.57; Topsfield 2002, fig.99.

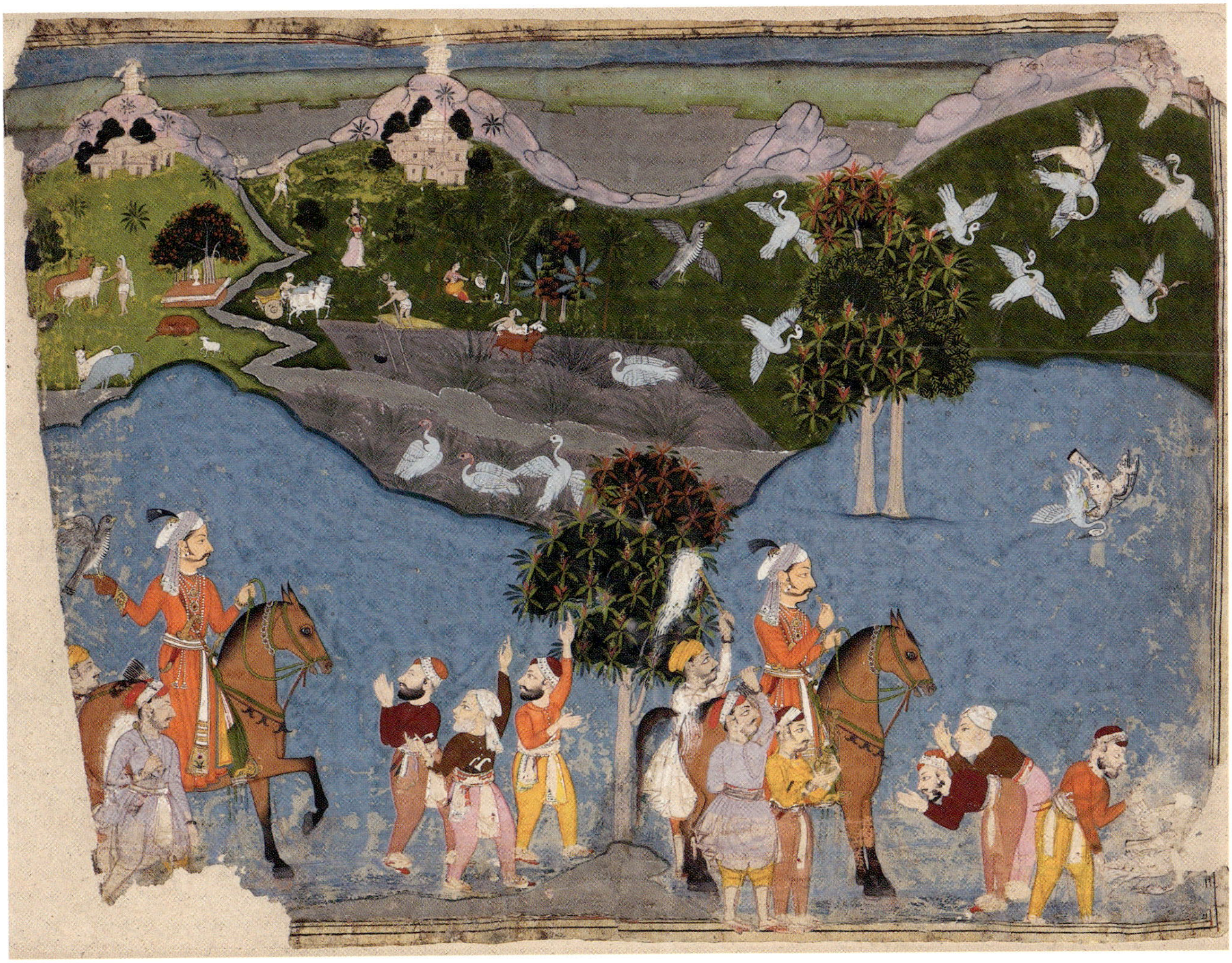

100 Sangram Singh Ranawat hawking

Udaipur, Rajasthan, *c.*1705–8
Gouache with gold on paper; 31 × 43.5 cm
Hodgkin Loan 78
Published: Hodgkin and McInerney 1983, no.34; Topsfield and Beach 1991, no.21; Filippi 1997, no.78

Sangram Singh, a noble of the Ranawat clan,[1] rides a well-groomed stallion on a hawking expedition. An attendant waves a yak-tail fan and others carry his shield and sword in cloth covers. The leading attendant and the huntsman walking ahead gesture forwards, as the deftly sketched hawk seizes a fowl in flight and brings it to the ground. As Howard Hodgkin remarks, "the unusual heavily shaded technique, with slight colour, is typical of a group of drawings made at Mewar in the late seventeenth and early eighteenth centuries. This is a particularly good example. Note the almost Romanesque group of attendants in the centre."[2]

Deriving from earlier Mughal and Deccani models, this use of heavy stippled shading with a largely uncoloured ground is found in many portraits of Maharana Amar Singh II (r.1698–1710) by his anonymous leading painter. Here the sensitively drawn horse and the statuesque human figures at least could be by that master's hand. The composition also is closely related to *Amar Singh hunting sarus crane* (no.99), for example in the way the hawk brings down its prey in consecutive stages. The sparse landscape, with a distant village and ploughman at far right, is here suggested by discreetly pink-shaded hill outlines and a few simple trees, with other trees and greenery crudely shaded with a dabbed cloth-pad.

1 Inscribed on the back in devanagari script: *ranovat sagaram syaghji*. A cadet branch of the ruling Sisodiya clan, the Ranawats were descendants of the offspring of Rana Udai Singh (1536-72). Sangram Singh Ranavat occasionally appears as a peripheral figure in later Udaipur court scenes. However some confusion could have arisen here between this Ranawat noble and Prince Sangram Singh, the son of Amar Singh, of whom this picture could well be a likeness a few years before his accession in 1710: for discussion, see Topsfield and Beach 1991, p.62.

2 Hodgkin and McInerney 1983, no.34.

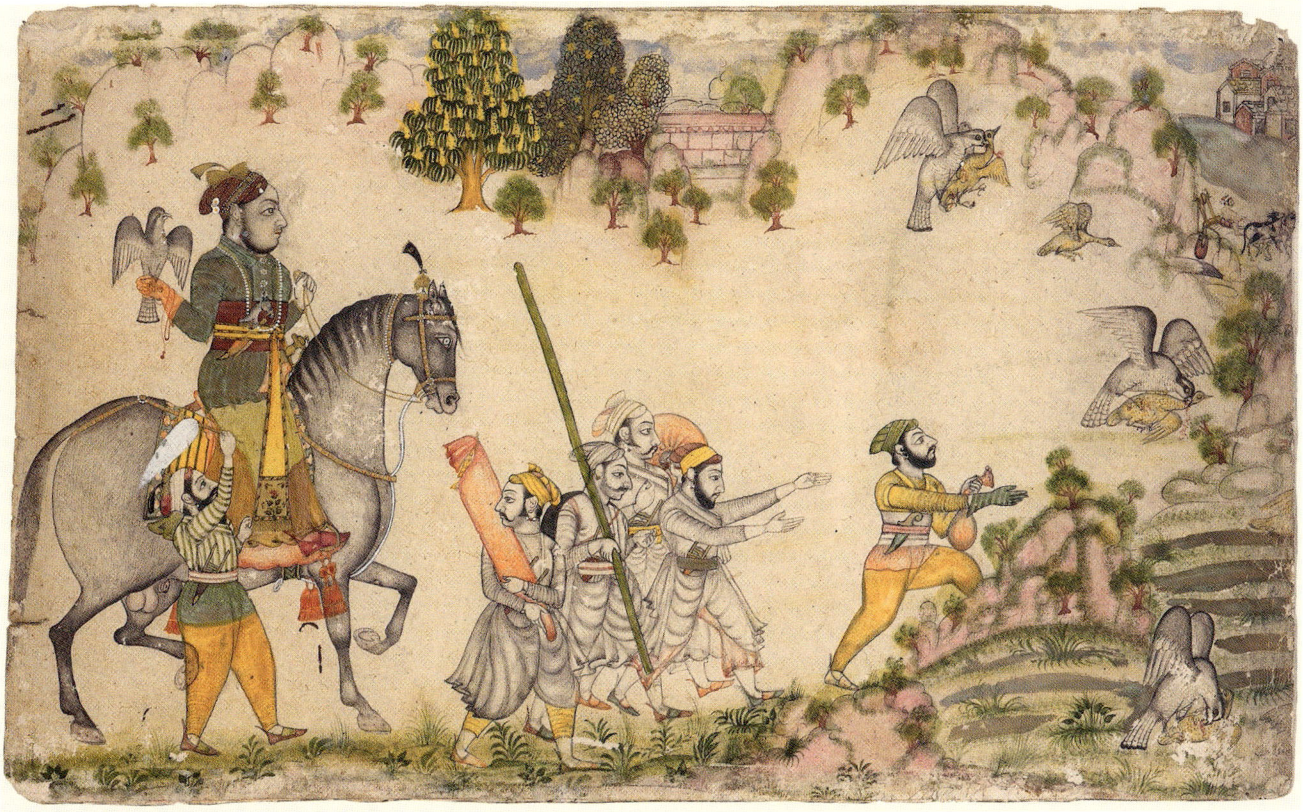

101 Maharana Jagat Singh in a lake palace garden

Udaipur, Rajasthan, *c.* 1750. By Jiva and Jugarsi[1]
Gouache with gold and silver on paper, 68.6 × 68.6 cm
Hodgkin Loan 20
Published: Filippi 1997, no. 20; Topsfield 2001, fig. 16; Topsfield 2002, fig. 161; Williams 2007, no. 19

At a time of growing threats from the Marathas to the south, the hedonistic Jagat Singh II of Mewar (r. 1734–51) sought solace in elephant fights, court festivals, and above all in developing his pleasure palaces on the islands of the Pichola lake at Udaipur. The lake palace of Jagniwas in particular was his personal creation. Inaugurated in 1746, it became his favourite resort in the last years of his life.[2]

Here we see Jagat Singh proceed along a corridor with courtiers and attendants, one of them supporting his trailing muslin robe. Painted elephants tussle in a frieze behind him, and the doorways and antechamber to the right and colonnade to the left are shown in an ad hoc, slanting perspective. In the central scene, the Rana has taken his seat under a canopy on a rich floral carpet set in one of the palace's courtyard gardens, shown by the artists in rectangular plan form. Cares of state forgotten, he contemplates his perfectly ordered trees and flowerbeds, and listens with rapt attention to the playing of his female musicians, their music mingling with the soft plashing of two hundred fountains.

Finally, Jagat Singh, or perhaps his more heavily bearded successor Ari Singh (r. 1761–73), is seen below at a lakeside balcony,[3] practising his archery on some generously sized fish.

1 Thus inscribed on the reverse in devanagari; entered into the Mewar royal collection in 1751.
2 Much remodelled since the 1960s, it is now the Lake Palace Hotel.
3 Compare Goswamy 1986b, no. 92.

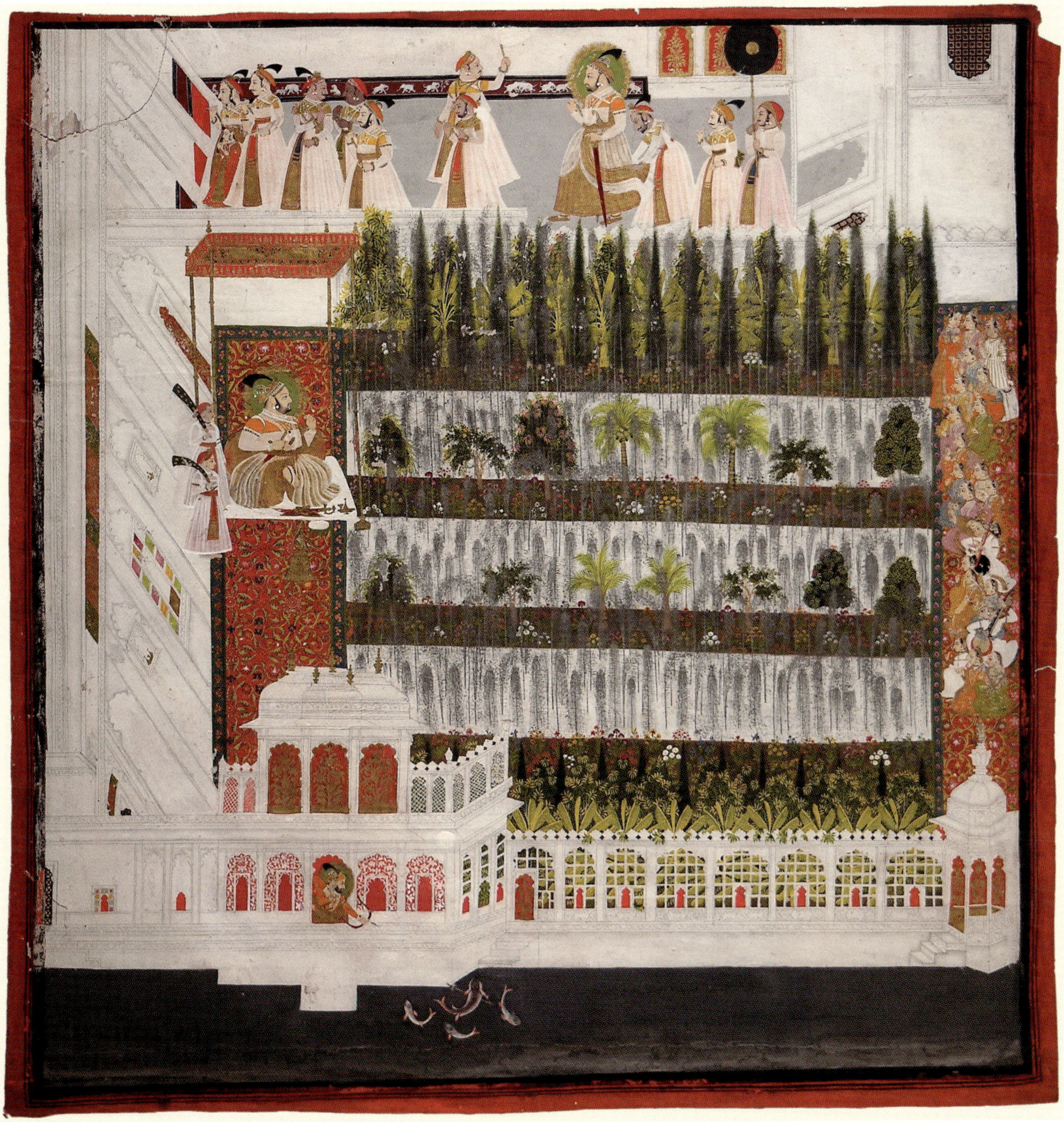

102 Jagat Singh and his queens at Jagniwas

Udaipur, Rajasthan, *c.*1750. By Sukha and Syaji[1]
Gouache with gold and silver on paper,
112.8 × 57.6 cm
Hodgkin Loan 24
Published: Topsfield and Beach 1991, no.39; Filippi 1997, no.24; Topsfield 2002a, fig.14

This elaborate painting celebrates Maharana Jagat Singh's favourite lake palace of Jagniwas and his leisure pursuits there (no.101). Somewhat damaged and light-faded,[2] it remains a striking example of the mid-eighteenth century Udaipur genre of lake palace subjects.[3] The elongated composition comprises five main scenes, evidently narrating the events of a day spent by the Rana in the company of his fourteen queens.

In the distance, Jagat Singh and his ladies have arrived by barge to worship at the Vaidyanath Mahadeva (Shiva) temple, on the western shore of the Pichola lake. Then at the lake palace of Jagniwas, Jagat Singh is greeted by his queens in one of two richly carpeted courtyards. Female attendants escort him, one holding up the ends of his robe. The same company then assembles on the roof terrace to the left, where a dancer and musicians perform. The Rana and queens each raise a hand as if to throw perfume or rose-water. In the central courtyard below, Jagat Singh and several of his queens watch six others perform the Rasmandala, the famous round dance of Krishna and the cow-girls. Jagat Singh was particularly devoted to these mystical dance dramas.

Jagat Singh's close male relations and courtiers meanwhile remain segregated from these purdah revels in a garden courtyard in the foreground. Seated in pavilions overlooking the water, they enjoy the lake breezes. Having joined them there, the Rana displays his skill as an archer by shooting a fish with an arrow. The arcade at the rear of this courtyard is shown with the imported Dutch or Chinese tiles which once adorned it. They are playfully reinterpreted by the artists as depicting Hindu deities and erotic scenes, including several exotic *firangi* (European) couples.

1 A devanagari inscription on the reverse reads: *sri ramji 1 / sri maharajadhiraja maharanaji sri jagat sighji ri surat ra pano jaganivas ra bhav ra kati vadi 7 some smat 1808 barasai kalami citaro sukho syaji*. ('Shri Ramji. Picture of the likeness of Maharajadhiraja Maharana Jagat Singh at Jagniwas; Monday the 7th of the dark half of Karttik, V.S. 1808; by the painters Sukha and Syaji'). Posthumously dated in late October 1751 like several contemporary Jagniwas subjects (no.60), it may have been painted earlier in the period 1746–51.

2 The painting was formerly trimmed at the edges and displayed in a frame, thus exposing it to light. The yellow and some green pigments have faded most, leaving the hills and vegetation with a pink tinge.

3 Topsfield 2001; Topsfield 2002, figs.138–40, 149, 158–61, 187, 189–90.

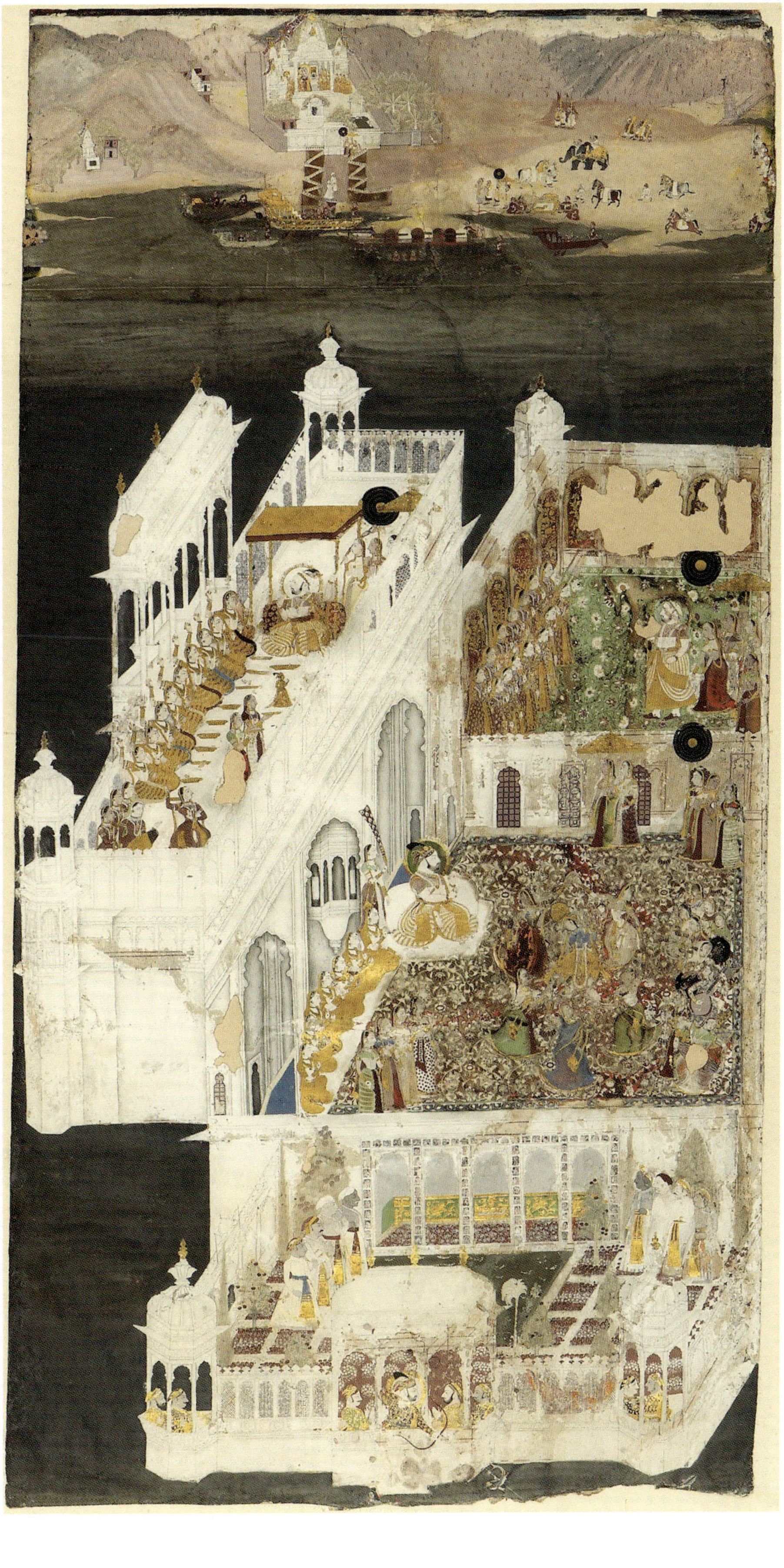

103 Rathor noblemen in durbar

Marwar, Rajasthan, *c.*1750–60
Gouache with gold on paper, 45 × 31 cm
Hodgkin Loan 18
Published: Filippi 1997, no.18

Fanned by an attendant and smoking a hookah, a white-clad Thakur of the Rathor clan rests against a throne cushion as he receives another nobleman in a durbar assembly on a terrace. Both wear a gold sunburst ornament on their turbans. Other courtiers and family members, many also wearing white and holding flowers, are ranged rhythmically in symmetrical facing rows, with their tall jutting turbans, black hide shields and protruding swords, against a bright red ground.

The main figure, gazing regally upward against the dark green background, has not yet been firmly identified. He is known from at least two further paintings, a comparable, slightly later durbar scene[1] and a procession scene on horseback.[2] In both he again appears with courtiers from his present entourage, though he has changed his hookah to a globular, silver-and-black Bidri ware model. The latter picture was formerly in the collection of the late Kumar Sangram Singh of Nawalgarh at Jaipur, who reportedly identified its subject as Kumar (Prince) Bakhat Singh of Junia, taking part in a Dassehra festival procession.[3]

1 Victoria and Albert Museum, London: Crill 1999, fig.56.
2 San Diego Museum of Art: Crill 1999, fig.57.
3 Unfortunately its inscription on the upper border is now mostly missing and unreadable. I am grateful to Sonya Quintanilla for this information.

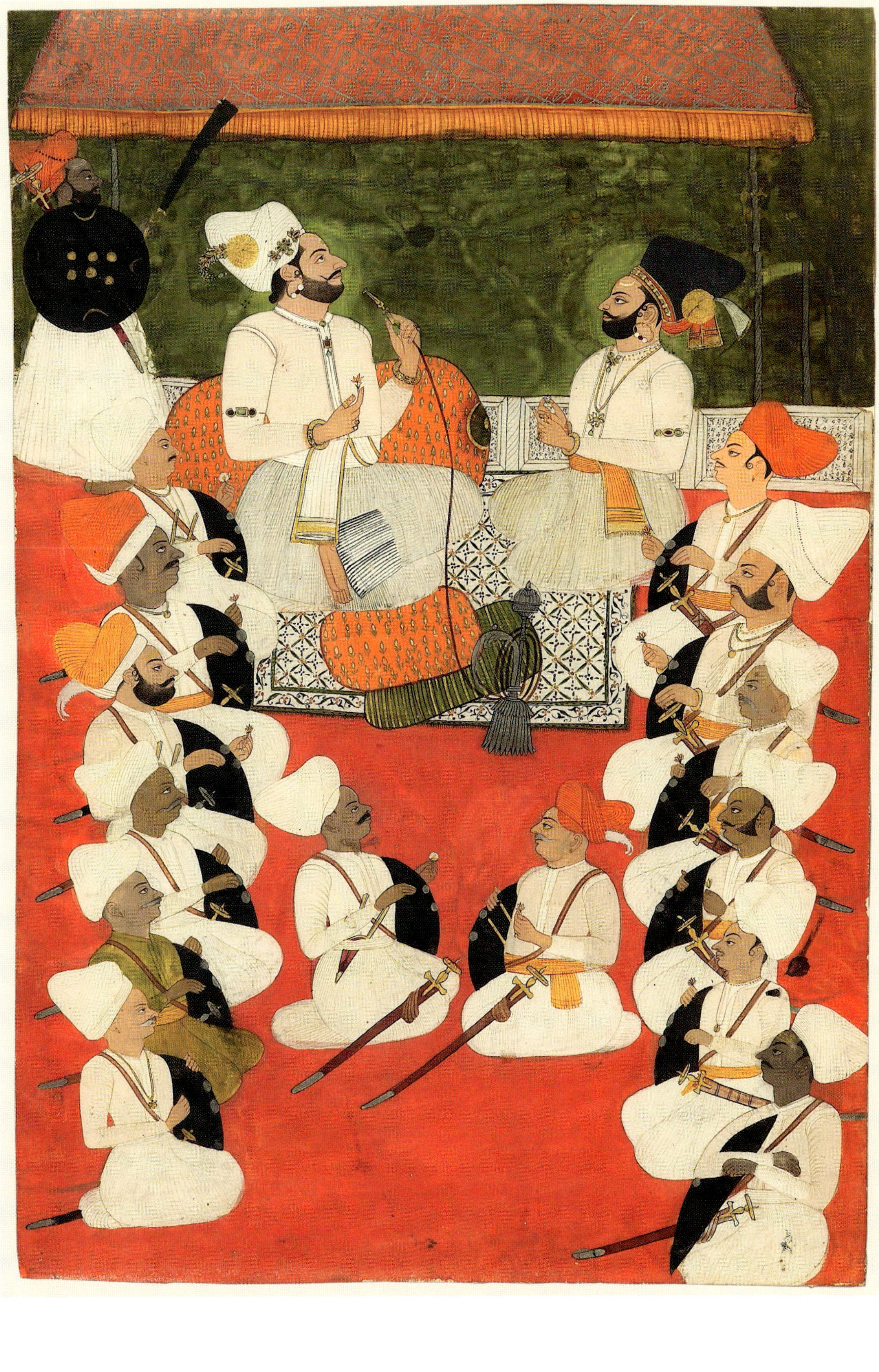

104 Maharaja Vijai Singh bathes with his ladies

Jodhpur, Rajasthan, *c.*1760
Gouache with gold and silver on paper, 40.7 × 58.7 cm
Hodgkin Loan 19
Published: Filippi 1997, no.19;
Diamond and Glynn 2008, fig.20b, p.274

Maharaja Vijai Singh of Jodhpur (r.1752–93) and his zenana ladies indulge in water-play in an octagonal bathing-pool. The bare-chested Raja, in voluminous green turban, drenches a concubine with his brass syringe, while other ladies demurely raise their hennaed hands to splash one another. Female attendants holding the royal sword and shield and other regalia stand to the right, while a band of female musicians plays to the bathing party on the left. On either side, bedchambers stand ready for the pleasant siesta that will ensue.

The setting for these pastimes is the palace at Nagaur, largely created by Vijai Singh's father Bakhat Singh (no.88). Born in 1729, Vijai Singh had grown up at Nagaur and he continued to revisit this important regional stronghold after succeeding his father to the Jodhpur throne in 1752. He would have been intimately familiar with its architecture and gardens, and also with a remarkable series of paintings that Bakhat Singh had commissioned of his daily life and courtly pursuits there. One such painting, dating from the late 1740s, shows Bakhat Singh celebrating the spring festival of Holi in this same tank.[1] Its composition has been closely followed, with many minor variations, in the present painting. The red powder thrown at Holi and the implements for scooping and propelling it are not seen here, apart from the Raja's trusty water-syringe. If not a Holi subject therefore, this is still a scene of decorous delight as well as pleasing architectural symmetry, centred on the figure of the Raja and the small terrace pavilion with sloping eaves where he would take his ease. A door in the wall behind it leads to a wooded garden beyond.

1 Mehrangarh Fort Museum, Jodhpur: Diamond and Glynn 2008, no.20.

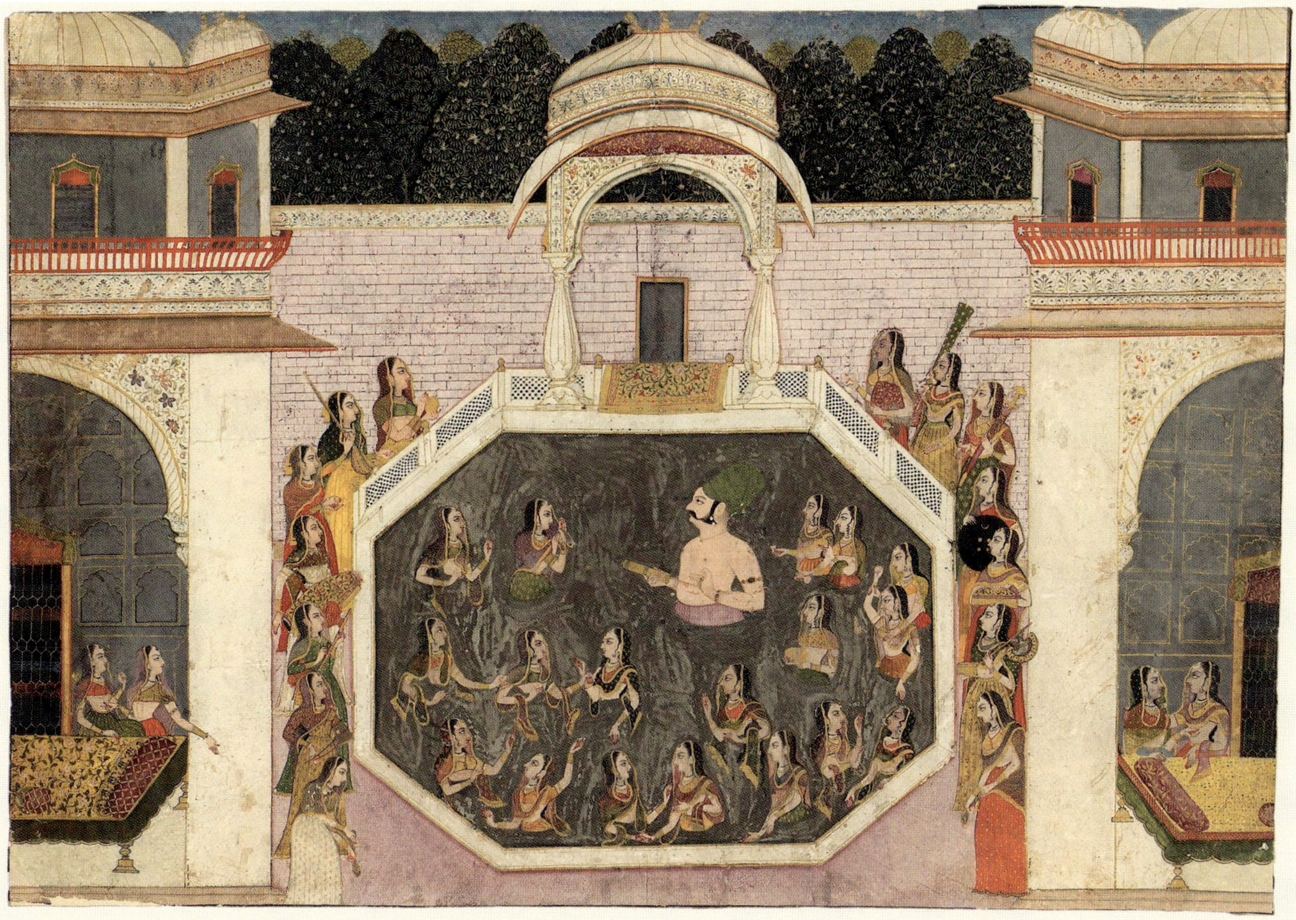

105 Maharao Madho Singh hunting wild boar

Kota, Rajasthan, *c.*1720
Gouache on paper, 50 × 62.2 cm
Hodgkin Loan 79
Published: Topsfield and Beach 1991, no35; Beach 1992, fig.137; Filippi 1997, no.79

See also detail, pp.182–83

Dressed in hunting green, Rao Madho Singh gallops in pursuit of wild boar, a favourite prey of Rajput huntsmen. Emerging with his hound from behind a tree, the Rao leans forward in the saddle as he thrusts at a fleeing boar with his *katar* dagger. The landscape around him is infused with an explosive energy. Trees, palms and stands of tall bamboo are rhythmically delineated or freely painted with single brush strokes. Colour washes or dabbed cloth-pad shading and extensive variations of green and blue-green tones are employed. A strip of turbulent lake with waterfowl in the foreground is rendered with a nervous, wiry line.

Vigorous as it is, this is not a scene observed at first hand. Madho Singh, the first ruler of Kota (r.1631–48), had lived in the previous century, and this large scale composition again derives ultimately from an early seventeenth century wall-painting frieze in the Badal Mahal of the Bundi palace.[1] Such historic subjects were seldom rendered with as much spontaneity and verve as here.[2]

1 Bautze 1986a, p.96, fig.12.
2 A further version, in the Kota royal collection, dates from the mid-eighteenth century and lacks the impact of the present painting: Welch ed. 1997, no.32; Bautze 1986a, fig.14.

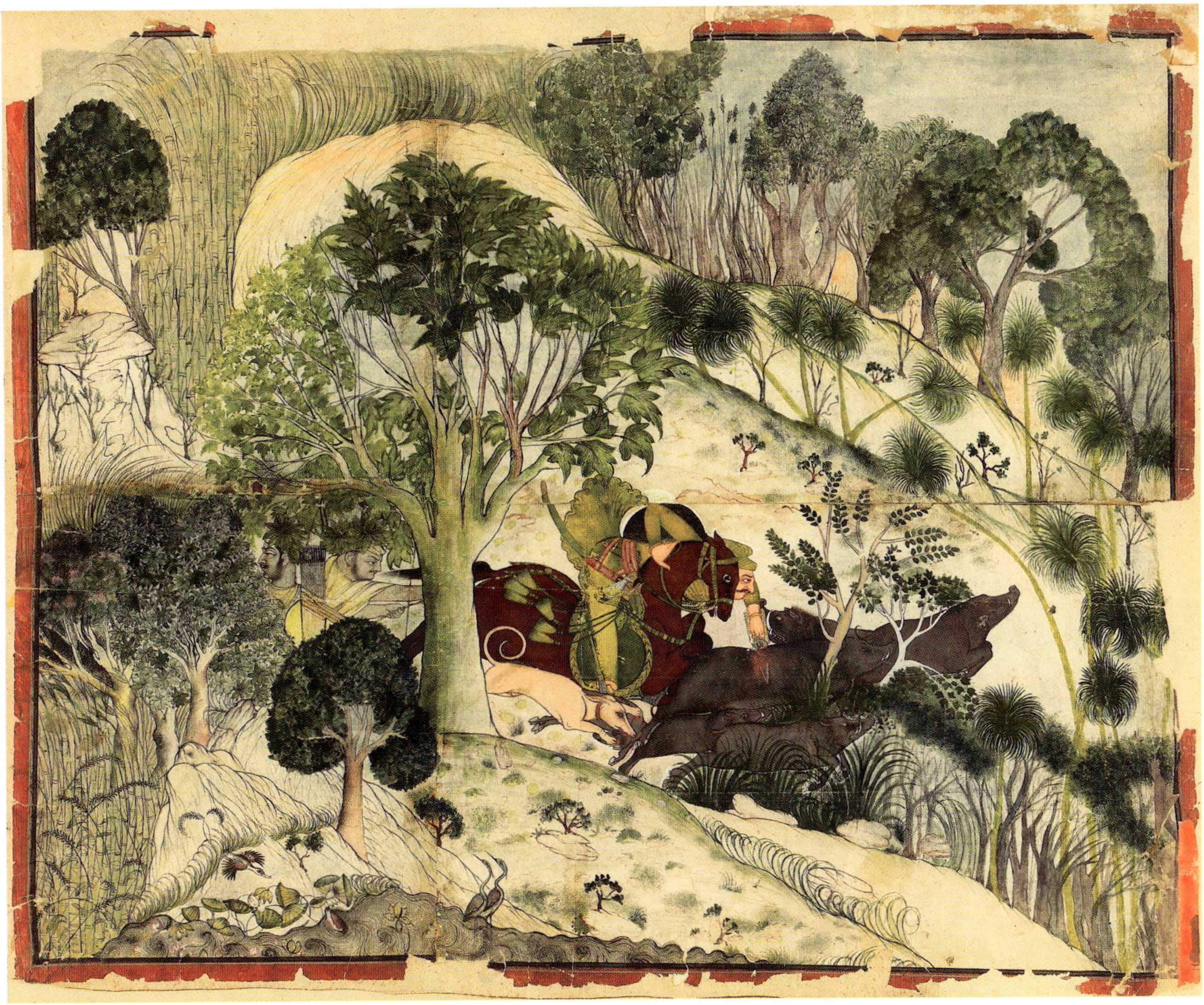

106 Elephant hunt

Kota, Rajasthan, *c.*1730–40
Gouache on paper, 46.3 × 52.1 cm
Hodgkin Loan 77
Published: Welch 1973, no.22; Falk et al. 1978, no.70; Topsfield 1984, fig.24; Topsfield and Beach 1991, no.36; Filippi 1997, no.77; Beach 2011b, fig.12

See also detail, p.275

This painting is a riot of elephant activity, and its subject is one of the main methods of catching a wild elephant. While the female elephants and their young frolic gaily in a lake and the older calves scramble among the distant rocks, the bull elephant of the herd rushes forward to confront the strange elephants which are approaching from the right. He tears up bamboos threateningly with his trunk as he runs. These interlopers are in fact tame elephants, ridden by hunters camouflaged with leaves. The wily hunters then manoeuvre to flank the bull on each side and lasso it with ropes, while horsemen riding ahead goad him with their arrows. Thus he is driven towards the tree in the top right corner, where a hunter waits to drop down ropes which will tie him to the spot. Abu'l Fazl, court historian to Akbar, describes this process: "... some experienced hunters throw a rope made of hemp or bark around their necks, and thus tie them to the tree. They are afterwards led off in company with some trained elephants, and gradually get tame."[1] The concluding act of roping the elephant to the tree is shown in detail in a very similar painting by the same artist, [2] which was evidently intended to follow this picture in sequence.

The artist shows as much sympathy with the revels of the free elephants as with the drama of the hunt. His landscape too is infused with restless energy, the waters seething in linear whorls and eddies, the trees and bamboo clumps surging or bursting with inner life. Such works represent the culmination of almost a century of inspired elephant paintings at the Kota court. Comparison with a spirited drawing of an elephant fight, dated 1725 and ascribed to the painter Niju,[3] suggests that the present work and its Dublin companion may also be by him.[4]

1 Abu'l Fazl, *Ain-i Akbari*, I, p.295; see also Edgerton 1931, pp.16–22, 87–91.
2 Chester Beatty Library, Dublin: Beach 2011b, fig.11; also Leach 1995, II, no.10.41, pp.997–1000; Topsfield 1981, fig.179.
3 State Museum, Lucknow: Beach 1974, fig.126.
4 As argued by Beach 2011b.

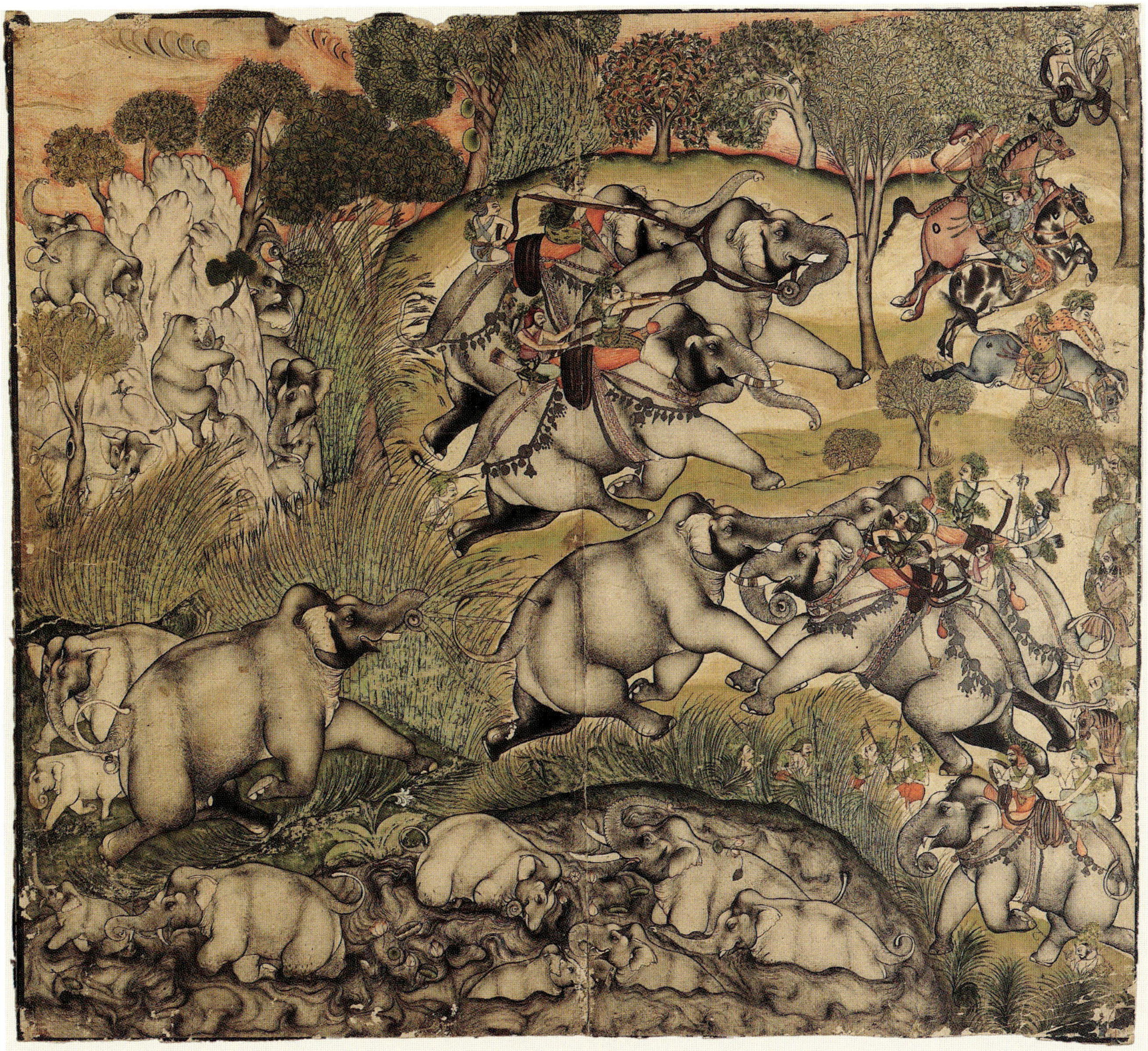

107 Shri Brijnathji and Maharao Durjan Sal hunting

Kota, Rajasthan, *c.* 1730–40
Gouache with gold on cotton cloth, 102.4 × 191.3 cm
Hodgkin Loan 74
Published: Topsfield and Beach 1991, no. 37; Brand 1995, no. 86; Filippi 1997, no. 74

A royal hunt is in progress in a wooded ravine, into which wild animals have been driven by beaters and drummers and musicians on elephants lining the cliffs above and below. Tigers, wild buffaloes and a pair of lions stand cornered in these rocky defiles. In the upper right corner, the hunt is led by Maharao Durjan Sal (r. 1723–56), who urges on his elephant in pursuit of a rhinoceros. Nearby on another charging elephant is the blue-skinned deity Brijnathji, a form of Krishna, whom the Kota rulers had adopted as their patron deity in 1719. Regarded as the true ruler of the kingdom, while the Maharao acted as his minister, Brijnathji was often depicted in paintings of court life or hunts.[1] The other nobles on elephants taking part in this grand imaginary hunting party include relatives and ancestors of Durjan Sal.

With its free-flowing narrative and vivid rendering of a Kota hunting-ground, this painting is similar in manner and scale to wall-paintings of hunts still found (with later repainting) in the Chattar Mahal apartment of the Kota palace.[2] This painting on cloth, which has also had slight restoration, was probably a hanging for display in a royal tent while the Maharao was living in camp, serving as a reminder of his richly painted palace apartments.

1 E.g. Bautze 1989.
2 Beach 1974, figs. 114–15; Singh, Brijraj 1985, figs. 47–48.

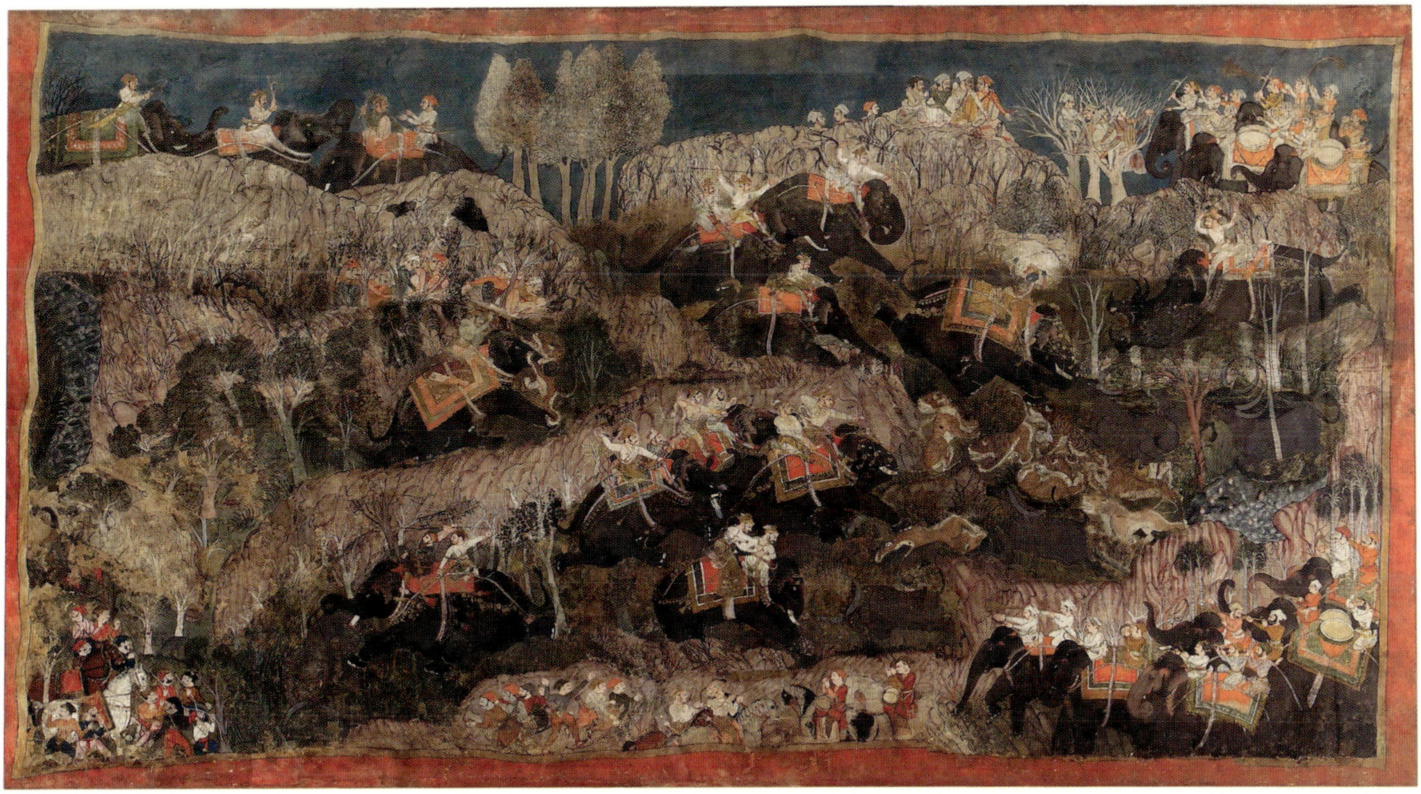

108–109 Elephants pushing cannons drawn by bullocks

Kota, Rajasthan, mid-eighteenth century
Brush drawing with colour on paper,
127 × 135 cm and 137 × 149 cm
Hodgkin Loans 60–61
Published: Filippi 1997, nos. 60–61

This pair of huge fragmentary drawings of an artillery detachment on the move may have been studies for a series of wall-paintings, possibly showing an entire army on the march. Impressive in their scale and rhythmical designs, they are only sparingly coloured in grey and orange or green tones. In each scene, five enormous carriage-mounted cannons are drawn by teams of several bullocks or oxen, while an elephant helps to propel each cannon from behind. Elephants have always served in India not only as the Rolls-Royces and battle-tanks of emperors and kings, but more widely as the equivalent of highly intelligent fork-lift trucks, extreme lifting and pushing being a speciality. Heaving the heavy artillery along was all in their day's work.

One of the uppermost cannons (no. 108) carries a triple-pointed flag of a type used at Kota. Astride each of the ten massive guns a gunner sits directing his team. Seven of these men are European specialist gunners, wearing a variety of exotic *firangi* ('Frankish') hats. The Indian gunners who ride on three lower cannons (no. 109) also wear turbans of differing types. This is evidently a sizeable army of diverse composition. These drawings may date from the mid-eighteenth century period when Kota was involved in a number of military campaigns, sometimes in concert with the Marathas who were becoming the dominant power in northern India at this time. One particular triumph was the battle of Bhatwara in 1761, when a small Kota force led by the able minister Zalim Singh assisted in defeating the far superior forces of Jaipur. The booty on that occasion included seventeen elephants, eighteen hundred horses, seventy-three cannons, and a prestigious Jaipur state flag.[1]

1 Welch ed. 1997a, p. 50, also ibid., no. 44, for a large-scale coloured drawing of a Kota military encampment in 1764.

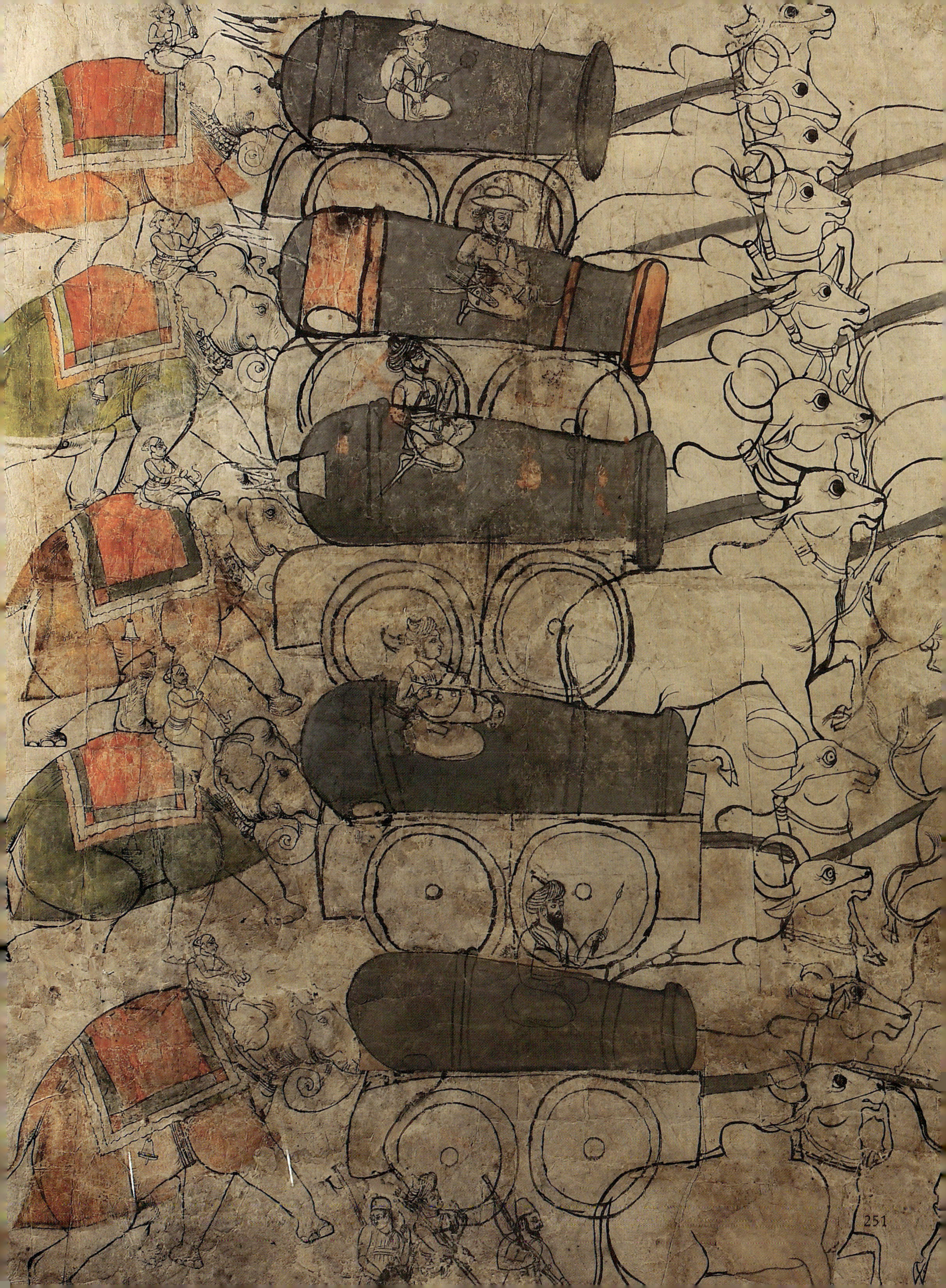

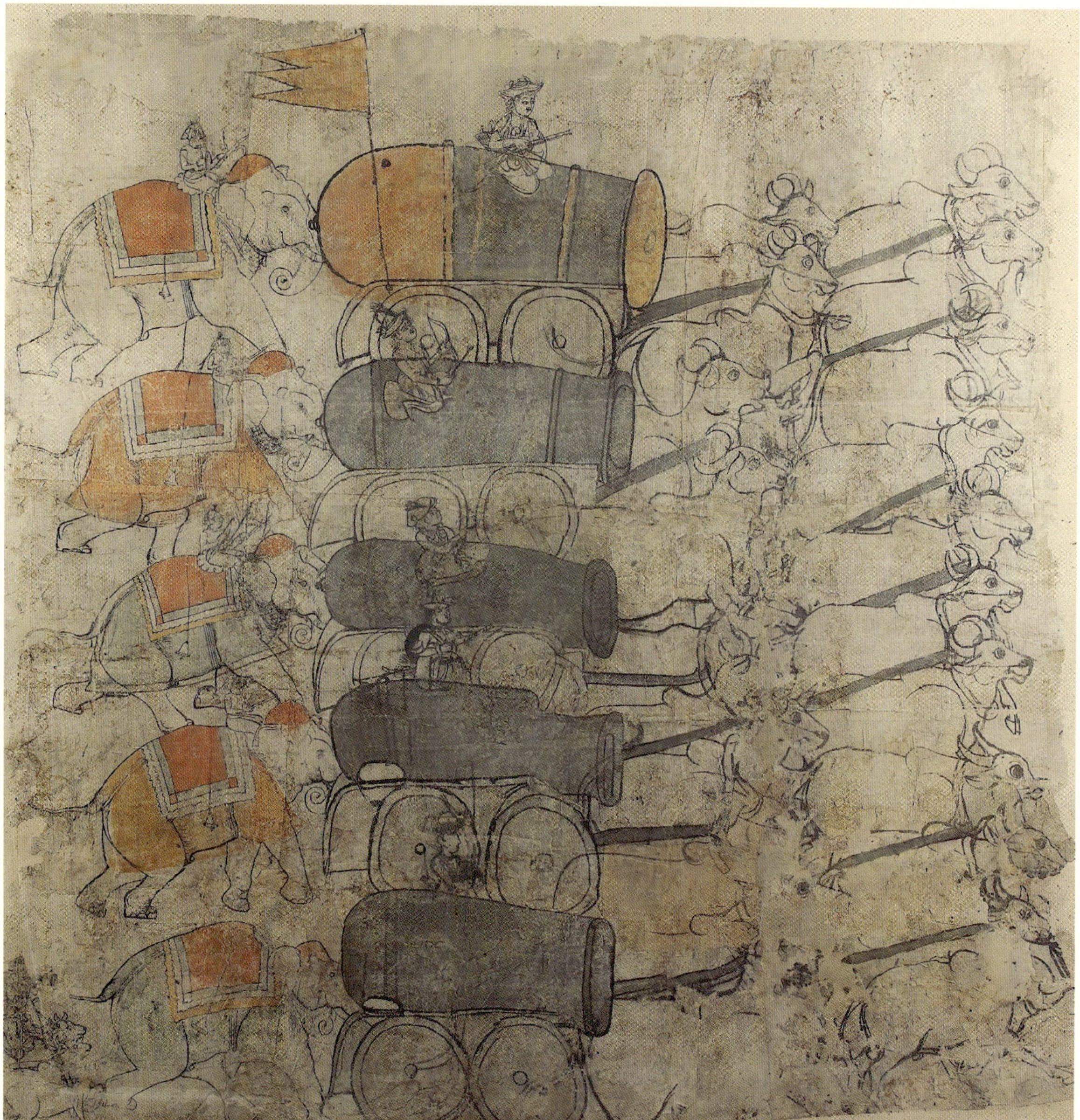

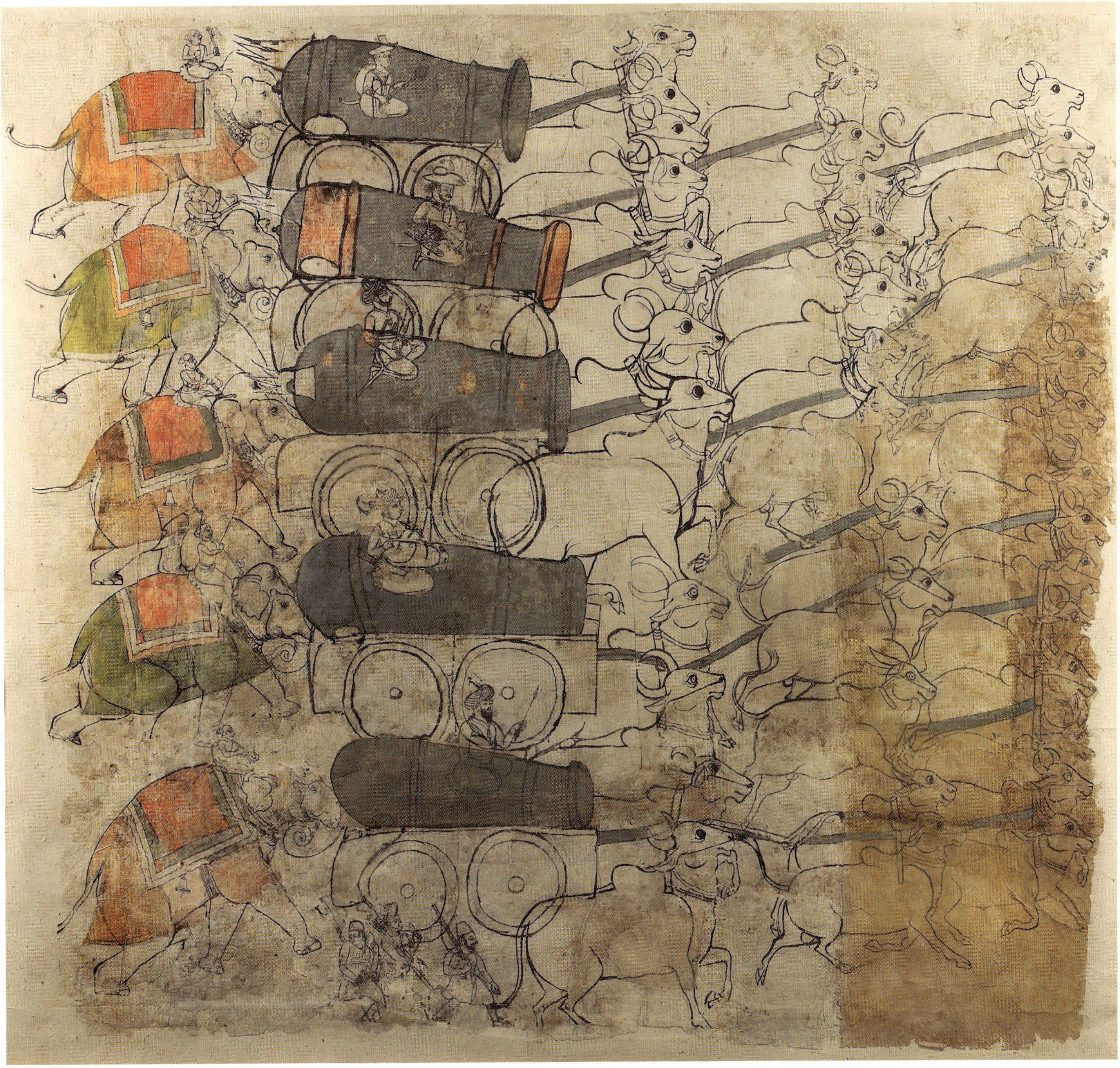

110 Rawat Gokul Das at the Singh Sagar

Deogarh, Rajasthan, 1806. By Bakhta[1]
Gouache with gold and silver on paper, 54 × 79 cm
Hodgkin Loan 80
Published: Topsfield and Beach 1991, no.40; Beach 1992, col. pl.P, p.217; Brand 1995, no.87; Filippi 1997, no.80; Topsfield 2002, fig.195; Beach and Singh 2005, fig.68; Beach 2011c, fig.6

This remarkable late work by the artist Bakhta (or Bagta) celebrates the leisure pastimes of Rawat Gokul Das (r.1786–1821) in and around the Singh Sagar ('Lion Lake') at Deogarh. Gokul Das shared the taste of his Mewar overlords (nos.101–2) for recreation in their lake palaces at Udaipur, where Bakhta himself had first worked over forty years before. Seen in modified plan form, this lake is less a conventional topographical view than a brilliant assemblage of minutely detailed scenes, linked together by the irregular shore-line.

Gokul Das appears four times, most prominently in the right foreground, where he shoots waterfowl accompanied by his uncle Gyan Singh and a courtier named Amarji. He appears three more times within the small pleasure palace on an islet in the lake. Here he converses with his ladies by their bathing-pool, performs his toilet in a corner turret and shoots some more fowl from another turret. On the shore to the left, the Rawat's escort take their ease beneath the trees, together with his elephant and the horses, camels and bullocks for the purdah carriages. Nearby cooks prepare a meal. Elsewhere grooms wash their horses in the shallows, dhobis (washermen) and fishermen are at work around the lake, and villagers in their fields.

Bakhta's treatment of landscape and wildlife is most vivid. The huge rocks in the foreground are fluidly outlined and writhe in molten, animated shapes. Between them, behind a wall, a luxuriant grove of flowering trees and plantains is alive with birds, peacocks and monkeys. Another notable passage is the further wooded islet in the lake, with its water-fowl and benignly basking crocodiles. Painted by one of the great Rajasthani artists towards the end of his long career, this work is a joyous celebration of the local landscape and of the ruler's pleasure in it.

1 Inscribed on the back in devanagari script (illus. Topsfield and Beach, p.104, fig.8): *mharavatji sri 5 sri gokal dasji ki surat: talav sig sagar kau bhav mhail sund / mudha agai kakauji ravat ?gyan sighji / tirai bhadau amarji [sam] 1863 ra: duti savan [bad] 12 saumai din panau najar vhau darikhanai barajya [del.: kalami ca] / kalami cataro bakhatau:* ('The likeness of Maharavat Shri Gokul Das at the Singh Sagar, accompanied by the uncle Ravat Gyan(?) Singh and Amarji; presented in the (?) pavilion on Monday 12th of the dark half of Shravan V.S.1863. By the painter Bakhta'). Below this, an indistinct inscription in red paint, together with a sketch of a face, also gives the artist's name, Bagta (*sic*).

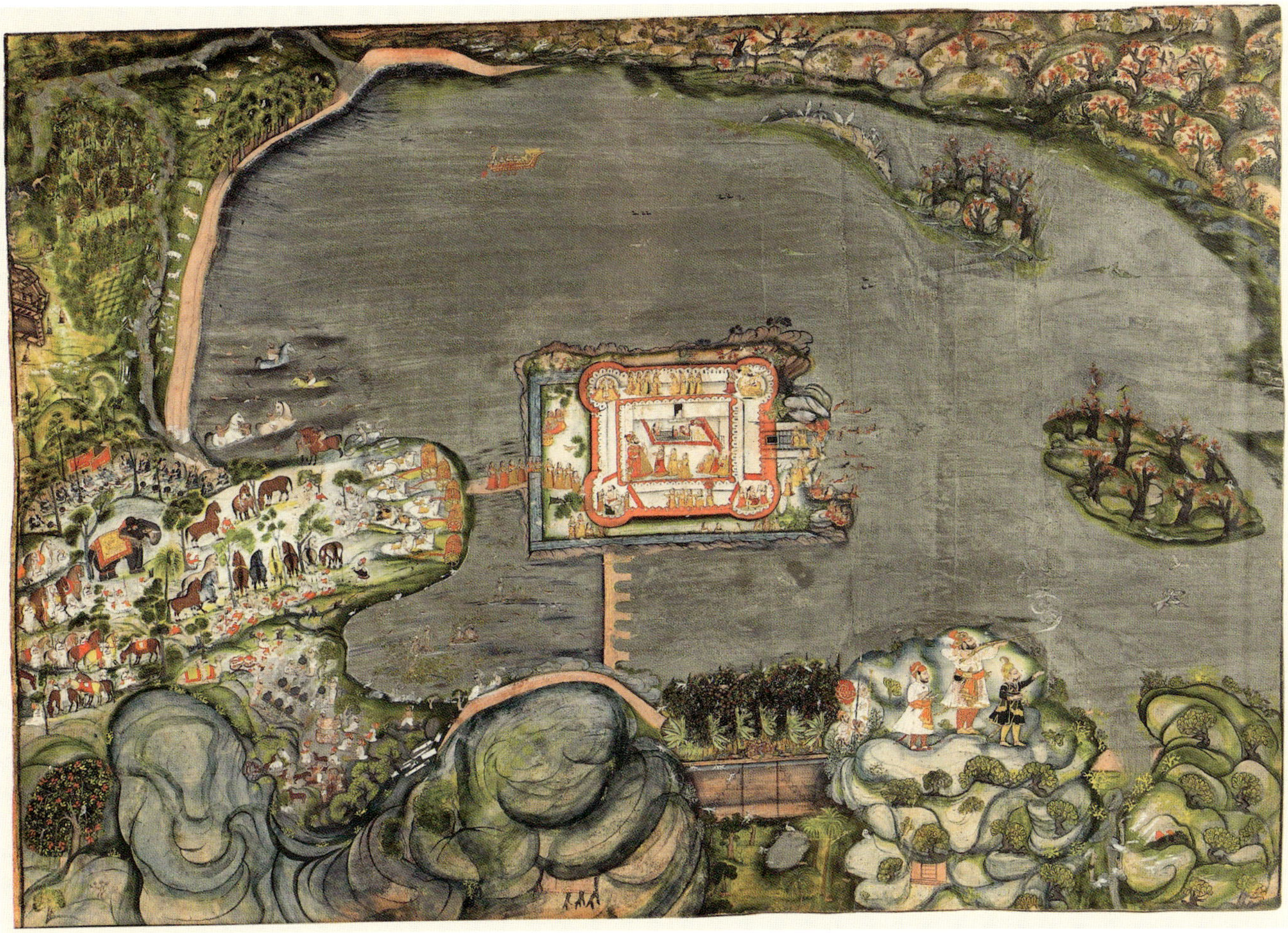

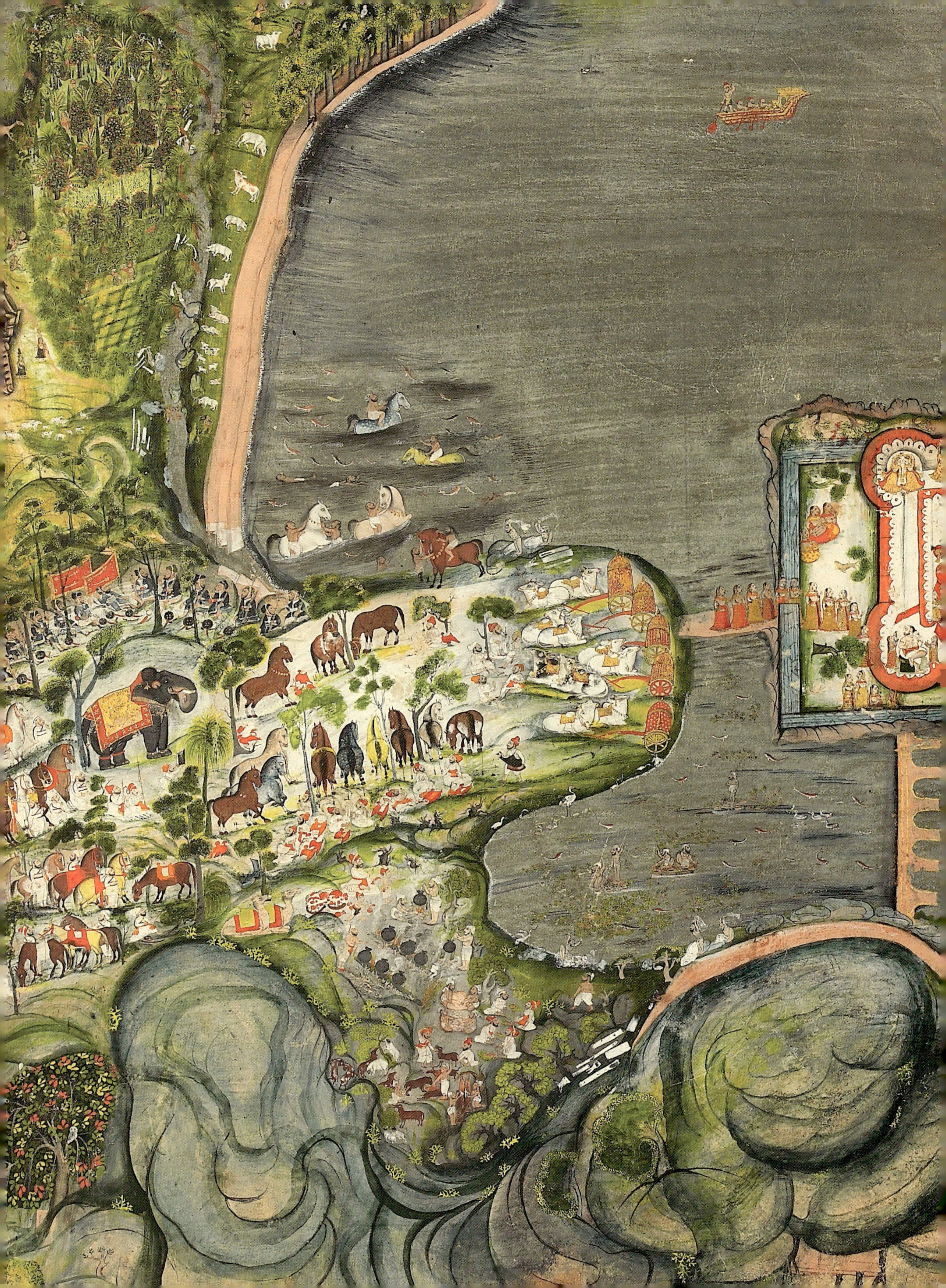

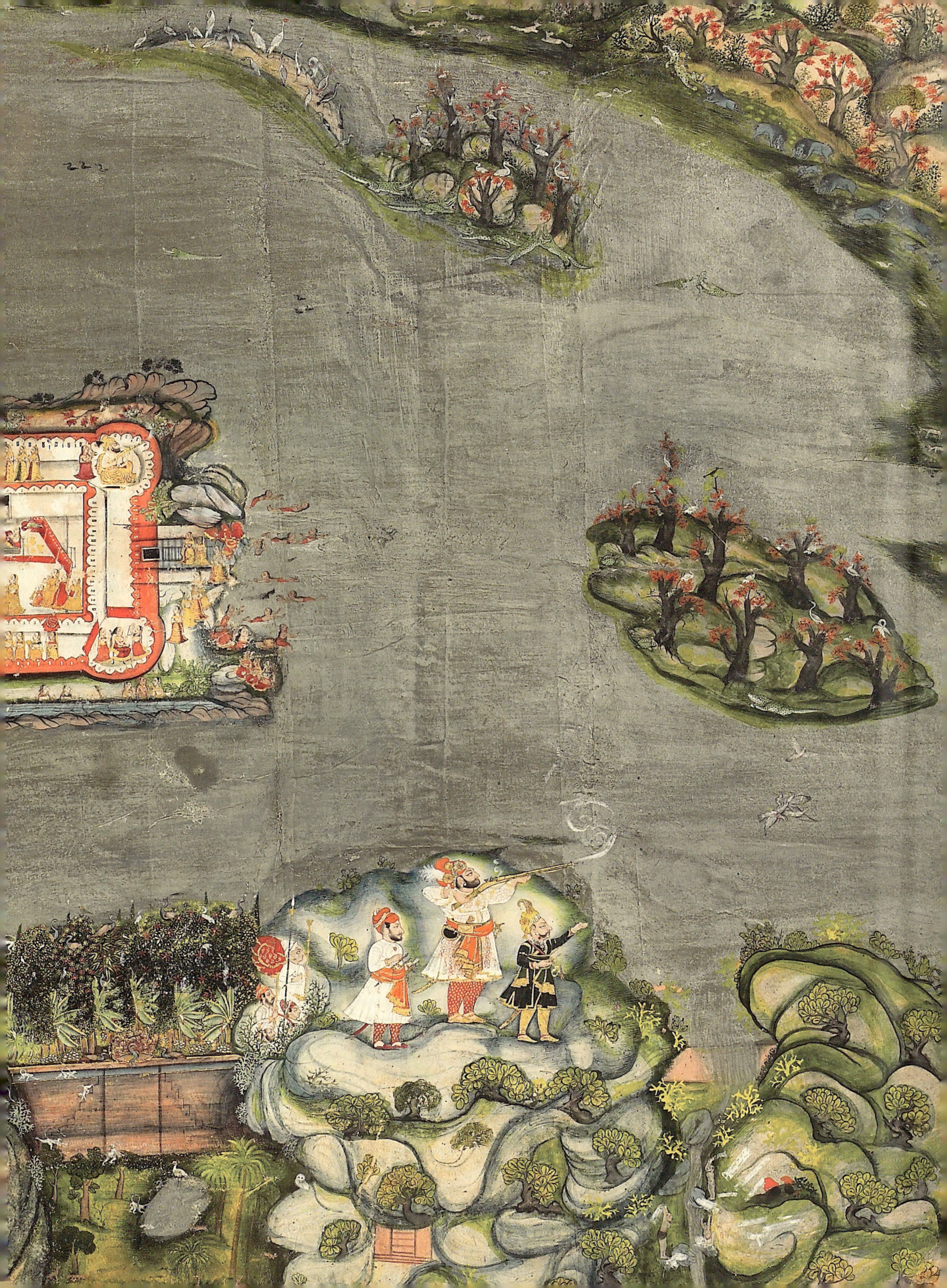

111 Maharaja Pratap Singh

Jaipur, Rajasthan, *c.*1790. Attributed to Sahib Ram
Brush drawing on paper, 71.5 × 58 cm
Hodgkin Loan 43
Published: Filippi 1997, no.43

Large in scale, these twin portrait studies of Maharaja Pratap Singh of Jaipur (r.1778–1803) can be attributed to Sahib Ram, his leading artist and head of studio.[1] In the unfinished study on the left, the Raja wears a court turban with heavily jewelled bands, plumes and a prominent peacock ornament, all quickly and deftly sketched. The royal profile and features are delineated with greater deliberation and a fine economy of line, each element precisely placed in a fluent sequence of rhythmical arcs and lines. The enlarged, tapering leaf-like eye and the brow curved like a bow belong to ancient Indian poetic traditions of beauty. The more playful curling ends of the royal moustache and the hair on each side of the ear add flourishes which save the composition from an over-geometric abstraction or Flaxman-like statuesqueness.

The second drawing reprises the subject with slight variations such as the added eye-lashes and a stronger accentuation of the profile with white outline wash. The turban is unadorned though other jewellery is worn, and there are preparatory marks for a royal nimbus. The Raja's lightly sketched hand holds the mouthpiece of a hookah tube, and he wears a cummerbund, a draped shawl and a garland sketched more broadly in long strokes of dark wash.

These highly accomplished drawings belong to a well-known body of similar works, probably cartoons for mural or large-scale panel paintings within the Jaipur palace.[2] Many depict scenes of the *Raslila* dance performed by Krishna with Radha and the *gopis*, a great predilection of Pratap Singh who was himself a prolific Hindi devotional poet. Reputedly a noble and upright prince, Pratap Singh lived in difficult times and was ill served by disloyal ministers and nobles. His greatest achievements were as a patron of art and architecture.

1 Aitken 2011; this picture is no.20 in her list of Sahib Ram's works, p.625.

2 First discussed a century ago by the pioneer scholar A.K. Coomaraswamy: Coomaraswamy, 1912, pp.20–21, pls.I–V. A head study of Pratap Singh closely related to the present picture formerly belonged to Coomaraswamy: Aitken 2011, fig.11; Coomaraswamy 1926, pl.CXV; compare also Pal and Glynn 1976, no.14 and cover illus.

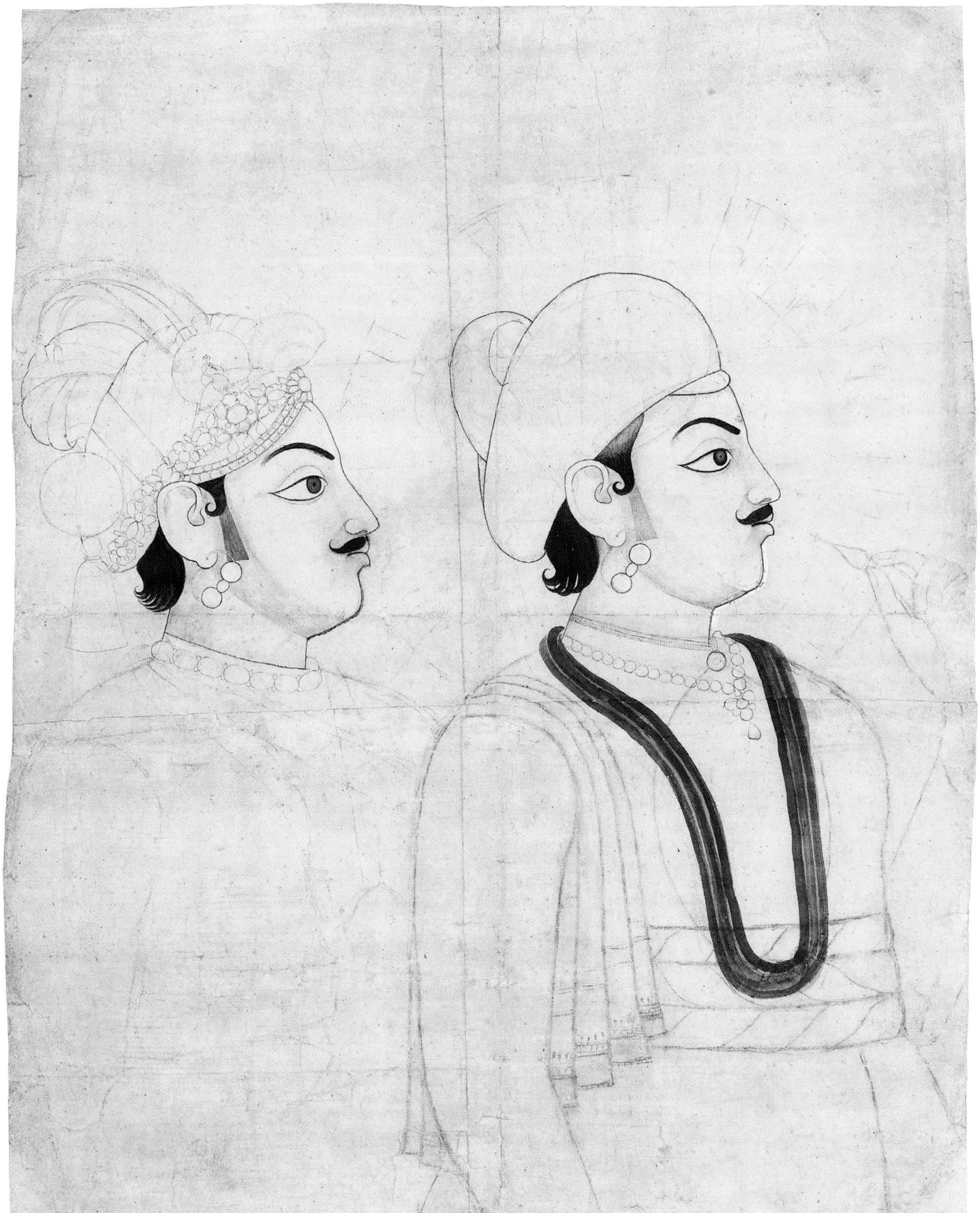

112 A court beauty

Udaipur, Rajasthan, *c.*1805–10. Attributed to Chokha
Gouache with gold and silver on cotton cloth
123 × 61 cm[1]
Hodgkin Loan 32
Published: Topsfield and Beach 1991, no.41; Filippi 1997, no.32; Topsfield 2002, fig.204; Williams 2007, no.25

Attributable to the distinctive and quirky Mewar artist Chokha, this flamboyant picture of an idealised heroine is all the more powerful for its large size and assured execution. Within a cusped arch a bejewelled beauty stretches her hands languidly overhead, with jutting bosom and out-thrust hip. Her huge lotus-petal eye is dreamily abstracted, the ends of her dark hair electrically wild. Her breasts are barely restrained by the transparent *choli*, and her flaring skirts, orange and crimson with tie-dyed lozenges, contrast vividly with the blue ground. Identified simply as 'a beauty', she is a supercharged version of the type of idealised female figures often found in Rajput palace wall-paintings. She may also represent a favourite queen or concubine of the hedonistic Maharana Bhim Singh of Mewar (r.1778–1828), and the chubby infant bidding for her attention could also be one of Bhim Singh's hundred or more children, the crescent moon at his forehead, an emblem of Shiva, suggesting his royal birth.

Chokha, the son of Bakhta (no.110), worked both at Udaipur and the minor Mewar court of Deogarh during the first quarter of the nineteenth century. His idiosyncratic works are full of brio and eclectic invention. Here the lady's profile and elongated eye derive from the full-blown Kishangarh style (no.97), while his voluptuous treatment of the female form recalls earlier Indian sculptural traditions. The beseeching child may derive from a similar source or else a European model. A related cloth-painting attributable to Chokha, of slightly smaller dimensions, is a standing portrait of a bare-chested Maharana Bhim Singh with a hawk.[2]

1 Inscribed above: *phutadya* ('A beauty'); with clerical valuations (10 rupees and 15 rupees respectively).
2 Ashmolean Museum, EA1985.31: Topsfield 2002, fig.203.

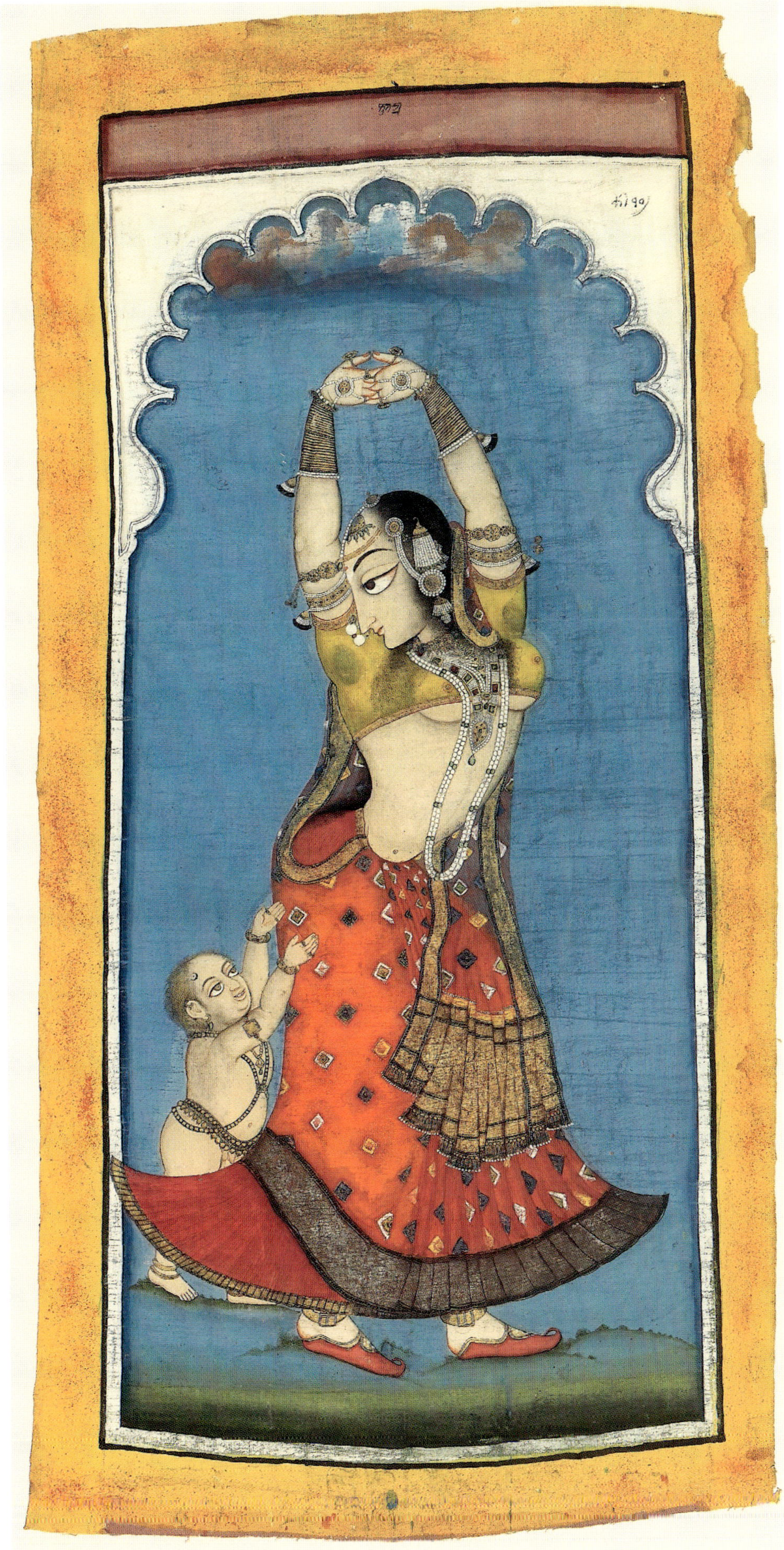

113 Sandhya Arati: Krishna returns to Nanda's house at dusk

Nathdwara, Rajasthan, late 19th century
Brush drawing with colour on paper, 49 × 121 cm
Hodgkin Loan 95
Unpublished

Partly unfinished, this impressive large scale drawing is a study for a temple hanging of the Vallabha sect, for the evening puja (worship) of Sandhya Arati, celebrated on the tenth of the dark half of the late summer month of Shravan.[1] The time is dusk or 'the hour of cowdust', when the young Krishna and his cowherd (*gopa*) friends return from the fields with their herd. The young god himself would have appeared in the largely vacant central area of the composition, with the *gopas* to the right with their cows.

The house of Nanda, Krishna's foster-father, is no simple village dwelling, but a vast palace complex, teeming with on-lookers within its numerous domed pavilions, balconies and windows. Nanda watches from the domed *chatri* pavilion above a gateway at the far left, where a *gopa* standing below announces Krishna's arrival. Krishna's foster-mother Yashoda, holding a ritual *arati* lamp, leads the female figures waiting at a doorway to greet the young god. Above the vacant area, an arcaded throne room has been made ready for Krishna by *gopi* attendants. Meanwhile deities in floating sky-boats, including Shiva and Parvati to the left, gaze down at this serene and harmonious scene.

Painted at the temple town of Nathdwara in Mewar, this drawing strongly recalls the earlier Kishangarh court style in its facial types with an elongated, upturned eye. The earliest known pichhavai depicting this general theme was in fact painted at Kishangarh in 1817.[2] The palatial buildings and lake with royal barges also recall the architecture of Kishangarh, as well of Udaipur, a short distance from Nathdwara. While the composition is a conventional one, its execution and brushwork show freshness and verve. The foreground figures and soulful-eyed cows are drawn with fluent strokes, the background figures are more cursorily yet deftly adumbrated. As well as being a setting for a devotional scene, this rambling *capriccio* palace scene conveys a lively sense of daily palace life and of traditional Indian urban life.

1 For Nathdwara *picchavais* of *c.* 1890–1900 depicting this subject, see Krishna 1984, pp.136–37, pl.6, and Krishna and Talwar 2007, no.6; for a later and garish example of *c.*1910–25, Lyons 2004, fig.50.
2 Bharat Kala Bhavan, Varanasi: Krishna 1984, pl.7, a Gopashtami festival subject.

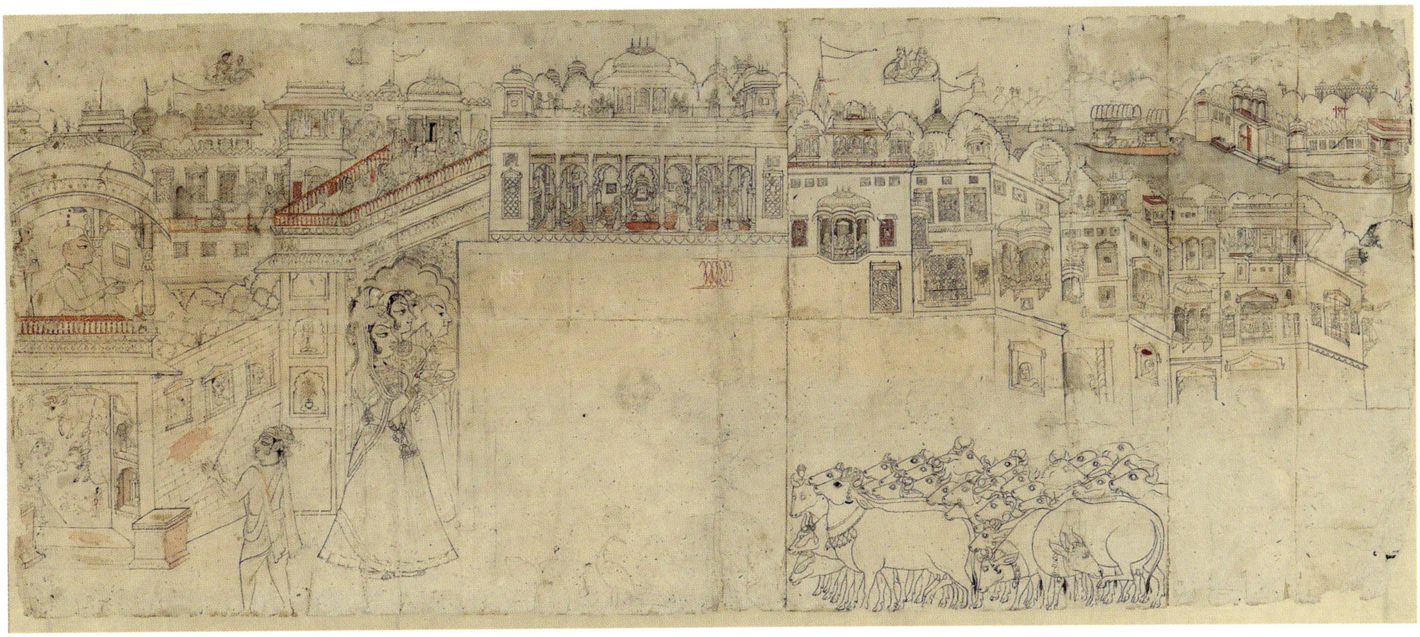

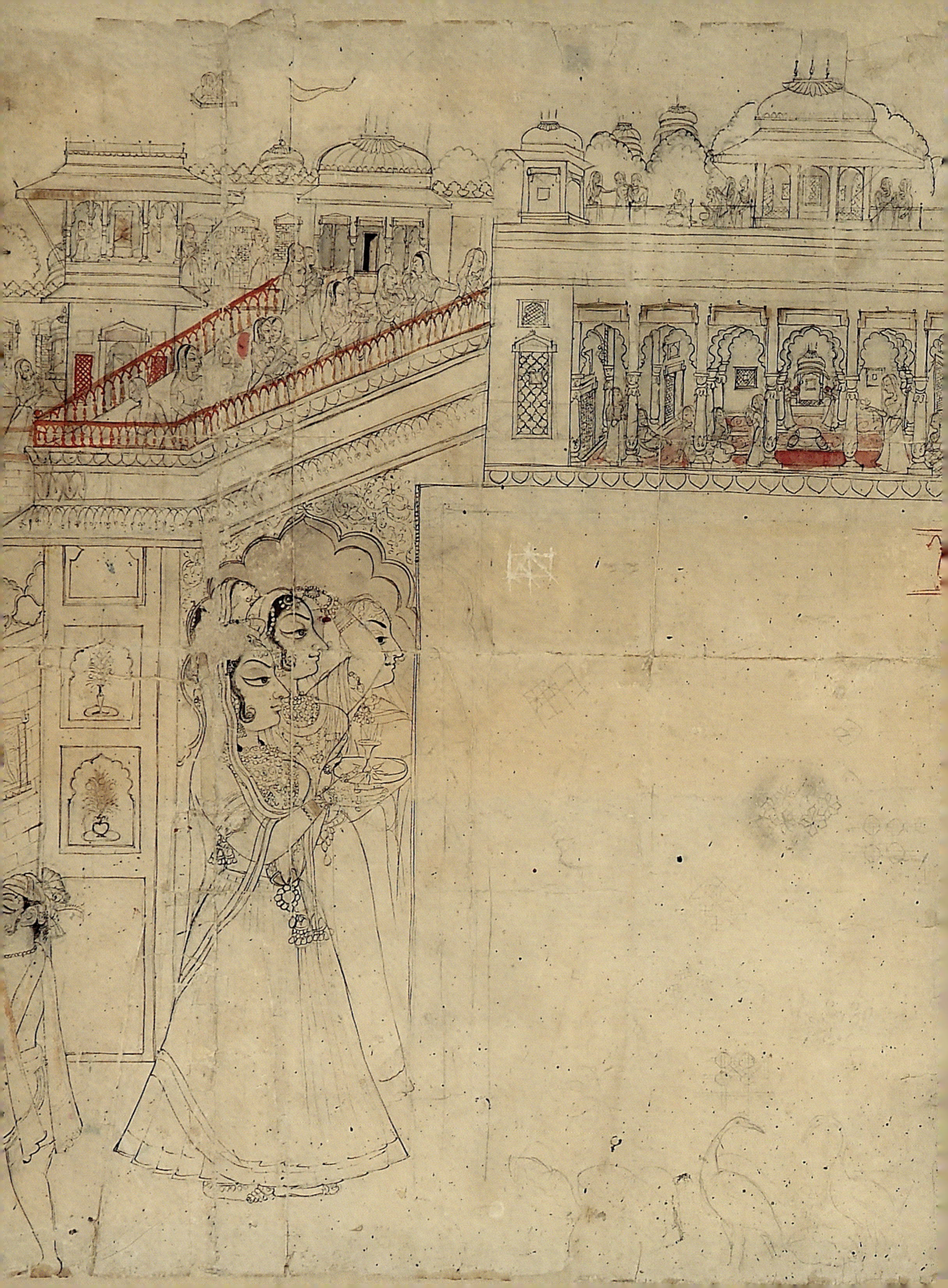

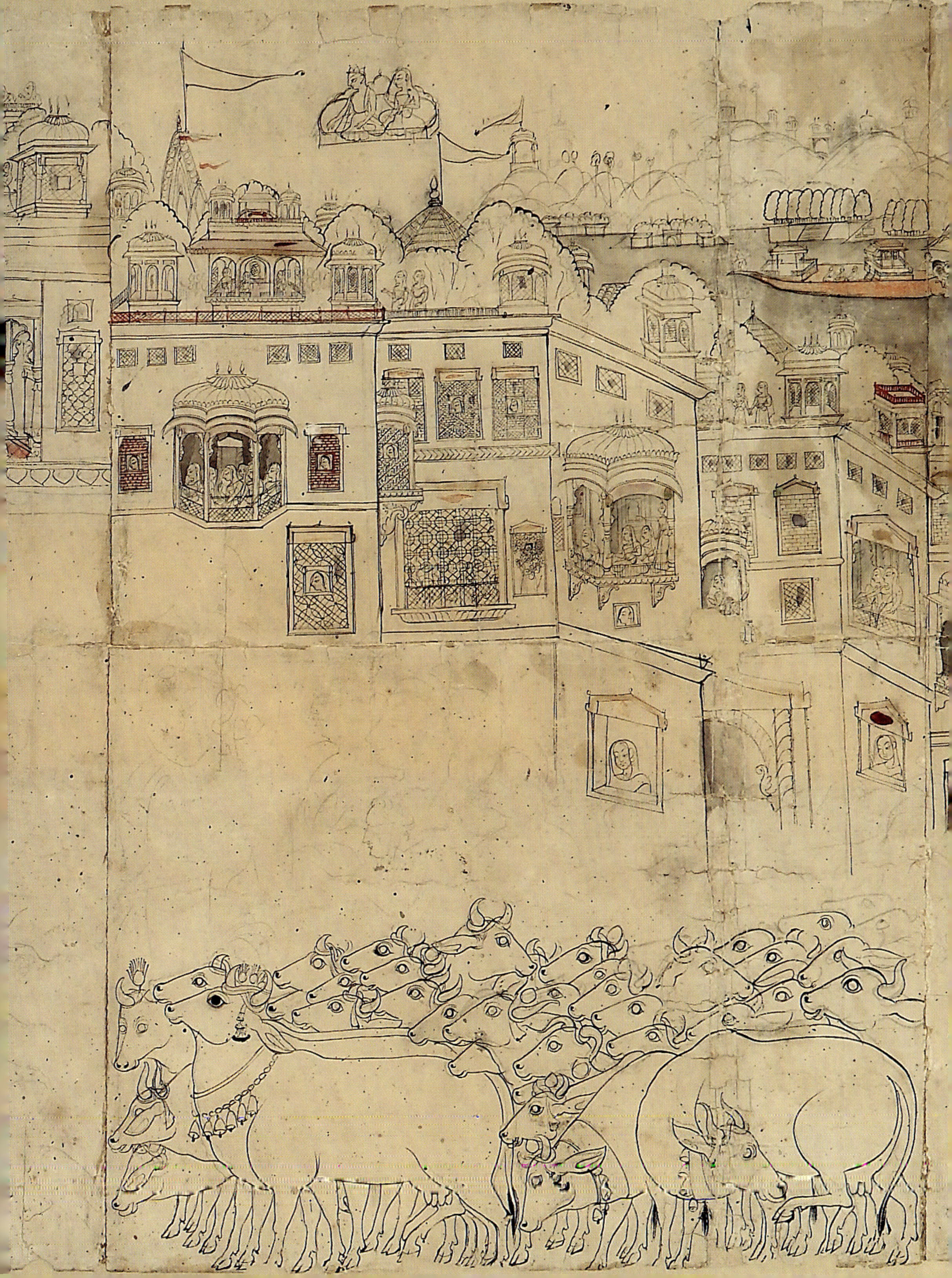

114 Maharao Ram Singh in durbar

Kota, Rajasthan, *c.*1850. Attributed to Kishan Das
Gouache with gold on paper, 40.5 × 30.8 cm
Hodgkin Loan 17
Published: Bautze 1990, fig.11 (detail);
Filippi 1997, no.17[1]

The flamboyant Kota ruler Ram Singh II, seated on the left, receives another chief, probably from a neighbouring Central Indian kingdom, at a durbar reception within a garden pavilion. Both men have radiant nimbuses and share the same enormous throne cushion. They and their entourages, ranged on either side, hold shields and swords, and the visiting party on the right includes two mustachioed warriors in helmets. Plantains and other flowering shrubs and trees are glimpsed above, between the pillars and the yak-tail fans waved by the attendants. In front of Ram Singh and his guest, silver double-candlesticks of probable Calcutta manufacture stand beside eight trays laden with fine textiles and jewellery. These ceremonial gifts are being presented to the Maharao. If the occasion were a wedding durbar these gifts could form part of a royal bride's dowry,[2] but it is unclear whether this is the case here.

This painting can be attributed to Kishan Das, an artist who depicted his patron Ram Singh with much bravura and often in unconventional ways,[3] such as riding his horse on the roof of the palace, or celebrating the Holi festival by hosing coloured water at his women and courtiers with the aid of a British hand-pumped fire-engine.[4]

1 Also Sotheby's sale cat., *The Bachofen von Echt Collection*, 29 April 1992, lot 30.
2 Compare Desai 1986, no.97, in which Ram Singh is received by the Jaisalmer ruler on the occasion of his marriage there in 1843.
3 Bautze 1989.
4 E.g. Topsfield 1980, no.35.

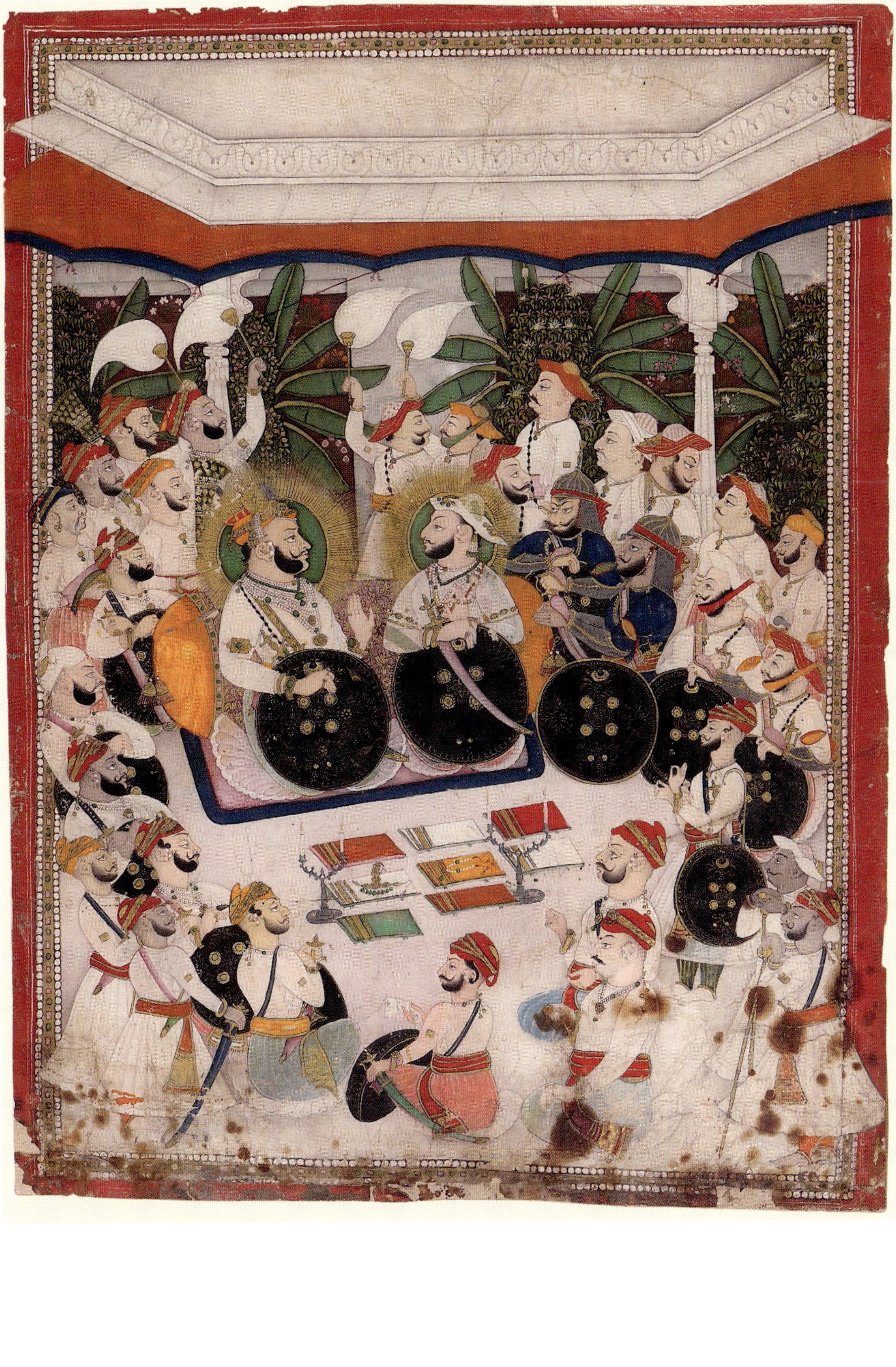

115 Maharao Ram Singh's marriage procession at Udaipur

Kota, Rajasthan, *c.*1851
Gouache with gold on cotton cloth, 92.6 × 69.5 cm
Hodgkin Loan 29
Published: Topsfield and Beach 1991, no.42; Filippi 1997, no.29

Maharao Ram Singh, seen twice on the left in his elephant howdah, arrives in procession at the Udaipur palace before his marriage to Phul Kunvar Bai, the sister of Maharana Sarup Singh. The Maharana, also shown with nimbus and mutton-chop whiskers (in reality he had a full beard), waits to greet him on the terrace in front of the palace. Then, whip and shield in hand, Ram Singh rides forward to strike the symbolic *torana* arch suspended over the zenana gateway, prior to claiming his bride. The Zenana Mahal, the women's wing of the palace, appears to the left of this gate, and a section of the main palace façade to the right, up to its small central doorway. The courtyard below is mainly thronged with the numerous Kota contingent, many of the nobles auspiciously dressed for the occasion in saffron and orange clothes. A military escort in British style uniforms stand by, a few playing musical instruments. A purdah palanquin, for a royal lady, and an open palanquin also stand ready. Meanwhile the palace musicians pound their *naqqara* drums and blow their *shehnais* with gusto around the gateway in the foreground.

This joyful occasion took place on 9 March 1851, when Phul Kunvar Bai became the eighth of Ram Singh's nine wives.[1] It may have been witnessed by the Kota artist, who also modelled his composition in some degree on an earlier painting of Ram Singh's wedding procession at Jaisalmer in 1843.[2] However the present painting is a more lively one and more full of incident. Even at the edges there appear unexpected details of ordinary life, such as a man touching the hand of an unseen lady at far right.

1 Shyamaldas 1886, II, pp.1944–45; Sharma 1939, II, p.588.
2 Welch 1997a, no.66.

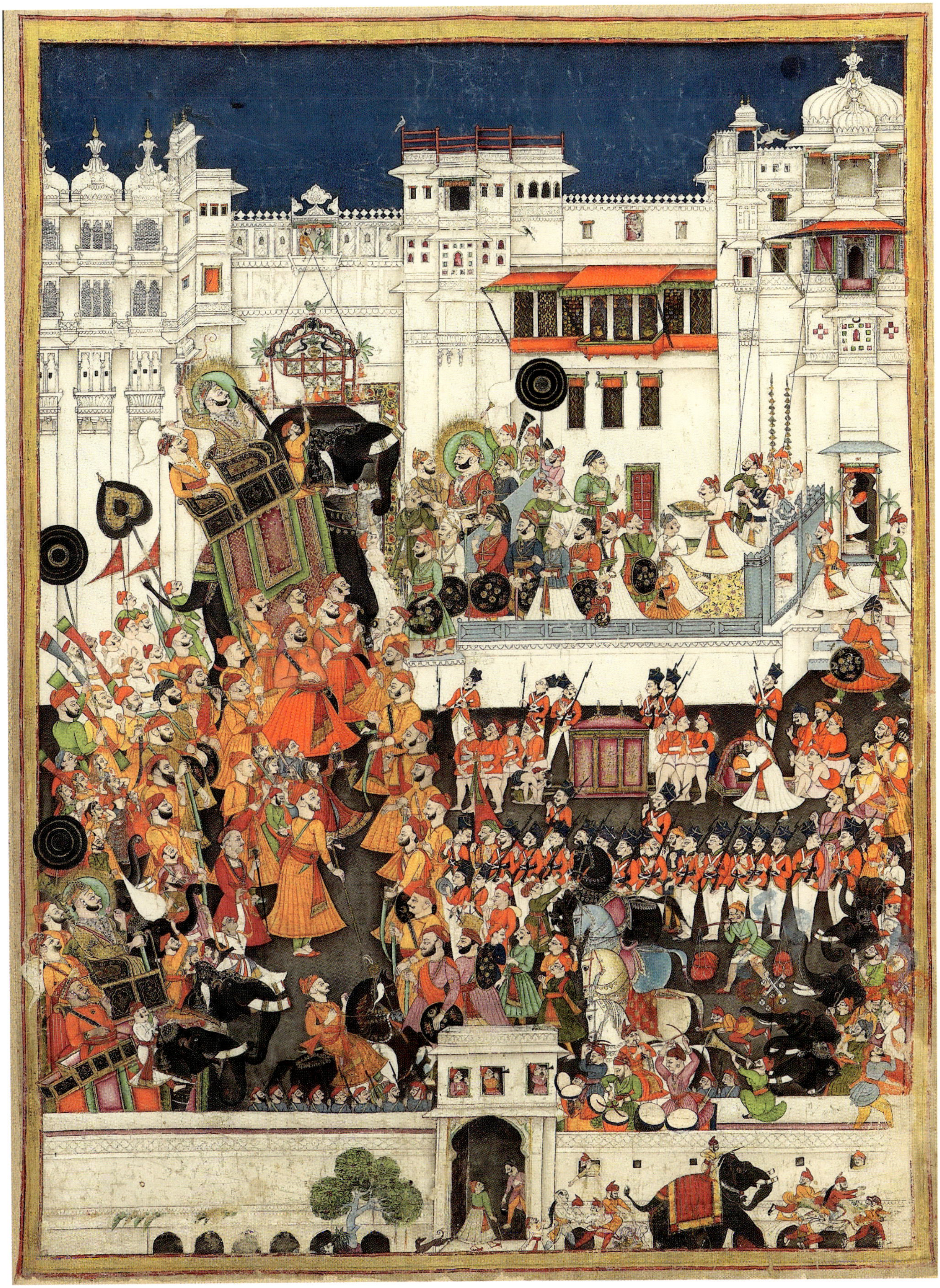

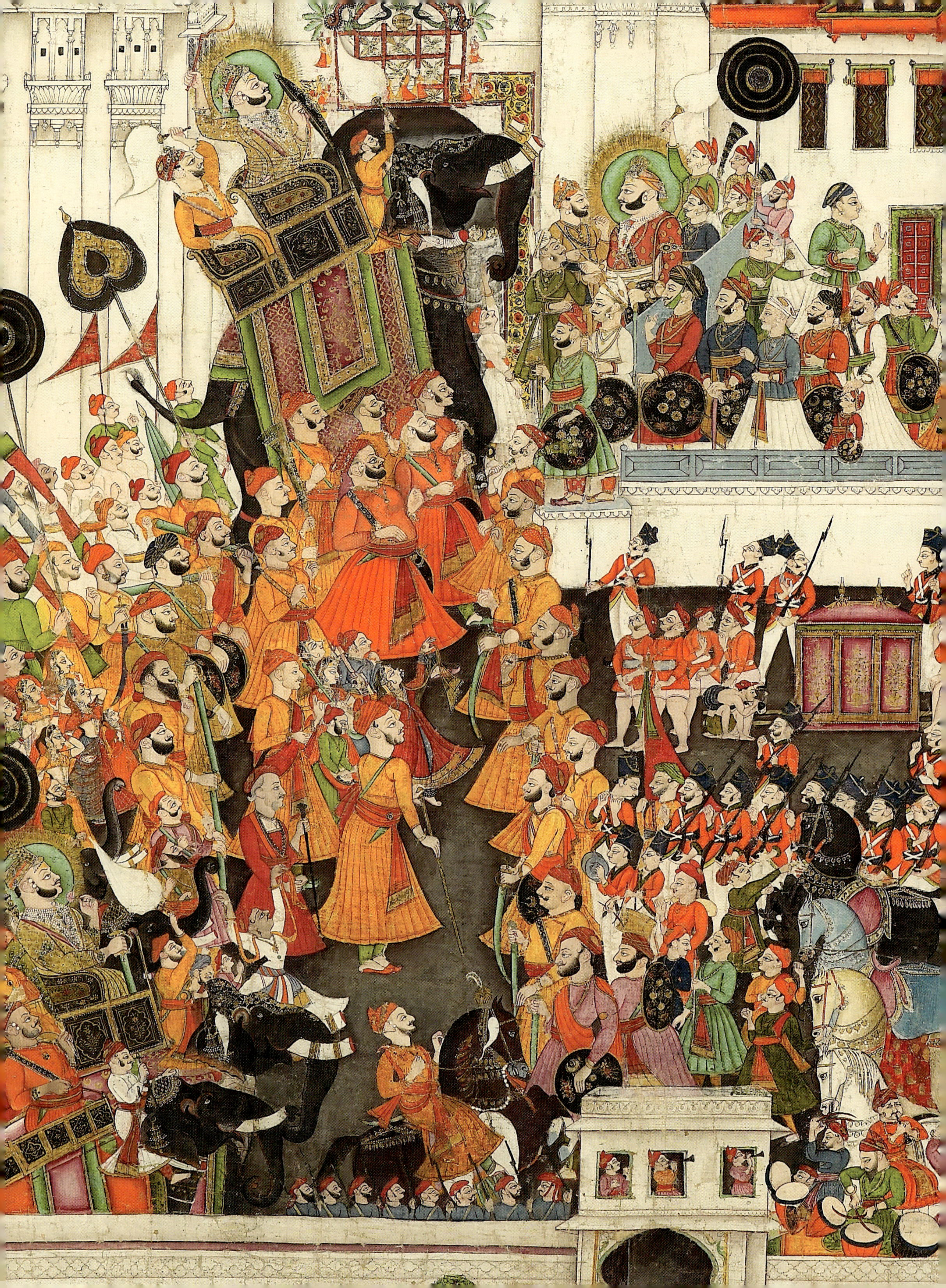

Appendix 1

About My Collection (1991)[1]

Howard Hodgkin

My collection really began when Wilfrid Blunt, my art master during the brief year I studied at Eton (1946), arranged two exhibitions at school. One was the stock of an Oriental bookseller called Luzac in Great Russell Street, which he borrowed, complete with price lists (consisting mostly of Mughal pictures). It made me realise that, even though the prices seemed huge to a schoolboy, such pictures could be bought. Among the Luzac paintings there was one I wanted to own – it cost all of five pounds, but Wilfrid Blunt very sensibly advised me that I could spend my money better on something else. He didn't think any of the pictures were really worth buying.

The other, far more remarkable show consisted of selections from the Royal Collections, as Blunt had some kind of inside track with the royal librarian at Windsor Castle nearby. The exhibition included Mansur's *Chameleon* (*c.*1600), one of the most extraordinary of all paintings from the Mughal dynasty (1526–1858). Blunt showed me illustrated Mughal manuscripts from the Royal Collection, which could only be viewed one opening at a time. He also let me see his own private collection of Indian and Persian paintings, which later as an art student I borrowed to make an exhibition. It was of mixed quality but again demonstrated that it was possible to buy Indian pictures – they were not something that simply existed on the walls of a museum. Wilfrid didn't speak much about Indian paintings – he didn't know much about them. So often when people talk about other people they talk about themselves. Wilfrid once commented about the Sitwells that they were marvellous at pointing you in different directions but what they said was usually a tissue of lies. He wasn't really creative enough to tell me any lies, but he was remarkably inaccurate. He loved collecting, and he wanted his pupils to become collectors, too: "If you enjoy art, there's nothing like having a bit of art at home."

For reasons I have often been asked about, but can't remember, I decided that I wanted to collect Indian paintings. I must have been about fourteen years old. To fund my first purchase, I went to the races, having got an advance on future payments, and put all my pocket money on two horses. I lost it.

I have no recollection of how I paid for it but I bought the painting all the same. It wasn't a very good picture, and it didn't remain in my collection for long – I soon exchanged it for something else. But I remember it was a hybrid, seventeenth-century 'Indo-Persian' picture from Aurangabad, India – very brightly coloured, very pretty, of people sitting around in a garden, drinking wine and lolling about in fanciful positions. It was not a very good picture, but I suppose a reasonably respectable picture for a beginner.

My chronological memory is poor, but I remember a few significant moments. The next one was when I bought, in a shop quite near the Victoria and Albert Museum, a portrait of Farrukhsiyar, the Mughal emperor (reigned 1713–19). It was a boring standing portrait and had little to recommend it, apart from the fact that it was in perfect condition, was on a contemporaneous album leaf, and had very pretty borders. I immediately carried it to the Indian Section of the Victoria and Albert Museum. There I met Robert

1 First published in *Asian Art*, Washington, D.C., Fall 1991; reprinted here (with minor revisions) by kind permission of the Director of the Arthur M. Sackler and Freer Gallery of Art.

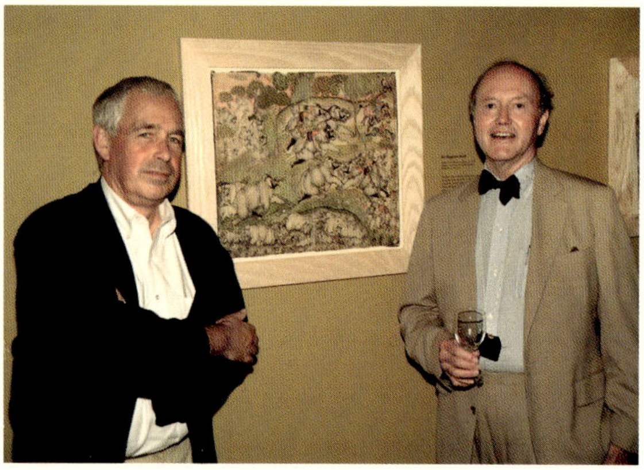

Howard Hodgkin with Stuart Cary Welch and the *Elephant hunt*, at the exhibition of Hodgkin's Indian paintings collection, Washington, 1991. (Photo: John Tsantes, courtesy Arthur M. Sackler Gallery, Washington, D.C.)

Skelton, then an Assistant Keeper, who shortly afterwards, and as a result of my taking this picture to show him, became a lifelong friend. He told me it bore the seal of Sir Elijah Impey, one of the important legal officers of the East India Company. I briefly flirted with the idea that a grand provenance, or at least a good one, makes a picture slightly better – it never does. But through meeting Robert Skelton, I eventually had the most memorable encounter of my collecting life.

Some years later, in 1959, I took Skelton a clutch of drawings. I had become very interested in Indian drawings partly because they were cheap and nobody else at the time seemed to care much about them. Sitting in Robert's office was a slightly plump, pink man, whose name, Cary Welch, meant nothing to me. Rather to my dismay, he looked through my collection of drawings and said, "Well, Beta minus" and grunted and then picked one out and said, "Alpha." I thought this was rather presumptuous, but I also liked that one best myself. His was a generous comment because as time went on I realised it wasn't terribly good. It was a Basohli portrait drawing of what was then thought to be the right period. Robert immediately suggested the three of us go to lunch, which seemed to be hosted by Mr Welch. I have very little memory of the lunch, except that Cary Welch did all the talking.

When Robert had to go back to the museum and continue a much-shortened working day, Cary insisted on taking me home in a taxi. He told me he had been rich since the age of twenty-one. His enthusiasm and charm were such that I didn't think he was much older than that then, though he must have been in his early thirties. We arrived at his small, rented mews house, filled with remarkably ugly Victorian furniture belonging to the landlord. But there were two or three large Indian paintings of breathtaking quality hanging on the walls. He introduced me to his wife and then lifted an enormous Harrod's dress box onto the table. It was filled with seventeenth – and eighteenth-century paintings from different Rajput kingdoms, unmounted, in heaps, as I was later to see them in India. After I had been there several hours, I shyly suggested that I should ring home. He said, "By all means; ask whomever you like to join us for dinner."

The dinner was very late and followed by a slide show, which was rather awkward because the only way you could look at the slides was to hold them up against the side of the lampshade. I remember going home at midnight, realising I had found the kind of new friend that one makes very rarely in a lifetime, and I was filled with a renewed lust to buy pictures.

After he moved away from London, Cary Welch frequently came to stay with me and my family. I never quite got used to his taking down whatever pictures I happened to have hanging up at the time and replacing them with his own most recent purchases, but it was very good training for me. At the same time he invariably ignored anything *I* had recently bought and wanted to show *him*. The more remarkable it was, the more he wished to pretend it wasn't there – not that he need have worried, because at that time he was acquiring masterpieces all over the world. I am now very grateful to him for this generous habit of replacing my pictures with his own; they were infinitely better than mine, and I learned a lot from looking at these great paintings closely. Cary talked incessantly about his pictures. I couldn't have had a better teacher. Though Cary is a scholar as well as a connoisseur, "ultimately he will be remembered as the Bernard Berenson of Indian art and for his great collection.

It's hard to think of another collection made on such purely visual grounds. So many collections of Indian painting are developed on an art historical or even a topographical basis. Though sometimes fascinated by iconography, Cary has said again and again, What you've got to buy is what gives you the biggest art buzz." I also thought that it was *art* (whatever that is), rather more than anything else, which appealed to me in Indian painting.

I started buying Indian pictures wherever I could. Gradually, people also began to bring them to me, and I acquired them in New York or wherever I happened to be. My collection didn't assume any form of its own until I began to see that the best was the enemy of the good. This was perhaps something I had seen when looking at Cary Welch's collection. Like many great collectors, he had vast accumulations of colour slides, things that have never appealed to me. I find them obnoxious and hard to look at, but it meant that sitting in Robert Skelton's sitting room one could look at a large number of pictures quickly and in detail and gradually acquire some sense of quality about a given school or the work of a particular artist.

It didn't take long for me to move from buying whatever I could that I quite liked to becoming very critical about what I already had. My collection, now about sixty paintings and drawings, at times has been even smaller – at one point it was down to about half its current size. Terence McInerney, a postgraduate student taught by Cary Welch who then became a dealer in Indian pictures, has over the last ten years become a great friend. Usually, without giving very specific advice, he has persuaded me that it was still possible to acquire good pictures. Without his help and encouragement my collection would be even smaller.

In the early 1960s I bought a page [cat. no.1] from the *Hamzanama* (Story of Hamza), which I saw reproduced in *Painting in India* by Douglas Barrett and Basil Gray (1963) when I had absolutely no money at all. I mentioned this to my late friend Bruce Chatwin, who was then working at Sotheby's. Bruce knew a dealer who knew the doctor of the woman in Switzerland who owned the picture. Bruce suggested that he could at least find out whether she would be interested in selling the picture and if so for how much. Eventually, entirely due to his intervention, I was able to buy the picture. I didn't have enough money to fly to Switzerland, so it was sent to me. And very disappointing it was. Though it was reproduced in glorious Technicolor in the book, in reality it looked rather grey. After a few years, however, I acclimatised myself to this masterpiece, which I now know is one of my best pictures. To pay for it I had to sell what was then almost my entire collection. I can't remember the exact number of pictures, but it must have been about sixty. Most were not very good and went for small sums of money to people I knew. Even now if I had to choose one picture from my collection, this would be it. It seemed to me to contain everything that I then loved in Indian painting, such as its (comparatively) huge scale, its architectural composition, and its total description of another world. But as a masterpiece it caused problems – masterpieces always do. I am a great believer in comparing one picture with another, and the presence of this picture could be quite destructive to the other. At home there was a mantelpiece opposite my bed on which I would put Indian pictures side by side. I would lie in bed, propped up on pillows at a comfortable angle, looking from side to side, left to right and back again, for hours and hours. During the time when most people read books I would just lie there thinking, "Is this one better than that one? No, it's not better than that one, take it away."

For a long time I thought I would probably never buy another picture, but eventually I got lucky and one or two other masterpieces came my way together with pictures that, though not masterpieces, I thought good enough. I became more and more skilful at making excuses for the ones that were slightly halt or lame. And I often went to quite ridiculous lengths to acquire things.

Disconcertingly, a collection begins to have a life of its own and to make demands on its owner that seem both impersonal and peremptory. For the most part it's really quite easy to resist the innocent charms of gap filling. But when a picture somehow demands to be bought (at whatever price) because it appears to be a great work of art of a kind not otherwise represented in the collection, it means trouble. I long wanted marvellous Basohli pictures, and eventually got some good ones. Early Mughal pictures were seemingly impossible to come by, and then by chance I managed to acquire the fragmentary painting on cloth *A Prince riding an elephant in procession* [no. 4], but my favourite and longest lasting enthusiasm has been for Kota painting.

Elephants are heavy animals but are depicted in painting from Kota as capable of such wild movement that they appear almost weightless – and how mysteriously they seem to haunt the rather conventional landscape. In one whole group of paintings and drawings elephants are being excited by fireworks. This possibly rather unpleasant spectacle did touch a nerve in Kota artists. Perhaps they were able to produce such extraordinary images of elephants in motion as a result of watching these displays. As a collector, my enthusiasm for these Kota pictures became my down-fall – my Waterloo. The acquisition of *Shri Brijnathji and Maharao Durjan Sal hunting* [no. 107] was such a traumatic event in my life as a collector that I felt I could go no further. It's the largest, most expensive picture I have ever bought – and the only one for which I have exchanged one of my paintings. This great, though fragmentary, picture finally enabled me to escape from the almost nagging lust that often keeps collectors in a slightly restless and unfulfilled condition for the rest of their lives.

At the moment, the prospect of another such purchase of equal scale, importance, and cost is unthinkable. So I am probably safe – and the exhibition of my collection at the Sackler Gallery is meant to celebrate the end of an obsession that has lasted more than forty years. Looking at the collection now, I realise that it has been making its demands for longer than I thought. Like Cary Welch, I had always been in search of art, but nobody can define that. For an artist there are elements of scale, form, and colour that are beyond verbal description. In Indian painting I have found much that for me could be found nowhere else, but I cannot tell you what – I can only metaphorically wave my arms at the pictures – and say look!

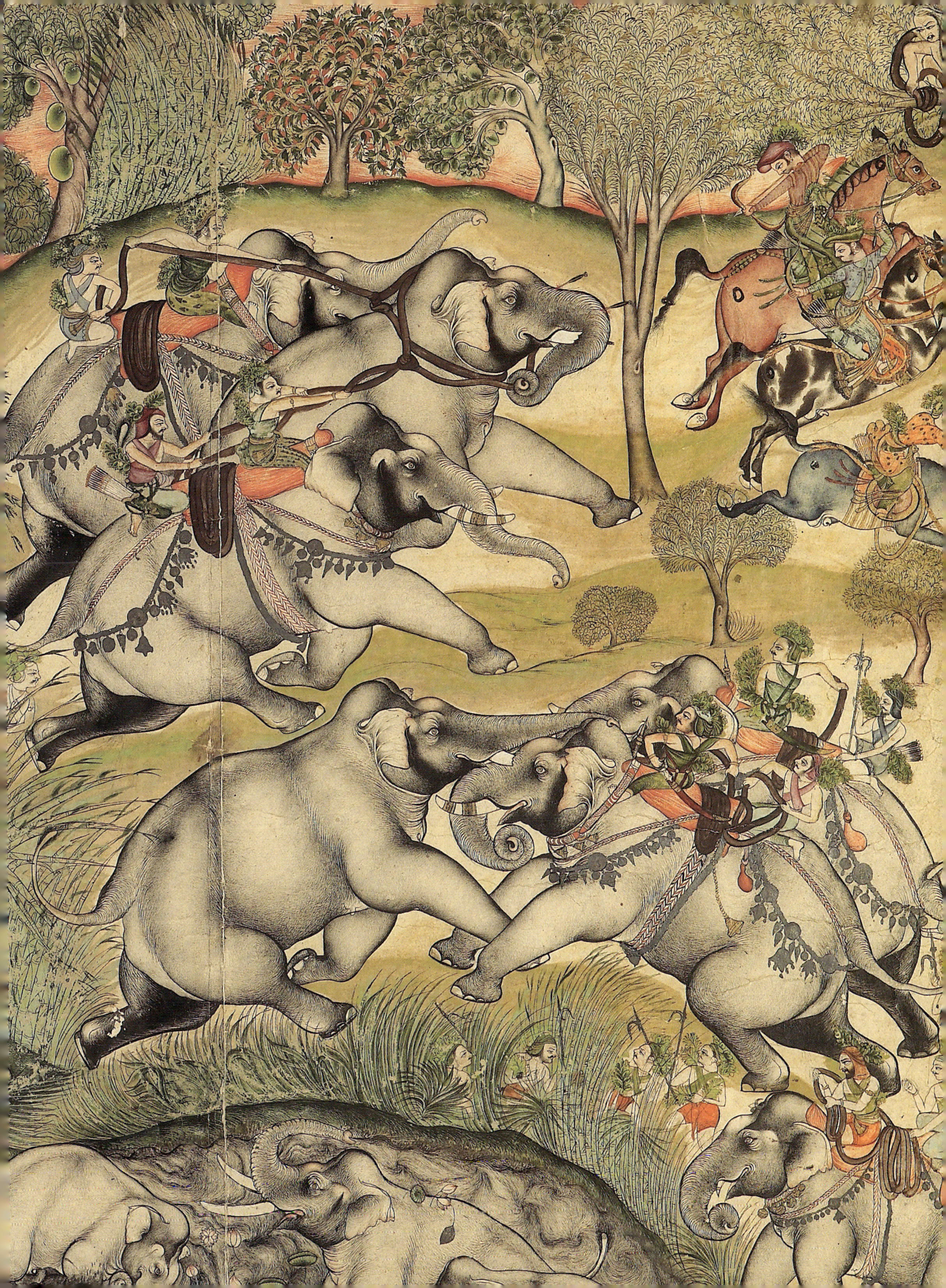

Appendix 2

On Collecting Indian Paintings (1991)[1]

Howard Hodgkin

I want to talk first this evening about the history of collecting. I think it's worth thinking about what collecting actually is. A great collection often seems to be the result of one very rich man going shopping. It isn't. It is really partly illness, an incurable obsession. It's partly – sadly in some cases – a desire for future or posthumous glory, perhaps more often for status while the collector is still alive. Also, and of course far more importantly it represents the human desire to get near works of art. At its worst it's greed, or the desire simply to possess, like a child at a party being given something to take home. But it's much more than that at its highest. It's difficult to think immediately of a collection which is sufficiently pure – made by people like Mrs Havemeyer, Gertrude Stein even or Nelson Rockefeller for a little while, and so on. There are moments in people's lives when the desire to possess works of art takes possession of them, and that is of course where – as an almost registered sufferer – I know all about it. But when you go into a museum and see the rather unfortunate result of some very rich man saying that his collection should be kept together and not mixed – as I'm sure the Director of the Museum would wish – with other works of the same kind, spare a thought, or a twinge of sympathy, for the poor man who probably ruined his personal life and spent far too much money, to make something that was his.

So first of all, collecting is the ultimate in possessiveness. Objects probably fare better than people at being at the sharp end of such emotion. They get nurtured and looked after and do not suffer from an obsessive love, unless they're repainted too much or interfered with. Painters, sculptors and architects throughout history have collected. I'm not knowledgeable enough to go through the whole history of artists as collectors, but it is a very strange thing that something that is so nearly an artistic activity in its own right has attracted and possessed so many artists. Please don't misunderstand when I name a few of them. We only really know about great artists and so those are the people I have to mention. I'm not for a moment joining myself onto them when I mention the names of people like Degas, Van Dyck, Rembrandt or the great English watercolourist Cotman. (Rembrandt in particular ruined himself by collecting works of art quite as much as by buying jewels for his wife).

The impulse to collect is thus a way of making art your own, but it's also a way of making art; a collection in the end is a work of art. A collection of extremely expensive French Impressionist pictures, recently bought and put in very grand Louis XV frames with little lights on top of them and very expensive price tags is obviously not a work of art. It's a work of self-aggrandisement. It's a way of saying look how rich, or how glamorous I am. But a collection which is made from passion, a collection which will never take no for an answer, when some new, desirable object comes along, is a very different matter. And for an artist it's a very difficult thing, because at what point do you say: 'I'm a painter', or 'I'm a sculptor' and not 'I'm a collector'? How much vanity comes into it? I don't know. Those of you who are collectors, or are going to

1 Transcript of a talk given after the opening of the exhibition *Indian Paintings and Drawings from the Collection of Howard Hodgkin* at the Arthur M. Sackler Gallery, Washington, DC, in September 1991; later published, with permission, in its present edited form in *The Ashmolean*, no. 23, Christmas 1992.

be collectors, probably do know; it's not something that I really like to try and measure, but it is certainly a disease.

I come from a family of collectors, and not very good ones mostly. I say that with pride really because they were so pure. (One thing I've forgotten to say is that to be a great collector, you don't have to collect great objects; and plenty of people who bought a lot of great objects haven't been great collectors). I have a great-grandfather who was nicknamed 'Rariora'. He made many different collections, including the first and still the best collection of documentary English pottery, about which he wrote a book which he was very proud of, called *Dated Examples of English Earthenware*. He collected the papers of the transvestite Chevalier D'Eon. He collected early printed books. His collection was published in a catalogue of three volumes. Among his other collections, particularly noteworthy were his objects called *lusus naturae*, small coloured stones which, when you looked at them carefully, had accidental pictures. His most celebrated example had a portrait of George IV: when you chopped the stone in half there was this king inside. In spite of the period in which he lived, his collection was more like a Renaissance *Wunderkammer* than something from the late nineteenth century.

Nevertheless, his son (my grandfather) and his wife introduced me at a very tender age to collecting. When I was a small child, sent away to boarding school, my grandmother would send me little antique watch keys or even the faces of eighteenth century watches in an envelope, to cheer me up at school. She thought a little bit of collecting would do the trick. I didn't really understand what was going on at all. As a child I was evacuated to America, and I stayed on Long Island for a while with a family where the mother was a dedicated collector of American antiques. But I didn't know what the word 'antique' was. I remember reading a comic at the age of seven, which was all about Mickey and Minnie Mouse. I was really taken by a picture of Minnie Mouse in her wonderful high-heeled clumpy shoes, holding up in one hand a little stool and in the other a telephone. She was saying: 'I just bought this great antique footstool' – I thought, what could this be? So I talked to the woman I was staying with, and she told me that 'antique' meant old and precious and admirable. Then I was taken to the museum and I was shown things in glass cases. So I thought 'antique' was something inside a glass case. After this I was taken to antique shops and started buying little things, all of which were complete rubbish. But I'm afraid that was when the collecting infection began to take hold.

Later I returned to England and went to school. My art master, Wilfrid Blunt, was rather in the tradition of my great-grandfather, a dilettante collector. He was the brother of the famous, and later sadly notorious, Anthony Blunt and was the complete opposite of him. He knew nothing about a great many things. And he was a wonderful teacher to schoolboys. He had a little glass case in the schoolroom in which every week he would put another object from his collection. After a while I realised he was very proud of these objects, particularly the way fresh-faced young schoolchildren would say: 'Please Sir, what is that?' Then he would say, in a sort of auctioneer / dealer's voice of great warmth and fruitiness, 'Oh, that's very rare. That's terribly important. That's very grand.' That added another aspect to the kind of objects people collect, which was I think quite important to me.

It was Wilfrid Blunt who first showed me what Indian painting was. He showed me several Indian pictures, and they were not very good. It was some years before I was willing to admit to myself quite how bad they were. But they were very interesting; and there is a lot to be said to coming first to a subject in that way, through objects of poor quality, not least because I could go to a shop and buy something almost as bad, and take it home and look at it and possess it. And so I did. I bought one bad picture and then another bad picture. Gradually I accumulated a lot of bad pictures. When I had accumulated quite a few, I began to realise that a collection was not just a lot of things, not one damn thing after another, like a collection of stamps or cigarette cards. It was something else. I didn't know quite what, but that was the first stirring that maybe there was more to it than this. I used to look at my pictures with increasing irritation. I remember picking them up and holding them, and sort of shaking them slightly, rather to say, 'Why aren't you better?' This was neither good for them, nor really very helpful.

But eventually I became friends with various other people who collected them. One of these was called Robert Erskine, and he was the sort of collector that has almost disappeared off the face of the earth. He had lots of money for a little while. Money on the whole is not very helpful if you want to make a collection, because I think it can open up too many possibilities: if you can buy *anything* then that makes it far more difficult to buy *something*. But Robert was very clever. He had wanted to collect seriously since he was even younger than me. Then one of his relations died at a fortunate age for him, and he suddenly had serious money to spend. And he spent it, as quickly as if he was living a loose life and having luxuries of every kind. Far from it: his luxuries consisted of things like pre-dynastic Egyptian sculpture, Boulle cabinets, bits of Greek pottery. And he was brilliant at it. The reason I say that he's the kind of collector that's almost disappeared is that he collected right across the board. His sense of quality was almost infallible. For example, he once bought for a very small amount of money a cardboard box full of shards of an archaic black-figure Greek pot. He spent the next six years of his life sticking them together. Then he realised there were some pieces missing; and the dealer he bought them from said: 'Oh, yes. I've got some pieces from the top of a wardrobe in Lord Elgin's house. I think they fit your vase.' They did; and they had the name of the artist. That huge vase is now in the British Museum.

Robert Erskine was the person who put me in touch with a network of ancient Parisian dealers who had their hands on the art market for a long time. The most famous of these was Charles Ratton, alias Uncle Charlie. He was the man who used to sell negro sculptures to Picasso or André Durand, and many of the props you see in Matisse's rooms, or Gertrude Stein and Alice B. Toklas' rooms, all came from Uncle Charlie. These vague bits of Tuscan furniture were, as it were, early products of Uncle Charlie, who over the years moved up and up in the world. Eventually as an old man he was selling things to the Rockefellers and other people and museums all over the world.

When eventually I sold that great heap of terrible pictures which I could never forgive for being so bad – and this was achieved with immense difficulty, by selling them to unsuspecting friends, or a kind relative who bought one of the larger, more doubtful pictures – it was Uncle Charlie who got the money and who went to Switzerland and brought back the *Hamzanama* painting, which is Number 1 in the exhibition catalogue. And it is a great masterpiece. It's such a relief to be able to say that. The *Hamzanama* is perhaps the greatest single achievement of Indian pictorial art apart from the Ajanta caves. The pictures in it vary tremendously in quality, and they're executed by many different artists. This happens to be a great picture from it. I have seen many other pictures from the series in Vienna and other places. It would be hard to say which page is the best, and I certainly wouldn't say that of mine, but it is a very good page from that manuscript.

But when I got it, having not had the money to fly to Switzerland and look at it beforehand, I was horrified. It arrived by mail; I had only enough money to pay its fare from Switzerland. I undid the parcel and there was this large, grey and slightly multi-coloured picture; from the side it looked crooked, and it was a mess. Perhaps that was when I began to really understand that condition isn't all that important, because I grew to love the picture. It was really only very dirty and had been stuck on different pieces of board so it had an uneven surface. Twenty years later it was properly cleaned and flattened, and turned out to be in wonderful condition. It now looks exactly like the coloured reproduction in the Skira book of Indian painting, which had first led me to buy it.

The acquisition of that picture turned me into a real collector; before that I wasn't even an apprentice collector. But once I owned that picture, Sherman Lee of the Cleveland Museum came to see me. People started treating me with a mixture of contempt and respect which I didn't entirely understand. And also at that moment, as I have written about, the great Cary Welch came into my life, and then everything hotted up tremendously. He used to come down and see me with all his latest acquisitions. He would take down from the wall any of my own Indian paintings that happened to be hanging, and put up his own instead. He would stay for weeks at a time and I would look at his pictures, because of course I couldn't look at mine. There was a time when I didn't dare look at my own pictures, even when I was by myself, in case they were not really good enough. When Cary looked at my pictures, he sometimes remained very silent. It was something like twelve years before I realised that those were the rare occasions when I had got something that he wanted.

I owe Cary Welch an enormous debt: nobody could have been more generous with his knowledge, and far more important, his feelings. Everything that I've ever done as a collector has been based ultimately on the strength of feeling. Cary's definition of what you had to buy was something that gave you a real 'art zap', and if it didn't do that, forget it. That actually is a very high ideal. It may not sound like it, but it is. He, like the rest of us, has often fallen short of it, because you can so easily buy something which you think is interesting or historically important. For Cary, who though he isn't by temperament a scholar has certainly behaved as one for much of his life, a picture can be 'very important' if it represents a missing link or another work by a painter whom you greatly admire. But in the last resort that's not what really matters, if you don't get some kind of nervous shock – I call it a shock to the heart, though I think it's somewhere rather lower down than the heart that this shock takes place. But if you don't get that, you shouldn't buy it. I think that applies to museum curators as well as private collectors.

But it is very difficult to stick to that ideal through thick or thin. To keep looking at a picture or an object constantly and asking questions of it is very hard work. I used to teach a lot, and I had a wonderful student who – though I never mentioned Indian painting or collecting to him – became a dealer, because he thought it was so horrible to be an artist. He said to me: "Look at you. Who'd want to be like you?" So he became briefly a brilliant dealer in Indian painting. I went to see him once. There were no pictures hanging on the wall at all, and I said: "Where are all your pictures?" He said – I wish I could imitate his accent: he was Australian and at really serious moments like that would always try and sound as lowdown and primitive as he could – "I got good pictures now." It was all said with great sarcasm. "I've had an art education. You taught me for five years. I've learned a lot about art." (By now I was feeling quite nervous). "And that's why there are no pictures on the wall. Because I've only got good pictures now. And good pictures ask too many questions." And he really had a point. They do. They are extremely demanding. And *you* ask *them* endless questions as well. So how much easier to acquire something which is decorative, which is charming or has iconographic interest, or the colours go with the drapes, and so on: it's a good buy; it's a bargain; it's a missing link in scholarship. All these distractions get in the way. To resist them all, to push them out of the way, you might feel is very easy, particularly if an object costs a lot of money or you had to change your life in order to acquire it. Somehow that doesn't make it easier. It makes it more difficult.

So Cary, during the years that he used to bring his pictures to stay, taught me lessons that I don't think I could have learned in any other way. In the years since, he has actually borrowed some pictures of mine for an exhibition that he was putting together. From then on I realised that he acknowledged that I too was a collector; to the extent that in a weak moment he once said: "Well, it's really only you and I", which actually is not true, but was again very generous.

What I'm trying to convey is that collecting is very,

very hard work. And strangely unrewarding, because if one has to – as several times in my life I have had to – break off a certain section of one's collection as if it were a piece of peanut brittle and exchange it for one, perhaps quite small, picture (though in my own case they're usually quite big, if possible), it doesn't necessarily make you like the new picture very much. You have to get used to it. In the end, you really have to forgive it, before you forgive yourself.

That takes me to the next thing, which is the awful autonomy of the collection. It's like Frankenstein's monster. It's like having something that you can't ever lock up in the cupboard, because it's always coming out again. Once you have bought one masterpiece or very good picture, the next picture you buy might not be quite as good – and, of course, for me it never was, until comparatively recently. But you feel it's got to be up there somehow; it's got to be nearly as good. Otherwise it just sort of shrivels and goes away. That happened for some years; and my collection grew very slowly.

It's all also a matter of luck. Kenneth Clark once pointed out that all collections are to some extent opportunist. You can only buy what is there. You can't behave like one of the Popes, who went around stealing great books from other people until they fell out from under his robe. So you only buy what you can. The trouble is in the end the collection makes you buy things that you don't want to buy. You think, I can't have that, it's too expensive, but nevertheless... Then you're in real trouble; and that's why you have to see if there's any light at the end of the tunnel. In my case, when Milo Beach suggested to me more than ten years ago that an exhibition such as this should take place, I remember very vaguely thinking that perhaps when that does happen, when, in the classic way, a collector has a published catalogue, then that's the end of it, that's when he'll stop collecting. So I thought, that's when I'll stop; and I have stopped – apart from a little mopping up here and there...

Finally, I would like to say a little about Indian painting, and about why I have bought the pictures I have. I'm not a scholar at all. I'm an artist, and my collection is the collection of an artist. Though I once made an exhibition [at the National Gallery, London in 1979] called, embarrassingly, 'The Artist's Eye', I don't think artists' eyes have any particular virtue, except that they exist independently of scholarship. That's not necessarily an advantage; and of course all my life as a collector, I've been rushing to sensitive and passionate scholars saying: "What do you think? What do you think?" But I can truly say that they've never made me reject something I've bought, even if they have sometimes given me tremors about it.

When I first saw Indian painting I thought of it as the most extraordinary phenomenon, because it was a system of representation, a microcosmic world, which was completely different, yet *not* completely different from our own. A lot of Indian painting is extremely representational, but in a way that is sometimes literal – like the kind of symbols you see on old maps that indicate, 'Here be trees', or 'Here be the city of so and so.' But it's often far *more* literal than that. I've never forgotten the first time I went to India and saw a pool surrounded by lilies, in a very unimportant, junky little yard somewhere; it wasn't the yard of a palace or anything. There were birds flying about and there were bright green trees. They were absolutely similar to the kind of pool, lilies, birds and trees that you would see in an eighteenth century Deccani painting. It was a sort of one-for-one representation. The only thing that would be missing in the picture would be light from a specific source. Nothing reminds one more forcefully that, even going back to fifteenth century Italian paintings, already light comes from one side and shadows fall on the other. In Indian paintings they don't. Shadows exist, but they're wherever the artist wants to put them, which I think naturally appealed to me as a painter as soon as I saw them as a child. It's the straightforwardness of Indian painting, the frankness of it which appealed to me enormously.

Whereas old European paintings tend to be covered in brown varnish and their colours may have changed a lot, Indian paintings – in spite of the remarks that everybody has made about the condition of my pictures (they're not as bad as people say) – have survived very well. And they are made in a very straightforward way. They are paintings on paper where layers of different colours have been built up. The drawing is of tremendous importance. It's all this kind of thing, which is really physical more than anything else, which appealed to me initially. The subject matter or narrative aspect has mattered much less. Recently I finally looked at all my pictures together, when they were being gathered for this exhibition. I was surprised to see that in fact they were genre scenes, the kind of painting that appeals to me less than almost any other in Western art. Nearly all my Indian pictures in one way or another show real life. I do of course have pictures that have Hindu religious subjects or mythological storylines, though not many; and I think that is only because most Indian painting is about mythological subjects, so that the style of each school is built up on that kind of traditional subject matter. What is marvellous to me and ever moving, is when the artist who's been making stereotyped images suddenly looks, as it were, slightly to one side, and starts looking at something, while still using the same wonderful strict tempo pictorial style which has been evolved to represent, for example, the Hindu pantheon. He just moves slightly to one side and uses the same language for the features of somebody that, if he doesn't know, he at least knows what they look like. That to me is very moving. And it's even more moving when it is applied to plants, animals, and of course to my great love in Indian painting, elephants. I don't think I possess a single picture of an elephant in which one could be quite certain, as one would be with a great Western artist, that Mr X – and remember that for the most part even when we know their names, Indian artists are rather anonymous compared to the one-man bands of the West – that Mr X has ever looked at an elephant, and sat there as if he was at a drawing school and sat on his little stool and held up his brush...never. It is all in the head. It is all the product of an infinitely refined imagination in the face of nature; and perhaps often at it's best – at its greatest – of only an adequate craftsmanship.

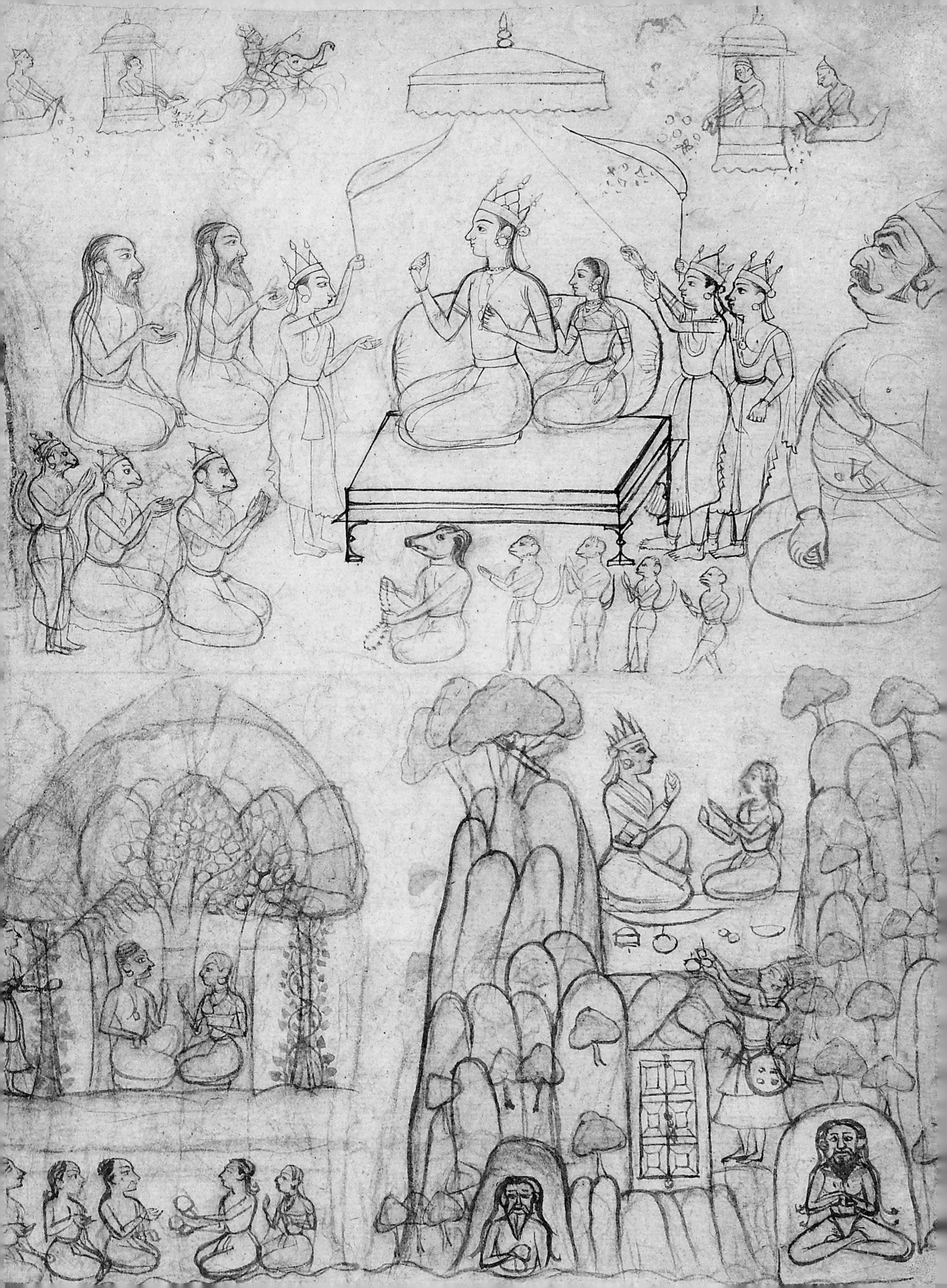

Appendix 3

On Indian Drawings (1983)[1]

Howard Hodgkin

This exhibition was arranged by an artist. A lot of nonsense has been written about the 'Artist's Eye' – it's certainly not superior but possibly a bit different. But anyway how would I know? As an artist I can choose what I like, a privilege for which I am grateful but one not available to the scholar or art historian.

My love for Indian drawing is something I want to share with other people. But it is based on feeling rather than knowledge, and so this exhibition is neither comprehensive nor historical. Few of these drawings come from museums because they don't have many. Most are from private collections, many from my own.

When I first became interested in Indian drawings and began to collect them I succumbed to the easy temptation of equating them with great European drawings of a kind I would never be able to possess. This one reminded me of an Ingres, that one was like a Rembrandt. The only advantage of these rather silly comparisons was to make me realise how unlike European works Indian drawings actually are. Tentatively at first, I began to see them as great drawings in their own right, executed in a language entirely their own.

But there were other attractions. They reminded me of India in a manner that was both intense and impersonal. The foreignness of the subject matter, and at the same time its curious familiarity, were moving in a detached sort of way. And my ignorance of style and iconography enabled me to enjoy these beautiful drawings without needing to worry about what they actually were. The subject matter retained its innocent enchantments: a ruler visiting a holy man in a garden, a prince hunting lions, an exquisite portrait of an animal. But inevitably as I learned more about them by making comparisons between one drawing and another the rot set in, and I started making value judgements. From then on I began to have endless conversations with friends on this fascinating subject. With Professor Cary Welch of Harvard, whom I first met many years ago when I first took some drawings to the Indian Section of the Victoria and Albert Museum for an opinion. He was typically forthright in his reactions. Not only has he a celestial gift of the gab when talking about Indian art, he is also a world authority on the subject; and his encouragement and enthusiasm have meant much to me over the years. Also with Robert Skelton, now Keeper of the Indian Section, who was also present on the same occasion and who has remained a constant and articulate prisoner's friend. (All collectors are prisoners.) And finally with Terence McInerney, who better late than never, opened my eyes to Mughal art.

Drawing is the most naked of the visual arts. Sometimes we can feel an almost physical contact with the artist and share in the workings of his mind and imagination. We learn to recognise and identify with certain marks on paper, traces of pencil and gouache, the speed of execution and the possibilities of various media, the genuine searches and intentional errors. The human element is paramount, so we feel we know when we are being told lies by the draftsman.

But our familiarity with these things can act as a barrier when we start looking at Indian drawings

1 Written as an introduction to the Hayward Gallery *Indian Drawing* exhibition catalogue, by Howard Hodgkin and Terence McInerney (London: Arts Council, 1983); reprinted here with minor revisions.

because at first they look so physically alike. For example, the emphasis on artistic personality, the self-revelation of a single human being, that is so familiar in Western art, is not often found in Indian art. And it is all too easy to equate the loose and calligraphic with an individual hand. Nor do we find human emotion expressed in any direct way. However, pantheistic feelings about nature abound, not only in images of animals such as the ubiquitous elephants, but also in the mysterious visual life given to the portrayal of plants and trees.

The Indian landscape, in so far as one can generalise at all is mostly quite empty and very dusty with a general tone and colour of beige and cream not unlike the tint of much of the paper that is used for these drawings. The sun and the light that come from it are so bright and hard that the edges of everything, whether leaf, stone, hill, building, animal or man, are very sharp. Even morning and evening pass in a flash. Shadows are cut-outs. The light is so bright that the modelling of surfaces is quite shallow. The scale is also different from what one is used to. The even illumination negates distance, so that the enormity of space is quite visible and everything looks and feels small.

Apart from the technicalities of drawing with brush and ink, there may be another reason for the almost totally linear foundation of Indian drawings. In an Indian situation, a tree is a tree. If it is depicted surrounded by blank paper, it is none the less representational. The one-to-one relationship between a drawn shape and its counterpart in nature is both finite and literal. There are no saving clauses, no sudden descents into mysterious calligraphy or romantic vagueness, no hopeful journeys into the unknown. All is clear and, if not exact, at least concrete.

The delicately coloured, unfinished landscape [reproduced on the cover of the *Indian drawing* catalogue] is of an astonishing fidelity to anyone who has been to Kota. But it lacks the enclosing envelope of light that we would expect to find in Western art. In this drawing, the trees cast no shadows. Likewise when we look at the modelling on an elephant's belly or, more rarely, on a man's face, it doesn't really reveal an effect of light. Rather like braille, it demonstrates the tactile quality of the form. Volume is more often implied than described. Indian draftsmen must surely be among the absolute masters of enclosing a weighty form between two simple lines, leaving the spectator to fill in what lies between.

Among the different subjects represented in this exhibition such as the durbar, tiger hunts, human and animal portraits, etc., elephants predominate. This is partly because I have a particular love of drawings of elephants. But there is also a better reason: good Indian drawings of elephants are more frequently encountered than drawings of any other subject. Human beings in particular are not nearly as elaborately or as enthusiastically depicted.

Perhaps the shifting volume and surface, the loose skin and the obvious structure inside it, the colossal weight which can defy gravity with a leap in the air and then sink to the ground in a heap like a mountain, were to the Indian artist what the changing forms and moods of the human body are supposed to have been to the Post-Renaissance European artist.

Bibliography

Abu'l Fazl Allami, *'Ain-i Akbari*, tr. H. Blochmann, repr. Delhi, 1965.

Aijazuddin, F.S., *Pahari paintings and Sikh portraits in the Lahore Museum*, London, 1977.

Aitken, M., 'Sahib Ram', in Beach, Fischer and Goswamy eds., *Masters of Indian painting*, Zurich, 2011, II pp.623–40.

Alderman, J.R., 'Paintings of Africans in the Deccan', in K.X. Robbins and J. McLeod eds., *African élites in India: Habshi Amarat*, Ahmedabad, 2006, pp.107–23.

van Alphen, J., and A. Aris eds., *Oriental Medicine: An Illustrated Guide to the Asian Arts of Healing*, London, 1995.

Archer, M., *Company drawings in the India Office Library*, London, 1972.

Archer, W.G., *Indian miniatures*, London, 1960.

—— *Indian paintings from the Punjab Hills*, 2 vols., London, 1973.

—— *Visions of courtly India*, Washington, D.C., 1976.

Arts Council, *In the image of man*, London, 1982.

Ashton, Sir Leigh, ed., *The art of Indian and Pakistan*, London, 1950.

Barrett, D., and B. Gray, *Painting of India*, Geneva, 1963.

Bautze, J., 'Portraits of Rao Ratan and Madho Singh Hara', *Berliner Indologische Studien*, 2, 1986a, pp.87–106.

—— 'Mughal and Deccani influence on early 17th century murals of Bundi', in R. Skelton et al. eds., *Facets of Indian art*, London, 1986b, pp.168–75.

—— 'Zur Darstellung der Hauptgottheiten Kotas in der Malerei der zweiten Hälfte des 18. und der ersten Hälfte des 19. Jahrhunderts', *Berliner Indologische Studien*, 3, 1987, pp.253–78.

—— 'Portraitmalerei unter Maharao Ram Singh von Kota', *Artibus Asiae*, XLIX, 3/4, 1988–89, pp.316–50.

—— 'Shri Brijnathji and the murals in the Chattar Mahal, Kota', in D.C. Bhattacharya and D. Handa eds., *Praci-Prabha: Perpectives in Indology, Essays in honour of B.N. Mukherjee*, New Delhi, 1989, pp.319–26.

—— 'The Ajmer Darbar of 1832 and Kota painting', *South Asian Studies*, 6, 1990, pp.71–91.

—— *Interaction of Cultures: Indian and Western painting, 1780-1910*, Alexandria, Va., 1998.

—— 'Early painting at Bundi', in A. Topsfield ed., *Court painting in Rajasthan*, Bombay, 2000, pp.12–25.

Bayly, C.A., ed., *The Raj: India and the British 1600-1947*, London, 1990.

Beach, M.C., 'Painting at Devgarh', *Archives of Asian Art*, XXIV, 1970–71, pp.23–35.

—— *Rajput painting at Bundi and Kota*, Ascona, 1974.

—— 'The Mughal painter Kesu Das', *Archives of Asian Art*, XXX, 1976–77, pp.34–52.

—— *The Grand Mogul: Imperial painting in India 1600-1660*, Williamstown, Mass., 1978.

—— *The imperial image: Paintings for the Mughal court*, Washington, D.C., 1981.

—— *Early Mughal painting*, Cambridge, Mass., 1987.

—— *Mughal and Rajput painting*, Cambridge, 1992.

—— 'Wall-paintings at Bundi: Comments and a new discovery', *Artibus Asiae*, LXVIII, 1, 2008, pp.101–43.

—— 'The Masters of the Chunar Ragamala and the Hada Master', in Beach, Fischer and Goswamy eds., *Masters of Indian painting*, Zurich, 2011a, I, pp.291–304.

—— 'Masters of early Kota painting', in Beach, Fischer and Goswamy eds., *Masters of Indian painting*, Zurich, 2011b, II, pp.459–78.

—— 'Bagta and Chokha', in Beach, Fischer and Goswamy eds., *Masters of Indian painting*, Zurich, 2011c, II, pp.733–52.

—— E. Fischer and B.N. Goswamy eds., *Masters of Indian painting*, 2 vols., Zurich 2011.

—— and E. Koch, *King of the World: The Padshahnama*, London and Washington, D.C., 1997.

—— and N. Singh, *Bagta and Chokha: Master artists at Devgarh*, Zurich, 2005.

Bernier, F., *Travels in the Mogul Empire AD 1656–68*, tr. A. Constable, 2nd ed., London, 1916.

Bibliothèque Nationale, *A la cour du Grand Moghol*, Paris, 1986.

Binney, E. 3rd, *Indian miniature painting: The Mughal and Deccani schools*, Portland, Or., 1973.

Boner, G., E. Fischer and B.N. Goswamy, *Sammlung Alice Boner*, Zurich, 1994.

Brand, M., *The vision of kings*, Canberra, 1995

—— and G.D. Lowry, *Akbar's India: Art from the Mughal City of Victory*, New York, 1985.

British Museum, *Paintings from the Muslim courts of India*, London, 1976.

van Buitenen, J. tr., *The Mahabharata*, vol.2, Chicago, 1975.

Chandra, P., 'A series of *Ramayana* paintings', *Bulletin of the Prince of Wales Museum*, 6, 1957–59, pp.64–70.

Cimino, R.M. et al., *Life at court in Rajasthan*, Florence, 1985.

Coomaraswamy, A.K., *Indian drawings: Second series*, London, 1912.

—— *Rajput painting*, 2 vols., London, 1916.

—— *Catalogue of the Indian collections: Museum of Fine Arts, Boston*, vol.5, Cambridge, Mass., 1926.

Craven, R.C. Jr. ed., *Ramayana: Pahari paintings*, Bombay, 1990.

Crill, R., *Marwar painting: A history of the Jodhpur style*, Bombay, 1999.

——, S. Stronge and A. Topsfield eds., *Arts of Mughal India: Studies in honour of Robert Skelton*, London, 2004.

—— and K. Jariwala, *The Indian Portrait 1560-1860*, London, 2010.

Cummins, J., *Indian painting: From cave temples to the colonial period*, Boston, 2006.

Dalrymple, W., *The Last Mughal: The fall of a dynasty, Delhi, 1857*, London, 2006.

Das, A.K., 'An introductory note on the emperor Akbar's *Ramayana* and its miniatures', in R. Skelton et al. eds., *Facets of Indian art*, London, 1986, pp.94–104.

Davidson, J.L., *Art of the Indian subcontinent from Los Angeles collections*, Los Angeles, 1968.

Dehejia, V. ed., *Devi: The Great Goddess*, Washington, DC: Arthur M. Sackler Gallery, 1999.

Desai, V., *Life at court: Art for India's rulers, 16th-19th centuries*, Boston, 1986.

Diamond, D., and C. Glynn, *Garden and Cosmos: The royal paintings of Jodhpur*, Washington, D.C., 2008.

Dickinson, E., and K. Khandalavala, *Kishangarh painting*, New Delhi, 1959.

Digby, S., 'A corpus of "Mughal" glass', *Bulletin of the School of Oriental and African Studies*, XXXVI, 1, 1973, pp.80–96.

Eastwick, E.B. tr., *The Anvar-i Suhaili or the Lights of Canopus*, Hertford, 1854.

Ebeling, K., *Ragamala painting*, Basel, 1973.

Edgerton, F., *The elephant lore of the Hindus*, New Haven, 1931; repr. Delhi, 1985.

Ehnbom, D.J., *Indian miniatures: The Ehrenfeld collection*, New York, 1985.

Emerson, J., *Images of Krishna: Painted Picchavais of the Vallabhaite sect*, Santa Barbara, 1987.

Falk, T., et al., *Indian painting: Mughal and Rajput, and a Sultanate manuscript*, London Colnaghi & Co, 1978.

Falk, T., and M. Archer, *Indian miniatures in the India Office Library*, London, 1981.

Filippi, G.G., *Indian miniatures and paintings from the 16th to the 19th century: The collection of Howard Hodgkin*, Milan, 1997.

Fondation Custodia, *L'Inde des légendes et des réalités: Miniatures indiennes et persanes de la Fondation Custodia (Collections Frits Lugt)*, Paris, 1986.

—— *Couleurs de l'Inde: Nouvelles acquisitions de la collection Frits Lugt*, Paris, 2002.

Gahlin, S., *The courts of India: Indian miniatures from the collection of the Fondation Custodia, Paris*, Zwolle, 1991.

Glück, H., *Die indischen Miniaturen des Hämzä-Romanes im Österreichischen Museum für Kunst und Industrie in Wien und in anderen Sammlungen*, Vienna, 1925.

Glynn, C., 'Seven inscribed Pahari portraits', *Los Angeles County Museum of Art Bulletin*, XXV, 1979, pp.38–55.

—— 'Early painting in Mandi', *Artibus Asiae*, XLIV, 1, 1983, pp.21–64.

—— 'The early Master at the court of Mandi', in Beach, Fischer and Goswamy eds., *Masters of Indian painting*, Zurich, 2011a, I, pp.407–24.

—— 'The "Stipple Master"', in Beach, Fischer and Goswamy eds., *Masters of Indian painting*, Zurich, 2011b, II, pp.515–30.

—— R. Skelton and A.L. Dallapiccola, *Ragamala: Paintings from India from the Claudio Moscatelli Collection*, London, 2011.

Goetz, H., *The art and architecture of Bikaner State*, Oxford, 1950.

Goswamy, B.N., *Rasa: Les neuf visages de l'art indien*, Paris, 1986a.

—— *Essence of Indian art*, San Francisco, 1986b.

—— 'Essence and appearance: Some notes on Indian portraiture', *Facets of Indian art*, eds. R. Skelton et al., London, 1986c, pp.193–202.

—— *Nainsukh of Guler*, Zurich, 1997.

—— and U. Bhatia, *Painted visions: The Goenka Collection of Indian paintings*, New Delhi, 1999.

—— and E. Fischer, *Wonders of a Golden Age: Painting at the court of the Great Mughals*, Zurich, 1987.

—— *Pahari Masters*, Zurich, 1992.

—— 'Manaku', in Beach, Fischer and Goswamy eds., *Masters of Indian painting*, II, Zurich, 2011a, II, pp.641–58.

—— 'Nainsukh of Guler', in Beach, Fischer and Goswamy eds., *Masters of Indian painting*, II, Zurich, 2011b, pp.659–86.

Gulbadan Begam, *The history of Humayun*, tr. A.S. Beveridge, repr. Delhi 2001.

Gray, B., 'A new Mughal painting on stuff', *Ars Islamica*, IV, 1937, pp.459–61.

Grube, E., *Islamic paintings from the 11th to the 18th century in the collection of Hans P. Kraus*, New York, n.d. [1972?]

Habighorst, L.W. et al., *Love for pleasure: Betel, tobacco, wine and drugs in Indian miniatures*, Koblenz, 2007.

Haidar, N.N., *The Kishangarh school of painting c.1680-1850*, D.Phil thesis, University of Oxford, 1995.

—— 'Bhawanidas', in Beach, Fischer and Goswamy eds., *Masters of Indian painting*, Zurich, 2011a, II, pp.531–46.

—— 'The *Kitab-i Nauras*; Key to Bijapur's Golden Age', in N.N. Haidar and M. Sardar eds., *Sultans of the South: Arts of India's Deccan courts, 1323–1687*, New York, 2011b, pp.26–43.

Heber, R., *Narrative of a journey through the upper provinces of India*, 2 vols., London, 1828.

Heeramaneck, A.N., *Masterpieces of Indian painting*, n.p., 1984.

Hickmann, R. and V. Enderlein, *Indische Albumblätter: Miniaturen und Kalligraphien aus der Zeit der Moghul-Kaiser*, Leipzig, 1979.

Hodgkin, H., and T. McInerney, *Indian drawing*, London, 1983.

Hurel, R., *Miniatures et peintures indiennes*, vol.1, Paris, 2010.

Hutchison, J., and J. Ph. Vogel, *History of the Panjab Hill states*, 2 vols., Lahore, 1933.

Inayat Khan, *The Shah Jahan Nama*, eds. W. Begley and Z.A. Desai, New Delhi, 1990.

Ipsiroglu, M., *Siyah Qalem: Vollständige Faksimile-Ausgabe der Blätter des Meisters Mehmed Siyah Qalem*, Graz, 1976.

Jahangir, *The Tuzuk-i Jahangiri or Memoirs of Jahangir*, tr. A. Rogers and H. Beveridge, repr. London, 1968.

Jain-Neubauer, J., *The Ramayana in Pahari miniature painting*, Ahmedabad, 1981.

Khandalavala, K., *Pahari miniature painting*, Bombay, 1958.

—— *Pahari minature paintings in the N.C. Mehta collection*, Ahmedabad, n.d.

—— M. Chandra and P. Chandra, *Miniature paintings from the Sri Motichand Khajanchi collection*, New Delhi, 1960.

Koch, E., *The Complete Taj Mahal*, London, 2006.

Kossak, S., *Indian court painting: 16th–19th century*, New York, 1997

Kramrisch. S., *Manifestations of Shiva*, Philadelphia, 1981.

—— *Painted delight*, Philadelphia, 1986.

Krishna, K., 'Painted picchavais', *Paroksa: Coomaraswamy Centenary Seminar Papers*, ed. G.M. Sheikh et al., New Delhi, 1984.

—— and K. Talwar, *In adoration of Krishna: Pichhwais of Shrinathji, the Tapi Collection*, Surat, 2007.

Leach, L.Y., *Indian miniature paintings and drawings: The Cleveland Museum of Art*, Cleveland, 1986.

—— *Mughal and other Indian paintings from the Chester Beatty Library*, 2 vols., London, 1995.

—— *Paintings from India: The Nasser D. Khalili Collection*, London, 1998.

Lee, S.E., *Rajput painting*, New York, 1960.

Losty, J.P., *The art of the book in India*, London, 1982.

Lyons, T., *The artists of Nathadwara*, Ahmedabad and Bloomington, 2004.

Malcolm, Sir J., *A memoir of Central India*, London, 1832; repr. Shannon, 1972.

Manucci, N., *Storia do Mogor*, tr. W. Irvine, Calcutta, 1907–09.

Martin, F.R., *Miniature paintings and painters of Persia, India and Turkey*, London, 1912.

Mason, D. ed., *Intimate worlds: Indian paintings from the Alvin O. Bellak collection*, Philadelphia, 2001.

McInerney, T., *Indian painting 1525–1825*, London, 1982.

—— 'Mysterious origins: The *Tantric Devi* series from Basohli', in V. Dehejia ed., *Devi: The Great Goddess*, Washington, D.C., 1999, pp.119–35.

—— 'Mughal painting during the reign of Muhammad Shah', in B. Schmitz ed., *After the Great Mughals*, Bombay, 2002, pp.12–33.

—— 'Chitarman II (Kalyan Das)', in Beach, Fischer and Goswamy eds., *Masters of Indian painting*, Zurich, 2011, II, pp.547–62.

Mehta, N.C., *Studies in Indian painting*, Bombay, 1926.

Menzies, J. ed., *Goddess: Divine Energy*, Sydney, 2006.

Michell, G., and M. Zebrowski, *Architecture and art of the Deccani Sultanates*, Cambridge, 1999.

Mittal, J., *Indian drawings: 16th-19th century*, New Delhi, 1989.

—— *Sublime delight through works of art, from Jagdish and Kamla Mittal Museum of Art*, Hyderabad, 2007.

Okada, A., 'Keshav Das', in Beach, Fischer and Goswamy eds., *Masters of Indian painting*, Zurich, 2011, I, pp.153–66.

Pal, P., *The classical tradition in Rajput painting*, New York, 1978.

—— *Elephants and ivories in South Asia*, Los Angeles, 1981.

—— and C. Glynn, *The Sensuous Line: Indian drawings from the Paul F. Walter Collection*, Los Angeles, 1976.

—— ed., *Dancing to the flute: Music and dance in Indian art*, Sydney, 1997.

—— et al., *Romance of the Taj Mahal*, Los Angeles, 1989.

—— et al., *Pleasure gardens of the mind*, Los Angeles, 1993.

Pasricha, I., 'Painting at Sawar and at Isarda in the 17th century', *Oriental Art*, XXVIII, 3, 1982, pp.257–69.

Patnaik, N., *A second paradise*, New York, 1985.

Randhawa, M.S., *Basohli painting*, Delhi, 1959.

—— *Kangra Ragamala paintings*, New Delhi, 1971.

Ray, N., *Mughal court painting*, Calcutta, 1975.

Robbins, K.X, and J. McLeod eds., *African élites in India : Habshi Amarat*, Ahmedabad, 2006.

Roe, Sir Thomas, *The Embassy of Sir Thomas Roe to India, 1615–1619*, ed. W. Foster, London, 1899.

Sarkar, J.N., *History of Aurangzeb*, Calcutta, 1924.

Schmitz, B., *Islamic and Indian manuscripts and paintings in the Pierpont Morgan Library*, New York, 1997.

Seyller, J., 'Model and copy: The illustration of three *Razmnama* manuscripts', *Archives of Asian Art*, XVIII, 1985, pp.37–66.

—— *Workshop and patron in Mughal India*, Zurich, 1999.

—— *The adventures of Hamza*, Washington, D.C., 2002.

—— *Mughal and Deccani paintings: Eva and Konrad Seitz Collection*, Zurich, 2010.

—— 'Deccani elements in early Pahari painting', in N.N. Haidar and M. Sardar eds., *Sultans of the South: Arts of India's Deccan courts, 1323–1687*, New York, 2011, pp.64–81.

Shah Nawaz Khan, *Maathir ul-Umara*, tr. H. Beveridge, Calcutta, 1911–14.

Sharma, M.L., *Kota rajya ka itihas*, 2 vols., Kota, 1939.

Shastri, H.P. tr., *The Ramayana of Valmiki*, 3 vols., London, 1957.

Shyamaldas, Kaviraja, *Vir vinod*, 2 vols., Udaipur, 1886; repr. in 4 vols., Delhi, 1986.

Singh, M.K. Brijraj, *The kingdom that was Kotah*, New Delhi, 1985.

Singh, Kumar Sangram, *Catalogue of Indian miniature paintings (Collection of Kumar Sangram Singh of Nawalgarh)*, (cyclostyle) Jaipur, 1965.

Skelton, R., *Indian miniatures from the XVth to XIXth centuries*, Venice, 1961.

—— *Rajasthani temple hangings of the Krishna cult*, New York, 1973.

Soudavar, A., *Art of the Persian courts*, New York 1992.

Spear, P., *Twilight of the Mughuls*, Cambridge, 1951.

Spink, W., *Krishnamandala*, Ann Arbor, 1971.

Spink and Son, *Indian miniature painting*, London, 1987.

Stronge, S., *Painting for the Mughal Emperor: The art of the book 1560-1660*, London, 2002.

Tandan, R.K., *Pahari Ragamalas*, Bangalore, 1983.

Tillotson, G.H.R., *The Rajput palaces*, New Haven, 1987.

Tod, J., *Annals and antiquities of Rajasthan*, ed. W. Crooke, 3 vols., London, 1920; repr. Delhi, 1971.

Topsfield, A., *Paintings from Rajasthan in the National Gallery of Victoria*, Melbourne, 1980.

—— 'Painting for the Rajput courts', in B. Gray ed., *The arts of India*, Oxford, 1981, pp.159–76.

—— *An introduction to Indian court painting*, London, 1984.

—— *The City Palace Museum, Udaipur: Paintings of Mewar court life*, Ahmedabad, 1990; repr. 2009.

—— ed., *Court painting in Rajasthan*, Bombay, 2000.

—— 'City Palace and lake palaces', in G. Tillotson ed., *Stones in the Sand: The architecture of Rajasthan*, Bombay, 2001.

—— *Court painting at Udaipur: Art under the patronage of the Maharanas of Mewar*, Zurich, 2002.

—— ed., *In the realm of gods and kings: Arts of India*, London, 2004.

—— ed., *The art of play: Board and card games of India*, Bombay, 2006.

—— and M.C. Beach, *Indian paintings and drawings from the collection of Howard Hodgkin*, New York, 1991, and London, 1992, repr. 1994.

Victoria & Albert Museum, *The Indian heritage: Court life and arts under Mughal rule*, London, 1982.

Waldschmidt, E. and R.L., *Miniatures of musical inspiration*, 2 vols., Berlin 1967, 1975.

Weber, R., *Porträts und historische Darstellungen in der Miniaturensammlung des Museums für Indische Kunst*, Berlin, 1982.

Welch, S.C., *The art of Mughal India*, New York, 1963a.

—— 'Mughal and Deccani miniature paintings from a private collection', *Ars Orientalis*, V, 1963b, pp.221–33.

—— *A flower from every meadow*, New York, 1973.

—— *Indian drawings and painted sketches*, New York, 1976.

—— *Imperial Mughal painting*, New York, 1978a.

—— *Room for Wonder*, New York, 1978b.

—— *India: Art and culture 1300-1900*, New York, 1985.

—— ed., *Gods, kings and tigers: The art of Kotah*, Munich and New York, 1997a.

—— *Rajasthani miniatures: The Welch collection from the Arthur M. Sackler Museum*, New York, 1997b.

—— and M.C. Beach, *Gods, thrones and peacocks*, New York, 1965.

—— and K. Masteller, *From mind, heart and hand: Persian, Turkish and Indian drawings from the Stuart Cary Welch Collection*, New Haven, 2004.

Wilkinson, J.V.S., *The Lights of Canopus*, London, 1929.

Williams, J., *Kingdom of the Sun*, San Francisco, 2007.

Wolfe, R.J., *Marbled paper: Its history, techniques, and patterns*, Philadelphia, 1990.

Worswick, C., and A. Embree, *The last empire: Photography in British India 1855-1911*, London, 1976.

Wright, E., *Muraqqa': Imperial Mughal albums from the Chester Beatty Library*, Alexandria, Va., 2008.

Zebrowski, M., *Deccani painting*, London, 1983.

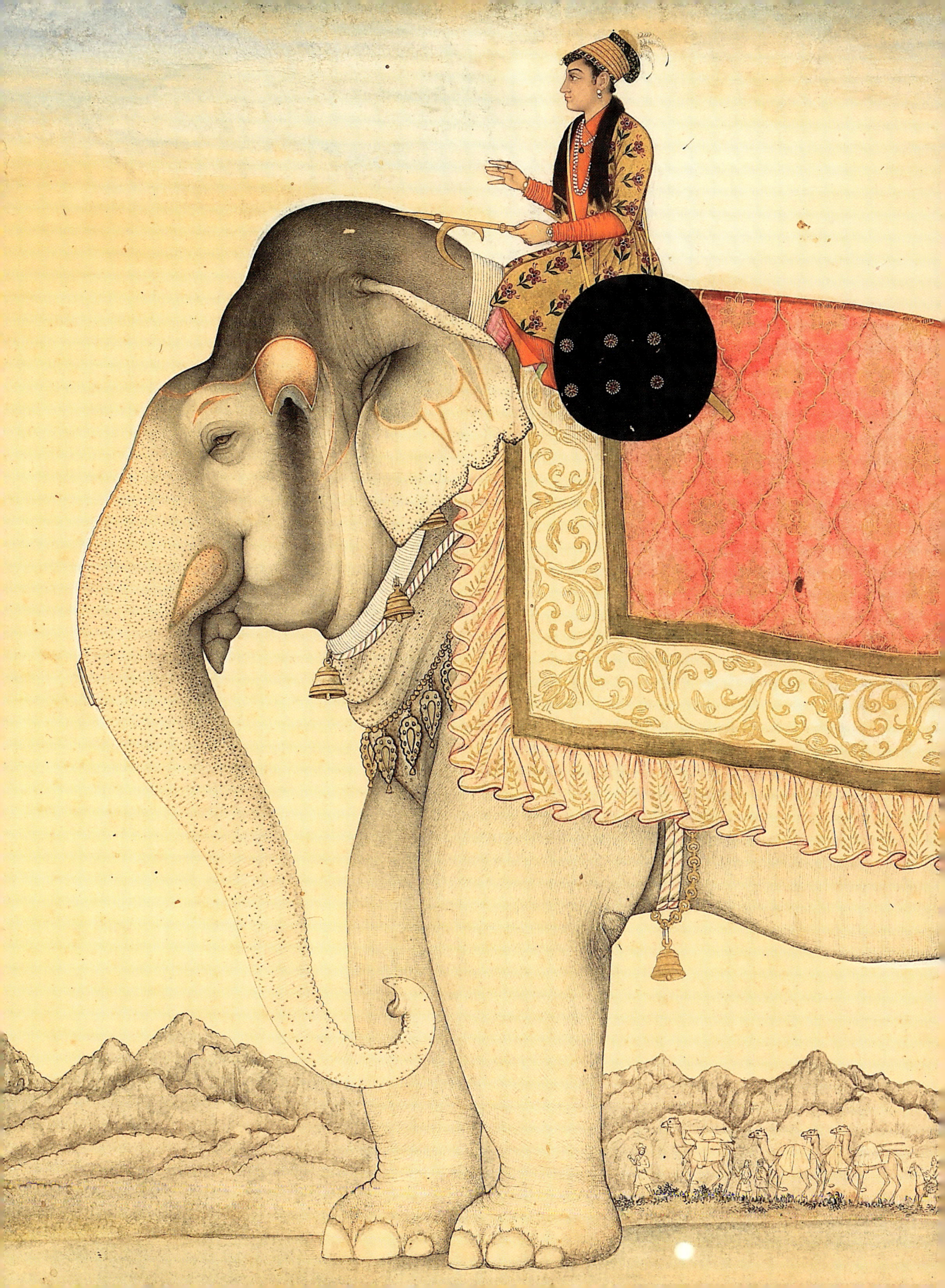

Acknowledgements

I am most grateful to Howard Hodgkin for making this exhibition and catalogue possible, as well as to Antony Peattie, Ann Marchini and Andy Barker for their kind assistance in the preparatory stages.

I am indebted to many colleagues for discussions of pictures in the Hodgkin collection and for other help: above all Robert Skelton, Catherine Glynn Benkaim and Milo Cleveland Beach, my collaborator on a previous Hodgkin catalogue; also Marcus Fraser, B.N. Goswamy, John Gurney, Jerry Losty, Adeela Qureshi, Julian Raby, Kenneth X. Robbins, Nabil Saidi and John Seyller. I thank also Ben Sheldon and Tony Gaston for their help in identifying birds, and Stephen Harris for flower and plant identifications.

I am grateful to Peter Willberg for his elegant catalogue design, and to all my Ashmolean colleagues for assistance of many kinds, not least David Gowers and his colleagues, as well as Jo-Hung Tang, for their photographic work.

I should mention finally that a number of pictures in the Hodgkin collection were already securely framed when I first studied them for this catalogue. As a result I was in some cases unable to view the reverse of the paintings and any inscriptions they may bear.

Andrew Topsfield